BEY

Also by Richard Lazarus

UNNATURAL CAUSES
THE CASE AGAINST DEATH

BEYOND THE IMPOSSIBLE

A Twentieth-Century Almanac
of the Unexplained

Richard Lazarus

For My Mother

A *Warner* Book

First published in Great Britain by Warner in 1994

A CIP catalogue for this book
is available from the British Library

ISBN 0 7515 1100 5

Typeset by Solidus (Bristol) Limited
Printed and bound in Great Britain by
Richard Clay Ltd, St. Ives plc

Warner
A division of
Little, Brown and Company (UK) Limited
Brettenham House
Lancaster Place
London WC2E 7EN

Contents

Contents

'When the impossible has been eliminated then,
whatever you have left, no matter how improbable,
must be the truth.'

Sherlock Holmes

Foreword

It is often said that truth is stranger than fiction, and so indeed it is. Anyone who doubts that statement need only read this book to become convinced. Science fiction novelists may contemplate the mysteries of space-time, describe the realms beyond the edge of the known universe, and take their readers on a rollercoaster ride through the centre of a Black Hole. But no fantasy ever written could compare with the oddities of the world which we already inhabit. A planet where men and women burst into flames while going about their everyday business, vanish into thin air in front of astonished witnesses and explode into pieces for no apparent reason. A world where fish, frogs and all manner of other animate and inanimate objects fall from the sky like rain; where water, blood or crude oil spurt from dry plaster walls; where pictures and icons suddenly begin to weep or bleed without warning. None of us considers these things possible, yet they happen nevertheless. Not in the mind of a master storyteller, but upon the surface of the planet we call earth. It would seem as though there were no scenario too ridiculous, no possibility too remote for the world we live in. What self-respecting author would have the audacity to create characters who are able to see into the future and step into the past, to take Polaroid snapshots using only their minds, plunge bodily into flames and emerge unscathed, or exhibit the very same wounds suffered by the crucified Jesus 2,000 years ago? Surely no writer would bother, for he could not expect his audience to suspend belief that far. Yet these are just a few of the amazing paranormal powers demonstrated by men and women during our own time. Their stories are told here, as are the experiences of those who have met the uncanny face to face in the form of space aliens, ghosts, extinct creatures, and a whole variety of phantasmagorical creatures of one type of another. Though they sound fantastic they are not fantasies. The twentieth century has been a unique period in the development of human knowledge. During the last nine and a half decades man has not only peered into the farthest reaches of the universe, but he has seen also into the microscopic world of the molecule. He has harnessed the energy of the atom and through research into DNA is at last unlocking the biological secrets of life itself. Away from the laboratory, man's thirst for knowledge has seen him journey into the remotest parts of the Arctic regions, traverse the deepest jungles and dive down to the ocean depths. A century which began before the advent of powered flight had, by the end of its seventh decade, seen a man walk on the moon. To most people mankind's scientific progress in the twentieth century has seemed like an upwardly curving graph-line of ever-increasing steepness. In the popular consciousness there are very few places man has not been, fewer that he has not seen, and little worth knowing that he does not already understand.

But is this sense of intellectual complacency a fair reflection of the real picture? Is humankind's comprehension of the world we inhabit really so all-embracing? The message of this book suggests that the answer to that question is a clear and unequivocal negative. For while man has developed and refined a system of scientific rules and certainties which appears to encompass the possible variations of most known phenomena, the plain fact is that not all events fit in with this regular and consistent pattern. As the reader of this book will soon become aware, every year of the twentieth century has seen its fair share of isolated incidents which fall outside the framework of natural laws as we have come to understand them. Otherwise ordinary men and women have demonstrated powers which science fails to recognise; unseen intelligences have made their presence known through a variety of mysterious and somewhat frightening manifestations; creatures long believed to be extinct have regularly appeared both in the sea and on land. Some of these happenings appear miraculous; others seem to have occurred through the agency of invisible forces which might best be described as diabolic. Many are neither particularly frightening nor uplifting to the human imagination; they are just so weird that the sheer fact of their reality – if true as reported – seems to turn upside-down at one stroke the very intellectual certainties that underpin our entire world view.

Taken altogether these oddities suggest that the physical world of matter we inhabit might occasionally and quite suddenly be interwoven with a different, more semi-substantial dimension: a place from which all manner of entities in various guises might suddenly appear and then disappear into again without warning. Another universe, even. It is these extraordinary occurrences which form the basis of a paranormal history of the twentieth century. Some of the examples contained within have been published before in books or magazines devoted to mysteries and the unexplained. Others have up until now remained unnoticed in the back copies of newspapers gathering dust on the shelves of the world's reference libraries. Many more were safely hidden from the public view within the files of government defence-related departments until the recent Freedom of Information legislation of the countries in question led to their wider circulation.

By focusing on a single enigma in each year I have, I think, managed to cover a fair proportion of the twentieth century's greatest mysteries. But no writer could achieve anything approaching a complete round-up of all the incredible events which have taken place during the past nine and a half decades, and certainly not in a single volume. What is more, every passing year throws up its own crop of fresh enigmas, some in keeping with the pattern of the past, others radically different. So I am not claiming to have written the definitive study of all preternatural happenings. One day perhaps another writer will publish such a book. Personally I have my doubts. The realm of the paranormal, like the visible universe itself, would seem to be expanding all the time.

1900

The Eilean Mor Episode

There are many stories of the sea which tell of vessels discovered adrift and deserted, in fine conditions and with all their lifeboats intact. Some of these tales turn out to be nothing more than that – stories concocted by sailors sharing a warm rum on a cold winter's night ashore. Yet many more have turned out to be entirely true and our own century, like the last, has seen countless ships abandoned for no apparent reason. Precisely what happened to their crews is one of the great mysteries, for it seems inconceivable that a group of rational individuals might jump overboard mid-ocean, giving up their only hope of survival. Nevertheless, the phenomenon continues to the present day as a careful reading of the Gazetteer at the back of this book will show.

In fact the vanishments which probably provide us with the strangest sea mystery of all concerned not seamen but lighthouse keepers. In the late nineteenth century the Eilean Mor lighthouse was built on the rocky expanse of Flannan Island to guide mariners safely round the Hebrides and the western coast of Scotland. It was manned by a duty team of two, and a third keeper was always on hand to act as a reserve in the event of illness or accident. With this failsafe precaution it was assumed that the 140,000 candlepower warning beacon need never go out. But in the first year of the century, on 15 December 1900, sailors navigating the icy waters of the North Sea watched in amazement as the Flannan Island lighthouse ceased to function.

First to report the mystery to the Scottish coastguard authorities was the captain of a steamer, the *SS Archer*, which had been sailing close to the Hebrides that night. However, due to the onset of rough weather it was several days before a relief vessel, the *Hesperus*, was sent to investigate. Among those on board was one Joseph Moore, the chief keeper in the area and a former duty officer on Flannan Island. Discussing the mystery with colleagues, Moore had been unable to imagine any circumstances which might cause the machinery to malfunction; what was more he was a personal friend of the three men on duty during December – Thomas Marshall, Donald McArthur and James Ducat – and knew them all to be experienced and able keepers who were unlikely to panic in a crisis.

When Moore had last seen them three weeks previously they had all been in good health and it seemed incredible that all three could have gone down with an illness serious enough to render them incapable of performing their duties. In fact, as Moore was to find out, something much stranger than sickness had struck the three men.

As the *Hesperus* approached the bleak island its crew saw that no preparations had been made for their arrival on the jetty, nor did repeated blasts from the ship's foghorn provoke any response. First ashore was Joseph Moore himself, striding purposefully towards the whitewashed walls of the lighthouse. Inside he found the place cold and empty yet otherwise normal. Everything was neat and in its proper place; even the wicks of the lanterns had been cleaned and trimmed, their bowls filled with oil ready to be lit at sunset. Checking the logbook for a clue to the mystery, Joseph Moore noted with astonishment that on the night of 14 December a storm had been described raging in the sea surrounding the island. This entry was inexplicable, for that night the weather had been comparatively calm, breaking only after the following night, when the absence of the light had first been noticed. Ducat had registered the last entry on 15 December. It said simply: 'Storm ended, sea calm, God is over all.'

Reporting this curious situation to the skipper of the *Hesperus*, Moore suggested that a full search should immediately be made of the small island. His advice was followed, but at the end of their investigations the crew of the relief vessel had found neither the lighthousemen nor any clue to their disappearance. The following day the *Hesperus* returned to the mainland bereft of survivors, bodies or explanations, leaving Joseph Moore alone on Flannan Island to man the lighthouse single-handed. During the next few weeks, as he paced the harsh, rocky terrain of the tiny island of Flannan, the chief keeper had plenty of time to ponder upon the fate of his comrades. Did they venture too close to the water, perhaps to be swept away by a huge wave? It was unlikely, for the men knew only too well the dangers of an angry sea. Had one become insane, killed the others and thrown their bodies from the rocks before following them to a watery grave? This possibility Moore weighed carefully in his mind before rejecting it. He knew the men personally to be of sound mind and body and, together with their families, he had waved them goodbye only weeks before.

And what of the storm mentioned in the log for the night of 14 December? It seemed impossible that such an inaccuracy could be made. None of it made any sense, and yet the fact remained that the men were gone. It was as if they had suddenly been overwhelmed by some extraordinary force and taken away against their will. Yes, thought Moore, that had to be the answer. But taken where, how, and by what?

And so the mind of Joseph Moore continued to be preoccupied by these macabre speculations during the lonely days of late December 1900 and early January 1901. Much later, months after he had been relieved of his solitary spell of enforced duty, Moore told friends how during those sombre weeks he had become aware of an unnaturally depressing atmosphere which seemed to pervade the entire island. Sometimes he even believed that while searching in vain for clues to the enigma he had distinctly heard the voices of Marshall, McArthur and Ducat calling to him on the wind. Whether or not this phenomenon was the product of his own imagination or the cries of the gulls circling overhead he could never be sure. But whatever it was, Joseph Moore could never be persuaded to return again to the bleak island of Flannan.

1901

Time-Warp at Versailles

Many people would like to step back in history to see for themselves how people in former centuries lived. Of course we know this is impossible and modern scientific thinking discounts the possibility of mankind ever building a time machine. Yet the experiences of certain select individuals would appear to fly in the face of everything we have come to believe about time and the physical universe.

During the Easter break of the year 1901 two middle-aged British schoolteachers, Annie Moberley and Eleanor Jourdain, were engaged upon a tour of Paris and the surrounding French countryside. Having never been to France before both women were enchanted by the splendour of the buildings in Europe's most celebrated capital. Yet it was during a trip to the Palace of Versailles that the two women were to undergo an experience which was to stay with them for the rest of their lives. Having explored the main palace and its outlying grounds, Miss Moberley and Miss Jourdain made their way through the world-famous gardens towards the Petit Trianon, Marie Antoinette's favourite home, which was situated elsewhere on the vast estate.

However, lacking a detailed ground plan the women

became lost and so, stumbling upon two men dressed in eighteenth-century garb whom they thought were groundsmen, they asked directions in French. Instead of helping, the men stared rather oddly at them and simply waved them ahead. Several yards on, the Englishwomen were passed by a young woman and a girl who were also wearing distinctly old-fashioned costumes, though this time of a surprisingly poor quality. Nevertheless, it did not occur to either of the schoolteachers that anything strange was happening until they came to a Temple D'Amour pavilion which was occupied by several more individuals dressed in the clothes of former times and speaking a French dialect unfamiliar to their ears. As they approached the Temple D'Amour it became clear to the women that some aspect of their own appearance seemed to startle the others. Nonetheless, one man proved friendly and with the assistance of gestures directed them towards the Petit Trianon. They found it after crossing a wooden bridge over a small gully. Yet having at last arrived at their destination both women were less inspired by the building itself than by the appearance of a person who was sitting sketching the outline of bordering woods. Strikingly attractive and wearing the distinctive high wig and long dress typical of an eighteenth-century aristocrat, the woman seemed more suited to be the subject of a portrait rather than the artist. Annie Moberley and Eleanor Jourdain were able to walk quite close to the aristocratic figure before she turned with a start. They smiled in greeting, yet she simply stared at them with an expression of fear and bewilderment. It was only at this point that the two Englishwomen at last realised they had somehow walked into the past. Recalling her own sensation, Miss Moberley described her surroundings as being in some way unnatural. 'Even the trees seemed to have become flat and lifeless. There were no effects of light and shade . . . no wind stirred the trees,' she wrote later. But just as if they had woken from a dream this eerie stillness seemed to lift and the surroundings and colours returned to normal. Within the blinking of an eye the aristocratic artist had vanished to be replaced by a scene in which a modern guide was escorting several ladies on a tour of the Petit Trianon.

Though they talked of little else during the rest of their stay in France, Annie Moberley and Eleanor Jourdain decided not to mention their experience to anyone else for fear of ridicule. However, a decade later, in 1911, having both become college lecturers in Oxford, they joined forces to write a full account of their extraordinary time-slip. When it was published the following year it proved a minor success and its authors became celebrities among the Edwardian psychical fraternity. Having by then thoroughly researched the history of Versailles, the teachers had long since come to the conclusion that they had indeed entered the past through some time-warp or invisible portal between dimensions. The probable year they had gone back to was, in their opinion, 1789. For the authors, the uncomprehending 'gardeners' were likely to have been the Swiss guards who were known to have been present at the court of Louis XVI, while the woman and young girl they had seen dressed in rags might have been French peasants living on the fringes of the palace grounds. The aristocratic lady seen sketching the woods was considered by them to be most probably none other than Marie Antoinette herself.

Sceptics – and there were plenty of them – ridiculed the story and insisted that the teachers had made it all up for the simple motive of profit. These critics were quick to point out that there was no single detail which could not have been researched in advance. Moreover, since there was no mention anywhere of a wooden bridge spanning a gully in any of the available records of the eighteenth-century palace, this vital aspect of their story seemed inconsistent with the known facts.

However, in the case of this last objection a vital clue was soon to emerge which was to lend credibility to the women's purported memories. During the 1920s a copy of the royal architect's original plans of the palace were found locked away in the bricked-up chimney of an old building in a nearby town. Hidden long before, possibly for safe-keeping, they had been kept beyond the gaze of any living person for well over a century. Intriguingly, the architect's plans included a wooden bridge over the gully which the women said they had crossed. Not surprisingly, the British authors claimed to have been vindicated and although it does not amount to conclusive proof that they had really stepped into the past, it became much harder to write the incident off.

Although the Versailles phenomenon remains probably the most famous example of a twentieth-century person finding the past replayed before his or her eyes it is by no means the only one. In October 1926 at a location near Bradfield St George in Suffolk, England, two other women walking together ventured into the grounds of a large Georgian house set back from a conifer-lined road. When they were told the next day that the place had been demolished in the later decades of the nineteenth century they returned to the spot. Sure enough, they found now that the road they had taken only the previous day was flanked by nothing but a ditch, beyond which lay a wilderness of tumbled earth, weeds, mounds and scattered trees. There was no sign of the mansion nor the regularly planted fir trees.

The United Kingdom provides us with many similar examples. During the summer of 1930, Dr Edward Gibson Moon, a country physician, was returning from a visit to Lord Edward Carson, who lived on the Isle of Thanet in Kent. Carson was very ill and Moon saw him almost daily, so he was well acquainted with the local countryside and especially the road running to the aristocrat's country house, Cleve Court.

On this occasion, having just walked out of Cleve Court's large semi-circular driveway, Dr Moon was somewhat surprised to find that the surrounding countryside looked very different. In the foreground both the land itself and the familiar hedgerow bordering it seemed strangely changed and in the distance buildings that normally provided landmarks seemed to have disappeared. The lane's tarmac surface had been replaced by a much narrower, muddy track stretching way across fields which were unusually empty of sheep. It was while the physician was still trying to come to terms with these apparently inexplicable changes that his attention was drawn to a man walking up the track towards him.

Carrying an old-fashioned flintlock musket and wearing breeches, riding boots, caped overcoat and top hat of a style long since out of fashion, the man was evidently an inhabitant of an earlier century. It seemed then to Moon as if the stranger saw him too, for he stopped mid-stride and gaped in amazement. Suddenly overcome by fear, Moon turned and looked back at the house he had just left. To his relief it seemed no different from usual and when he turned once more to look at the vision ahead of him the countryside had returned to normal and the musket-carrying visitor had vanished.

So what should we make of such experiences? Are they fact or fantasy? Individual cases of retrocognition can possibly be explained away as hallucinations, though this does not of course explain why the witness should suddenly find himself hallucinating. Cases in which more than one witness sees the same vision at the same time – like the Versailles example – are more puzzling, since it is less easy to imagine how two people might share the same vision coincidentally. By far the most convincing examples of all, however, are of those where a particular location becomes the focus of several experiences shared by a whole string of astonished witnesses. At a spot near Haytor Vale, a small town on the eastern edge of Dartmoor in Devon, a phantom cottage has been sighted by local people and walkers several times during the present century. On one occasion a surveyor for the Ordnance Survey Department saw the building for himself while looking down upon the Devon countryside from a high vantage-point. Yet when he combed the vicinity later that day he could find no trace of any building on the spot he had marked on his map, though county records suggested that a small dwelling had indeed existed there during the earlier part of the previous century.

Given that people sometimes disappear mysteriously, vanishing literally as if into thin air, some parascientists have contended that invisible time-warps might have swallowed people up, sending them back permanently into former eras. There, unbeknown to those they have left behind, they remain, leaving no evidence to suggest their true fate. It is an intriguing theory certainly, but since there seems to be no historical record of people turning up suddenly in clothes of styles that we would now recognise as contemporary to our own age, the hypothesis remains improbable. However, there may be one or two instances where a sudden flashback to a scene from the past may have led to disaster for the percipient. On one dark night in March 1979, English motorist Mrs Barbara Davison had a lucky escape when she narrowly avoided a serious accident on the Sevenoaks by-pass in Kent. Driving alone along a road with which she was perfectly familiar, Mrs Davison was astonished to see the carriageway ahead of her suddenly blacked out and another, smaller road appear, seemingly leading away to her right. Bravely ignoring the evidence of her eyes, she continued driving left into the darkness where she knew the real road must be. Within seconds she was through the black patch and everything had returned to normal. Had she followed the phantom road she would have driven straight into the path of oncoming traffic. The Kent woman's experience (which she reported to a local newspaper) was found to have been matched by those of at least three other drivers travelling on the same road that evening. Yet the fact remained that no right turn had existed at the spot for more than twenty years. Like Barbara Davison, none of these motorists had attempted to turn right, but local journalists investigating the phenomenon found that no fewer than four fatal accidents had taken place on the same stretch of road during the previous eighteen months. In each of these tragedies drivers had inexplicably swerved across the grass-covered central reservation of the dual-carriageway by-pass. Police road traffic experts had tried at the time to ascertain whether moonlight or the headlights of oncoming vehicles might have caused some illusion which had led the drivers to steer in the wrong direction. They had found no natural explanation for the crashes.

1902

Enigma in the Atlantic

The possible existence of under-sea civilisations is a subject which has long excited the imagination of science-fiction writers. It is not hard to see why. Since the bottom of the world's oceans remain largely unexplored, one can easily imagine that underwater cities built by advanced subterranean beings might exist undetected by man. However, while stories based around such a possibility remain popular in science-fiction literature, a number of real-life incidents which have taken place during the present century would seem to suggest that the bottom of the sea may really be hiding secrets that would not be out of place in a Jules Verne novel.

In the early hours of the morning of 28 October 1902 the British merchant vessel *SS Fort Salisbury* was steaming north through the Gulf of Guinea some distance off West Africa in the South Atlantic. The sea was calm and the sky above clear, so the ship's lookout had no difficulty in making out two red lights as they appeared from out of the water several hundred yards ahead and away from the ship's starboard side. Focusing on the lights through binoculars, the lookout observed them to be illuminating a huge, dark object which, though clearly a seagoing vessel, was of a type he had never before seen. Becoming concerned about a possible collision, he alerted the helmsman and called Second Officer A.H. Raymer, who hurried on deck to see the mysterious craft for himself.

In the event the second officer had only a few brief moments to view the object before it submerged. Yet it was enough for him to confirm the basic details of the lookout's sighting.

Writing afterwards in the ship's log, Raymer described the manifestation as being 'a little frightening . . . we couldn't see too much detail in the darkness but it was between 500 and 600 feet in length with two lights, one at each end. A mechanism of some kind – or fins, maybe – was making a commotion in the water. We could see its sides were scaled as it slowly sank from view beneath the waves'. Talking later of his experience, Raymer considered the possibility that they had seen the upturned hull of a capsized vessel, and firmly rejected it. He was too experienced a sailor to make such a mistake, he reasoned, and in any case, no ships had been lost around that time in the seas off West Africa.

The possible misidentification of a marine animal was an even less likely prospect. Although each witness on board the *Fort Salisbury* had independently noticed that the object's surface seemed to be scaled rather than smooth, the chances that they had seen a huge species of fish were less than zero since it would need to have been many times larger than the largest-known aquatic creature, the blue whale. Moreover, as an Admiralty source commented, fish do not tend to come complete with illuminations.

So a mechanism it must have been, and given its behaviour it was evidently a submersible craft of some type. The only problem with this theory was that in the year 1902 no nation on earth possessed the technology to create a submarine of such size. In 1888 the first fully operational naval submarine had been launched by the French, which was driven by a single screw powered by an electric motor, and weighed only 30 ton. Two years later the Germans, who were the real masters of early submersible technology, launched a 200-ton vessel, yet this did not go into full production until 1905. The Royal Navy, which launched its first underwater vessel in the same year as the incident off New Guinea, was way behind the Germans in terms of technical sophistication. And so the sighting, unexplained at the time, remains an enigma today.

More than ninety years after the incident no one has come up with an answer that seems to make a shred of sense. What can safely be said, however, is that the year 1902 provides us with merely the first of many reports of unidentified submarines being in places where it seems logically impossible for them to have been or behaving in a way inconsistent with any man-made model.

On 12 January 1965 airline pilot Bruce Cathie was flying over Kaipara Harbour north of Helensville in New Zealand when he noticed what he thought at first to be a stranded whale in the waters below. On closer examination the pilot realised it was a metallic structure 100 feet long, seemingly resting in water which he estimated to be about five fathoms deep. Although it was clearly a submarine, Cathie thought there was something distinctly odd about the vessel's shape so he reported it to the New Zealand Navy. He was told that the object he claimed to have sighted could not possibly be a conventional submarine since the tide in the harbour had been out at the time and the water over the estuaries and mud flats was in any case always too shallow for a submersible vehicle to penetrate that far into Kaipara Harbour. Cathie's mystery was soon to be augmented by other curious Antipodean sightings. On 11 April of the same year two men inspecting a wrecked fishing boat at Wonthaggi Beach eighty miles from Melbourne, Australia, saw two strange submarines surface half a mile offshore at a distance of about one hundred yards apart. After watching them for some fifteen minutes the men saw them submerge once more. Yet they were later told by officers of the Australian Naval Intelligence Department that 'in view of the locality and configuration of the coastline the objects were unlikely to have been submarines'. They were equally unlikely to have been optical illusions, for three further reports of strange 'submarines' off the seas north of Brisbane came in during a five-day period that same month. Once again the Australian Navy investigated all three incidents and came to the same conclusion: that the objects were not any type of conventional vessel, since no responsible skipper would be prepared to risk his ship in an area full of submerged rocks and other underwater hazards.

Some reports have proved even harder to explain. In 1963 a US Navy exercise involved in the detection and tracking of underwater craft picked up a peculiar sound-trace off Puerto Rico in the South Atlantic, some 500 miles south-east of the continental United States. Sonar operators on destroyers accompanying the aircraft-carrier *Wasp* apparently latched on to a submersible object driven by a single propeller which was able to reach speeds of over 170 knots, though the world record for a man-made submerged nuclear sub was a mere 45 knots.

Precisely how a propeller-driven vehicle could achieve speeds exceeding that of the fastest man-made submarine by nearly four times is hard enough to imagine, yet the enigma was further compounded when the mysterious sonar target dropped down to depths of over 27,000 feet, which at the time beat the record dive by a conventional submarine by several miles. When details of the incident eventually came to light, the US Navy declined to comment. Since that time they have never seen fit to speculate on the origin of the mystery craft and if they are any closer to discovering the truth they have chosen not to say so. Somehow I doubt whether that situation is likely to change. The idea that alien life-forms may be observing us from distant planets is enough to terrify many people. The prospect that advanced civilisations of unknown creatures may secretly be inhabiting our own planet at this very moment and living unnoticed only a few miles from our coastlines is far more disturbing.

1903

Barisal Guns Over the Ganges

Throughout the present century there have been many reports of mysterious detonations coming from the upper atmosphere. Where these booming noises are clearly unrelated to thunder, scientists have tended to look towards natural explanations such as earthquakes or avalanches, and more recently man-made causes such as bomb-testing or the sonic booms of aircraft breaking the sound barrier. Doubtless many sky booms have their origins in these mundane circumstances. But some remain unexplained.

During the summer of 1903 administrators working for the British Raj in India were puzzled by the sound of curious artillery-type booms which echoed out of the still air above the Ganges Delta. With villages few and far between and with firearms scarce among the native people, there seemed no reason for these sounds, which tended to occur during mornings when the weather was typically clear and calm. Englishman G.B. Scott, investigating the phenomenon for *Nature Magazine*, found that the local people were as mystified about the sounds as the administrators. Scott, who heard the noises himself on several occasions, had his first encounter with the 'Barisal Guns' during a walk with friends along the riverbank at Chilmari in May. Initially they were, so he wrote in his account for *Nature Magazine*, just like those made by a heavy cannon roughly ten miles off down the river. But the sounds moved closer until the men were startled by three quick successive violent reports, evidently close by, and apparently coming from the air about 150 yards above the water. Curiously, nothing was visible to the witnesses, and when they asked a group of local boatmen working nearby whether they had also heard the booms the Englishmen were somewhat surprised to find that although they had, the sounds had appeared to them to have come from an entirely different direction.

The publication of G.B. Scott's report in *Nature Magazine* led to a flurry of interest in the phenomenon and, partly as a response to the Englishman's article, a Belgian named Ernest Van den Broeck undertook wider research, managing to establish that similar unexplained booms had been reported throughout the previous century around coastal areas from Iceland to the Bay of Biscay. Van den Broeck himself believed that the most likely energy behind the sounds was a peculiar kind of discharge of atmospheric electricity – a form of clear-sky thunder. While meteorologists favoured the atmospheric theory, geologists became convinced that the sounds were allied to earthquakes, perhaps emanating from the interior zones of the earth's molten core where vast quantities of liquid rock or magma were assumed to be in constant flux. Another natural theory, favoured by the twentieth century's earliest oceanographers, held that coastal regions and river deltas were the most likely setting for the sounds to be heard because they were caused by the settling of the earth beneath the steadily accumulating weight of sediment washed out to sea. Last and least favoured among these early hypotheses was the idea that a fracturing of subterranean strata through large-scale earth movement and the bursting of rock through temperature-induced stress might be responsible.

In fact time and the march of scientific knowledge has tended to weaken all of the explanations. The clear-sky thunder mooted by Ernest Van den Broeck has been neither proved to exist nor replicated under test conditions, despite numerous attempts. Though the molten interior of the earth's core is now known to transmit earthquake waves, it is now accepted that such tremors do not always – or even usually – coincide with an outbreak of the artillery-type noises first termed as the Barisal Guns. We can now say with confidence that river deltas are neither unique nor even especially typical locations for the sounds, and so scotch the 'accumulating weight of sediment' theory. And finally, since the lowlands of the Ganges Delta do not suffer the sort of extreme temperature fluctuations necessary to fracture rock strata, the last of the early hypotheses could hardly apply.

While the nineteenth century saw many reports of clean-air concussions these extraordinary bangs and booms do seem to have become more frequent and more widespread through the past ninety-odd years. During the 1920s and 1930s residents around upstate New York became used to a sound they termed the 'Guns of Seneca Lake'. According to one investigator, the direction from which the sounds came was always vague and whenever observers moved towards the locality from which they assumed the sounds had come the detonations would just start off again somewhere else. Another American example would seem to focus on the Connecticut River Valley, between the towns of Moodus and East Haddam. In these examples shocks produced by the aerial explosions actually shook houses, and so violently that many residents referred to them as earthquakes. Yet none of the other signs usually associated with earthquakes seemed to accompany the Moodus noises, which led some experts to wonder whether conventional earth tremors were really the cause or an effect of the sounds.

During the winter of 1977 people living on the Atlantic coast of the United States heard many examples of clear-air detonations, a few of which could be traced to sonic booms from the new British Concorde airliner which was beginning its controversial transatlantic flights in the face of American public disapproval. Although air layers of various temperatures and density had been proven to conduct sound much farther than it would normally carry, many aviation officials doubted that the Concorde explanation was the likely cause of more than a small percentage of the explosions heard in the skies above the East Coast cities.

During the same decade strange booms in the skies above the West Country of England and Wales were being blamed upon tests involving the world's first supersonic jet-liner. However, there is no way that Concorde flights could conceivably be held responsible for the bizarre explosion which occurred in the Berwyn Mountains near Llandrillo, Clwyd, at just after 8.30 pm on 23 January 1974. Witnesses close to the epicentre of the explosion reported seeing a blue-green streak of light crossing the sky immediately before the enormous crash was heard. Believing that a plane had collided with a mountain face, police went to search but found neither wreckage of a terrestrial craft nor signs that a meteorite had fallen to earth. Yet, incredibly, it afterwards emerged that a global seismology unit based at the Institute of Geological Science in Edinburgh had recorded an earth tremor of magnitude 3.54 on the Richter scale, centred upon the precise spot near Llandrillo where the aerial phenomenon was reported. This remarkable event, which has never been explained, was repeated two and a half years later when on the night of 6 August 1976 people living in the same area of Wales were again terrified by a gigantic explosion in the sky above and a display of bizarre aerial lights. It was afterwards established that the boom was heard over about a ten-mile radius and close to its centre it was so violent that in the words of one witness, Mr V.C. Worthington, 'The earth shook as though from a heavy impact.' Many local people afterwards spoke of the sky above the Berwyn Mountains lighting up brightly and staying that way for several minutes, yet once again an extensive search revealed nothing that might account for the happening.

It remains unclear whether the curious phenomenon of loud detonations in clear skies has a natural origin as yet undiscovered or a supernatural one. If scientists were willing to spend time and energy on the subject we would perhaps soon know the answer. However, as with so much that is unexplained, such willingness has not been forthcoming. Ninety years after they were first heard, the Barisal Guns of the Ganges Delta remain as mysterious as ever.

1904

Spring-Heeled Jack: Man or Monster?

Some said he was a superman, others a devil. At the height of his career of terror he was as infamous and feared as his namesake Jack the Ripper, though there the comparisons between the two individuals must end. Today it is hard to believe that he existed at all, but if the stories hold substance then he must surely have been something other than a man.

Although this sounds like the opening of a cheap sensationalist novel or a children's comic story it perfectly described the true-life antics of a figure whose remarkable, if rare, appearances terrorised Victorian and Edwardian England from London to Liverpool. Known by the nickname Spring-Heeled Jack, the extraordinary caped character apparently flew through the air in great leaps, jumping over walls and high gates with seeming ease, effortlessly resisting all attempts by police and military forces to apprehend him.

Jack first appeared on Barnes Common in south-west London for three consecutive nights during February 1837. In these early sightings he invariably sprang out upon men and women walking down back-streets alone or in pairs. Although no attempts at robbery or violence were reported, the encounters seemed genuinely scary. The very sight of

Spring-Heeled Jack's ghoul-like visage and glowing red eyes was apparently enough to cause women to faint and to leave their male companions trembling with fear. When alerted to the phenomenon the police authorities originally put the tales down to a prankster – until one of their own constables saw the creature for himself and confirmed that reports of his unearthly appearance were all too real. What was more, the officer had observed with his own eyes the demonic figure's ability to jump over a 12-foot wall in a single gravity-defying effort.

A year later he was reported to be haunting the back-streets of Bow, on one occasion attacking a woman named Jane Allsop. Reliving her ordeal afterwards for magistrates in Lambeth, Miss Allsop described her assailant as hideously disfigured with glowing eyes like balls of fire. The same incredible features were to be mentioned again and again as the extraordinary bounding figure was sighted all over southern England and the Midlands during the 1850s and 1860s. Newspapers labelled Jack Public Enemy Number One and the Lord Mayor of London gave the monster official recognition, offering a substantial reward to anyone who could apprehend him. As sightings spread from London to the Home Counties groups of vigilantes were organised to catch the beast and on one occasion the ageing Duke of Wellington apparently went out on horseback to join attempts to hunt it down.

It was all to no avail. During the 1870s army authorities in Aldershot set traps after sentries reported being attacked by a man with glowing eyes and icy hands who could spring over a wall 14 feet high. When they did manage to corner him he was shot several times at point-blank range but bounded away laughing, leaving no blood on the ground where he had been hit. All those present agreed with the conclusion of the *London Morning Post* that this intruder was no ordinary mortal.

Four months on, the creature was again cornered and fired at, this time by residents of Newportin, but once more escaped unhurt, and a mere seven days later he appeared again, this time to evade a mob in the city of Lincoln.

The year 1877 marked Spring-Heeled Jack's last appearance during Victorian times and as the years passed and memories faded, people began to doubt that he had ever really existed. Yet his most spectacular appearance was still to come. On the afternoon of 10 September 1904 police in the Everton district of Liverpool were called upon to investigate curious reports of a strangely clad figure seen running along the rooftops of some terraced houses. By the time they reached the scene a large crowd numbering several hundred had gathered to watch the extraordinary performance of superhuman athleticism. High above them the man, apparently defying gravity, went leaping from building to building, covering as much as 30 feet at one jump. Ignoring requests to come down he finally crouched cat-like on all fours, and with one tremendous effort vaulted clear across the road, disappearing behind the houses opposite. All efforts during the rest of the day to find him proved in vain and the remarkable character has not been seen since.

Ninety years after this last appearance what can be said of these fantastic stories? It would be comforting to write off Spring-Heeled Jack as a product of mass hysteria or overheated imagination, yet the sheer number of witnesses – particularly in September 1904 – weakens the rationalists' argument. His prodigious ability to propel himself upwards and over great distances would – unless the reports were hugely exaggerated – seem impossible for even the fittest human athlete and the span of sightings over a sixty-eight-year period must in any case rule out the activities of a single person.

The possibility that Jack was actually an alien of extra-terrestrial origin has been mooted by the UFO lobby. But against this it must be said that none of the descriptions handed down appear to conform to those of the aliens so regularly given by witnesses to close encounters in recent times. That Spring-Heeled Jack might really have been a ghost or an entity from another dimension seems on the face of it to be the most plausible explanation of all, although set against this hypothesis it should be remembered that during his bouts of known activity he used strength and speed to resist capture rather than apparition-like characteristics.

In truth there is no explanation that seems remotely satisfactory and it is probable that this is one enigma that will never be solved. Unless, of course, he decides to return . . .

1905

Fires from Heaven

On the morning of 26 February 1905 the Hampshire County Constabulary were called in to investigate a bizarre fire which had claimed the lives of an elderly married couple living in the small English village of Butlocks Heath near Southampton. The charred corpses of Mr and Mrs Edward Kiley had been discovered by firemen after neighbours noticed smoke pouring from the couple's bungalow. The rescuers were too late to save either resident yet it was the peculiar manner of their deaths rather than the fact of their passing which so profoundly shocked the firemen. For although the bodies of Mr and Mrs Kiley had been consumed by flames to a point where they were no longer recognisably human, carpets, curtains and other combustible materials in the room where they had died remained largely undamaged. Moreover, the absence of any naked flame or other likely cause of the blaze defied logical explanation. At the subsequent inquest photographs of the Kileys' blackened forms, still sitting upright in their favourite armchairs, chilled the blood of jurors and the local coroner could only comment that the couple had probably lost their lives by some sort of accident, though 'by what means we are unable to say'.

The Butlocks Heath incident is far from unique. In every year, from every corner of the globe, there will emerge a small but significant group of fire tragedies which do not fit into any recognised category. Often because the circumstances surrounding these deaths are so bizarre they remain unclassified, while in other cases the very fact that they occurred is officially covered up. Spontaneous human combustion, the burning from within of living human bodies, is labelled a myth by every official department that comes into contact with it. So deep is the determination to hide it and so wide is the conspiracy that camouflages evidence of its reality that over the years doctors, scientists, pathologists, policemen, nurses and members of the fire brigade and ambulance services have all at various times been conscripted into an extraordinary web of deceit. Ostensibly, the cover-up exists to protect the general public from the knowledge of a distressing and unpredictable form of natural danger. The true reasons are rather more complex.

Spontaneous human combustion (SHC) apart from being one of the most horrific forms of death, is actually impossible; impossible in the sense that its multifarious paradoxes defy virtually every established physical law.

'A fact against nature' is how one doctor has aptly described it, and so great are its contradictions to logic that most scientists remain inhibited from conducting experimental studies. There is simply no way that burning human tissue could generate the immense levels of heat necessary for the calcination of bone structure, yet this fact is regularly observed in cases of SHC even when victims have incinerated inside undamaged clothing. Today, more than two centuries after the phenomenon was first identified by doctors, few medical figures are prepared to discuss it and the vast majority of the population remains blissfully unaware of its deadly presence in our midst. Only the friends and relatives of its victims and those witnesses who have experienced the awful effects at first hand are any the wiser.

Examples of the cover-up are easy enough to find. In 1972 an English forensic scientist named Dr Keith Simpson was interviewed by journalists after he had investigated an horrific combustion of a woman named Edith Thompson, who turned into a ball of fire before the amazed eyes of several witnesses in an old people's home. Ignoring the bizarre aspects of the woman's death, Simpson simply denied any evidence of the SHC phenomenon, claiming that in forty years of medical practice he had never once seen or heard of any fire deaths that could not be explained rationally. Instead of stonewalling awkward queries some officials have chosen to put forward ludicrous natural explanations. When in January 1979 the body of a Yorkshire widow was found burned entirely from the knees upwards, a police spokesman insisted that something must have fallen on her from the open fire, despite the fact that the grate was empty. Similarly the sudden inferno which engulfed another Yorkshire woman in May 1981 was blamed laughably on a lighted cigarette, even though the woman did not smoke.

This official refusal to accept the often irrefutable evidence is saddening, since those left behind through such an unnatural bereavement often flounder in a morass of superstition and whispers of heavenly retribution while at the same time being denied any hope of coming to terms with what they know. Witnesses may be pressured into changing their stories to fit in with a natural explanation and there is even some evidence that a few are being driven to madness or suicide as a result.

Whatever the experts might claim, spontaneous human combustion definitely exists and students of the paranormal have now collected several hundred witnessed examples from around the world which have taken place during the twentieth century.

Among these perhaps the most compelling of all are the testimonies of those who have suffered an outbreak of the unnatural flames and survived. Though extremely rare, there can now be no doubt that such partial combustions do occur. In December 1916 Thomas Morphey, an American hotel owner from Dover, New Jersey, found his housekeeper Lillian Green smouldering on the floor of his living room; she was still conscious yet unable to account for the flames that briefly engulfed her. In 1942 Aura Troyer, an Illinois bank clerk, was discovered ablaze inside the vault where he had been working. Speaking afterwards of his ordeal Troyer could only say that it had 'happened all of a sudden'.

Both of the victims described above suffered very serious injuries to their whole bodies. Scarcely more fortunate was another American, Jack Angel, who in November 1974 was inexplicably burned while asleep in his motorhome at Savannah, Georgia. Angel went to sleep on 12 November and awoke four days later with his right hand charred black and less serious burn spots to his chest, legs and back. There was no trace of fire in the van and Jack Angel was able to remember nothing of the incident. Yet another person to suffer an attack of the unnatural fire was Mrs Jeanna Winchester, who burst into flames while riding in a car in Jacksonville, Florida, on 9 October 1980. Though Winchester herself suffered severe injuries, the white leather seat on which she had been sitting remained undamaged and investigating fire officer T.G. Hendrix commented that he had never see anything like it in twelve years in the force. Speaking of her ordeal several weeks later in hospital, Mrs Winchester reluctantly admitted spontaneous combustion must have been to blame. 'At first I thought there had to be a logical explanation, but I couldn't find any. So I guess it really was me burning. But why did it have to be me?'

The American woman is not the only person to ask herself the same question, for while the existence of SHC is now being conclusively established, it has been far less easy to imagine the possible cause. Some believe it is linked to geomagnetic field anomalies, others to atmospheric phenomena like ball lightning. However, there is a third body of opinion which suggests an even more frightening possibility – that the force behind the internal fireball is directed by a malevolent intelligence.

Once again the year 1905 provides an English example which has been used by several writers to promote this theory. In December of that year a series of curious events, culminating in the unexplained slaughter of more than 250 chickens and geese on a Lincolnshire farm near Binbrook, began the same week that a young servant girl burst into flames in the kitchen of the Rev. A.C. Custance, who lived in a neighbouring district. Neither the girl's death nor the attacks on the livestock were satisfactorily explained. The fowl had each been slaughtered in the same hideous fashion: the skin around their necks had been pulled off from head to breast and their windpipes drawn out of position and snapped. Could it be possible, wondered some theorists, that some invisible entity, malevolent and sadistic of mind, had systematically destroyed the lives of the innocent girl and the defenceless creatures, killing them in the most repulsive ways imaginable – by fire and slow strangulation respectively? In his book *Lo!*, veteran collector of anomalies Charles Fort made clear his own suspicion that a being of incendiary appetite temporarily became manifest in Edwardian rural England. 'If we accept that in Binbrook Farm something was savagely killing chickens, we must accept also that whatever we mean by a being was there.' Of the girl herself Fort wrote: '. . . unknown to her something behind her was burning her and she was unconscious of her own scorching flesh'.

It is not hard to see why Charles Fort's conjectures were for many people difficult to accept. But whatever we think of his analysis, the existence of spontaneous human combustion can no longer be seriously questioned.

1906

The Jonah Syndrome

According to the dictionary definition, a coincidence occurs when two or more unrelated happenings share eccentric correlations of time, place and circumstance. Conventional mathematicians will always argue that coincidences are both natural and predictable for, since there are millions of people in the world doing billions of things every day, it must be perfectly obvious that totally unconnected events will sometimes come together in a way that may very well seem astonishing to those directly involved. Viewed from this perspective coincidences become little more than natural and inevitable occurrences. Despite the mathematicians' bland assurances, however, those caught up in the middle of genuinely sinister coincidences remain stubbornly unconvinced of this, as do writers like myself who have made it their business to study the peculiar phenomenon of synchronicity.

Perhaps the strongest evidence for the existence of an underlying force behind coincidences comes when we consider the manifestations of jinxes. This specialised form of ongoing coincidence occurs when one factor – a person or object, or even a name or a number – is surrounded by a spider's web of apparently interweaving variables which amount to rather more than chance groupings. Generally speaking, these coincidences tend to do more harm than good.

Easily the strangest of all jinxes is the Jonah Syndrome; whereby luckless individuals become the focus of tragic events while personally remaining immune. Quite unaffected themselves, they inexplicably trigger accidents, illness and death in those they live and work with, and people with this unwanted gift of promoting misery often find themselves vilified by society and falsely accused of the most heinous crimes.

By far the most infamous Jonah – and probably the most prodigious in the level of misery she spread – was Typhoid Mary, a young American servant girl who, it seems, may have been solely responsible for an epidemic which claimed the lives of some 40,000 people in the early part of this century. Her history of contamination began in 1906, when members of several wealthy New York households were stricken with typhoid. A cook named Mary was discovered to have worked in the kitchens of all the affected residences, and while they could not explain her own immunity to the disease, health inspectors considered her to be the cause of the outbreak. She was imprisoned in an isolation cell for three years. During her incarceration all tests to justify the health inspectors' opinions proved negative, however, and Mary was eventually released on the condition that she avoided domestic service in future. Sadly, she did not take that advice. Five years later a number of people suddenly became ill in the city's Sloanne Maternity Hospital. Typhoid was diagnosed and the luckless Mary was discovered to be working in the kitchens under an assumed identity. Once more she was detained, this time without reprieve. Typhoid Mary ended her days in solitary confinement, reviled as one of the most prolific killers of all time. Yet recently medical figures have begun to doubt that the girl was the cause of the outbreaks. Why, for instance, had no one been affected in the intervening years when, as we now know, she had worked in jobs handling food? Why was typhoid never detected in her body in all the tests carried out over a period of many years? The mystery was never solved but the indisputable fact remains that Typhoid Mary was at the epicentre of all the outbreaks. Could she simply have been very unlucky, the unknowing victim of a force every bit as deadly as typhoid, yet far more subtle?

We will never know whether the American girl was really a Jonah. However, few could doubt that her contemporary Jeanne Weber truly deserved the title. Weber, a Frenchwoman from the lower classes, was labelled 'The Ogress' for her apparently unconscious ability to bring about the deaths of children in her care. In 1906 she was accused of murdering a total of four infants, two of whom were her own sons. Each child had expired in her custody yet medical evidence supported her plea of innocence, since the individual inquests recorded the deaths to have been a result of separate and unrelated natural causes. However, her acquittal in 1906 was not the end of the story. Several months after her release from prison, Jeanne Weber was staying at the house of a friend who had a small boy. On only the second day of her visit the child choked to death while sitting on her lap. Once more suspicion fell upon her and she was charged with infanticide. But after two trials failed to produce a shred of evidence linking her with the cause of death she was freed.

While the two cases from 1906 remain the most famous examples of Jonahs we have, readers doubting the existence of the phenomenon should not make the mistake of believing that similar medical enigmas do not arise today. In February 1980 a similar talent for promoting sudden illness and death in the young was displayed by Miss Christine Fallings, an eighteen-year-old epileptic from Blounstown, Florida. On the second day of that month Fallings, who earned spare-time money as a baby-sitter, telephoned the state police to report the death of a baby in her care. The cause of the infant's death was found to be encephalitis, a brain inflammation. One year and one day on, having moved to Lakehand, Christine Fallings watched in astonishment as two young brothers went into convulsions the moment they were introduced to her for the first time. The boys recovered in hospital, yet within a few days another child she was sitting for had died of myocarditis, a heart condition. The next week another of her charges ended its life the same way. Finally, on 12 July 1981, a little girl died in Christine Fallings' arms moments after being given an inoculation for whooping cough. Following this last tragedy the distraught teenager gave up the idea of working with children. Extensive medical tests were subsequently carried out upon Fallings, all of which proved conclusively that she was not carrying any known communicable disease.

1907

A Ghost That Sought Justice

Just as the ghost of Hamlet's father walked the battlements of Elsinore Castle urging his son to seek vengeance upon his murderer, so many real phantoms have returned for the express purpose of seeking justice.

On 11 October 1907 Mrs Rosa Sutton of Portland, Oregon received a letter from her son James, lieutenant in the US Navy, who was based at the Naval Academy in Anapolis, Maryland. Although the contents of James Sutton's letter gave no hint of trouble, his mother suddenly felt herself becoming almost overwhelmed with an intense feeling of distress and fear for her son. For no reason she could explain, she was certain that he was in great danger.

Mrs Sutton was reassured by her physician and members of her family, yet the next day a letter was received confirming her dreadful premonition. Lieutenant James Sutton had, it stated, been involved in a drunken fight with some friends after a party had got out of hand. Enraged by an insult, he had returned to his quarters to get a pistol and in the course of an attempted arrest had shot himself. Yet rather than being recorded as an accident, his death was being put down officially to suicide.

In the event this grim piece of news was not the only shock Rosa Sutton was to receive that day. Almost before the death of her son had sunk in she became aware of his ghostly figure, draped in a long army overcoat, standing in the corner of the room. 'At that instant,' Mrs Sutton would later write, 'young Jimmy stood before me and said as clear as I have ever heard: "Momma, I never killed myself . . . my hands are as free from blood as when I was five years old."' The apparition vanished, saying nothing more. Mrs Sutton fell into a dead faint. But by the time she recovered she had got a clear mental impression of the real events that had claimed her son's life. Through some sixth sense she now knew that he had been attacked from behind by a group of men who beat him on the head with the butt of a gun, kicking his face and ribs repeatedly. One of them had then picked up his own pistol and shot him. There was now only one priority in the bereaved mother's mind: to clear the name of her dead boy from any trace of dishonour.

Since Mr Sutton had not shared his wife's vision he assumed that shock had simply induced a hallucination. But when in the following weeks Rosa Sutton persistently claimed to see further visitations in which the dead James described in graphic detail the men who had attacked him, her husband began to change his mind. He finally became convinced of the psychic presence when his youngest daughter Daisy reported a dream in which her brother showed her a picture of a man named Utteley whom he said had been the murderous gang's ringleader. Shortly afterwards when the family received a photograph of James Sutton standing among a group of fellow officers Daisy immediately recognised the face of the same man. Sure enough, enquiries proved that it belonged to a Lieutenant Utteley, the officer named in her dream. And so, spurred on by their dead relative's persistent materialisations, the Sutton family applied to the military establishment to have their son's case reopened. It proved to be a painstaking process, but finally, in 1909, when James Sutton's body was exhumed from Arlington National Cemetery and reexamined by US Navy pathologists, it was proved that the young officer had been severely beaten about the face and chest in a manner which corroborated the apparition's account. This startling new evidence conflicted with the earlier testimony of Navy doctors who had reported to the inquest of Lieutenant Sutton's death, and brought into question the court's verdict of suicide. Yet it was not enough to convict those men named by the officer's ghost as his assailants. With the second-hand testimony of a discarnate spirit ruled inadmissible in a court of law the Sutton family had to content themselves that their relative's honour had been partially restored. As for James Sutton himself, it appears that he was satisfied, for he never returned in ghostly form again.

Phantoms who return to seek vengeance for their own deaths might seem more like the stuff of historical fiction than fact. Yet curious though it may seem to most people, the spirit world has assisted police in solving many violent crimes and has sometimes helped in the tracing of the spirit's own murderer. Typical of this syndrome was the now-famous case which came to court in Evanston, Illinois in 1979.

The trial centred on the brutal murder of one Teresita Basa, a Filipino nurse who had been stabbed to death in her apartment two years previously. Initially there had seemed little chance of ever solving the crime. Forensic evidence was inconclusive and conventional police enquiries had offered little clue to the identity of the assailant. All that was clear was the motive: robbery, for Teresita Basa's expensive jewellery had been stolen.

It was not until many months after the murder that police investigations took a dramatic and unexpected turn. Remy

Chura, a speech therapist, spiritualist and close friend of the dead woman, began having the same persistent dream. In these nightly visions Teresita's spectral form would appear over Chura's bed asking her friend to avenge her death. The nurse named her murderer as one Allan Showery, a small-time thief who had called on the fateful day posing as a TV repairman. According to Teresita's dream ghost, Showery had now given her stolen jewellery to his girlfriend, a woman whom she also named. Before disappearing Teresita would always implore her old friend to go to the police with this information.

For some time Remy Chura did nothing, sure that her story would be ridiculed. Eventually, however, she relented. It was the right decision. Although the homicide investigation officers found Chura's tale fantastic, Allan Showery was in fact known to them as a persistent offender and they called him in for questioning. To begin with he denied any knowledge of the killing, but his manner aroused enough suspicion among his interrogators for them to instigate a search of his girlfriend's flat. The raid revealed a large quantity of stolen goods, including a ring which proved to be an heirloom from Teresita Basa's collection. Under pressure Showery broke down and confessed to the slaying, though at the trial he changed his plea to not guilty on the advice of a lawyer certain that a ghost's testimony would be thrown out of court.

In the event the hearing made legal history. Showery's defence attorney insisted that the testimony of a disembodied spirit was not admissible. The presiding judge, Frank Barbero, ruled otherwise. Faced with the condemning evidence of his unseen victim, Allan Showery changed his plea to guilty and was sentenced to fourteen years in jail.

1908

Cataclysm at Tunguska

The morning of 30 June 1908 saw one of the most extraordinary and mysterious events to have occurred since the world began. Something travelling with terrifying velocity and containing enormous destructive power visited itself upon the remote Tungus region of Siberian central Asia, devastating a total area of some 700 square miles in an explosion which would seem to be unparalleled in human history. Reports at the time show that the blast was heard 500 miles to the west and its vibrations felt as far away as the western United States. Seismic readings in Great Britain registered successive shock-waves of earthquake proportions and the night skies across Europe were lit up as if it were day. Strangely, however, it was not until March 1927 that an expedition to investigate the Siberian blast was undertaken.

Led by the eminent scientist Leonid Kulik of the Soviet Academy of Sciences in Leningrad, the Russian team had become fascinated with reports which spoke variously of a cylindrical object exploding in mid-air, of a blast so great that it flattened whole forests on both banks of the river, and of a hot wind which sucked away buildings and tents and scorched whole herds of reindeer. Although the Russian scientists thought these tales must be greatly exaggerated, it was clear that something very remarkable indeed had fallen to earth in June 1908.

In fact, what was found exceeded all the expectations of Kulik and his men. When they reached the vantage-point of the Khlandi Ridge, a position some 35 miles from the area where they had estimated the explosion to have taken place, the scientists were faced with a scene of utter devastation. Before them to the limits of the horizon, perhaps some 16 to 20 miles in distance, mighty trees had been flattened in unbroken regimentation and all were lying in one direction – towards them. Kulik immediately realised that if this was the result of a meteor strike upon the earth's surface then the crater left would be prodigious in size. However, to his astonishment, when the expedition finally reached the epi-centre of the blast (an incredible 37 miles from the first signs of the devastation) they found not only an absence of crater but a whole area of trees virtually unaffected for a circum-ference of almost a mile. Since there was no sign of impact damage it was obvious that the explosion had taken place some miles above the ground, just as several eye-witness accounts had indicated. Yet this behaviour was untypical of meteorites, and if the object was not a meteorite then what could it have been?

Although he made three more visits to the area Leonid Kulik never found a solution to the riddle. Indeed it is a question that continues to baffle scientists today, although there has been no shortage of theories. Among these undoubtedly the most controversial is the space vehicle hypothesis. This postulates that the Siberian blast was caused by the exploding nuclear reactor of an extra-terrestrial craft which had suffered a critical malfunction in flight. Though it might appear fanciful at first glance, the extra-terrestrial hypothesis has been taken seriously by several scientists, for the following reasons: first, among the several hundred documented eye-witness reports of the catastrophe many mentioned the descending object manoeuvring and changing direction as it travelled over Lake Baykal. If these reports were accurate one would have to conclude that the object must have been under intelligent control. Secondly, post-war aerial surveys of the affected Tungus Region have revealed stark similarities between the blast pattern there and those evident in the cities of Hiroshima and Nagasaki after the atomic bombs were dropped. The central area of relatively undamaged landscape was most obvious. Likewise, the 'shadowing effect' whereby natural contours helped protect both animate objects and buildings, seemed to be a feature of each explosion. Thirdly, and much the most curious, was the way that new species of plants and animals seemed to emerge and grow more quickly in Siberia, as indeed they did following the Hiroshima and Nagasaki attacks. In all three cases it would seem likely that the bizarre genetic aberrations were caused by radiation. Lastly, and perhaps most striking of all, was the way in which eye-witness accounts of the pillar of smoke rising above Siberia paralleled the infamous mushroom cloud now so familiar to all mankind.

Some Soviet scientists have been at the forefront in promoting the extra-terrestrial hypothesis. Noticing that H-Bomb tests conducted by the USA and USSR during the 1950s produced magnetic disturbances in the upper atmosphere leading to spectacular displays of aurora lights on the opposite side of the planet, Dr Vasilieyev of Tomsk University pointed out that a similarly dramatic aurora display was watched by, among others, the British explorer Ernest Shackleton, who was trekking across Antarctica at a point which seemed to be the magnetic opposite of Tunguska on 31 June 1908. Another Russian, Professor Zolotov, has since confirmed that silicate globules found embedded in tree bark in Tunguska contain exotic elements such as itterbium, which could hardly be terrestrial in origin, but which might conceivably be found in the hull of an inter-planetary vehicle. Like Vasilieyev, Zolotov has now come to believe in the spaceship theory.

Another possibility – and to many mainstream scientists a much more plausible one – is that the Tunguska explosion was the result of a comet, the dirty cosmic snowballs of gas and dust which on rare occasions enter our solar system to appear as stars with great incandescent tails, remaining visible for weeks or months before hurtling away on their never-ending celestial journey. The possibility that such an enormous inter-stellar traveller might have strayed into the earth's gravitational field cannot be entirely ruled out, nor can we dismiss altogether the original assumption of most scientists that the blast was created by an enormous meteorite. Nevertheless, on the evidence we now have, both of these natural solutions seem to be deeply flawed. To begin with neither of them could possibly explain the witnessed accounts which described the object changing course over Lake Baykal moments before it exploded. And even if we dismiss these observations as unreliable, there are plenty of other objections. How, for instance, could a comet produce the appearance of a nuclear explosion and leave damage patterns so remarkably like that of a man-made weapon? Perhaps more significantly, it seems impossible that the purported approach of this galactic monster could have gone unnoticed by more than a hundred observatories around the world which were in operation in June 1908, all of which failed to make a sighting of any unusual celestial object. If, on the other hand, the source of the devastation was an approaching meteorite, one wonders why the massive lump of rock would have vaporised 5 miles above the Siberian forest instead of impacting and leaving a huge crater as other giant meteorites have done in the past. Even assuming that this is what must have happened, there is no explanation for the evident lack of debris which must have resulted from the break-up of an object weighing many thousands of tons.

And so the full story of Tunguska remains unwritten. All that we can be sure of, and be eternally grateful for, is that the explosion occurred in perhaps the least dangerous area possible in terms of the risk to human life. Apart from a few hundred herdsmen, some subsistence farmers and the odd nomad, the loss to our race was minimal. Had the disaster taken place over a city the size of New York or Tokyo, the death toll would have been counted in millions, and even if the object had exploded over the sea its effect would have been much worse, creating tidal waves of skyscraper proportions like those which followed the Krakatoa volcanic explosion thirty years earlier.

On 30 June 1908 the world was lucky. Next time it may be a very different matter.

1909

Airship Wave Over Massachusetts

The first wave of UFO sightings to occur during the present century came not in 1947, as most people erroneously assume, but some thirty-eight years earlier. During 1909 reports came in from Europe, North America, South Africa, Japan, New Zealand and various other parts of the globe. Witnesses to these events spoke of seeing large oblong objects with powerful downward searchlights cruising high above them through the night-time sky. Although at the time the stories were widely ridiculed by newspaper editors and sceptics alike, with hindsight they would appear to mark the beginning of a phenomenon which would one day grip the imagination of people across the planet. Since many of these early UFO sightings were made by multiple witnesses they were almost certainly not hallucinations; and because virtually identical descriptions were made by citizens of different cultures living many thousands of miles apart it would be difficult to put the tales down to mass hysteria or the urban myth syndrome.

One of the best documented reports from America took place in December 1909, when policemen walking their pre-dawn beat at Worcester, Massachusetts were alerted to a fiery light hovering overhead. During the following nights the same manifestation was seen by residents in two other towns and on 23 December it made an appearance at much lower altitude over the city of Boston. Many New Englanders afterwards claimed that the single light had partly illuminated a much larger object of elongated shape while the accounts of other witnesses (who had presumably viewed the craft from a different angle) spoke of a more rounded object with portholes. Whatever it looked like, the flying vision reappeared the next day and then again on Christmas night as it travelled serenely over small settlements to the south-west of Newhaven, Connecticut.

Following the New England sightings many conjectured that the mysterious skyborne visitor was an airship built by some eccentric inventor. For a while suspicion focused on a Worcester manufacturer of engineering equipment named Wallace F. Tillinghast, who had claimed earlier that year to have built a successful flying machine. The rumours died down when it became clear that Tillinghast's prototype could never have left the ground, and in any case anyone who took the time to compare the reports from the United States with those being made elsewhere around the planet would soon have realised that no single culprit could have been responsible for so widespread a plethora of sightings. In particular both New Zealand and Britain seemed besieged by cigar-shaped objects of varying sizes throughout 1909. During the six weeks from the end of July to the start of September hundreds of people reported low-flying craft over both the North and South Island of New Zealand while witnesses in more than forty towns across Britain reported strange shapes and lights in the night skies during a period from the third week of March to the second week in May.

A typical British sighting and one of the most publicised at the time was that of a police officer, Constable Robert Kettle, who was alerted by the steady buzz of a high-powered engine emanating from above his night-time beat along the streets of Peterborough in the early hours of 23 March. Looking up, PC Kettle could clearly make out the shape of a long oblong craft with a bright light attached to one end, gliding silently over the rooftops until he lost sight of it. Kettle later described how, as he looked up, he could see men waving from a smaller section of the craft suspended by rope or wire from the main section. Two lights on the ship came on and shone down, illuminating the ground as the craft gained altitude and sailed away in the direction of Derby.

Among these British encounters easily the most compelling was that of a Welshman named Lethbridge, who claimed to have met two curious figures standing next to a grounded 'cigar' while on an evening hike in the hills near Caerphilly, Mid-Glamorgan. Dressed in fur caps and coats, the men, of human appearance, 'jabbered furiously to each other in a strange dialect' before taking fright at the witness's approach and hurrying back inside their machine. The craft then rose quickly into the sky with a downdraught of hot air which almost forced the Welshman to his knees.

In the decades that have followed the rush of anomalous aerial sightings during 1909 there have been many speculations which have sought to explain the phenomenon in a natural way. One hypothesis centres upon possible secret test flights of zeppelin airships, the large dirigibles which history has shown the Germans were then developing. Although no official German military documentation has been found to support this theory, the machines' characteristic cigar shape (and the clearly human-like appearance of the occupants seen by Lethbridge) certainly seems to fit it. However, the big problem with the zeppelin hypothesis comes when we consider the distance between the areas in which these flying ships were seen. For while it is quite possible to imagine a prototype dirigible travelling from Germany to any part of

Britain, we can say for absolute certainty that airship technology had not advanced to a point where a voyage from Europe to either North America or New Zealand would have been possible. Unpalatable as it may be to those who prefer to deny the existence of UFOs, historians of this period have long since admitted that no mechanisms of human design could have been responsible for the bizarre wave of airship sightings that gripped the world during the year 1909.

Which leaves us with one further question. If we didn't send them, then who did?

1910

Many Happy Returns

The year 1910 was a momentous one in the life of Adela Samoa, a doctor's wife from Palermo, Italy. It began with sadness when her five-year-old daughter Alexandrina died on 15 March of tuberculosis; it was to end in joy when the following December she gave birth to twin girls. As a devout Catholic the Italian mother might well have considered her pregnancy to be Heaven-sent, a gift from the blessed Virgin Mary to whom she silently prayed every Sunday in the cathedral. But to Adela Samoa the link with the earlier tragedy was not merely fortuitous but absolutely essential. A month after she had lost Alexandrina the girl had appeared to her in a dream cradling a baby in her arms, telling her mother that she was coming back. Immediately Adela became convinced that she must be pregnant despite an ovarian operation the previous year which had left her – in the opinion of medical experts – unlikely to conceive ever again. Sure enough, the mother was right to trust her own instincts, and when the first of the two girls to be born in December bore distinctive birthmarks in the same place as her dead child, she was named Alexandrina in tribute to the memory of the first girl.

Initially Adela's husband had assumed his wife's dream to be the product of grief and insisted she put aside all thoughts of reincarnation. Yet with the passage of time even he was forced to admit there was something odd about the affair. With every day the second Alexandrina seemed more and more like her predecessor, playing the same games and sharing an aversion to the same food; moreover, like Alexandrina the first she was left-handed even though her twin sister was not. Even so, it was not until the girl was aged eleven that the Samoas came to genuinely believe her to be a reincarnation. One day in the spring of 1921 Adela told her daughters that they would be visiting the town of Monreale the following week. Immediately, Alexandrina pronounced that she had already been there and described the town with remarkable accuracy. It was, she said, the place where you saw 'red priests' unlike any in Palermo. When her mother asked how she knew all these things Alexandrina expressed surprise and replied that Adela had taken her there when she was young, accompanied by a woman she described as 'the neighbour with scars on her forehead'. Adela knew that neither twin had ever visited Monreale. Indeed, the only time she herself had been there was many years before, when she had been accompanied by her first child and a friend who was suffering at the time from an unsightly outbreak of cysts on her forehead. Casting her mind back to that day Adela recalled seeing in the main square of the town a line of Greek priests wearing bright-red vestments of a type unknown in Italy. The first Alexandrina had been particularly interested in them. From that moment on nothing would ever convince the mother that the soul of the first girl had not truly been returned to her in the body of the second.

This incident from earlier in the century is one of many examples where children seem able to remember incidents from previous lives which seem impossible to explain unless one accepts rebirth in some form or other. A later example from the United Kingdom bears a particularly strong similarity to the Samoas' experience. In May 1957 two sisters, Joanna and Jacqueline Pollock, aged eleven and six respectively, were killed when a car mounted the pavement in their home town of Hexham, Northumberland. Soon after the tragedy the girls' father, John Pollock, became convinced (for reasons which he has never been fully able to explain) that their souls would return in the bodies of other children. So when in 1958 his wife Florence announced that she was pregnant once more his belief grew into the certainty that she would give birth to twin girls. John Pollock's feeling was so strong that he even argued with the gynaecologist who told his wife that she was carrying a single child. Once more parental instinct proved the more trustworthy guide: on 4 October Mrs Pollock gave birth to twin girls. Again, as in the case of the Samoas, a physical mark reinforced the parents' belief. The eldest of the twins, named Jennifer, had a line on her forehead in the place where her dead sister Jacqueline had cut herself badly after falling off a bicycle; the same girl also had a birthmark on her head which corresponded to a similar blemish on the skin of the deceased daughter. The other twin, Gillian, had no birthmarks whatsoever, yet this in its own way was also slightly odd, since the twins were monozygotic – formed from the same egg.

With the Pollock family, as with their Italian counterparts of a half-century before, it would be memory recall which finally tipped the balance towards total belief in reincarnation. When the girls were just four months old the family moved to Whitley Bay, which is situated some miles from Hexham, and did not return to their old district until three years later, when John Pollock took his family back on a day trip.

Both husband and wife were amazed by the way in which

their young children showed recognition of the parks and play areas frequented by their elder daughters. They were even able to recognise the road in which the family used to live and their elder sisters' school. Apparently this trip helped to trigger something in the girls' minds, for within weeks they were suffering from nightmares of a disturbing intensity. On these occasions, after waking, they would recall the sudden deaths which had ended their previous lives, describing the scene of the accident in graphic and accurate detail. These dreams would continue for many months until, having reached the age of five, Jennifer and Gillian ceased to be tormented by the trauma. Now long since grown into adulthood, the sisters remember nothing of their former lives, yet John and Florence Pollock remain convinced that their dead daughters did return, just as John sensed they would.

1911

Omens of Doom

The myths and legends of many ancient civilisations hold the appearance of certain birds to be portentous of death. According to the Roman Chronicles of Plutarch, ominous signs and portents preceded the assassination of Julius Caesar, among their number being the stygian screech owl which perched in the city's main square around the Ides of March. Later, at the emperor's funeral, a strange and unnatural bird supposedly flew into the Hall of Pompey carrying a sprig of laurel in its beak, only to be torn apart by a flock of predatory wonders who suddenly descended upon it from out of thin air. Likewise, in Shakespeare's play *Macbeth*, the regicide of Duncan is heralded by the night-long shrieking of 'the obscure bird'.

Today most people in the West would scoff heartily at such an idea. Yet during the present century there have been several incidents which support the idea that birds of ill omen are rather more than simply an old-fashioned superstition.

Grim reapers of the feathered kind have been regularly seen to mark the last moments of one particular English bishopric, the See of Salisbury. If mediaeval accounts can be believed huge white birds of a type unlike any native British species have often been seen hovering over the countryside before the last days of the incumbent bishop. The first sighting of the white omens of Salisbury took place in 1414, when a flock of the creatures descended on the cathedral roof in time to mark the laying to rest of the local church leader. Many times since they have been sighted, including two occasions in the last century. One Victorian observer described them as being like albatrosses but with dazzling white wings, while another nineteenth-century witness said they moved 'woodenly' through the sky like gigantic overgrown gulls. But perhaps the most convincing account is that of Miss Edith Oliver, an elderly spinster who was returning home from choir practice on the morning of 15 August 1911, the day on which the then bishop, Harold Wordsworth, died unexpectedly. Like most local parishioners Miss Oliver knew of the birds' significance, and upon seeing them she turned back to Salisbury Cathedral to warn her spiritual superior. In the event she was too late, for she reached her destination only to learn that the bishop had died suddenly of a heart attack.

Speaking later of her experience, Edith Oliver expressed her conviction that the creatures she had seen were of a truly supernatural origin and rejected any suggestion that they belonged to some species native to Britain.

Although it is the houses of the aristocracy which have tended to attract the most famous omens, these preternatural visitations are by no means the exclusive preserve of the rich and powerful. Frank Podmore, a founder member of the British Society for Psychical Research, wrote of a doctor's daughter who had repeatedly seen a 'strange, tiny, graceful-looking bird with a very slim head' every day for a week prior to a death in her family. During its regular visits the bird tapped on the window of the house to announce its arrival yet significantly it was never seen to eat and ignored water and breadcrumbs put outside. After the family's bereavements the bird was seen no more.

The oddity described by Podmore is far from unique. For years writers interested in curiosities have noted cases where flocks of birds have descended upon the roofs of houses in which a death was imminent or subsequently occurred unexpectedly. The eminent psychologist C.G. Jung encountered several of these oddities while researching *Synchronicity*, his classic study of coincidences.

A particular example involved the death of one of Jung's own psychiatric patients. After the man had gone to work his wife was alarmed to see a flock of seagulls descend upon the roof of their home. To the woman the birds' arrival was ominous since a similar phenomenon had accompanied the death of both her mother and grandmother. Although she feared mainly for her own life, it turned out to be her husband's end that had been foreshadowed. Later that same day she learned that he had collapsed at work and died of a cerebral haemorrhage.

Omens of doom do not always appear on the wing. For more than five centuries foxes have been the messengers which stalk the deathbeds of an old Irish family, the Gormanstons. Indeed, so famous is the phenomenon that a fox is incorporated into the family's coat-of-arms. According to ancient tradition foxes are seen to gather in large numbers around the time of the demise of a Gormanston male. And this is no mere folk legend: examples of the phenomenon have been witnessed on three occasions this century. Perhaps the most celebrated account took place on 8 October 1907, when more than a dozen creatures gathered to bay and cry their strange lament below the walls of the Gormanstons' castle home. Inside the fortress walls the fourteenth viscount was slowly slipping away from the mortal plane. Later, an even larger group of foxes was seen lurking for several hours in broad daylight in the castle gardens and on the day before the viscount's funeral a similar sight befell mourners who arrived at the chapel where the Irishman's body lay. Even after the service the curious vigil continued: a solitary vixen was seen to sit beside the viscount's grave for more than a week after the burial. One witness commented at the time that it seemed as though the creature was guarding the man's last resting-place.

Clearly such behaviour on the part of ordinary foxes would be highly unusual since the animals do not gather in large numbers, nor do they habitually hunt as a pack in broad daylight. Yet the Gormanston foxes quite possibly had nothing in common with the natural creatures at all, for they entered the castle grounds through an unknown route, disappeared and reappeared without warning or explanation and, according to one report from a local farmhand, were seen to pass a flock of geese without attempting to attack them, the very opposite of foxes' normal behaviour pattern.

To some people the arrival of portentous creatures such as these can be explained in terms of coincidence and the overheated imaginations of the superstitious. Others see such visitations as providing further evidence of the existence of a level of reality other than our own. Viewed in this light omens of doom appear only fleetingly because, like apparitions, they are not truly of this world.

1912

A Predictable Disaster

Some parapsychologists have conjectured that disasters attract (or perhaps we ought to say project) premonitory influences in direct proportion to their size. The greater the scale of the tragedy the higher the likelihood of previsions, or so claim the experts. Certainly some of the major disasters of the twentieth century, such as London's 1975 Moorgate tube disaster and the tragic Aberfan landslip of 1966, have provided much evidence to support this theory. An even more striking example surrounds the sinking in 1912 of the *SS Titanic.* Literally hundreds of people claimed afterwards to have foreseen the catastrophe and so widespread were these accounts from sources around the world that an entire book was devoted solely to premonitions foreshadowing events of that terrible night when more than 1,300 men, women and children slipped beneath the icy waters of the North Atlantic. Yet unmentioned among these psychic glimpses was a far stranger form of prediction that had taken place not days but some fourteen years earlier. In this case the maritime disaster on a scale unprecedented in peacetime was not only foreseen but described in quite meticulous detail. The man responsible was not a seer but a British novelist named Morgan Robertson.

Robertson's version of events was contained in a story entitled *Futility*, published in 1898. In the book a great liner is bound for America on her maiden voyage and, despite a reputation for unsinkability, strikes an iceberg and goes down with a huge loss of life. The author called his fictional vessel *Titan*, and the similarity in names is only one of many details which bear a truly eerie comparison to the real events. Like her fictional predecessor, the *Titanic* was reckoned to be the largest vessel afloat yet carried too few lifeboats. Indeed, the dimensions of the two vessels bore an uncanny likeness, while their berth capacity, number of funnels, turbines and propeller screws were all exactly the same. In almost every imaginable sense the two ships were identical. More importantly so was their dark destiny, for both ships rammed icebergs in exactly the same spot in the North Atlantic.

Futility was not a great publishing success and even if it had been it is doubtful whether its uncanny preview of the *Titanic*'s fate could have helped to avert the disaster. Yet a reading of the book may just possibly have saved the lives of at least one crew crossing the same stretch of water many years later.

In April 1935 a young seaman called William Reeves was standing watch in the bow of the tramp steamer *Titanian* bound for Canada out of Tyneside, England. Alone at his post around midnight, Reeves, who had read *Futility* the previous month, apparently began to brood on the similarities between the real and fictional incidents. Neither offered much comfort since his own ship was crossing the same stretch of ocean and in the very month of April when both Morgan Robertson's vessel and the pride of the White Star Line had descended to their watery graves. When out of the blue it suddenly occurred to Reeves that the exact date of the *Titanic*'s sinking – 14 April 1912 – was the day of his own birth, the coincidence solidified into an overwhelming sense of dread that he too was to become part of some awful trick of fate. Without being able to offer an explanation to his colleagues he shouted out a frantic danger warning and the tramp steamer's engines were turned full astern. At the very moment that the ship churned to a halt a huge iceberg could be seen towering menacingly out of the night's blackness. Had Reeves' warning come even a few seconds later the *Titanian* would certainly have followed those other similarly named ships to the bottom of the sea.

Incredibly, even this is not quite the end of the bizarre fact-follows-fiction coincidences that surround the 1912 tragedy. In 1886 a British journalist named E.W. Stead had written yet another story about a liner which sank after striking an iceberg in the North Atlantic. Though in this case the ship's name was *Majestic*, yet the name of the captain of the ship, E.J. Smith, was the same as that of the real captain of the *Titanic*. Curiously enough, the British journalist, who later became interested in all aspects of psychic phenomena including the role of precognition in our lives, did not notice the forewarning of his own fictional account. In fact E.W. Stead became a passenger on the *Titanic* and lost his life in the tragedy.

1913

Phantom Stone-Throwers

While just about everything in the world of the paranormal seems very odd to most people, there are some events which are even more strange than most. Attacks by invisible stone-throwers are a prime example of this second category.

For a four-day period beginning on the morning of 30 January 1913, a house in Marcinelle, a residential area near the Belgian town of Charleroi, became the focus for a variety of pebbles and stones thrown accurately through windows and doors. When Mr Van Zanten, who owned the house, was first alerted to the mystery by the unmistakable sound of breaking glass, he initially assumed it to be the work of children living in the neighbourhood. He alerted the police and they began to watch the house. However, instead of ceasing, the bombardment continued and indeed intensified. Yet no one was caught throwing the missiles and there seemed no explanation for their origin. Reporting in writing to his superior, one of the Belgian police officers described how he had seen a stone arriving straight through the middle of a large window pane followed by others spiralling in a parabolic motion designed to shatter the remaining shards of glass so that the whole pane was broken up methodically. In another window a projectile was caught in the fragments of the hole it had made only to be subsequently ejected by another stone passing neatly through precisely the same point without causing further damage. In the officer's opinion, either the stones were being thrown preternaturally or the unseen attacker had an extraordinarily accurate throw. Having by then lost all his windows, Mr Van Zanten had come to the same conclusion. Yet while the householder was much bewildered by the destruction to his property he took consolation in the fact that none of his family had been injured. Indeed his two children, both aged under five, seemed unperturbed by the mayhem around them and when a piece of brick finally did strike a human target – Van Zanten's father-in-law – it caused no pain and left no mark.

A full police search of the local area failed to uncover anything suspicious and on 2 February, to the Belgian family's great relief, the bombardment stopped, as mysteriously as it had begun.

Amazingly, the tale described above is only one of literally dozens of cases of invisible stone-throwers that have been collected by mysteriologists throughout the century.

In October 1901 stones were falling in prodigious numbers on Harrisonville, a small town in Ohio, causing widespread alarm; four years later, in Port of Spain, Trinidad, stone showers in and out of doors accompanied a whole range of poltergeist phenomena centring upon a reputedly haunted house. In 1907, the Irish town of Magilligan, County Derry, saw stones regularly hitting the roofs and windows of a cottage owned by one Mr McLaughlin. As with the case from 1913, eye-witness accounts tend to support the theory that the energy involved in these incidents was intelligently directed. In 1929 a Fortean researcher named Ivan T. Sanderson had a first-hand experience of a stone-thrower's intelligent behaviour on the Indonesian island of Sumatra, where he was staying with a friend who found small pebbles every morning on his verandah. Sanderson suspected that a poltergeist might be to blame, so the next evening, to test his theory he marked several small stones with lipstick and threw them into the darkening jungle which bordered his host's garden. Moments later, the same objects landed at his feet. Sanderson considered this to be absolute proof that a supernatural agency lay behind the phenomenon, since no human eyes could have detected, within such a short period of time, and returned the stones thrown into the tangled foliage.

Sometimes the sheer distance the stones are propelled defies belief. In January 1923, following the four-month bombardment of a farmhouse in the Ardèche region of France, one local politician wrote: 'No mortal hand could have done this. It is impossible for a man to throw rocks across a field 440 yards long, still more impossible for anyone to have been hidden undetected.' In 1977, officials in Spokane, Washington, were equally baffled by persistent reports of rocks falling upon a house owned by a Mr Billy Tipton. The following year Tipton moved to Hazlitt, New Jersey, where his home once more became the focus for a skyborne onslaught.

Fortunately for those at the centre of the happenings the activities of phantom stone-throwers is usually short-lived. Even so there have been some notable exceptions, and it is these persistent outbreaks which prove beyond doubt that the stories are not simply a product of someone's imagination.

In Britain, perhaps the most compelling evidence for the objective reality of the poltergeist phenomenon was the nightly blitz of a row of five houses in a street in the Ward End district of Birmingham. Early in 1982, having received numerous complaints of windows being smashed by stones thrown at the backs of houses in Thornton Road, the West

Midlands Constabulary set up a team to watch over the afflicted premises. The police assumed that local youths were responsible for the nocturnal attacks, yet instead of finding human culprits they discovered an enigma which has defied explanation until this day. Although the vigilant police heard the regular crashing of flying projectiles against the roof tiles and bricks of the houses under surveillance, they could find absolutely no evidence of anyone hurling the objects. Sophisticated equipment such as night-sights and image-intensifiers proved of no practical value and, by the end of 1982, after 3,500 man-hours of fruitless observation, the police had got no nearer to solving the crimes. Today, the visitations have ceased to plague the residents of Thornton Road but the mystery remains unsolved.

Outbreaks of inexplicable activity on the scale described above confound the claims of sceptics who insist that phantom stone-throwers are really no more than attention-seeking children hurling objects behind the backs of investigators. Could an entire police force be fooled for so long? Difficult to believe though many of these stories may sound, there can no longer be any reasonable doubt that ghostly stone-throwers do exist. Nor are they becoming any less active: during the past ten years reports have come from over a dozen countries including Czechoslovakia, Italy, South Africa, Kenya, Brazil and Western Australia.

1914

The Jinxed Mercedes

There is a theory widely held by paranormal investigators that runs of ill fortune marking the history of certain inanimate objects can usually be traced back to an initial tragedy. According to this hypothesis, negative thought-patterns can in some yet to be understood way psychically imprint themselves on the material world we see, touch and feel. This idea remains unproven, yet for evidence of such a force we surely need look no further than murderous history of the Mercedes-Benz limousine which featured in one of the most historic tragedies of the century.

The double killing of the Archduke Franz Ferdinand and his wife in Sarajevo while they were travelling in the car proved to be the spark that lit the fuse of the First World War. It also began a separate and quite astonishing legacy of destruction centred firmly on the vehicle itself.

Immediately following the outbreak of hostilities in Europe the Mercedes passed into the hands of a distinguished senior officer in the Austrian Cavalry, General Potiovek. Used as a general staff car the Mercedes proved an unlucky omen, and its owner's fortunes in battle turned sour. After presiding over a catastrophic defeat at Valjevo Potiovek resigned his commission and retired to his country retreat where he quickly went insane. The car, meanwhile, was passed on to a subordinate officer in the same regiment for whom it was to prove an equally unlucky possession. Early in 1915 the captain who had acquired the car drove into the back of a truck and was killed along with his driver and two other soldiers. After the Armistice was signed the Mercedes passed out of the armed services into civilian hands. Its first owner following the war was the governor of Yugoslavia. Although it was used only rarely the car still managed to become involved in several accidents during its official duties, the most serious of which occurred in the autumn of 1919 when it overturned on a bend killing its chauffeur and causing the governor himself to lose an arm. In 1923, having been auctioned by the authorities, the car became the property of a prosperous doctor. After two years of apparently trouble-free motoring he too met his death at the wheel, crushed to death as the car again overturned. Two peasants standing by the roadside also perished. And so the bloody saga continued. Of the car's last four civilian owners only one did not die in a fatal accident while driving it. The single exception, a wealthy jeweller, took his own life.

Others also suffered, including a Serbian farmer who fell under its wheels and a garage owner who died in a crash while testing the car after a service. The limousine's final owner, Tibor Hirschfield, died in a head-on collision with a bus as he returned from a wedding, along with his four passengers. All in all it would appear that a staggering twenty-two people lost their lives in accidents involving the Mercedez-Benz. Happily for the world's motorists the car is now safely installed in a Vienna museum.

Although the above-related tale is probably the worst case on record of a jinxed car it is certainly not unique. The Porsche racing car in which film star James Dean was killed in 1955 acquired a similar reputation. Bought by a garage owner named George Barris, the wrecked automobile slipped as it was being unloaded from the breakdown truck and broke the mechanic's legs. Considering the car to be damaged beyond repair, Barris initially decided that it should be broken up for spare parts, but unfortunately this did nothing to lessen the jinx's power. The engine was sold to a doctor who was also an amateur racing enthusiast, and in the very first event he entered following his own car's refit he was killed. Also killed in the same event was the driver of another car that contained parts from James Dean's cannibalised Porsche.

Meanwhile, back at the garage, someone had the bright idea of restoring the shell of the original car and exhibiting it as James Dean's death carriage. This ghoulish suggestion was soon put into practice and the car was towed on the back of a trailer across the southern states of America, where it proved to be a great attraction. However, unlike its former owner the jinx was far from dead and the truck pulling the sideshow was involved in several bizarre accidents. In Sacramento the car fell off its mounting, breaking a teenager's hip; en route to another destination it rolled off the back killing a pedestrian; in Oregon a truck carrying the car crashed into a shop; in New Orleans the Porsche fell off some stationary mounting supports and broke into several pieces. Finally, in 1960, the machine was permanently lost after it fell off a train while travelling to an exhibition in Los Angeles.

1915

The Battalion That Disappeared

While the flower of Europe's youth was being crucified on the barbed wire of the Western Front a smaller but no less bloody conflict was being fought between the Turks and the British in Southern Europe. The Gallipoli campaign of the First World War was mounted by the Allies in order to assist the Russian Army fighting in the Caucasus. Although it lasted only twelve months it cost many thousands of British and Commonwealth lives and resulted in the resignation of its architect, Winston Churchill. Among the hardest hit were the regiments of the Australian Commonwealth troops but it was the loss of a battalion of British soldiers from the 1st 5th Norfolk Regiment which provides us with the most extraordinary mystery of 1915.

The multiple vanishment quite literally into thin air of a total of 145 men might sound a fantastic fabrication, yet the incident was witnessed by, among others, a platoon of twenty-two volunteers of the number three section, First Division Field Company NZEF who, fifty years afterwards, broke their silence to sign an affidavit attesting to their recollections.

Briefly, what the Anzacs claimed to have seen can be described as follows: On the morning of 21 August the Allied forces were ordered by their Commander-in-Chief, Sir Ian Hamilton, to advance across Suvla Plain and ascend Hill 60, a Turkish stronghold. All that morning the lower slopes of the hill were shrouded in a curious mist, a meteorological phenomenon which, apart from being unprecedented in that region, appeared to defy natural law since it remained unaffected by a stiff breeze blowing from the south-west. Into this swirling mist a company of men from the 1st 5th Norfolk Regiment advanced, never to emerge. Then, according to the signed testimony of the Anzacs who watched in amazement from their positions lower down, the peculiar mist seemed to swirl ever more swiftly around in circles until it assumed a dense, solid-looking cloud shaped rather like a loaf of bread which rose into the sky leaving the slopes of Hill 60 devoid of men. The strangely shaped cloud then drifted away across an otherwise clear sky – against the direction of the wind!

Upon the cessation of hostilities in 1918 the British military authorities sought the return of prisoners captured in the battle of Suvla Bay. Turkey duly handed over its POWs but it became clear that although many British soldiers were captured during the battles which took place on 21 August 1915, no contact was made with the 1st 5th Norfolk Regiment.

Indeed, no captured British prisoners ever claimed afterwards to have seen or heard of any of the men who made up the battalion that disappeared on that fateful August day. Further evidence which tends to corroborate the extraordinary assertion of the Anzac veterans appeared in 1967, when a declassified edition of the final report of the Dardanelles campaign was at long last made public. Although it was heavily censored by the Ministry of Defence there remained some details which clearly lent credence to the story of an unnatural vanishment. In the MOD's final report the loss without apparent cause of a large body of men on the slopes of Hill 60 is conceded and the official description of the weather in Suvla Bay on the morning in question bears out the New Zealanders' version of events. The slopes of Hill 60 were, said the official report, 'wrapped in a strange and unnatural mist that rose up in a way astonishing to behold'.

Of course, this incredible story is too much for many people to swallow. In a campaign which is known to have cost the lives of tens of thousands on both sides, it is certainly easier to contend that the company was simply wiped out by the machine-guns of the Turkish defenders. Yet this explanation is unconvincing since it does not account for the lack of corpses on the battlefield and ignores the testimony of more than twenty surviving witnesses who had the courage fifty years later to tell the true version of events as they saw it, even though it left them open to ridicule.

The mass disappearance syndrome in which hundreds or even thousands of people vanish without warning or explanation seems to be a very rare phenomenon and for that we must be grateful. But the Suvla Bay incident is not unique in the annals of the supernatural history of the twentieth century.

In December 1937 China had been at war with Japan for more than six months. With the invaders pushing northwards to advance upon Nanking, a forward guard of approximately 3,000 Chinese troops was deployed to defend a vital bridge south of the city. Taking up entrenched positions, the troops waited for the expected Japanese onslaught. It never came. What did occur was much more alarming. On the morning following his tactical deployment the Chinese commanding officer, General Li Feu Siea, was awoken by a frantic subordinate who told him that radio contact had been lost with the division guarding the bridge. Fearing that his men had been overrun, Commander Feu Siea gave orders for an immediate reconnaissance to be made of the forward lines. He was prepared for the worst, yet the tale his officers returned to tell was so strange he could hardly believe it. For what they found was simply lines of empty trenches devoid not only of life but of death also. No corpses or other signs of a recent battle remained to suggest an explanation for the men's whereabouts. Li Feu Siea was baffled, for he knew that if the soldiers had deserted en masse they must have recrossed the bridge, but they had not done so. Southwards lay the enemy and certain destruction. So what had become of them? The Chinese puzzle was never solved. Two days after the division vanished hordes of Japanese swarmed across the bridge into the city. The assault that followed culminated in the rape of Nanking, a massacre unequalled in the bloody history of Asian warfare, and the loss of the 3,000 men defending the bridge was forgotten in the general carnage. However, many years later, following the end of the Second World War, an official investigation by the Chinese government could uncover no evidence to suggest a logical explanation for those strange happenings in the final days before Nanking fell. A later enquiry set up by the communist regime of Chairman Mao Tse Tung established categorically that none of the Chinese defenders who held the bridge in 1937 was ever seen or heard of again.

1916

Lest We Forget

Apparitional encounters have been reported so frequently throughout history that only the most stubborn sceptic could dispassionately view the evidence and come to the conclusion that there are no such things as ghosts. However, while most parapsychologists readily accept that phantom forms are seen with great regularity there is still considerable debate as to the precise nature of the phenomenon. One American parapsychologist has coined the phrase 'semi-substantial' to describe the ambiguous reality of ghostly apparitions. It seems particularly apt, for although ghosts can affect the physical environment of mass they fleetingly inhabit (lifting solid objects and so on) they are also often seen to appear and disappear suddenly, or fade in and out of view slowly, passing through closed doors, walls and solid objects, floating or gliding rather than walking. The same US researcher contends that ghosts exhibiting a less solid appearance may be returning via a different method, possibly through the mental projection of their own minds on to the minds of the observer – a sort of telepathically spawned hallucination. Yet another variety are, he feels, not really true ghosts at all but the place-memories of earlier events trapped in the psychic ether;

energy imprints, in other words.

Perhaps no single hypothesis is comprehensive enough to account for each and every type of ghostly manifestation. But whichever supposition we lean towards, the undeniable fact remains that some visionary entities do seem to return with purposeful intent and are apparently driven by a form of autonomous consciousness, a part of the human psyche which has survived the death of the brain and whose continued existence is independent of the blood, bone and tissue which has been destroyed.

In traditional ghost lore, many of the most dramatic and convincing apparitional encounters have taken place during times of great conflict, the ghosts involved being the spirits of those who have lost their lives on the battlefield. This concentration of wartime examples may be rather more than coincidental, for it is an enduring belief among cultures around the planet that those who die violently are more likely to return in phantom form than people who end their lives peacefully through natural causes.

Ghostly encounters from our own century tend to reinforce this ancient belief. A classic example of a soldier's ghost returning, in this case to fulfil a promise, is recalled by British author Robert Graves in *Goodbye to All That*, an account of the writer's experiences in the French battlefields of the First World War. The phantom in this instance was that of a young infantryman, Private Challoner, whom Graves had befriended while they were both undergoing training in Lancaster. Challoner's battalion was subsequently posted to France in March 1916, a few weeks before Graves' regiment, and on the day he was due to embark the young soldier had cheerfully told the future author that they would definitely meet again in France.

In fact Challoner was killed in a battle near the town of Festubert some days before Graves' troopship crossed the

Channel. A month or so later, however, Graves insists that he clearly saw the young man walk past the window of his billet room, smoking a cigarette. According to his account in *Goodbye to All That*, Challoner recognised his old acquaintance, saluted and walked on. When a shocked Graves reached out of the window, he saw only a smouldering cigarette butt lying where Challoner's ghost had passed a few seconds before. Typically, the writer ends his description of the incident with a classic understatement: 'Ghosts were numerous in France at the time.'

A strikingly similar example surrounds the last moments of Wilfred Owen, the First World War poet who appeared in London at the moment of his death in France at around twelve noon on 4 November 1918. A veteran of the Somme, Owen survived the great battles of the trenches only to be killed a few days before the Armistice ended the conflict.

Knowing the war to be close to its end, Owen's father had been hoping his son would be spared, but when he saw him suddenly appear as a shining figure dressed in his officer's uniform he knew in his heart that the young soldier would not be coming home. Sure enough, a week after Mr Owen saw his son's apparition he received an official telegram stating that Captain Wilfred Owen had died of injuries sustained in battle. If accurate, the time of his son's death in a French field hospital would appear to coincide exactly with the appearance of his spectral form in England.

Seven days later the poet's ghost was to return once more, appearing this time to his brother Harold, then serving as an officer on board *HMS Astraea*, a British cruiser anchored in Table Bay off the coast of South Africa. While ill with malaria Harold Owen was lying on his cabin bunk when he saw his elder brother's figure materialise just a few feet away from him. According to the naval officer's written account of the event, his brother's eyes were 'alive with the familiar look of trying to make me understand', and when Harold spoke the ghost's face 'broke into a sweet and most endearing dark smile'. Wilfred Owen's spectre vanished after a few seconds leaving his brother profoundly astonished that he should have appeared in his cabin. Yet the younger man wrote afterwards that he had felt no fear during the encounter, only an 'exquisite mental pleasure at thus beholding him'. Overcome with tiredness, Harold Owen fell into a deep sleep and when he awoke he knew with absolute certainty that his brother was dead. The following week a letter arrived from England confirming the news.

1917

Miraculous Visions at Fatima

The miraculous comes in many forms and never has this been more true than in the twentieth century. At the same time as churches have seen their influence diminish and ordinary men and women come to question the existence of God in increasing numbers, the appearance of signs and wonders has continued to take place unabated. Carved effigies have been seen to move, Madonnas to weep, images of the Crucifixion to bleed. Pictures of Christ have appeared suddenly and in the most unexpected places, huge crosses have been seen to float in the sky and the sick have been healed. To unbelievers none of this makes any sense and religious phenomena in their multifarious forms are often written off as the hysterical imaginings of the enraptured faithful. But in fact many of these miracles have now been proven to have taken place beyond any measure of reasonable doubt, leaving us with little choice but to accept that, in certain special circumstances, and for a brief period of time, faith in God can bring about a genuine transcendence of physical laws.

Without doubt the most famous Heaven-sent omen of the last hundred years was the so-called Miracle of Fatima. On 13 May 1917 a vision of a beautiful lady appeared to three poor shepherd children tending their sheep outside the small village of Fatima in Portugal. The children apparently saw, standing upon a glowing cloud that hovered above an oak tree, the shining figure of a young woman who told them that God had chosen them as his messengers and they must meet her in the same place on the thirteenth day of each month until October, when they would receive a very special communication. Believing the glowing form to be that of the Holy Virgin Mary the three youngsters, Lucia dos Santos, aged ten, and a brother and sister, Francisco and Jacinta Marto, nine and seven respectively, immediately returned home to tell their parents of the vision. Though bemused, the adult members of their families were sufficiently impressed by the children's certainty to accompany them to the spot on the thirteenth of the following month. They were not alone. In all, some fifty local people who had heard the story were gathered when the vision of Our Lady returned on 13 June. Though the children were the only ones to actually see the woman's figure, all the others present did apparently see a strange transformation in the sky and hear heavenly music emanating from the clouds.

News of the strange goings-on at Fatima spread throughout southern Portugal and an even larger crowd, numbering several thousand, turned up for the repeat performance the following month. Once again many of those present reported witnessing a strange light in the sky and other mysterious phenomena. Meanwhile, the Catholic Church, which had initially derided talk of the heavenly visitation, became concerned at the way so many people had come to believe in the children's story. And so when 13 August arrived the local Catholic archbishop had Lucia, Francisco and Jacinta arrested for interrogation before they had a chance to go to the appointed place.

Despite considerable pressure and no little amount of

bullying the three children steadfastly refused to change their version of events and two days later the authorities had little choice but to release them. And on 25 July the glowing lady appeared to them again, this time on a hillside near Valinhos. She told them they would see her for the last time on 13 October when she would impart to them the promised message of monumental importance. By that time considerable excitement and controversy had grown around the children's visions and a crowd of no fewer than 70,000 people joined them on the wet and dismal afternoon of 13 October in the hope that they too might see the apparition for themselves and at last have God's existence proven to them. But the faith of those gathered was to be reinforced in a quite different way.

As before the shining lady herself remained invisible to all but the children themselves, yet in the sky above, the dark clouds were suddenly parted to reveal a brilliant sun radiating all the colours of the rainbow. There was a peal of deafening thunder and a blinding flash of light far brighter than anything seen before by witnesses. Yet what was to come was even more extraordinary. For then the sun itself began to move across the sky in a spinning motion, casting off revolving beams of coloured lights. It plunged crazily towards the earth then returned upwards like a bouncing ball in a way which was both terrifying and wonderful to behold. Some people fainted, some screamed, most simply fell to their knees and prayed. Eye-witness accounts suggest that after a few seconds the sun returned to its normal position but twice more repeated the same fantastic manoeuvre, all the time casting an unearthly luminosity over the crowd, before the display ended. Afterwards people on the hillside found that their clothing, which had been soaked through in an earlier downpour, had become quite dry.

Shortly after their brief moment of fame two of the

children involved in the enigma, Francisco and Jacinta, died during the influenza epidemic of 1918. Lucia learned to write and imparted the three secrets the shining lady had told her on that day to the Pope. The first refers clearly to the end of the horrors of the First World War, while the second appears to predict the outbreak of the Second World War and its conclusion with a weapon of unheard-of power which created a great unknown light. Lucia's record of the vision's last warning has never been made public by the Roman Catholic hierarchy and remains securely locked away in a vault deep within the heart of the Vatican. Only the encumbent Pope is privy to the dire prophecy it is reputed to contain.

The events of Fatima were never to be repeated, and much controversy surrounds the whole purported occurrence. While it is unnecessary to point out that the sun could hardly have moved from its position in the galaxy, nor the earth from its axis, the fact remains that tens of thousands of people did afterwards attest to the evidence of their own eyes, that the sun danced on that remarkable day in October 1917. Many of these were not devout Roman Catholics, and even in the case of those who had gone there in sublime anticipation of witnessing something wonderful it is not easy to imagine why they should all have seen the same event if it had been simply a hallucination.

1918

Without Trace

The sea remains a place of grim secrets and baffling enigmas. Although maritime safety standards have improved dramatically during the present century every year sees the disappearance of between five and ten large ships, leaving no trace or explanation for their loss. Why these tragedies continue to occur on such a scale we cannot safely say, yet simplistic natural explanations often seem insufficient.

Among the many mysteries of the sea few have caused so much controversy among sailors as the inexplicable disappearance of the American vessel *USS Cyclops*, a 20,000-ton collier which vanished with a cargo of manganese ore in late March 1918. With the loss of 304 lives, the demise of the *Cyclops* proved to be the US Navy's worst disaster of the First World War, yet it seems unlikely that the ship fell victim to the mines or torpedoes of the enemy. With a length of over 500 feet the cargo ship should have been able to withstand the most severe Atlantic storms. Instead she vanished in fine weather.

Very few of the known facts of the last voyage of the *Cyclops* seem to make sense. Twenty-four hours after leaving port from Barbados, where she had delivered a quantity of coal and taken on some 10,000 tons of manganese ore to be used in the manufacture of arms, the *Cyclops* passed the liner *Vestris*, engaged on her usual run from Buenos Aires to New York. The message from the cargo vessel indicated that all was well on board. But neither the *Cyclops* nor any of the 300 souls she carried were ever seen again by human eyes. When she was posted overdue orders were sent to search the area of the vessel's known route. No wreckage was found and the US Naval authorities seemed unable to suggest a plausible reason why she might have sunk.

Mines were not believed to present a hazard to shipping in that part of the South Atlantic and U-Boat activity was thought at the time to be confined to more northern waters.

In the many years that have passed various scenarios have been suggested for the demise of the ship: a sudden localised hurricane, a bomb planted by saboteurs and even mutiny among the crew have all been mooted. There is no evidence to support any of these hypotheses and a US Navy investigation conducted in the months following the Armistice confirmed that no enemy surface vessel or U-Boat had been in the vicinity of the *Cyclops* during her last voyage. That a rough sea could have broken up the vessel seemed most unlikely since she had already proved herself a rugged ship, battling through countless Atlantic gales during the eight years following her launch in 1910. In any case, as the official enquiry showed, there were no reports of storms anywhere off the east coast of central America during late March or early April. Joseph Daniels, Secretary to the Navy, wrote of the disaster: 'There is no more baffling mystery in the annals of the Navy than the disappearance of the *USS Cyclops*.' President Woodrow Wilson, who took an active role in trying to uncover evidence that might provide a solution to the mystery, finally had to concede that 'Only God and the sea know what happened to that great ship.'

Almost three-quarters of a century later the statesman's words still ring true. However, the *USS Cyclops* is simply one of many huge ships that have vanished during the twentieth century in circumstances which can only be described as baffling. On 17 June 1984 the Panamanian-owned *Artic Carrier*, a 17,000-ton cargo vessel, left Brazil with a full cargo of various commodities. She was last heard of 300 miles north-east of Tristan da Cunha in the South Atlantic. What fate befell her we cannot say, although we know for certain that no mayday message was sent and neither bodies nor wreckage were recovered.

It was as if the ship had never existed. A paragraph in Lloyd's List sums up the enigma to perfection: 'The real reason for her loss, as unexpected as it was sudden, will probably remain a mystery.' At the end of October 1979 a ship four times bigger than the *Artic Carrier*, the Norwegian ore-carrier *Berge Vanya*, disappeared at a position estimated to be some 600 miles due west of Cape Town in apparently pleasant weather conditions, and while crossing some of the busiest shipping lanes in the world. That the sea could have devoured the *Berge Vanya* before she could send a mayday signal to nearby ships or even fire a single SOS flare into the night sky was hard to accept. Even so, no one saw the great leviathan go down and there have few conjectures as to the force that destroyed her.

The loss of the *Orient Treasury*, a 28,000-ton bulk carrier flying the Panamanian flag, provides another odd story. Carrying a cargo of chrome when she sailed from Masinloc in the Philippines on 12 January 1982, the *Orient Treasury* successfully reached Port Said before she vanished. Amazingly a committee of investigation concluded that the vessel might have been the victim of pirates, though no buccaneers were known to have operated in those waters for more than a century. Why such an extraordinary claim should have been made without a shred of evidence to support it beggars belief. As one journalist afterwards commented, 'They appear to be grasping at straws.'

And so the list of lost ships goes on and on, with each seafaring nation recording its share of disasters which seem to defy belief. One of the most spectacular misfortunes to have struck the British merchant fleet concerns the last voyage of the UK-built 170,000-ton combination carrier the *Derbyshire*, which sailed from the US port of St Lawrence, bound for Kawasaki in Japan, in 1980. With a mass twice as big as the *Titanic*'s and a length three times that of a football pitch, the *Derbyshire* was among the largest ships ever to fly the red ensign. Built to carry crude oil, bulk or iron ore she was loaded with 157,000 tons on her voyage to the bottom of the sea. The great ship was manned by a crew of forty-two and skippered by an experienced captain, Geoffrey Underhill, so the trip should have presented no problem for her. Yet it did, and why we shall never know. The *Derbyshire*'s last radio message on 8 September put the vessel's position some 700 miles south-west of Tokyo and estimated her time of arrival at Kawasaki at around noon on 11 September. It was the last anyone heard of her. Whatever fate befell her must have happened so suddenly that it gave no one a chance to send a mayday signal. As one English journalist commented at the time, 'There was a routine radio signal – then oblivion.'

Just why such gigantic ships should simply vanish in fine weather without sending a distress signal and leaving no signs of wreckage whatsoever is beyond the ken of most maritime experts. Today's vessels are certainly better built than their nineteenth-century predecessors and while the early steam era saw many ships break up as a result of poor design methods, today's mighty iron-clads are constructed to rigorous safety standards and surveyed under strict supervision before they are given the necessary certificate of seaworthiness. There are no longer bands of wreckers or fleets of pirates to harm them and the possibility of sudden unexpected severe weather conditions has been greatly lessened by satellite early-warning systems and reliable radio transmission apparatus. Nevertheless, vessels of all sizes, including the most massive steamships, continue to vanish without apparent cause. As the list of lost ships continues to grow longer some mysteriologists are coming round to the conclusion that the sea is hiding dangers which have yet to be recognised.

1919

Death Bones in the Outback

Throughout recorded history there has remained a universal superstition among the races and civilisations of our planet. According to this belief select groups of individuals within a particular society are said to possess the unique power to harm others, either through the sheer force of their will or by using some secret magical art. In some parts of today's world, including Haiti, Australia, Africa and areas of eastern Europe, belief in curses and spells is as strong as ever and although most enlightened Westerners would dismiss the idea out of hand eye-witness accounts suggest that there really have been occasions when healthy people have turned sick and died for no apparent reason.

Among the best-known methods of supernatural murder is the bone-pointing ritual practised by the Aboriginal Australians. Early settlers to the subcontinent were amazed at the rapidity of death brought about by the secret methods of the Aboriginal sorcerers called Mulunguwa. This extraordinary form of execution had already been in existence for several thousands of years and continues to be used today. The weapons used, ritually loaded killing bones, or *kundela*, are usually the femurs of large lizards, kangaroos or emus, but some are also fashioned from wood. Their design, like the material used, varies from tribe to tribe. Usually, *kundela* are quite small, from 6 to 9 inches long, pointed at one end and shaved to a smooth roundness. They are hardened in a charcoal fire and the blunt end is wrapped around with human hair and then charged with the Mulunguwa's psychic energy. Once the weapon has been made ready it is given to the Kurdaitcha, the tribe's ritual killers. These frightening figures clothe themselves with kangaroo hair, which they stick to their skin with human blood, and may afterwards don masks of emu feathers to make their appearance even more strange.

Operating like a team of Mafia hit-men, in groups of two or three, the Kurdaitcha are relentless and seldom give up the hunt for a condemned man. When they finally corner their prey, they approach to within 15 feet or so, one member holding the exposed bone. Pointing it like a pistol, he thrusts the *kundela* forward while the Kurdaitcha utter a succession of piercing chants. Once the spear of thought has pierced their intended victim they retreat, knowing that death will follow, as certainly as if the man had had an actual spear thrust through his heart.

Descriptions of those who suffer the agonies of the *kundela*'s after-effects make unpleasant reading. One early Antipodean anthropologist, Dr Herbert Basedow, wrote of a man he knew to be cursed ending his life as a pitiable sight. 'His cheeks blanched and his eyes became glassy while the expression of his face became horribly distorted . . . when he attempted to shriek the sound choked in his throat and all one saw was froth at his mouth. His body began to tremble and the muscles twisted involuntarily . . . soon after he fell on the ground and began to writhe in mortal agony . . .' For the man Basedow described, death came as a relief.

Many psychologists believe that it is the consequences of extreme fear itself which set the body's natural production of adrenaline, thereby reducing the blood supply to the muscles and constricting smaller blood vessels in the process. This intense fear would, according to the beliefs of such medical practitioners, begin a potentially disastrous cycle of reduced blood pressure and reduced circulation, which, if unchecked, could prove fatal. So, provided the victim himself believes that the deadly magic is unassailable and as long as his own closed community subscribes to the same belief, it is perhaps not so hard to see why the Australian Aboriginals' curses should achieve their devastating effect. The Western experts say that the boning ritual is, in effect, a form of psychosomatic suicide rather than a true psychic murder.

One or two incidents recorded during the present century suggest that the killing method of the Aboriginal hit-men is not necessarily irreversible, while others simply reinforce the terrible power which the bones have. In 1919 Dr S.M. Lambert was working with the international health division of the Rockefeller Foundation at the remote Mona Mona Mission in northern Queensland. In a report published several years later Dr Lambert concluded that the boning method of murder left no trace of physical wounds nor any medically acceptable cause of death. Initially, he had dismissed all talk of invisible killings out of hand, yet during the autumn of 1919, after one of his missionary helpers, a native convert named Rob, fell victim to a curse laid by a local witchdoctor named Nebo, Lambert found his mind being changed very quickly. Soon after the bone was pointed at him Rob became seriously ill and extremely weak, though an examination by Lambert discovered no sign of fever nor any symptoms of a recognised disease. He tried to reason with the man to no avail. Seeing Rob's life ebbing away by the hour, he went to the witchdoctor and threatened to cut off his tribe's supply of food. Reluctantly, Nebo agreed to visit Rob and cast a spell releasing him from the effect of the bone's power. By the following morning the mission worker had completely recovered and was once again in full possession of his physical strength.

Sometimes, however, the boning ritual claims its victim despite the attentions of the white man's medicine. In 1953 a sick Aborigine named Kinjika who had angered his tribe and had been boned as a punishment, was transferred by air from his local Arnhem Land to the Northern Territories. Kinjika had not been injured or poisoned and appeared not to be suffering from any known disease, but doctors in Darwin quickly realised that he was dying and guessed that fear of the curse was to blame. However, no one within the modern hospital seemed able to help him and nothing psychiatrists said could convince the man that he had more than a few days to live. In fact the native survived for a further seventy-two hours before expiring in an agonised convulsion. An autopsy on Kinjika's body revealed no wounds and no sign of poison.

Three years later, in mid-April 1956, again from Arnhem Land, the same hospital received another Aboriginal patient, named Lya Wulumu, who had fallen ill in a similar fashion. Examinations including X-rays, blood tests and spinal taps detected nothing abnormal and doctors treating the man could find no clue to his deteriorating condition, apart from the boning ritual. According to one specialist who treated him it was as if the man's life was slowly running out of his body, like sand from an hourglass. Psychiatrists tried hypnotism to reinforce a conviction that he could beat the curse but as his strength slowly failed he was placed in an iron lung. Once again the doctors' efforts were to no avail. On the third day after he was admitted Lya Wulumu lost his life in a writhing, twitching, vomiting heap, just one more tragic testament to the efficacy of the notorious Aboriginal bones of death.

1920

The Curious Case of the Amphibious Elephants

As the world's largest land creature it is unsurprising that the elephant features among the main attractions in zoos and game reserves around the world. But size is only part of the reason for the elephant's perennial popularity. It is rarely aggressive unless endangered, and there is much in the animal's nature to admire: children and adults alike marvel at the gentle sensitivity with which even the most massive of elephants will use its trunk to take a bun or piece of fruit from a human hand.

While it has long been known that the elephant is among the most intelligent mammalian species, it has only recently been discovered that it has a unique capacity among land mammals: the ability to emit sub-sonic signals below the threshold of human hearing using a vibration of the bones in its forehead. These signals, not unlike those emitted by whales, can travel over huge distances and convey a variety of messages. Thus a mother elephant is able to call to her calf or warn other members of her herd of imminent danger without showing any outward signs of alarm.

The comparison between the sub-sonic sounds transmitted by elephants and the complex songs sung by whales is almost certainly coincidental, for clearly the former is a land mammal and no zoologist has ever seriously put forward a case for the modern-day elephant having evolved from a marine species. Yet astonishingly there is now strong evidence that elephants do sometimes enter the water, not merely for a brief wallow in a pool or in order to cross a river, but actually to swim in the open sea itself, sometimes travelling great distances in the process. So unlikely does this possibility seem that wildlife experts have traditionally scoffed at the very mention of amphibious tuskers, but for the mysteriologist prepared to take facts at face value, the case for believing in the ocean-going elephant is now overwhelming.

The first real evidence we have of a seaborne elephant comes from the eye-witness account of a South African farmer living on the Natal coast near Margate. On the morning of 1 November 1920 Hugh Balance was looking out to sea when he saw a violent commotion in the water at a distance he reckoned to be about a third of a mile from the shore. Having run to fetch his binoculars Balance could make out an apparent fight between two killer whales and a third creature that raised itself out of the water on a number of occasions. As the battle continued a growing crowd of people gathered to join the farmer, who was at last and to his own amazement able to make a positive identification of the third animal.

The others present were dumbfounded when Balance insisted that it was an elephant, but when they looked through the field glasses for themselves they could only confirm his opinion.

According to a full account of the affair published subsequently in a provincial South African newspaper, the unequal offshore struggle continued for some time before the whales swam away leaving the third animal floating lifelessly on the surface. During the night a heavily mutilated carcass drifted on to the beach near Tragedy Hill, where it was examined and found to be certainly elephantine in form with a distinctive trunk and tusks. The body lay there rotting for several days until a team of oxen dragged it back to the sea, where it was washed away by the outgoing tide.

When the full report of the Natal incident appeared in the London *Daily Mail* an expert from Regent's Park Zoo wrote off the story as a hoax. Yet several readers who had returned from the colonies wrote in to describe their own sightings of elephants swimming in estuaries or the wide mouths of rivers, while an expatriate New Zealander pointed out that an elephant carcass had been washed up on a beach in Queensland, Australia, during the latter half of the last century. Still, it would be fair to say, very few people who knew the habits of elephants well were prepared to countenance the possibility that such heavy quadrupeds could swim in waters out of their depth for any length of time. But since then the century has produced many more examples which point to exactly that likelihood.

In 1930 the carcass of a small elephant-like animal with a long trunk was washed up on Glacier Island, Alaska, and in 1944 the headless corpse of what seemed to be a fully grown male was washed ashore at Machrihanish Bay on the west side of Kintyre, Scotland. Since neither of these locations was anywhere near the natural land habitats of either Indian or African elephants, it is not hard to imagine the bewilderment of those people who found them.

In 1955 two more elephants – believed to be of the Indian variety – were washed on to a beach near Wellington in New Zealand, while during the same year another was found beached at high tide near Sen Zu Mura on the Japanese coast of Oshima. Sixteen years later the sea carried another elephant's body to England. It landed in Widemouth Bay, not far from Bude in Cornwall, in March 1971. Just a few months afterwards the crew of the trawler *Ampula* working out of the

North Sea fishing port of Grimsby were amazed to find a ton of young African elephant in their nets together with the usual catch of cod and herring.

Just how these huge exotic land mammals might have found their way into oceans thousands of miles away from their natural habitat is hard to imagine, but the sheer fact of the phenomenon is beyond question. Could it be that they had died on land and had fallen close to a shore to be washed away by a tide? Might they have fallen into rivers and drowned, and then been carried out by strong currents into the open sea? Did they escape from captivity and fall overboard from ships carrying them alive to foreign zoos? There is absolutely no proof for the last hypothesis and precious little for the former.

If anything, evidence seems to suggest that these elephants had spent much of their time in the sea alive. Although an elephant's skin is very tough, exposure to salt water might be expected to bring the body to a state of advanced decomposition rather more quickly that they could be carried from their native shores to the extreme northern or southern climes where the examples listed above were found. Yet these elephant carcasses appeared, with one exception, to be in pretty near-perfect condition. The problem is that the alternative solution (that elephants can swim in the open sea) seems to many experts to be a hundred times more incredible still. Zoologists, for their part, would have no truck with the idea.

Then in 1976, to add further fuel to the mystery, an Englishwoman who signed herself simply 'Mary F.' submitted two remarkable photographs and an accompanying letter of explanation to a local newspaper in Cornwall. She claimed the photographs depicted a 'sea serpent' she had sighted off Trefusis Point at the mouth of the River Fal, but in fact they seemed to show quite clearly the outline of an elephant's head and trunk rising above the waves. Indeed, 'Mary F.' wrote in her letter that the creature had seemed very much elephantine in its shape, size and movement, yet for some reason the witness never drew the obvious conclusion. Incredible though her story was, many local people remember that five years earlier a dead elephant had been washed up on the coastland at nearby Bude and thus were more willing than most Britons to believe the woman's story and accept the photographs as genuine.

Could an elephant have gaily swum around the world's oceans and eventually ended up off southern England? It seemed unlikely, but the pseudonymous woman had been quite certain that the thing she had sighted in the water was definitively alive.

As it was to turn out, an event just three years later would finally prove that elephants can and do swim successfully in waters of great depth many miles out to sea. The August 1979 edition of the *New Scientist* included a photograph taken the previous month by Admiral R. Kadirgama, which showed a local species of elephant swimming 20 miles off the coast of Sri Lanka. With its trunk waving in the air and its four legs underneath achieving a steady motion, the elephant was clearly in no difficulties. So, faced at last with the undeniable evidence, sceptical zoologists around the world were forced to eat their words and accept that elephants sometimes swim out to sea. When in 1982 the crew of an Aberdeen fishing boat pulled in a dead elephant about 32 miles out of their North Sea port nobody in the zoological fraternity was particularly surprised. On the other hand, for the half-dozen Scottish trawlermen aboard the vessel, the world 'surprise' hardly suffices!

1921

Footprints in the Snow

During the early months of 1921 an expedition of British climbers was attempting an ascent upon the treacherous North Face of Mount Everest, when, having reached an altitude of 17,000 feet, they were surprised to see three large figures moving along on hind legs in the snow field above them. Although the figures were clearly non-human, a more precise identification proved impossible and by the time the explorers reached the spot the only thing left behind was some huge ape-like footprints in the snow. Longer and a good deal broader than those made by the climbers' own mountain boots, the impressions showed three broad toes and an even broader thumb to the side. One was measured and found to be 13 inches wide by 18 inches long, although because of the quickly melting snow the exact size of the original print could not be determined with complete accuracy. Dumbfounded by the vision and the traces left behind, the leader of the expedition, a British officer named Lt Col Charles Kenneth Howard-Bury, was astonished to learn from his Sherpa guides that the illusive creatures were well known to local people, who called them Yeh-Teh, or Man-Beast.

The Sherpas described the animals as being basically

human-like in facial appearance, with large pointed heads, long arms which hung below the knees and a covering of brownish-red hair. They kept themselves to themselves, living around the tree line and only occasionally venturing upwards into the realms of perpetual snow. Basically shy creatures, the yeti were considered by the Nepalese to be usually harmless, although there had been stories of them pilfering food from villages, preying on yak herds and sometimes, on very rare occasions, attacking humans. It did not take the British officer long to realise the significance of this discovery. Not only were these creatures quite evidently an unknown species, if the descriptions of his guides were accurate, they were quite unlike any existing life form known to zoologists.

When Lt Col Charles Howard Bury returned from the Himalayas to report details of his sighting to journalists, it excited exactly the level of interest he had anticipated. Within months news of this 'abominable snowman' had spread throughout the world and the legend of the Nepalese man-beast was on the lips of newspaper readers everywhere. Zoologists quickly became divided on the question of whether a race of unknown human-like monsters might live secretly in one of the more remote areas of the planet. But the majority were quite clearly against it. Though Charles Darwin in his evolutionary theory had postulated the possibility that a 'missing link' still existed somewhere in the huge uncharted mountains of Soviet central Asia, few had taken his idea seriously. And since it was generally believed that all the larger animals of the world had been found and catalogued it seemed incredible that such a remarkable creature could have remained undetected for so long.

Yet evidence for the existence of the yeti continued to accumulate as the century wore on. In 1925 a Greek photographer named N.A. Tombasi reported the sighting of a huge hairy man-beast which walked upright and occasionally stopped to uproot rhododendron bushes in the mountains of Sikkim. When it realised it was being watched the creature quickly disappeared, but Tombasi claimed to have found tracks in the snow unlike those of a human being or any known animal species.

Although the following two decades would see a virtual absence of yeti reports, in 1951 a British Everest reconnaissance expedition on a mission to evaluate routes for an attempt to ascend Everest the following year, found more tracks at an altitude of 18,000 feet which followed a line along the edge of the Menlung Glacier. According to the expedition leader, Eric Shipton, the tracks, which lasted for nearly a mile, were evidently not made by a human being. Instead, a bipedal creature of great weight and with an enormous stride seemed responsible. An experienced climber who had scaled mountains throughout the world, Shipton was a reliable enough witness and his photographs of the freshly made tracks, clearly showing the spoor of a large mammal, reignited the controversy surrounding the yeti's existence. In the climber's own opinion the tracks were probably made the night prior to their discovery or earlier that day because there was no sign of blurring around the edges, which showed well-defined toe marks. Shipton was positive that the creature which made them must have been a very large biped and since the shape of the spoor differed markedly from those of a bear, it was almost certain that they were made by an unknown creature.

Others disagreed. Sceptics were quick to point out that melting snow often enlarges small, well-defined tracks into bigger ones and that given this scenario the tracks Shipton photographed might conceivably have been made by a langar monkey, a species known to sometimes live at considerable heights. In order to test the theory Professor W. Tschernezsky of Queen Mary's College, London conducted an exhaustive analysis of the Shipton footprints using a reconstructed model which he compared with bears, various monkey spoors, and those made by early man. None were comparable.

For a brief time it seemed that the case for believing in the yeti's existence was becoming unassailable; yet by the beginning of the 1960s the position had swung back towards the sceptics' viewpoint. Several expeditions financed by London newspapers and led by experienced teams of British climbers failed to find either the snowmen themselves or their tracks. One reputed yeti scalp turned out, embarrassingly, to be pieces of goatskin mounted on tough hide. Sir Edmund Hillary, who was knighted for his personal conquest of Everest in 1953, mounted his own abortive yeti-finding expedition in 1960 and came back convinced that stories about the animal were nothing more than fascinating fairy-tales moulded by local superstition and nurtured by the Western media.

And yet, just when the case for believing in the creature's existence was beginning to fall apart, the number of sightings by Westerners increased. In 1970 a member of a team climbing Annapurna, Welshman Don Whillans, was alerted by his Sherpa to the approach of a yeti. He turned round in time to see the creature drop behind a ridge and afterwards discovered a set of freshly made tracks in the soft snow. Later that day Whillans again saw the creature, or another of the species, bounding along with an ape-like gait; he watched it for some time as it travelled over a distance of half a mile before disappearing into the shadow of some rocks. Formerly doubtful of the yeti legend, Whillans was now certain in his own mind that the animal he had seen was not a known monkey or bear. In 1975 a Polish trekker named Janusz Tomaszczuk had a rather more dramatic encounter while he was hiking in the foothills of Everest. In contrast to the shy behaviour of the yetis previously sighted by Westerners, the creature Tomaszczuk saw advanced upon him menacingly until the Pole's frightened screams drove it away.

In addition to actual sightings the past twenty years have seen the emergence of more examples of clearly defined tracks backed up by extremely convincing photographic evidence. In 1978 Lord Hunt, a distinguished British climber and leader of the first successful expedition to scale Everest, photographed huge footprints 14 inches long and 7 inches wide which he found in a side valley below the world's highest mountain. Hunt, who had seen similar tracks on several occasions before and had heard for himself the creatures' high-pitched yelping cries piercing the still mountain air of the Himalayas, firmly believes that there can be no explanation other than the existence of an unidentified species.

The following year, 1979, another British expedition found fresh footprints in the Hinken Valley and heard scream-like calls several nights running. The team leader, Squadron Leader John Edwards, took a number of very clear pictures of the tracks which, in the opinion of several experts, provided the firmest evidence to date that the abominable snowman was real.

Yet the question-mark against the existence of the legendary Himalayan man-monster remains unanswered. The Sherpas, who make little distinction between the metaphysical world and objective reality, believe the yeti can make itself invisible and reappear at will. Were this to be true it would easily explain why the world is still waiting for a convincing photograph of the creature, let alone a live example, caged and tagged. Without doubt the brief history of the abominable snowman is entangled in a web of fantasy, legend and most recently commercialism. Searches for the creature have provided much-needed foreign revenue for one of the world's poorest countries and newly-built hotels are named after the yeti in the towns which lie in the foothills of the mighty Himalayas.

Sceptics may scoff but the fact remains that the footprints have been reported, and more importantly photographed, on many occasions; droppings have been analysed, and sightings by unimpeachable witnesses, including several Western climbers, continue to be made. Inconclusive this evidence may be, but can it be dismissed?

1922

Invisible Assailants in London's West End

For many people the possibility of suddenly being attacked by an unknown assailant is one of the nightmares of modern-day life, and given the increase in violent crime this fear would seem to be well founded. In the late twentieth century armed robberies, muggings and motiveless beatings appear in our newspapers with ever-growing frequency. Along with the increasing willingness of criminals to resort to barbarity, racial tensions, social deprivation and the slow cancer of drug and alcohol abuse is gradually eroding the social framework of our inner cities, bringing with it civil disorder, riots and a rise in nihilistic street gangs. Against this background of mounting crisis, serial killers drift like evil spores on the wind of social upheaval, killing and mutilating individuals at random in order to satisfy their twisted sense of personal gratification.

When senseless and vicious attacks take place without warning the police are faced with an uphill struggle to convict those responsible. The one thing that would appear certain is that when violent crimes take place the perpetrators as well as the victims are bound to be human. Yet, as we are about to see in this short chapter, even this apparently obvious assumption might sometimes be erroneous. The nature of some physical assaults is so bizarre that even the latest and most sophisticated methods of crime detection offer no chance of tracking down the assailants.

Early in the morning of 16 April 1922 a man was brought in unconscious to London's Charing Cross Hospital, bleeding profusely from a deep stab wound to his neck. Stabbings in the West End of London were rare in those days, particularly in broad daylight, and the physicians treating his injuries were shocked. But this incident proved to be a crime of an even stranger variety than doctors had first expected. For it was an assault that lacked an assailant.

When he regained consciousness the injured man, an office clerk on his way to work, claimed to police that no one had been close enough to administer the thrust, nor had anyone jumped out upon him. He was quite certain. They assumed that he must have been mistaken until a witness to the incident, which had taken place at a turning off Coventry Street in London's West End, corroborated the victim's strange testimony. Still, were this to be the only piece of evidence, they would have been forgiven for rejecting the apparently supernatural nature of the crime. However it was not.

Two hours after the office worker was admitted, another man bearing knife wounds staggered into Charing Cross Hospital, again speaking of an invisible attacker. Finally, that evening, a third victim of the phantom knifeman was treated by the hospital's doctors. A full police enquiry was launched, only to discover that each assault had occurred at precisely the same spot – the turning off Coventry Street. Beyond that the constabulary was unable to offer a solution and when a full report of the bizarre crimes appeared in the following week's *Daily Express* newspaper, a police spokesman was quoted as admitting that the men's injuries defied rational explanation.

Most puzzling of all, it emerged that the last of the three victims seemed to have been stabbed in the back at a point below the left shoulder blade – yet his jacket showed no signs of penetration whatsoever.

The mysterious violations that took place during the daylight hours of 16 April 1922 echoed the bizarre circumstances surrounding the murder of Englishwoman Lavinia Farrar twenty-one years earlier. Discovered lying in a pool of blood on the kitchen floor of her Cambridgeshire home in March 1901, Farrar was found to have been stabbed repeatedly through the heart. Yet incredibly her dress remained intact. Could it be that she had had the strength to put on clothes after stabbing herself? wondered detectives. It seemed unlikely, for she was seventy-two years old, blind and a cripple. The assailant, whether human or otherwise, was never identified.

Another victim whose injuries bore the hallmarks of an unnatural murder was English farmworker Charles Walton. The agricultural labourer was found dead on the afternoon of 14 February 1945 in a field on Meon Hill near Lower Quinton in Warwickshire. To those who found him it was immediately evident that he had been killed by a pitchfork: there were deep slashes on his chest and throat forming a cross shape. Yet since the man was believed to have no enemies, had not been robbed and was unlikely to have taken his own life in such a ghastly manner, the mystery of his death remained beyond the wit of even Scotland Yard's best detectives to uncover. Some locals suggested witchcraft might be involved, and others pointed to the fact that the place where Walton's body was found was reputedly haunted by spectral figures, one of which was regularly seen – according to local folklore – carrying a large pitchfork.

Publicly the London detectives derided all such talk as superstition. Privately, they themselves began to wonder whether a supernatural murder really had taken place after several of their men saw the ghostly form for themselves.

Anyone who finds the above-related stories hard to swallow might care to trawl through the pages of Charles Fort, that veteran chronicler of the unusual. There you will find listed outbreaks of invisible throat-cutters, unseen stranglers and even, in China, the odd plague of demon pigtail choppers! Since Fort was writing in the early years of the present century most of his examples are taken from the Victorian era. Yet a contemporary survey of newspaper clippings from around the world shows that such incidents are as likely to occur today as ever in the past. Indeed, the correlations of time and space between some deaths for which the cause remains unknown makes one wonder whether these malign invisible forces are beginning to use even more subtle methods of dispatching humans. Within the space of an hour on the afternoon of 7 July 1988, two young Canadian Indians, Alexander Eagle and Charles Brian Able, suddenly fell down dead while walking close to the steps of the main city hydro-sub-station in Cecil Street, Toronto. Although the men had both seemed perfectly fit they had each suffered a complete circulatory collapse. Yet despite three months of forensic testing for poisonous or toxic chemicals, drugs and alcohol, experts were unable to find a cause of death for either man. The following October the *Toronto Star* described police bafflement after the discovery of an unconscious thirty-year-old Indian on the steps of the same building. Having been taken to hospital the man died later the same day, and doctors were unable to suggest a reason for his sudden demise.

Were these men's deaths linked only by a cruel quirk of fate or was there a more sinister force at work? And if the second possibility is true, what mind is directing that energy?

1923

The Boy King's Curse

The discovery of the tomb of Tutenkamen was without doubt the archaeological find of the century. For the first time in history a royal tomb of ancient Egypt was seen in all its magnificent splendour complete and intact. Yet the world-wide sensation over the tomb's riches was soon to be replaced by stories about its curse.

The expedition which uncovered the last resting-place of the boy king was headed by two Englishmen – Lord Carnarvon and Howard Carter – who had been on the pharaoh's trail for more than fifteen years. Carnarvon was an amateur archaeologist who financed the expedition from his own pocket. Carter, on the other hand, was a dedicated and highly regarded professional in the field of Egyptology. Together they had searched for the ultimate prize; together they would regret their success. Neither man could claim to have been ignorant of the curse: in August 1922 Carnarvon received a warning from the famous mystic and clairvoyant Count Louis Hamon. Hamon described how he had received a cryptic message through his spirit guide. The message, relayed through automatic writing when Hamon was in a trance state, read: 'Lord Carnarvon not to enter tomb. Disobey at peril. If ignored will suffer sickness. Death follows.' The English peer, normally not a man given to superstitious beliefs, was nonetheless sufficiently concerned to contact his associate in the venture. When asked for advice, Carter told him that such talk was not for sane men. So, dismissing all thoughts of supernatural evil, Carnarvon went ahead with his plans. The story of Count Hamon's warnings soon reached the pages of the press, however, and by the time the archaeologists set sail for their destination, tales of impending doom had captured public imagination around the globe.

For more than two months nothing was discovered in the Valley of the Kings and it began to appear increasingly likely that yet another mission would end in failure. Then one morning a team of native workers led by Carter found some steps leading down into the sand which, when uncovered, revealed the tomb's entrance. Without at first realising it the explorers had also found another warning, for above the tomb's entrance was an inscription in hieroglyphics which, when decyphered by experts in the Cairo Museum, read: 'Death will come to those who disturb the sleep of the pharaohs. They shall sicken, they shall thirst.'

Once aware of the inscription's significance Carter's Egyptian work crew became afraid and refused to go on. It took some time to hire enough men willing to continue the excavation and then only at greatly inflated wages. Meanwhile, Carter ignored the warning and cabled the exciting news to his partner, who had returned briefly to his Hampshire home to conduct some pressing business. The excavation was finally completed in mid-February 1923, and it was on the morning of the 16th of that month that the tomb was at last opened. Howard Carter and Lord Carnarvon were the first to enter, followed by distinguished archaeologists from around the world, all drawn magnetically towards the unique event. As it turned out they were not to be disappointed. The boy king's grave consisted of four rooms – two ante-chambers, the burial chamber itself and a treasure room piled high with fabulous riches. The lid of the pharaoh's sarcophagus was lifted to reveal an inner compartment of solid gold. The archaeologists were staggered. Clearly this was the most remarkable find of all time, its historical value exceeding every expectation. For Carnarvon and Carter it was the greatest moment of their lives, the consolidation of their long search.

As stories of the hidden gold and jewels were telegraphed around the world, mention of the tomb's inscription took second place and the legend of the curse faded into the background. Not for long, however. On 6 April 1923, only eight weeks after his moment of supreme triumph, the fifth Earl of Carnarvon suddenly died. His passing from the mortal plane was attributed to an infected mosquito bite which had in turn brought on a severe attack of pneumonia. Was this the curse at work? asked the newspapers. It looked distinctly possible for, coincidentally, the golden death mask of Tutenkamen had a blemish on its cheek in exactly the same spot where the English aristocrat suffered his fatal insect sting. Moreover, the Earl's passing was accompanied by some decidedly strange events, not only in Egypt but in England too. To begin with a phenomenal vision, a so-called 'wild man', was seen several times running naked around Carnarvon's Hampshire estate during the first week of the month of April. Odder still, the hour of Carnarvon's death in a Cairo hotel coincided with an unexpected power failure which plunged the entire city into an eerie darkness. Meanwhile, at precisely the same time in England, the Earl's pet dog let out a pitiful yell and died.

The unexpected demise of Lord Carnarvon was an auspicious beginning for the boy king's curse since it accounted for one of the two men most responsible for the tomb's defilement. Next to die was not Carter, however, but one of the aristocrat's closest friends, George Gould, who was unable to make the funeral but travelled to Cairo the following month to pay his last respects at Carnarvon's grave. While in Egypt Gould visited another burial site: the tomb of Tutenkamen. Within six hours he had collapsed into a coma and a day later, to the bafflement of doctors, he too was dead. No reason could be found for his illness. The second mystery delighted the popular press of the day and as other members of the excavation team began to die off one by one the newspapermen gleefully kept account. Within six years twelve of the original twenty-two people present at the opening of the tomb had themselves been laid to rest. These included Carnarvon's wife, also a victim of a poisoned insect bite; the Earl's half-brother, who committed suicide; Professor Newberry, who had opened the royal sarcophagus and subsequently died of heart failure within months; and Professor Derry, who had conducted an autopsy on the mummified remains and who first concluded that the boy pharaoh had probably been murdered. When Arthur Weighall, who wrote a book on the subject of the curse, himself fell victim in 1930 only two men of the group who had witnessed the opening of the tomb were left alive. One of these was Howard Carter, who died nine years later. The other, an Englishman named Richard Adamson, lived to a respectable old age although intriguingly his life was not entirely without tragedy. Having denounced the legendary curse of Tutenkamen as superstition in a radio broadcast during the 1930s the Englishman returned home to find his wife had died suddenly. Ten years later Adamson wrote an article voicing the same sceptical viewpoint; on the day it was published his son broke his back in a plane crash. Lastly, when he agreed to appear on British independent television to 'explode the myth of the curse once and for all', Adamson's taxi was involved in a near-fatal crash in the London rush hour.

Like Richard Adamson, most Egyptian experts remain sceptical about the possibility of an actual curse, choosing to blame the bizarre string of deaths on coincidence. But their disbelief did nothing to save them. During the early 1960s Mohammed Ibrahim, director of the Cairo Museum for Antiquities and the man charged with personal responsibility for the Tutenkamen treasures, derided the curse as a contemptuous invention. Yet in 1966, after he was instructed by his government to arrange for an exhibition of the relics in Paris, he apparently felt a strong sensation of foreboding.

The museum director even told a friend how he had been warned in a dream to stop the treasures leaving the country. Mohammed Ibrahim did his duty and defied the threat. The Paris show went ahead as planned, yet two weeks after it opened in the Louvre, the museum director was killed in a car accident outside the Egyptian capital. Once more the curse would seem to have claimed vengeance.

Ibrahim's successor was Dr Gamal Mehrez, also a famous authority on Egyptian history. Since interest in the curse had been revived, Mehrez went out of his way to emphasise his personal unbelief. At the age of fifty he was, he claimed, living proof of the non-existence of the curse since he had himself been working with the antiquities all his adult life. But, tragically, history was about to repeat itself. In 1972 Dr Mehrez was, like his predecessor, charged with the task of transferring the Tutenkamen treasures abroad, this time to London for an exhibition at the British Museum. He complied despite receiving an extraordinary anonymous note warning him of his own certain death if he went ahead. On the evening that preparations were finalised for the transport of the tomb relics, Gamal Mehrez was found dead in his office. An autopsy showed that he had suffered a massive circulatory collapse.

Archaeologists are on the whole an unromantic bunch and if you mention the curse of Tutenkamen you will most probably be met with a tirade of derision. Yet for the celebrated few who stepped inside the pharaoh's funeral chamber on that fateful day in February 1923 the legend was real enough.

1924

Ghosts on Film

It is disappointing (although perhaps not that surprising, since ghosts usually arrive unannounced) that 160 years after the development of the photographic process, cameramen have only rarely been able to trap conclusive evidence of human survival after death in the eyes of their lenses. Faulty equipment, misidentifications, slow or double exposures have all been proved responsible for so-called mysterious photographs. Moreover, just as fraudulent mediums have done much to discredit the cause of spiritualism, phantomagraphic hoaxers have wrought considerable harm to the overall case for the belief in ghosts. In the right hands the camera *can* lie, and many photographs that were once considered inexplicable by those who passionately believe in the afterlife have long since been exposed as cheap fakes.

However, the history of psychic photography is not quite the unmitigated catalogue of 'fraud, folly and fabrication' that one notable critic termed it to be. Some exposures really do deem to contain quite startling evidence of survival. Of these, easily the most interesting examples are those in which figures or images of faces appear on family snapshots taken under normal conditions, in situations where the photographer has noticed nothing untoward at the moment the picture was taken. During the twentieth century there have been many such examples of ghostly forms appearing spontaneously on developed negatives.

In the summer of 1925, a holiday portrait of Lady Palmer, taken by a companion during a visit to the Basilica at Domnesy in France, clearly showed a pair of priests outlined in the background. The figures were dressed in robes unlike any used by local priests for more that seventy years, yet the women insisted afterwards that they had been completely alone in the chapel. Another example of a 'phantomagraph' was the picture taken in 1954 by the Rev. Kenneth Lord in his own parish church of Nealy Hall, Ripon, where a straightforward interior shot of the church altar produced the distinct shape of a cloaked and hooded figure. Lord insisted that no person had been in his viewfinder at the moment he pressed the button, and the shape was too clearly human to be a shadow or optical illusion.

Weird images continue to crop up with what seems to be increasing regularity. In the autumn of 1990 during a holiday to the Austrian Tyrol, Englishman George Todd took several pictures of a group of friends sharing a meal in their hotel. When he had the prints processed in his own home town of Scunthorpe he was amazed to see an extra guest at their table. The mysterious woman's form, slightly out of focus yet undoubtedly smiling, seemed to be floating just in front of the others present, and the fact that two beer glasses on the table were clearly visible in front of her precluded the possibility that the photograph was simply an amalgam of Todd's picture and another holiday snap.

An equally odd picture was published for the first time in a British Sunday supplement in October 1991. Taken on the previous New Year's Eve in London's Covent Garden shopping area by a family named Webb, it clearly captured not only the couple's three-year-old daughter but also a floating phantom figure of a schoolgirl dressed in black. The girl's form, seemingly legless, was partly obscured by other solid objects, indicating precisely her position and physical reality within the three-dimensional framework of the picture. When it was carefully studied by Vernon Harrison, former president of the Royal Photographic Society and world-renowned expert on forgeries, he pronounced it to be genuine beyond reasonable doubt.

But perhaps the most famous example of ghost photography was taken in 1924. It also remains the most convincing, not only because of the quality of the image produced but also since the apparitions involved were witnessed at the time not just by the photographer but by dozens of people, all members of the same ship's crew. On 2 December 1924 an American-owned tanker, the *SS Watertown*, was steaming south towards the Panama Canal from San Pedro, California when tragedy struck. A leak of gasoline asphyxiated two seamen working in the hold. Two days later, the victims, James Courtney and Michael Meehan, were buried at sea and the ship continued its voyage.

The following morning something very strange was noticed by the ship's first mate. Looking through binoculars the officer could clearly make out the faces of two men bobbing up and down in the waves off the *Watertown*'s starboard bow. Larger than life –about 6 feet across – they appeared to be keeping pace with the tanker. Alerted to this anomaly the ship's captain, Keith Tracy, ordered the vessel to be steered closer to the visions. It soon became clear that the moving shapes in the water were unquestionably the faces of the two dead sailors consigned to the waves the previous day. To the considerable discomfort of the terrified crew the apparitional visages continued to be seen alongside the ship for several days; only when the ship entered the canal zone just off Balboa did they finally vanish.

If the joint testimonies of all those aboard the *SS Watertown* were the only evidence to emerge from this curious incident then it would still be an extraordinarily impressive ghost sighting. However, they were not. Captain Tracy had with him a box camera on the voyage and took a roll of film of the watery apparitions. Several exposures clearly show the faces of James Courtney and Michael Meehan drifting on the sea. All those who later saw the pictures, both officials of the company which employed them and the friends and relations who grieved for their loss, agreed afterwards that the photographs showed the unmistakable features of the two dead seamen.

1925

The Cruel Torment of Eleonore Zugun

A few hundred years ago everyone believed in the Devil. In the Middle Ages it was universally accepted that Lucifer was a real being, Lord of the Nether Realm and served by an army of spirits whose purpose was to overthrow God's creation. Christ called them demons and cleansed those possessed by them with the power of the Holy Spirit. St Paul warned the early Christians that the final battle between mankind and its old enemies – 'the superhuman forces of evil in the heavens' – was about to begin. The belief in the existence of objective forces of evil was not confined to the Christian world, either. The same basis for this superstition has its roots in most of the myths and legends of the major world faiths. Islamic tradition, for example, holds that demons or *djinn* were created out of the primeval substance before man walked on earth and that the same spirits will exist after mankind is no more.

Jewish belief in demons, or *D'Bukkiem*, is enshrined in the Kabbalah. Hindu and Buddhist texts tell of similar entities tormenting their human victims as do the early writings of the Hellenistic and Mesopotamian cultures. Modern society considers itself to be too sophisticated to believe in such mumbo-jumbo and today even many churchmen prefer to think they are too enlightened to hold on to such ridiculous superstitions.

Yet while the world's belief systems have moved on to embrace new terrors, the old enemies of mankind do not seem to have quite gone away. Unbelievable though it may seem to most people, the past hundred years have thrown up a number of examples of strange events which can in no circumstances be explained unless we consider the possibility of the diabolic.

In February 1925 Eleonore Zugun, a twelve-year-old peasant girl living in the northern Romanian village of Talpa, apparently became possessed by an entity which her aged grandmother took no time in identifying as the Devil. In Eleonore's presence small objects began to jump up and transport themselves through the air; stones showered down on the roof of her home; windows shattered for no apparent reason and the atmospheres of rooms where she was present turned icy cold. When her parents took her to a priest for exorcism the ceremony did nothing to quell these violent disturbances. Observers watched in amazement as heavy items of furniture moved in bizarre gyrations and several eye-witnesses felt the force of heavy blows upon their heads. But by far the greatest malice was reserved for young Eleonore herself. The invisible tormentor attacked the child on a daily basis and scratches and welts appeared on her face, neck and arms. On one occasion her hands turned purple with as many as twenty-five apparent bites. With her parents helpless and going out of their minds with worry, the girl was given refuge in the local monastery but when the extraordinary activities continued even there she was diagnosed as an hysteric and moved to a lunatic asylum.

To begin with doctors and psychiatrists assumed that the strange contusions which regularly appeared on the girl's flesh were the result of self-inflicted wounds, yet careful observation of the girl and regular examinations proved otherwise. As evidence that the phenomenon was genuine began to gather the story became the focus of considerable newspaper interest and drew the attention of paranormal investigators across Europe. In the late autumn of 1925 Harry Price, the English psychic investigator, made a series of studies into the case of the young Romanian. Following his first meeting with the child in Vienna, Price's case notes clearly indicate the effect the spirit had upon its victim.

'During the first few minutes of my preliminary observational period, Eleonore gave a short, sharp cry of pain whereupon deep indentations or teeth marks appeared on the fleshy part of the forearm some distance above the wrist ... forming together an elliptical figure. If the reader will bite the fleshy part of his own arm, he will get an exact representation of what we saw.'

Another English investigator to visit Eleonore Zugun and become convinced of the phenomenon's genuineness was Colonel W.W. Hardwick. Hardwick's own account of his observations include the following report:

'Eleonore was tying up a box when she gave a gasp and moved her right hand towards her left wrist – distinct teeth marks appeared on her wrist, then scores like scratches appeared on her right forearm, cheeks and forehead. Shortly after, a series of marks like some type of lettering appeared on her left forearm, all rising to distinct white inflammatory swellings within three or four minutes, fading slowly. The girl was under close observation and could not have produced these herself by any normal means.'

Due to the activities of her unwanted persecutor the Romanian girl became something of a cause célèbre among those who delved into the psychic world and, accompanied by a Viennese countess named Zo Wassilko-Serecki, who befriended her, she travelled to many European cities including London, Paris and Munich to demonstrate the phenomenon in front of scientists, journalists and medical specialists. Though some remained dubious of the authenticity of her condition Eleonore was never seen attempting to cause the marks herself and it seems highly unlikely that, given the number of sceptical witnesses who investigated her case, the strange scratches, bites and swellings that regularly appeared on her body could have been produced by any other than preternatural means. Some suspected that a ghost might have become attached to her own psychic aura while others believed that only an emissary of the Devil himself could have behaved so cruelly. Today many parapsychologists would contend that emotional disturbances within the pubescent girl's young mind were actually to blame for the horrible attacks which plagued her, and it is certainly interesting that the wounds of her body stopped appearing a few months into 1926, when Eleonore began to menstruate for the first time. Whatever the real truth of the matter, the fact remains that the case of Eleonore Zugun remains one of the most convincing examples of a paranormal outbreak to have occurred at any time during the modern era.

1926

Strange Signs and Wonders

From the earliest days of her childhood in the small community of Konnersreuth in Bavaria, Therese Neumann was considered to be a saintly child. She never missed mass and always said her prayers dutifully, kneeling before the crucifix on her bedroom wall or the Madonna that her mother kept beside her bed. It seemed to neighbours that God was testing the Neumann family's religious faith when at the age of twenty Therese was struck down by a mysterious hysterical illness, leaving her bedridden, blind and paralysed. In fact the ordeal only intensified her love of God and six years later, on Good Friday 1926, few of those who knew Therese Neumann could doubt that she had truly been touched by the spirit of the Lord. Following an apparent vision of her namesake, the child saint Therese of Lisieux, Neumann was suddenly and miraculously cured of her symptoms and was able to resume a normal life once more. A normal life, that is, except for one curious after-affect: each Friday from that moment on during every single week of her life Therese Neumann would exhibit the miracle of stigmata, a replica of the physical wounds suffered by Christ during his crucifixion. During these twenty-four-hour periods she would go into a trance when she would relive the whole scene at Calvary, following the Son of God's footsteps and inwardly watching the crucifixion process up to and including the moment of the Messiah's death. People who witnessed Therese's ecstasy described her shedding little tears of blood and claimed to actually see deep wounds and holes open up involuntarily upon her hands, feet and brow. Those who suspected fraud were soon convinced that no self-inflicted wounds could be responsible, so deep were the holes that appeared in her flesh and so copious the blood which followed.

By the time Therese Neumann died in 1962 she had been investigated by a whole range of interested parties including mystics, physicians and journalists. Over a period of thirty-six years not one single person had ever seriously attempted to claim let alone prove that something other than a supernatural, divine or otherwise paranormal force was behind the evidently real and visible wounds that appeared on her body every Friday.

Although Therese Neumann remains one of the most famous cases of stigmatics on record her life is of course by no means the only concrete evidence we have that the phenomenon exists. When Italy's most venerated stigmatist, Padre Pio, was laid to rest at San Giovanni Rotunda in southern Italy in September 1968, he had bled constantly from the hands and feet for more than fifty years. The wounds had first appeared on the afternoon of 20 September 1918, three days after Padre Pio and his fellow Capuchins celebrated the feast of the stigmata of St Francis. Monks found Padre Pio lying unconscious on the floor of a small chapel with blood pouring from five places: both palms, soles of his feet and his left side. Over the next half-century these wounds never seemed to close and although they never stopped bleeding neither did they become infected.

It was the belief of Padre Pio's congregation that he wore

the imprint of the Saviour's wounds because of his burning love for God and his devotion to the mass. While the interpretation of the phenomenon is clearly based on religious fervour there can be little doubt that the atmosphere of intense reverence and adulation that marked the priest's unbringing played a major part in the appearance of the stigmata. Indeed, some psychiatrists have put forward the theory that a background of intense religious devotion allied to a traumatic childhood is a common factor to virtually every noted stigmatic to have emerged this century.

One example that would seem to fall into this category (though here, unusually, it involved a Baptist rather than a Catholic) was that of Cloretta Robinson, a black schoolgirl from Oakland, California who began to exhibit dramatic stigmata a few weeks before Easter 1972 when aged ten. The marks first appeared during a lesson in religious education at school and inexplicable bleeding continued from the girl's feet, chest and forehead as well as from her hands. A subsequent investigation undertaken by psychiatrist Joseph E. Lifschutz, confirmed that Cloretta was deeply religious, the Bible being virtually her only reading. Moreover, while she claimed never to have heard of the phenomenon of stigmata before her own bleeding began, she had spent the weeks before Easter reading a book called *Crossroads* by John Webster, a highly charged book about the crucifixion. In Lifschutz's opinion it was improbable that the girl could have repeatedly injured herself in a manner that had deluded the doctors treating her. It was much more likely, he concluded, that the sheer power of mental and emotional force (whether conscious or unconscious) had brought about the dramatic changes in her physical state. It was, he wrote, 'no longer possible to dispute the power of mental and emotional forces to control physical matter'.

True no doubt. But why do so few devotees exhibit these

marks and what precisely is the process through which they can form, sometimes within a matter of minutes? There is much in the physical phenomena of mysticism which remains unexplained.

1927

Seeing the Future

In the opinion of most scientists the march of time is inexorable and unchanging. In a world where so much is uncertain we can at least be sure that day will follow night, that one year will follow the next. The present becomes past, the future becomes present. No man can know for certain what lies around the corner for none can know those things which have yet to happen. Almost all of human experience supports this viewpoint. Yet on very rare occasions some men and women seem to have stepped back into former times or glimpsed knowledge of things to come. These moments of preternatural insight cast into doubt many of the certainties we have regarding the forward motion of linear time. For this reason, and also because they are impossible to test under laboratory conditions, most scientists tend to dismiss the stories out of hand and spend little time hypothesizing about their origin. Yet a select few have chosen the opposite path, trying to create a new theory of time which embraces strange and mysterious aberrations.

John William Dunne made his name as a pioneer aircraft designer – he was the man who built the first British war plane. But it is as a writer and time theorist that he is best remembered today and it is in this field that he has excited the interest of mysteriologists everywhere. Although Dunne had been interested in predictive dreams and kept a personal record of his own 'night-time revelations of the future' since before the turn of the century, it was not until 1927 that he published his ideas in a book entitled *An Experiment with Time*, which can fairly claim to be the first genuine attempt to look at the subject of prediction on a serious level. Dunne's concepts – which he called 'serial time' – were complicated and controversial, though to many not entirely implausible. Basically, the writer considered a human mind to be conscious only of what it is doing and thinking at that precise moment; past and future become irrelevant. At the same time, according to Dunne's conjectures, a person's mind might be conscious of what he is doing – aware of itself – at any given moment; not only that, but it must be aware of being aware and so on and so on, ad infinitum. Thus to Dunne the human mind became a mental hall of mirrors. If one accepted this hypothesis it was not hard, claimed the writer, to go a step further and accept also that mankind's perceptions of time might be misleading, which in turn opened up the possibility that the sense of time we experience during our waking life would be quite different to that experienced during sleep.

Although elements of his own dreams often came true they were largely unremarkable until, late in 1916, while working for the British Army, Dunne awoke with a vision of unprecedented clarity in which he saw an explosion in an armaments plant. Two months later, in January 1917, a gigantic blast occurred in a London bomb factory, killing seventy workers and injuring more than a thousand. Soon afterwards the then aircraft designer had another dream in which he vividly saw an as yet unpublished newspaper headline recording a death toll of 4,000 people in a volcano eruption in the Far East. Within a week he was reading the same headline at his breakfast table. Only one detail was different: the estimated dead already numbered 40,000, ten times the figure he had foreseen.

Although J.W. Dunne was by no means the first person to dream the future, *An Experiment with Time* was, in 1927, the only published account of the subject written by a person of scientific reputation. It marked the beginning of several studies into precognition which have led parapsychologists towards a re-evaluation of the universe we inhabit and the concept of linear time which most of us still believe in. These studies tend to suggest that premonitions of disaster happen rather more frequently than is generally assumed and that a subconscious foreknowledge of impending danger might even be an effective defence mechanism common to us all.

In 1966 Dr J.C. Barker, an English psychiatrist from Shrewsbury, set out to discover whether large-scale disasters attracted a disproportionately higher number of premonitions. Taking as his focus the Aberfan coaltip tragedy, which claimed 144 lives on 21 October of that year, Barker appealed via the science column of the London *Evening Standard* for doomwatchers to contact him. Over one hundred letters were received, of which thirty-five were judged to be reliable, in that those who had had a prevision had spoken to others of their dreams prior to the actual event. The dreams seemed different in style – one woman saw about a hundred black horses charging down the hillside pulling hearses; others spoke of a suffocating sensation and a black mist appearing before their eyes; some heard the screams of the struggling children – yet in substance they all told the same story. Analysing the data, Dr Barker came to believe that premonitions could one day be used to warn of impending disasters and provide a practical method of avoiding them.

Across the Atlantic, meanwhile, an American parapsychologist, Professor William Cox, was producing a body of evidence which suggested that people were already using this remarkable psychic faculty, though hardly any were consciously aware of it. Conducting a series of statistical surveys on the numbers of rail passengers using trains which subsequently crashed, Cox found that the proportion travelling on the doomed trains was invariably lower on the day of the accident than was usual for that particular run. Data from over one hundred accidents spread over a six-year period produced statistical differences and variations that were far higher than anything that might be explained in terms of mere chance. Indeed, using a computer Cox estimated that the odds against these sets of figures occurring coincidentally were well over 1,000,000 to 1. The parapsychologist concluded that whether people realised it or not they were predicting future trouble and taking evasive action.

To most scientists the idea that we can see tomorrow remains a nonsense, and a dangerous nonsense at that. 'If prevision be a fact,' one Nobel Prize-winning academic has flatly stated, 'then it undermines the whole theoretical framework of the universe.' But as more and more evidence gathers to show that the human mind can, in special circumstances, act as an antenna for future events, so the fortress wall of outright scepticism is slowly showing cracks. Doubtless the process will continue until at some point, perhaps by the middle of the next century, the majority of scientists will agree with the prophecy of Albert Einstein that 'the separation between past, present and future has the value of mere illusion'.

1928

Evil Shadows

The more macabre manifestations of the paranormal have provided a rich seam of material for Hollywood scriptwriters and the popularity of the horror genre shows no sign of diminishing. Many of the screen's biggest hits have been based directly or indirectly on reports of genuine phenomena, perhaps most notably *The Exorcist*, in which the sex of William Peter Blatty's fictional child host was changed from the original story, but little else. Is literal possession by invisible entities at the root of such claimed phenomena? Although most scientists and psychiatrists remained united in their dismissal of spirit possession, there is now a growing body of evidence to support the theory that an intrusion into the human psyche by unseen minds is only too possible.

One of the most detailed and therefore one of the most convincing cases of demonic possession focused upon a woman from the American Mid-West whose real name, for reasons of her own protection, was never made public. She was baptised a Catholic, and despite having been notably pious as a child, in her late teens 'Mary' began to hear strange inner voices, voices which urged her to blaspheme during mass and commit immoral acts. She was seen by several doctors who diagnosed hysteria, but Mary began to manifest signs of demonic possession as she grew older and nothing the medical practitioners did seemed to help. So in 1928, when she was forty years old, the woman reluctantly agreed to undergo an exorcism at a Franciscan convent in Earling, Iowa. She was told that the ceremony was to be conducted under the direction of Father Theophilus Reisinger, a sixty-year-old monk, and Father Joseph Steiger, an experienced exorcist. Although both men had seen possessed people before neither was prepared for what was to follow.

To begin with a large room had been made ready for Mary's arrival at the convent and a number of nuns stood by to assist the two priests. But as it was to turn out the combined strength of even a dozen pairs of hands would not always be enough to restrain the unfortunate woman. On the very first morning of the ritual Mary exhibited a number of preternatural signs which those present recognised to be unquestionably the hallmark of the Beast. From her mouth issued forth a series of deafening howls sounding like a pack of wolves, while her body became hideously twisted at every joint.

As the exorcism continued for the next few days vast quantities of excrement and vomit would fill the room even though the victim had taken only a spoonful of milk to sustain her during the whole of the previous day. Sometimes Mary disgorged various other materials, including shredded tobacco leaves and foul-smelling birds' feathers. Some of the nuns were so shocked by what they saw that they fled in terror but the priests worked determinedly around the clock until at last there was a breakthrough when several demons came forth to proclaim their identity. One called himself Beelzebub; another named herself as Mina, a ghost who was damned, she said, for murdering four of her children in her earthly life. Yet another demon, Judas, confessed that he had intended to drive Mary to suicide. What convinced the priests that these entities were real and not simply fragments of Mary's own subconscious mind was the way each one seemed to possess an uncanny knowledge of information not known to their host.

One day the demon called Beelzebub gleefully told Father Steiger that he would suffer an accident the following Friday. In fact the priest's car crashed over a railing as he was crossing a bridge on the way to visit a sick parishioner. Steiger was only slightly hurt but his fear that the demon had planned the event was reinforced when upon his return and without his mentioning the incident to anyone else, the demon was able to describe with accuracy the scene of the crash, laughing at the priest's misfortune.

Though identified, the spirits present in the body of Mary were proving much harder to get rid of, and for two weeks the solemn ceremony was repeated every day without any sign of further success. Yet just as the priests were reaching the point of exhaustion the woman's condition attained a favourable crisis. On 23 December at about 9 pm Mary broke free from the grip of her attendants and flew to the ceiling. The convent's sisters shrank back in awe at the extraordinary levitation but Fathers Reisinger and Steiger seized the moment to press home their advantage and within a few seconds the woman fell once more to the bed, free at last of her unseen tormentors. Sitting up she opened her eyes and quietly smiled. 'By Jesus' mercy,' she said, 'praise be Jesus Christ.'

Can such an amazing story be explained by anything other than the preternatural?

For many doctors and psychiatrists possession remains a diagnosis that reeks of medieval superstition and should therefore never be considered. Such sceptics would readily point out that extreme psychological conditions such as epilepsy, hysteria and schizophrenia can produce the very same convulsive seizures, muscular rigidity and foaming at the mouth that have characterised accounts of apparent possession from our own century and before. During these attacks the patient's face may become distorted, bloated and violently discoloured, while strange guttural noises can be produced by a sudden spasm of the throat muscles.

Schizophrenic patients might manifest several different personalities acting autonomously and with apparent indifference to each other, each demonstrating idiosyncratic speech patterns and individual memories. So, say the sceptics, when one looks at the bewildering range of phenomena that can be explained naturally one hardly needs to try to find a supernatural solution to the enigma of possession. Yet this is really only half the story. For there are many characteristics which distinguish the possessed from those who are mentally ill. To begin with the hallucinations, muscular spasms and seizures evident in hysterics usually last no more than five minutes, while a demonic attack may continue for days or even weeks unabated. Still more important are the attendant phenomena which cannot be explained in psychological terms. Levitation, insensibility to pain, the exhibition of superhuman strength and the contortion of limbs into impossible positions – all of which were contained in the American example from 1928 – are just some of the manifestations of unnatural powers which psychiatrists cannot account for. The occasional accompaniment during exorcisms of various poltergeist-type phenomena is equally mysterious.

One other example of possession from the present century is worth consideration because, like Mary's, it shows that purely psychological explanations are sometimes inappropriate. When she was sixteen years old a South African Catholic girl named Clara Germana Cele, who was studying as a residential pupil at Marianhill Order Mission School in

Uzminto, a township about 50 miles south of Durban, began to behave wildly. On 20 July 1906 she attacked other students who were present, broke one of the heavy posts on her bed with her bare hands, growled and grunted like an animal and seemed to be conversing with invisible beings. She was placed in a room on her own but during the next few days her behaviour worsened and she began to manifest the undeniable signs of diabolical possession. A cup of holy water began to boil when it was brought close to her and a wooden cross burst into flames as it was carried into her room.

Other impossible physical manifestations were her repeated levitations. In the words of one witness Clara floated often 3, 4 and up to 5 feet in the air, sometimes hanging vertically in space and other times horizontally, in a rigid position.

Some people tried to forcibly pull her down, holding on to her feet, but it proved impossible. An even more disturbing physical capacity which terrified the attending priests and nuns was the girl's curious ability to transform herself into a snake-like creature, whereby her whole body would become as flexible as rubber, writhing and hissing along the floor. During these occasions her neck elongated to several times its normal length, enhancing her serpent-like appearance, and on one morning, having entered this repulsive state, she slithered rapidly across to a nun and bit the woman on the leg.

Formal exorcisms began on 10 September 1906, performed by Father Erasmus, the girl's own confessor, together with Father Mansuet, the mission rector. As in the case of Mary, Clara Germana Cele's possession ended with a spectacular demonstration of levitation which took place before no fewer than 170 witnesses in the mission chapel. The Devil's exit was also marked by an incomparably foul stench and loud bell-like percussions which shook the framework of the church to its very foundations.

Afterward prayers were said in relief and thanksgiving that the young girl's soul had been freed at last from the Devil's claws.

1929

Highways of Death

In January 1929 a new German highway between Bremen and Bremerhaven was opened. With a two-lane carriageway on either side the new highway was much wider than its predecessor and was therefore considered to be much safer for the motorist. However during the following months the road became the focus of an extraordinary catalogue of carnage for which there seemed no logical explanation. Within a twelve-month period of its opening more than a hundred cars crashed on the Bremen–Bremerhaven link – in nearly every case at a straight stretch of carriageway near a kilometre stone marker, number 239. Were this to be the only oddity it would seem strange enough, but it was not. When questioned afterwards by police, surviving motorists would recall how they felt their cars being guided off the road by an invisible force as they approached marker 239. As more time passed the accidents continued until on a single day, 7 September 1930, nine cars left the road at the jinxed marker. It had been a clear, dry, fine autumn day and there were no natural hazards to explain the extraordinary turn of affairs.

Considering the mystery some German scientists believed that a powerful electro-magnetic underground pulse was the source of the problem, but their theory lacked evidence. Only after stone marker 239 was removed and the ground where it had stood showered with holy water did the accidents cease.

The idea that certain stretches of road with black-spot reputations might in fact be sites where the power of evil has built up into a localised psychic dark region will seem ridiculous to most people but not to English exorcist Dr Donald Omand. During the late 1960s the Anglican clergyman claimed evidence linking road accidents in particular places to odd compulsions on the part of motorists. His theory, outlined in a book, *Experiences of a Present-Day Exorcist*, held that latent demonic influences had the power to possess drivers, leading them to deliberately commit suicide by impulsively swerving into the path of oncoming vehicles. While his hypothesis attracted open derision from many of his peers in the Church, it was supported by, among others, a leading Austrian psychiatrist.

Donald Omand was originally alerted to the black-spot phenomenon after a nurse reported the strange story of a dying motor crash victim. According to the driver's deathbed testimony, he had been proceeding along a clear stretch of road when he had begun to see white spots coming towards him.

Suddenly, and without reason, he felt an irresistible urge to steer his car straight towards an oncoming truck. The nurse's curiosity became heightened when the truck driver, who suffered only minor injuries, spoke of feeling a similar irrational compulsion. His curiosity aroused, the British clergyman made a study of several hundred cases of head-on collisions, visiting hospitals and convalescent homes to talk to survivors of road accidents as well as checking police records. The same odd compulsions to commit suicide were apparent in a small but significant minority. These oddities Omand attributed to a form of possession, and noticing that particular stretches of road were mentioned repeatedly, he personally visited them and conducted exorcisms on each black spot.

In 1971 a BBC TV crew made a documentary film about the clergyman's ideas, accompanying him on the exorcism on a stretch of road between Charmouth and Morcombelake in Somerset, England which had earned a dreadful reputation for accidents although there was no apparent reason why it should attract them. In their back-up research for the film, which was shown the following year, the BBC team found that, while there had been seventeen accidents in a sixteen-month period prior to the ceremony, in the following six months there had been none.

The beliefs of the Rev. Donald Omand will be rejected by most people as ridiculous superstition. Yet in fact a trawl through various oddities and strange stories reported through the present century will show that the phenomenon of ghoulish entities influencing drivers to crash on particular stretches of road predates the activities of the Anglican exorcist. Again in England, this time in rural Devon, a road leading to the sleepy village of Postbridge earned itself a reputation for danger after several serious and apparently causeless accidents occurred there in 1921. In March one Dr Helby, a doctor at the nearby Dartmoor Prison, was flung off his motorcycle and died of a broken neck; a few weeks later a motor coach swerved on to a grassy bank, ejecting several passengers in the process. The coach driver described how as he had lost control he had felt invisible hands pulling at the wheel. In July two men on a motorcycle recorded having a similar sensation while coming down the same hill in Postbridge and on 26 August a young Army officer, again riding a motorcycle, was badly injured in the most bizarre incident of all. Talking of his experiences afterwards the officer insisted that he had quite clearly seen and felt a pair of large, hairy hands close over his own black leather gloves, forcing him to steer away from the road. He considered himself lucky to be alive and felt certain that some supernatural entity had contrived to destroy him. He might just have been right.

1930

The Village That Vanished

The possibility of the complete and permanent vanishment of human beings into thin air is something that most of us would prefer not to dwell upon. Yet as we have seen already in some of the mysteries covered so far in this book, there have been incidents in which solid flesh-and-blood human beings have apparently vanished – not metaphorically, but quite literally – into space. What happens to these people after their disappearance is anyone's guess, for the precise nature of the force which claims them seems to be beyond our comprehension. Psychic whirlpools, vile vortices, time-slips and portals between dimensions have all been suggested by paranormal writers, but in truth none of these theories seems satisfactory.

The vanished lighthouse men from Flannan Island, the lost British battalion of the Gallipoli campaign and the missing defenders of Nanking are just a handful of examples among thousands which seem to make little sense to our rationalist minds. But perhaps the most bizarre of all modern-day disappearances was the thin-air migration of an entire Eskimo village from their traditional homeland on the shores of Lake Anjikuni in 1930. To this day the Canadian authorities have never been able to solve the riddle or make contact with members of that tribe or their descendants. It was quite literally as if they had never existed.

The mystery emerged in November 1930 when a fur trapper named Joe Labelle snowshoed into the Eskimo village to find the familiar shanty-style huts devoid of population. Only two weeks before when Labelle had last been there the village had been a noisy settlement teeming with life. Now, instead of the usual friendly welcome, an unearthly silence greeted him. Unable to find a single soul the trapper looked desperately for clues to explain the situation. He searched in vain. Tied to their normal mooring-places were the Eskimos' kayaks; in their homes were the villagers' essential items, their rugs and their rifles. On the cold camp fires stood the usual pots of congealed stew made from the caribou meat which formed the tribe's staple diet. All was just as it should have been, except for the people. It was as if the entire community of over 2,000 had suddenly left in the middle of an otherwise normal day. But there was one other detail notable by its absence: Labelle saw, to his utter astonishment, that no tracks led away from the encampment.

Feeling, as he later described, a strange sick feeling of dread growing in his stomach, the grizzled trapper made his way to the nearest district telegraph office and alerted the Royal Canadian Mounted Police. The Mounties had never heard anything like it. Immediately an expedition was dispatched to investigate the village and a search was begun across the borders of Lake Anjikuni. The second measure failed to locate the lost tribe while the first served only to deepen the mystery further. Arriving in the deserted encampment the Canadian Mounties found two chilling pieces of evidence, both of which strongly suggested that an unnatural event had occurred. To begin with it was discovered that the Eskimos had not taken their sleigh dogs with them as Joe Labelle had originally assumed. Instead, the frozen carcasses of the huskies were found buried deep inside a snowdrift on the camp's perimeter. They had starved to death. Next, and in some ways even more incredible, was the discovery that the graves of the tribe's ancestors had been opened up and the bodies removed.

Both of these details baffled the authorities. Clearly the Eskimos could not have travelled without using either one or other of their means of transport, their sleighs or their kayaks. Nor would they have left their faithful canine servants to a slow and painful death. Yet gone they were, and the dogs had been abandoned to their fate. The second enigma – the open graves – was to confound ethnologists familiar with tribal ways, since tomb disturbance was unknown among the customs of the Eskimos. Besides, the ground was frozen hard as iron and was virtually undiggable by hand. As one high-ranking officer in the Mounties said at the time: 'The whole affair is physically improbable.'

More than half a century later that verdict still holds true.

1931

The Riddle of Teleka Ventui

Among all the hidden faculties of the human mind one of the strangest must be the manifestation of xenoglossia, the phenomenon through which people suddenly and without warning find themselves capable, either consciously or in a trance, to communicate in recognisable human languages or dialects which they have never learned. Although psychiatrists treating schizophrenics have long since explained the way a single human mind can create a whole range of alternative personalities which appear to be different people, it is hard to see how the more extraordinary cases of xenoglossia could be the result of a similar schism in the normal consciousness of the subject involved. After all, becoming competent in a foreign language takes painful training or practice and involves the use of a vocabulary, syntax and system of grammatical rules very different from one's own. When a foreign language proves to be one that has not been used for hundreds or even thousands of years the possibility of a natural explanation seems even less likely.

Probably the most bizarre example of xenoglossia to emerge during the past century involved a young English girl from Blackpool who in 1931 became overshadowed (intermittently possessed) by the personality of Teleka Ventui, a Babylonian woman whose earth life had taken place during the eighteenth dynasty of ancient Egypt – approximately 1400 BC. The child, pseudonymously known in the files of the British Society for Psychical Research as Rosemary, was able to speak during her moments of possession in a curiously old-sounding dialect, and it was this oddity which led the psychiatrist treating her, Dr Frederick Wood, to copy down some of her phrases and send them to Egyptologist Howard Hulme. To Frederick Wood's surprise Hulme confirmed that they were far from gibberish. Indeed, the Egyptologist wrote back to say that the utterances demonstrated a remarkably high degree of grammatical accuracy and contained many archaisms, peculiar popular terms, ordinary elisions and figures of speech appropriate to pre-Christian Egypt. 'It was,' he claimed, 'very evidentual that the mind controlling Rosemary must have considerable knowledge of the language and customs which characterised Egypt under Pharaoh Amenhop III.'

To probe the enigma further Howard Hulme went to Blackpool to interview 'Teleka Ventui' at first hand. He was armed with a set of twelve questions concerning small details of everyday Babylonian life which required detailed answers – the sort of replies only he and perhaps a dozen other historians around the world might be able to deliver with confidence. In his presence the small girl from the north of England was able to do just that in a tongue unheard outside academic circles for thousands of years. Over a ninety-minute period the girl also wrote down sixty-six accurate phrases in the last language of the Hieroglyphs. By the end of the session Hulme was convinced that he had really heard a voice speaking from across the sands of time.

Although the case of 'Rosemary' remains the most famous and best documented it is by no means the only twentieth-century example of dead languages echoing from the mouths of modern speakers. In 1930 a New York physician named Dr Marshall McDuffie discovered that his own twin toddlers were able to converse in an unknown vernacular. He had assumed it to be their own special language until a professor of ancient languages who visited the household as a guest heard the McDuffie children speaking and pronounced it to be Aramaic, a language current at the time of Christ.

More recently regression hypnotists have found patients with similar xenoglossiac abilities. One American eleven-year-old studied by Dr Morris Netherton, a Californian past-life regression hypnotist, was able to talk at length in an ancient Middle Eastern dialect, while in Toronto a thirty-year-old Canadian child psychologist regressed back to his days as a Viking warrior, recording his adventures in Norsk, the precursor of modern Icelandic. The same subject also remembered living as a young man in Mesopotomia in AD 650 and proceeded to write in the language of the day. Samples were verified by experts in ancient Middle Eastern culture in Washington, who confirmed the language to be Sessamid Pavlavi, a form not used since AD 651 and which bears no relation to modern Persian. Not surprisingly, these learned men were unable to offer even a tentative explanation for the way in which the Middle Eastern vocabulary, with its own peculiar set of grammatical rules, had entered the mind of the modern psychologist.

Whether cases such as those described above are the product of discarnate minds channelling their thoughts through the brains of the living or whether they indicate a form of mental transmigration remains a subject for speculation. What we can say with absolute certainty, however, is that no current model of the human consciousness can satisfactorily account for them.

1932

The Cherbourg Dinosaur and Other Modern Sea-Serpents

It is easy to see why the sea provides us with so many mysteries. Over seventy per cent of the earth's surface is covered by water and all but three per cent of this is over 200 metres deep. Since light does not penetrate more than a few hundred feet down the ocean's bottom remains largely hidden and submarine exploration into the very deepest regions is both difficult and expensive. The unknown vastness of the great deep is yet to reveal its secrets and so it is not surprising that many cryptozoologists remain convinced that there may be gigantic unidentified creatures living beyond our sight. Throughout the present century there has certainly been no shortage of people claiming to see ocean-going monsters as a brief glance through the Gazetteer will show. These include descriptions of giant crocodiles, super otters, enormous eels, Chinese dragons, tremendous tadpoles, many-humped reptiles and various examples of long-necked prehistoric-type lifeforms. While such tales inspire fascination among many ordinary people most serious-minded marine scientists have greeted them with hearty hoots of derision. Just as mammalian zoologists usually reject out of hand stories of Big Foot and the Yeti, so their marine counterparts flatly refuse to consider the possibility that an unknown species of large sea creature could have escaped detection for so long. Given the enormity of the world's oceans, this steadfast determination to reject several thousand eye-witness accounts of weird animated forms strikes many mysteriologists as being deeply unscientific. More importantly, it flies in the face of some evidence which is not simply difficult but actually impossible to deny. For while you can always cast doubt upon the testimony of eye-witnesses, it is difficult to argue with the reality of an unidentified carcass weighing several tons.

On 28 February 1932 residents living to the west of Cherbourg on the French Channel coast discovered a long and heavy carcass washed up on the beach at Querqueville. With a long thin neck and small head much like that of a camel and two big flippers at the front of its 30-foot long body, the creature resembled nothing the locals had ever seen before. Most people who came to view the corpse immediately assumed it to be a still-living dinosaur. The following week the skipper of a local ship, *Tugboat 177*, told newspapers that he had seen the creature alive several days before it had been washed up, swimming rapidly in the sea not far from Querqueville. At the time he had described it to friends as having a camel's head on a long neck.

Were this to be the only report of an anomalous carcass to be found during modern times it might be possible to dismiss the tale as a clever hoax. However, this is far from the case.

Seven years earlier, in 1925, the decomposing body of an enormous animal with a 30-foot neck, a huge head and a duck-like beak was found on a beach at Santa Cruz, California. Although some biologists who examined its skull concluded that it was probably the remains of an extremely rare beaked whale from the North Pacific, their identification is far from convincing. During the Christmas period in 1941 two odd carcasses were washed up on the Scottish shores and formally identified by scientists as the decomposing remains of enormous sharks. Local people remained sceptical, however, and spoke to journalists of seeing animals with long necks, pointed tails and body hair which resembled the texture of coconut fibre. In January 1945 a similarly described monster some 25 feet long and weighing a ton ended up in Thurso Bay not far from Dounreay on the north Scottish coast. A contemporary newspaper account tells how no expert had been able to identify the creature, which had a long, tapering neck and relatively small head, similar to that of a swan.

As the century wore on prodigiously sized carcasses of an unidentifiable nature continued to make their way on to shores around the world. Late in 1948 a jellyfish-like animal with no eyes and a tough skin was washed ashore on Dunk Island, Queensland, Australia. It was said to weigh several tons. In January 1950 an even larger creature with massive walrus-like tusks drew the attention of curious townspeople to a beach near Attaca, Egypt, having been cast up by a three-day gale in the Gulf of Suez. Biologists who witnessed the phenomenon for themselves admitted bafflement. Once again in southern waters, yet another unusual carcass arrived on a beach at Tema on the west coast of Tasmania in August 1960. With a strong tide burying it and exposing it many times during a year-long period the gigantic mass of animal tissue weighing many tons was available for examination by numerous experts, yet no firm conclusion was reached as to its identity. Ten years later, in 1970, a 30-foot long sea-serpent was found at a beach at Scituate, Massachusetts, and in April 1977 fishermen aboard the Japanese vessel *Zuiyo Maru* pulled in a decomposing monster while they were working off the Pacific coast of New Zealand's South Island. In this last case numerous pictures were taken of the creature's decomposing, 34-foot long, clearly reptilian body. Although both sketches and photographs depicted a creature with an elongated neck, four flippers and a thin tail, some experts concluded that the tantalising find was nothing more than the badly rotted corpse of a basking shark. Others, however, continued to believe that it must have been something far less mundane. Michihiko Yano, a fishing company executive who had been on board the *Zuiyo Maru* at the time, continued to insist that the animal his company's vessel had netted was actually a plesiosaur, a long-extinct marine reptile of a species known to have lived off eastern Australia 100,000,000 years ago. Backing up his conviction was Professor Yoshinori Imaizumi, director general of the animal research department at the Japanese National Science Museum, who stated categorically that in his opinion the remains were 'not a fish, whale or any other mammal, but most certainly a huge reptile of prehistoric dimensions'.

The possibility that marine saurians might still exist was further strengthened in June 1983 when a British schoolboy on holiday at a Gambian sea resort discovered yet another anomalous carcass washed up by the tide. Teenager Owen Burnham made careful sketches of the creature, which was over 15 feet long, before it was chopped up for meat by local people. When marine experts at Cambridge University saw these sketches, the 'Beast of Bungalow Beach', as it became known, was identified as mostly resembling a young kronusaurus, a species which was known to have lived in Atlantic waters between 136,000,000 and 65,000,000 years ago. Though the possibility of the existence of a living fossil excited their interest, the testimony of one teenager was of course less than conclusive proof of such an important discovery. Lacking any way of objectively corroborating the boy's story, the Cambridge scholars simply shrugged their shoulders and went back to studying jellyfish.

And so the reality of sea-serpents remains an enigma. We

cannot say with any degree of certainty that they exist, yet at the same time regular sightings from around the world and, much more significantly, the occasional appearance of anomalous corpses washed up on beaches provide compelling evidence that there truly are giants in the sea. Perhaps one day a prehistoric creature will rise from the depths and take a stroll down Fifth Avenue like Ray Harryhausen's animated monster did in the film *The Creature from 20,000 Fathoms*. However, I have my doubts . . .

1933

The Quest for Nessie

Loch Ness is without doubt a place which deserves a mystery. Nestling deep in the Scottish Highlands, surrounded by rugged mountains which rise in sheer faces 2,000 feet from its sides, the loch is one of three great lakes that fill the Great Glen, a massive geological fault which all but severs northern Scotland from the rest of Britain. With a surface area of some 14,000 acres and black depths reaching down to over 900 feet in places, Loch Ness is easily the largest body of fresh water in Britain and the third largest in Europe. But while the lake is truly massive it is even more mysterious. Beneath those dark waters, rendered virtually opaque by peat leached from the land, a huge creature is believed by many to reside; a creature which should have become extinct 100,000,000 years ago.

Although the Loch Ness Monster is now easily the world's best-known phantom animal and by far the most regularly seen, the legend of the Scottish creature did not make headline news until 1933. On 11 May of that year a Mr Alexander Shaw and his son were standing on the lawn of Whitefield House when they saw a wake on the surface about 500 yards out, followed by the emergence of what appeared to be the back of an animal near Urquhart Bay, directly opposite them. Both men had the impression of something long and undulating stretched out in front, while behind water was thrown up as if by a long tail. Other witnesses the same week were the Clement family of Temple Pier near Drumnadrochit. Mr Thomas Clement described it as an animal some 40 feet long with four flippers, a long tapered neck and low humps. On 27 May the creature appeared once more, this time at Cherry Island, where Mrs Nora Simpson watched it from a distance of about 45 yards for some ten minutes before the animal sank. Mrs Simpson's description tallied with that made by the Clement family.

The next report was to be somewhat more dramatic. On the afternoon of 22 July Mr George Spicer, a London company director, was driving with his wife along the shore road towards Foyers. Shortly after they passed Whitefield, an animal with a long neck and large body jerked itself from out of the bracken on the hillside to their left, crossed the road and submerged into the water. Both witnesses stubbornly refused to accept that their eyes had been playing tricks on them or that the animal was really one of a known species, such as a horse.

Soon others were coming forward claiming that they had seen the peculiar creature on land, and these stories, together with numerous accounts of sightings in the loch itself, ensured that the subject gained nationwide coverage. The possibility of an investigation was raised by the local MP in the House of Commons and Bertrand Mills Circus offered a £20,000 reward for the animal captured alive. Then in November the mystery took a new twist after a walker, Mr Hugh Gray, managed to capture the creature on film from a vantage-point on the loch shore near Foyers. Gray himself described the object as a living creature of considerable dimensions and technicians at Kodak examined the negative and certified that it had not been tampered with. Just over a month later, on 12 December, a newsreel crew working with Scottish film productions took a cine film of an animal passing through the shallow water just off Inverfarigaig. Swimming at a distance of about 100 yards from the nearest camera, the monster could be seen moving towards the right, getting further away as it passed and seemingly diving as it left the camera's view. Though mostly underwater it very clearly appeared to be a large reptilian whose long neck shape matched the consistent and clear reports that had been coming in throughout the year.

As usual most scientists remained sceptical. When shown the prints of Hugh Gray's still photographs zoologist Professor Graham Kerr of Glasgow University thought they were 'unconvincing as a representation of a living creature', while another expert, J.R. Norman of the British Museum, felt they were more likely to show 'a bottle-nose whale, a species of shark, or just mere wreckage'. Several scientists suggested that dark objects seen on the loch's surface were probably rotting tree trunks raised to the surface by the gasses of natural decomposition, while it was the firm opinion of the director of the aquarium at London Zoo, E.G. Boulinger, that 'The case of the Loch Ness monster is worthy of our consideration only because it presents a striking example of mass hallucination . . .'

But although most of the scientific establishment repudiated Nessie as a stunt perpetrated on a credulous public by charlatans and eager newspaper editors, the sightings continued. By the time Rupert Gould, a retired naval officer, published his own investigation of the mystery in June 1934 there had been forty-seven separate sightings from sixty-nine independent witnesses.

In the decades since the first rush of sightings interest in the phantom serpent of Loch Ness has increased rather than diminished. As every year goes by the mountain of solid evidence from eye-witnesses and photographers grows larger. The total number of sightings is now reckoned by some writers to exceed 3,000. Moreover, during the latter part of the century sophisticated attempts to prove the monster's existence have served to heighten the probability that something strange really does exist beneath those dark waters.

In 1969 a British independent television news team using state-of-the-art sonar searching gear picked up a positive contact for two minutes that was widely interpreted as a large animal. The following year, in 1970, a side-scan instrument developed by engineer Martin Klein detected submerged moving objects up to fifty times the size of the largest fish known to inhabit the loch. In 1972 an underwater camera and strobe flash triggered by movements within sonar range produced a provocative image of the flipper-like limb of an unseen creature estimated to be some 8 feet long. Three years later a similar sonar-activated device set up by a Boston monster-hunter, Robert Rhines, produced pictures which seemed to show the long, curving neck and bulbous torso of a huge reptile. The year 1987 saw the most comprehensive sonar probe ever undertaken in the loch. Two dozen boats dropped a sweeping sonar curtain into the lake for a three-day period, continuously scanning the depths. Not far from Urquhart Castle, the sonar's graph recorder showed something large moving slowly more than 180 fathoms below the surface. Even sceptical sonar engineers who were working for the team of monster-hunters admitted that an unknown species could well be responsible for the anomalous trace.

Still the evidence builds up. In July 1992 sonar mapping operations at the loch's bottom picked up an apparently huge solid target moving some 50 feet under the water. According to the captain of the Norwegian ship carrying the equipment this sonar trace could not conceivably have been coming back from a shoal of fish, nor was it in his opinion a false echo reading. Two weeks later, some British newspapers published a colour photograph of a long saurian neck emerging from the waters of the loch. Although the picture, taken by a motorist standing on a road which runs alongside Fort Augustus, was too fuzzy to provide conclusive proof of an animate creature, experts at the Kodak laboratory and at the RAF photo laboratory in Scotland all accepted that the snap had not been retouched.

1934

An English House of Horror

Britain is traditionally considered to be the home of haunted houses; it also has its fair share of damned ones. A habitation which has regularly brought misery to its occupants is Kelvedon Hall, a sixteenth-century mansion situated in the Essex countryside some 30 miles north-east of London. The hall, which is currently owned by a former British cabinet minister, the Rt Hon. Paul Channon MP, began its legacy of doom in 1934 when it was converted briefly into a convent school. In the very first year after the Sisters of St Michael took over the building, a number of inexplicable accidents and fires occurred. Then during the summer term of that year a chain of tragic deaths rocked the establishment. The first to die was a child who contracted tetanus poisoning after a playground fall. Within weeks another pupil died of a cerebral haemorrhage. The suffering continued the following term: in September a Sister Premauesi was found drowned in the mansion's pond; a fortnight later another child died after a bout of pneumonia picked up during a spell of mild weather. The nuns who ran the school prayed hard for a change of luck, yet their run of ill fortune was not over, for in late October a paying guest at the house, Mrs Margaret

Gallivan, fell to her death from a third-floor window.

An inquest returned an open verdict on the unfortunate Mrs Gallivan but the Sisters of Saint Michael were certain that sinister powers were at work. Within a week of the woman's accident the mother superior closed the school and moved her nuns out. She was quoted in the local paper as believing that there was something 'evil and terrible' about the place, adding that her Sisters in Christ felt the same way. A spokesman for the local diocese was meanwhile reported as saying that the whole matter was 'uncanny to the last degree' and a Roman Catholic exorcist subsequently visited the hall before it was sold in 1937 to the Channon family. Clearly its new occupier, Sir Henry 'Chips' Channon MP, immediately felt the same vague unease about his acquisition for he asked the Bishop of nearby Brentwood to bless the property. For a while at least the blessing may have done the trick, since Sir Henry, a member of the wealthy Guinness dynasty of bankers and brewers, lived to a prosperous old age. However, after Paul Channon inherited both his father's Westminster seat and his country home, the curse of Kelvedon Hall began to assert itself once more.

In 1986 Channon's daughter Olivia was found dying in her student flat at Oxford. An autopsy confirmed that she had swallowed a lethal cocktail of alcohol and heroin. In the resultant scandal Channon lost not only his child but the chances of cabinet promotion. Subsequent events suggested that the effect of the jinx was spreading somewhat wider, into the area of Paul Channon's ministerial responsibilities. After becoming Secretary of State for Transport the Essex MP was dogged by an unprecedented series of transport disasters throughout the United Kingdom, culminating in three major train crashes in the winter of 1988–89. With his political reputation coming under pressure Channon used a Parliamentary debate on 6 March 1989 to restore confidence in the public transport system. Yet at the precise moment that the minister rose in the House of Commons to begin his speech another two trains collided in Glasgow, killing and injuring more than fifty people. The following July Channon's misery was complete when, upon the publication of an independent report critical of his role in the aftermath of the Lockerbie 747 terrorist bombing, he was sacked unceremoniously by Margaret Thatcher.

Although Kelvedon Hall must surely be the most outstanding example of a jinxed home it is by no means the only one. Another particularly unhappy residence was acquired by a widow, Mrs Penelope Gallencault, in the spring of 1972. Situated on the banks of the River Thames in the picturesque village of Bray in Berkshire, the place seemed friendly enough to begin with, yet friends staying for weekends found they could not sleep in their rooms, which they described as having a spooky and unnaturally cold atmosphere. Mrs Gallencault's feelings were not cheered when she found out the place had once been used as a location for a cheaply made British horror film. As it turned out the real horror was about to begin, for during the next two years tragedy would strike repeatedly in the life of Penelope Gallencault. In the first instance a neighbour was found dead in her garden, his body lying undiscovered for a full week. The following month one of Mrs Gallencault's cats was found dead with its neck inexplicably broken. Then, incredibly, her two young sons both drowned in separate incidents within the space of a month. First Charles was found in the house's bath, while his younger brother Richard escaped from his playpen and fell into the river which ran along the back of his mother's property. For the young widow the shock was almost too much to bear, yet the cycle of grim coincidence was far from complete.

At the very same spot where her younger child had fallen to his death a man's body was washed up the following week.

And the next year the gruesome round was further compounded when on 30 September 1973 a visitor to Mrs Gallencault's home inexplicably fell in the river and met his death in precisely the same way.

Not surprisingly the woman began to talk of her home as having an aura of evil and the local priest, the Rev. Sebastian James, curator of St Michael's Church, Bray, was moved to speculate that the place might have been used to practise black magic at some point in the past. The police were equally mystified, one senior officer admitting that their own men had noticed an indefinable eeriness about the place. Some detectives apparently became convinced that the deaths were more than just a bizarre series of unconnected incidents, even though no physical evidence existed to support the hypothesis. Indeed the forces of law and order were probably wasting their time for it is doubtful that the culprit – if culprit there were – could have been held within a prison cell.

1935

Fire Walk in the Home Counties

Among the numerous superhuman feats of mind over matter, surely one of the hardest to understand is that of incombustibility. Ancient records show that the practice of fire walking was firmly established in many parts of central and southern Asia by about 500 BC. Over the centuries it spread westward to the Mediterranean countries, and elsewhere tribal cultures in north America and across the Pacific region have developed their own fire-walking rituals. To the Western scientists who first heard of the ceremonies it tested credulity that men, women and sometimes even children could walk across scalding stones and burning ash to emerge unscarred, yet the tales told by early white settlers and missionaries were simply too numerous to ignore. And so throughout the present century academics and medical figures have been desperately trying to find a rational explanation for the bizarre phenomenon.

In 1901 the American professor S.P. Langley of the Smithsonian Institute witnessed native priests engaged upon a fire walk in Tahiti. When one red-hot stone was removed from the pit to determine its heat, it boiled water in a bucket for upwards of twelve minutes, leading Langley to estimate its temperature to be about 1,200 degrees Fahrenheit. In 1922 the French Bishop of Mysore in India, Monsignor Despatures, attended a fire walk undertaken by a Muslim mystic in the courtyard of a local maharajah's palace. Extraordinarily, according to the Bishop's account, the mystic was able to confer his personal incombustibility upon members of the maharajah's bandsmen, who marched in columns of three bare-footed through the rising flames without any sign of injury.

Still many people who had not witnessed the phenomenon themselves refused to believe such things were possible and reckoned instead that mass hallucination on the part of the assembled witnesses must be at the root of the enigma. So in the autumn of 1935, when British psychic investigator Harry Price announced that he was going to undertake a comprehensive investigation of the mystery, it drew considerable interest. In early September a prodigious fire pit was prepared in the garden of SRP member Alex Dribell, who lived in Carshalton, Surrey. Constructed with seven tons of oak logs, a ton of firewood, a load of charcoal, ten gallons of paraffin and fifty copies of *The Times*, it was deliberately designed to test the psychic powers of the most devout mystic.

Price's subject was a young Indian from the province of Kashmir called Kuda Bux, who had reputedly performed similar feats on many occasions in his native subcontinent. Captured on 16-millimetre film for posterity and watched by a phalanx of learned professors from the University of London, the bare-footed Kuda Bux walked steadily and deliberately across the length of the glowing pit's surface several times. A physicist present confirmed that the body of the fire was 1,400 degrees centigrade – beyond the melting point of steel – yet a careful examination of the Indian's feet by three doctors revealed no signs of blistering whatsoever. When two of the investigators attempted to place their bare feet at the furthest edge of the pit they had to retreat with bad blistering and bleeding.

The British scientists who witnessed the Carshalton fire walk were baffled and bewildered at the logical contradictions it threw up. Certainly the young Kashmiri who undertook the ordeal was no trickster, for he had not used oils or lotions to protect the soles of his feet. Indeed, his feet had been washed and dried by a doctor immediately prior to the test. Investigators were intrigued to notice that despite Kuda Bux's numerous fire walks in the past his soles did not seem to be excessively callused or protected by hardened skin. Nor in this case did the subject seem to be in the sort of ecstatic or exalted mental state that had been commonly observed during religious ceremonies elsewhere in the world. In the opinion of Harry Price, the only possible conclusion was that Kuda Bux had conclusively proven his personal mastery over fire with a calm confidence and unhurried stroll through wood and ash of unimaginable temperatures.

Since that autumn afternoon in Surrey over sixty years ago, a number of natural theories have been put forward to explain the phenomenon of apparent incombustibility. Some scientists have contended that fire walking is actually a gymnastic feat rather than a supernatural one, for the soles of those who cross the coals are never in contact with them for long enough to produce a burn. Other scientists believe that the sweat of the walker's feet would in itself produce a quenching effect, thus forming a protective layer between the walker's skin and the top surface of the fire. Yet these ideas, while perfectly fine in theory, remain far from conclusively proven in practice. And when a group of German scientists from the University of Tubingen attempted to join Greek fire walkers at the annual festival of St Constantine in Langadhás they were forced to retire rapidly with third-degree burns.

So the fire walk remains stubbornly beyond the comprehension of twentieth-century science. Though it flies in the face of every known law of medical science and would seem to be beyond the pain threshold of human endurance, the fact remains that every year men and women place their feet with faith and confidence upon live coals and red-hot ash. Such demonstrations of the sheer power of human will would appear to be common to Buddhists, Hindus, Christians and Muslims alike and can be seen in locations as far apart as China, Tibet, India, Japan, the Philippines, Fiji, Mauritius, Polynesia, north America and a number of European countries.

1936

The Nazi Hoodoo

Hoodoo vessels have been part of seafaring folklore ever since the days of the Vikings. When early mariners were obliged to rely heavily upon luck and a fair wind this was only to be expected, yet many are surprised to find that even in the relative safety of modern-day sea travel, tales of jinxed ships continue to chill the spines of the most level-headed and experienced sailors. If the dark history of one twentieth-century vessel is anything to go by, we should perhaps think twice before laughing at their fears.

The star-crossed career of the German battlecruiser *Scharnhorst*, launched in October 1936, is undoubtedly the most outstanding recent example of a floating hoodoo. The Nazi warship's curious catalogue of disasters had begun even before she set sail when, for reasons which were never fully explained, she rolled over in dry dock while still only half completed, crushing sixty assembly workers to death in the process and injuring a further 110 men.

At her launch another death occurred when, watched by Adolf Hitler himself, she inexplicably broke away from her 7-inch steel cable moorings and smashed into two barges, badly damaging them both. One of the fastest and most heavily armed ships in the führer's fleet, the *Scharnhorst* should have been a key asset in the dictator's plans for world domination. Reality was very different.

Three years later, in the vessel's first contact with the enemy – the bombardment of Danzig – a forward gun turret exploded killing nine men and injuring another dozen; the following day the air-supply system in another forward gun turret aboard the *Scharnhorst* broke down, suffocating twelve more victims. Although the warship had still to receive one hit from an enemy round she had already claimed almost a hundred German lives among those who had built and manned her.

During her short-lived career the *Scharnhorst* took part in several engagements with units of the Royal Navy, yet surprisingly, given her massive fire-power, she did not actually manage to sink one enemy vessel. A year after she first saw action the ship was engaged in the bombardment of Oslo. Early on in the battle, the *Scharnhorst* was struck by a lucky Norwegian shell that damaged her steering mechanism and she had to retire. Limping away from the fray she sought safety in the estuary of the River Elbe, only to collide with a passenger liner, the *SS Bremen*, which capsized in the mud to be finished off by British bombers soon afterwards.

The ship's career was proving inauspicious to say the least, and when this latest accident was blamed upon an unexplained radar failure the *Scharnhorst*'s crew began to talk openly of the hoodoo. But far worse was to come. A few months later, on the battlecruiser's return to active service, lookouts failed to notice a disabled British patrol boat as it slipped close by during the hours of darkness. The English vessel's skipper was quick to realise the danger the German ship presented to merchant convoys in the North Atlantic and raised the alarm. Soon a squadron of British warships was closing in upon their unsuspecting prey.

Having just had her turbines refitted and with greatly superior fire-power, the Nazi iron-clad should have struck fear into the hearts of her pursuers. Instead her skipper decided to run for cover. As the night closed in the *Scharnhorst* took an unlucky hit below the water line and found herself losing power. Now she was a sitting duck and a series of torpedoes soon followed, striking her amidships. Her magazine ignited and the huge ship exploded into flames. At 7.45 pm the pride of Hitler's navy slid beneath the waves at a point north-east of North Cape, Norway. Of the 1,460 men aboard the German vessel, only thirty-six survived and all but two of them were taken prisoner. Incredibly for these two sailors, even then the jinx of the *Scharnhorst* was not quite dead, for having reached the Norwegian shore on a raft and believing they had escaped captivity, a bizarre death awaited them. As they attempted to make a hot drink using an emergency oil heater salvaged from the dying ship, the mechanism blew up in their faces, killing them both instantly. Only then was the story of the century's most notorious hoodoo vessel finally at an end.

1937

A Meeting of Minds

On 12 August 1937 an aeroplane piloted by a pioneer Russian aviator, Sigismund Levanevsky, took off from Moscow Airport with a crew of five on a flight over the North Pole to Fairbanks in Alaska. But Levanevsky's mission – to test run the possibility of an intercontinental cross-polar route for the planned introduction of a passenger service – was doomed. Several hours after their departure from Moscow the pilot radioed to report trouble with his starboard motor and the rapid loss of altitude. As his words were drowned in an indistinct crackle it became clear that they would be forced to land upon the vast polar wastes, and a Consolidated flying boat was dispatched to zigzag over the frozen ocean to find them. However, after thirty days it returned having discovered no sign of the flyers or their aircraft.

Still the Russians did not give up hope and they hired an intrepid Australian explorer named Sir Hubert Wilkins to continue the search for Levanevsky and his crew. A Lockheed 10E plane with extra fuel tanks and special navigational aids for night flying was made ready in New York. On the day before Sir Hubert Wilkins was due to resume the search, however, he was approached by an elderly and somewhat eccentric writer named Harold Sherman, who put forward a curious proposal. Were the men still alive, said Sherman, could it not be possible for them to transmit information regarding their current latitude and longitude through some means of human telepathy so that a rescue plane might be sent immediately to pick them up at that point? While not entirely a disbeliever in the idea of telepathy, Wilkins saw little prospect of such an outcome. But what about in fifty or a hundred years, suggested Sherman. Could it not be possible that human minds would be developed to the point where such a rescue could be effected? Wilkins admitted that such an eventuality might one day come about and allowed himself to be persuaded by Sherman to undertake a series of experiments during his Arctic rescue mission to see whether his own mind could contact the American's at specifically agreed times when they would concentrate on each other. So on three nights a week – Mondays, Tuesdays and Thursdays – between 11.30 pm and 12.00 midnight, Eastern Standard Time, the pilot would consciously relive and review the outstanding events that had occurred on his expedition that day; meanwhile Sherman, sitting alone in his study, would allow his mind to wander and record his own mental impressions of what Wilkins had experienced. An objective evaluation of their evidence was to be given by Dr Gardner Murphy, a friend of Sherman's and head of Columbia University psychology department. Murphy collected and annotated Sherman's notes, filing them away until Sir Hubert's personal log could arrive for comparison.

In the event the Australian's lengthy rescue mission proved full of exciting adventures and near-disasters as he flew low over and often landed upon the pitted surfaces of the frozen Arctic river valleys. For thousands of miles he had to fly blind sorties in conditions of near-darkness through layers of endless impenetrable cloud from which mountain peaks would suddenly loom. Virtually every day brought with it new hazards and he narrowly avoided disaster a dozen times. Yet the end purpose of his mission remained unfulfilled: the crash wreckage and the bodies of the Russian flyers were never found. Meanwhile, in his New York apartment, Harold Sherman was receiving a dramatic series of mental impressions which in the fullness of time would be seen to correlate closely with the real activities of the Australian explorer thousands of miles to the north. Some were quite stunning in their accuracy. For example, on one occasion Sherman's notes described how he had seen Wilkins robed in a black dinner-jacket, surrounded by many other men and women in military attire and evening dress. To Sherman the vision had seemed impossible, yet he had disciplined himself to record even his most bizarre impressions. Months later Wilkins' own account of that date showed that he had been met at Regina by the governor of the province and invited to attend an officers' ball, for which the governor himself had lent Wilkins a dinner jacket for the occasion.

As one might expect some of these sessions were more fruitful than others, yet only the most committed sceptic could doubt that some hitherto unknown form of mental transference must have been responsible. The full progression and results of the long-distance telepathy experiment were carefully monitored by Dr Gardner Murphy and witnessed as true in sworn affidavits signed by other prominent academics in New York. Its influence exceeded the expectations of the men involved. Although they had embarked upon the tests in the personal belief that communications between minds might one day become possible, neither man had had any idea that their own mind links would mark the beginning of a fundamental shift in scientific thinking towards the existence of a new kind of mental energy.

Throughout the following decade scientists working in

laboratories in universities across America, Europe and the Soviet Union spent endless hours working with students, clairvoyants and others who claimed special psychic powers to find out whether there really was any scientific basis for the idea of telepathy. From the very beginning many of their results were spectacular. For example, American professor J.B. Rhine, working at Duke University with a volunteer economics student named Adam J. Linzmayer, found that his subject could accurately describe the symbols on a hidden playing card nine times in a row, a feat which carried odds against of roughly 2,000,000 to 1. Over a much more detailed and lengthy series of tests the same subject scored more than twice as many hits as one would expect through the simple workings of chance. Rhine's hundreds of fruitless hours working with non-psychic individuals made him certain that telepathy was a gift possessed only by (or at least only developed in) very few people, yet when a psychic star emerged it seemed to prove once and for all the existence of mind-transference. One notable student named Hubert Pearce averaged no fewer than nine correct playing-card hits out of a standard run of twenty-five; on one run he actually scored a total hit ratio of one hundred per cent.

Despite his impressive results J.B. Rhine met much opposition from mainstream researchers who refused to accept that ESP was a valid branch of science. This lingering hostility manifested itself in various forms. Some said that Rhine's collection of data was sloppy and his reports written up in a partisan style. Others accused him of not applying appropriately vigorous and stringent controls to his subjects within the laboratory. One even hinted darkly that Rhine might have joined with his associates and students to perpetrate a fraud on a grand scale. Needless to say, none of these charges were ever proven and little or no evidence emerged to support them. But the damage was done.

J.B. Rhine continued his work doggedly up to the year of his death, 1980, and a statistical breakdown of his decades of research at Duke University undoubtedly upheld the probability that extrasensory perception really does exist. However, in the eyes of most of his peers Rhine's overall body of evidence fails to make the case beyond reasonable doubt.

Doubtless the quest for incontrovertible evidence will go on, and perhaps one day it will even succeed in changing the sceptics' minds. Yet like many researchers working in the field of the paranormal, I cannot help but wonder whether that final conclusive piece of ESP evidence will prove to be as hard to find as those Russian flyers whom Sir Hubert Wilkins sought so long ago in the year 1937.

1938

Three Fingers of Fire

As I wrote in an earlier section every year of the twentieth century has seen several cases of spontaneous human combustion. However, some twelve-month periods have seen far more, though it is not clear why this should be. For instance, during 1938 American journalist Frank Russel uncovered no fewer than thirty-nine examples of fire deaths whose circumstances seemed reminiscent of the classic SHC type.

Russel's trawl included several of the most well-witnessed burnings on record. Typical was the curious death of Englishwoman Miss Phyllis Newcombe, who exploded into flames during a dinner-dance at Chelmsford's Shire Hall, Essex, on 27 August.

Miss Newcombe, twenty-two years of age on the night of her immolation, had been dancing with her fiancé, Henry McAusland, when at around midnight her dress suddenly burst into flames. There was considerable panic and by the time the fire had been smothered with a tablecloth the unfortunate young woman had been reduced to little more than a charred skeleton. Afterwards, the county coroner, Mr L.F. Beccles, described the incident as the most mysterious he had ever known, but nevertheless he believed that a cigarette must have ignited her ballgown rather than accepting the statements of eye-witnesses who steadfastly maintained that it was Phyllis Newcombe herself and not her garments who had been ablaze.

Another English death that Russel uncovered was the sudden combustion of Mrs Mary Carpenter, who perished while holidaying on a cabin cruiser on the Norfolk Broads on 29 July. In full view of her horrified husband and children Mrs Carpenter was engulfed in flames and reduced to a charred corpse within the space of two minutes. The wooden structure of the boat remained undamaged and investigating officers from the Norfolk fire brigade admitted they could not understand how the tragedy had happened.

However, easily the most curious fire deaths Frank Russel found had taken place several months earlier on 7 March. It was a day when the fiery persecution seemingly struck down three men in as many minutes, hundreds of miles apart. First to die was Willen Ten Bruik, an eighteen-year-old Dutchman who was driving his car through the small town of Ubbergen near Nijmegen. The second, a middle-aged Englishman named George Turner, was driving a lorry along a by-pass outside Chester.

The fire's third victim, a seaman named John Greeley, was at the helm of the *SS Ulrich*, a merchant steamer bound for Liverpool. The *Ulrich* was 700 miles from her destination when the unnatural flames began to consume her helmsman and researchers have estimated that her position lay at a point exactly equidistant from those of the other victims. In other words, Greeley began to burn when his ship had reached the apex of an enormous equilateral triangle, the other locations being at the base angles. Why such a factor of distance should matter to the force behind spontaneous combustion remains obscure, yet the fact can hardly be coincidental. It is also true to say that each man was engaged in a markedly similar activity at his moment of death – steering a vehicle – although once again why this should make any difference is hard to imagine.

While Frank Russel's pre-war research assisted in building the case for belief in spontaneous human combustion, he never went as far as to analyse his data to suggest possible causes behind the phenomenon. Much later other writers would fill this gap. In 1975 Fortean writer Livingstone Gearhart drew up six charts showing how a period of intense solar activity during 1938 correlated with several of the examples of spontaneous combustion contained in the article by Frank Russel. Gearhart went on to point out that global averages in magnetic-field variation can show quite dramatic dips and surges during such periods of high solar activity and speculated upon the possibility that these might match geographical patterns of SHC distribution. Although he failed to prove his case conclusively this analysis of the 1938 burnings has perhaps come closest to making sense of an otherwise incomprehensible horror. Yet even Livingstone Gearhart could offer no rational explanation for the way three men hundreds of miles from each other should have suffered the same fate on 7 March. In the words of the journalist who first discovered the mystery, it was as if 'a galactic being of unimaginable size had probed the earth with a three-pronged fork . . . three fingers of fire which burned only flesh'.

1939

Black Dogs

One of the most commonly reported creatures from the realms of psychic phenomena is the black dog of rural England and Wales. Black dog legends have their roots deep in the heart of British folklore and the animals are known by a variety of names in different parts of the country, including Black Shuck, Shriker, Trash and Padfoot. Stories involving these dogs usually follow a simple scenario: the percipient, walking alone and usually at night, becomes aware of the presence of a large black dog with flashing red eyes either barring his way or trotting down the road towards him. Sometimes the observer will be unaware of the dog's phenomenal reality until it vanishes before his eyes, either dematerialising into a mist, fading ghost-like from view, or suddenly exploding in a flash of light. But most often the creatures are immediately recognised as being unnatural because of their size (sometimes said to be as big as a calf), their huge glowing eyes, or because they simply impart to the witness a dreadful sense of overwhelming supernatural evil.

In centuries past black dogs were seen as malevolent spirits in canine form, manifestations from hell intent upon human destruction, and there are numerous legends of black dogs serving as an omen of death in English counties as far apart as Lancashire, Yorkshire, Derbyshire, Suffolk and Norfolk. Such tales would have been written off as fantasies or allegories of yesteryear were it not for the all-too-frequent and well-witnessed examples which have continued to crop up throughout the twentieth century.

One of the most clearly described encounters with a black dog was that of farm labourer Ernest Whiteland, who saw one as he was walking home one late August evening in 1939. Whiteland was returning home after visiting a friend in the Suffolk village of Bungay, and having reached roughly the halfway point of his homeward journey along the lonely road between Maltings and Ditchingham Station, Whiteland noticed a sizeable black object coming towards him on four legs. Peering through the gathering gloom he at first thought it was a small Shetland pony, but as it approached he realised it was a large canine with a long, black, shaggy coat. No great lover of dogs, Whiteland moved into the middle of the road so that it might easily pass by, but when it got level with him it simply vanished. Wondering if his senses had betrayed him, Whiteland spent a few minutes looking around for the dog until at last a sudden sensation of fear came over him and he proceeded to cover the rest of the journey home with a stiff pace. The following morning he discovered the area was believed in years gone by to be haunted by a ghostly canine apparition known to local people as Black Shuck.

Coming as it did so close to the town of Bungay, Ernest Whiteland's experience is particularly interesting, because by far the most dramatic of all black dog sightings centres on precisely that area. On Sunday 4 August 1577, according to an account recorded by eye-witness Abraham Felming, a fearful prodigy appeared while a service was taking place in the local church. Clearly visible to all among the terrified assembly the monster let out a single hideous bark before rushing headlong through the worshippers, burning to death two men who were kneeling in prayer. When the dog reached the end of the church it apparently disappeared in a violent flash and the building's stone floor still bears today the deep scratch marks supposedly made by the animal's claws. For most modern people an account so fantastic is to be treated with extreme scepticism. This is understandable. But before we let our own prejudices reject the tale out of hand, we should not forget the remarkable consistency with which similar creatures seem to haunt twentieth-century Britain. And, even more remarkably, the circumstances of many of these sightings would appear to buttress rather than diminish the ancient legends of black dogs presaging death.

In July 1950 author Stephen Jenkins saw a giant dog baying and howling on a road near his Devon farmhouse the day before his brother passed away. A similar creature was seen in 1928 by a student from Trinity College, Dublin, who was visiting England at the time. In this instance the dog's appearance would seem to have indicated the demise of the Irishman's father, who was gravely ill. Other twentieth-century examples of black dogs being seen immediately before a death come from Buxton Lamas in Norfolk and the Isle of Man. In the most recent case of a fatal encounter, in 1978, a couple saw a canine spectre on a road near the village of Exford, Somerset, and their family was plagued by death and misfortune for months afterwards.

A careful reading of the details of several sightings reinforces the essentially supernatural nature of the phenomenon. A dog seen by a girl in Bredon, Worcestershire during the Second World War was said to have had eyes like coals which lit up inside, while in 1907 a Somerset woman was menaced by a dog she saw near Budsley Hill, an animal of prodigious size with 'eyes like saucers'.

It is unlikely that anyone who sees a black dog could forget the experience. An omen witnessed by a man near Leeds in 1925 was said to have emitted a sulphurous vapour as it barked, while a similar creature which jumped out at a Norfolk woman during the same year had a 'hot breath of noxious odour'. In 1972 a pony-sized black dog visited a Dartmoor farmhouse causing structural damage to the building's wall, roof and electrical circuits, as well as terrifying the occupants.

The examples listed above are merely a handful among hundreds of sightings of British black dogs recorded over the past ninety years. They show no sign of abating, even though most of us have long since given up our belief in the existence of such supernatural creatures. From the accounts of eye-witnesses it must be perfectly plain to even the most sceptical reader that such reports cannot merely be the misidentification of a normal species of canine and it would be quite wrong to imagine that the only witnesses to see these visions are feeble-minded country types or those predisposed to belief in the legends. It is quite true to say that black dogs are usually seen in quiet rural areas, favouring lanes and ancient sites, trackways, churchyards, and other out-of-the-way places, and the fact that their appearance usually comes about during the hours of darkness, in lonely unlit locations, and to individual witnesses rather than groups of people, raises the possibility of a hallucination. Yet if they are illusory why should these particular visions remain so consistent? And why should the same stretches of road or same churchyards be so persistently haunted by these phenomenal creatures, often being seen by individuals who have no prior knowledge of the legend surrounding the spot?

The plain truth is that although these phantom animals have no logical place in our modern way of life there is good reason to assume that they are as real as you or I.

1940

Min-Min and Other Spook Lights

At regular intervals during the present century a ghostly luminous phenomenon has haunted Alexandria Station, an 11,000-square-mile range in the remote outback of south-west Queensland, Australia. The curious dancing forms of light, known as Min-Min (named after a public house in the nearby town of Boulia), have never been explained but their curiously watchful behaviour has led many an Australian witness to claim to have been followed or even chased.

Some believe they have seen the activities of the earth-bound dead. Others feel that the lights are alien lifeforms or even tiny UFOs. Science, which ought to provide us with the answer, is at a loss to account for them.

One of the earliest written accounts of the Min-Min lights, though by no means the first reported sighting, was published in March 1940. In it the witness, a stockman travelling between Boulia and Warenda, first noticed a strange glow emanating from the middle of a graveyard. As he stopped his vehicle he watched the hovering luminescence gradually form into a ball the size of a watermelon and then move towards him. Afraid for his life, the stockman took off in a hurry back towards the direction of Boulia, the nearest civilisation, and afterwards claimed that the light followed him all the way to town.

Since the publication of this account from 1940, glowing spheres have startled many travellers along the lonely stretches of road that criss-cross the vast expanse of Alexandria Station, leaving little room for doubt that something extremely strange occasionally manifests itself there. Nor are the Min-Min lights in any way unique. Mysteriologists have uncovered several locations around the world where balls of light variously labelled will-o-the-wisps, ghost lights or spook lights, are regularly seen.

These low-level nocturnal lights are by no means always round in shape; often they appear like flames or candlelight which flickers on and off, moving about as if attempting to entice the witness into following them.

The most famous examples are probably the American varieties, the Saratoga and Marfa lights of Texas, the Brown Mountain lights and Maco lights of North Carolina, and the Hornet spook lights of Missouri. Such concentrations of sightings in highly localised areas tends to rule out the possibility that the ghost-like phenomena are examples of ball lightning and descriptions in any case suggest that these light globes are not filled with the huge levels of electrical energy which characterise lightning balls. Exactly how these light forms do emanate is much less clear. In Britain the occasional appearance of low-level nocturnal lights has been documented since before Shakespeare's time and given all sorts of colourful names such as Jack O'Lantern, Corpse Light or Corpse Candle. Although the superstitious believed that they were lights held by the wandering ghosts of evil-doers who had been murdered or executed, the standard scientific explanation was that they are caused by methane gas given off by swampy ground and spontaneously ignited.

Unfortunately for the rationalists, attempts to create an

artificial swamp and ignite the methane given off have failed to duplicate the typical characteristics shown by will-o-the-wisps. Not to be outdone, some naturalists have suggested that the luminosity might in fact be the result of phosphorescent fungi or bacteria attached to the wing feathers of owls! Other natural explanations to emerge more recently have included lights from radio-active mineral deposits, electrical phenomena akin to St Elmo's Fire, and the misidentification of car headlights travelling in the distance. Such simple explanations might well be responsible for a few sightings but since not every appearance occurs over swampy ground, near the habitats of owls or close to highways, these theories fail to offer an all-embracing solution to the enigma. They also do not begin to account for those cases in which ghost lights have apparently shown intelligent purpose.

On 16 July 1952 two American police patrolmen riding late at night on a deserted road in Maryland were startled by a yellow light which came directly towards them. As they stopped so did the light, and it continued to hover about 20 feet in front of them. When they edged the car slowly forwards the light retreated, gaining speed as they accelerated in chase. After matching their speed for a time it seemed to give up and drifted away over the countryside. Similar behaviour has been recorded by motorists travelling along a stretch of road known as Spook Light Road near Neosho, Missouri, while North Carolina's most famous ghost light at Maco is most commonly seen haunting the coastline and railway track where the ghost of a man decapitated by a train in 1868 has also been repeatedly seen. In Arkansas, the Girdon light also has a ghost story, the victim this time being a foreman battered to death at a point along the railway track which the light frequents. Meanwhile, at Screven, Georgia yet another light which hovers above a railway track is commonly seen at a location where a flagman was killed in a train accident.

Although they only seldom seem to present a source of danger, glowing lights hanging in the air near to the site of an earlier tragedy offer the unsettling possibility that forms of life might exist on a level previously unknown to earthly science. Depending upon your point of view that idea is either challenging or sinister.

Certainly in Britain, where will-o-the-wisps are still regularly seen in many areas of the countryside, folklore holds that they attempt to lure people into bogs and unsafe areas of marshy ground. Such behaviour is distinctly anti-social, yet conversely some interesting stories have emerged from elsewhere in Europe to suggest that the phenomena can sometimes prove useful. In November 1977 a married couple climbing Mount Snezka, Czechoslovakia's highest peak, lost their way and found themselves in serious difficulties when it began to snow heavily. Realising their position was becoming serious the two climbers were suddenly confronted by a large blue globe which floated several feet off the ground, shining with a clear, warm light. Although frightened, each climber seemed to know by some instinct that the manifestation had appeared in order to lead them safely down the mountain and, according to their later testimony, this is precisely what it did, staying ahead of them a few paces all the way to the lower slopes. Only when the first houses of the nearest town came into view did the helpful light form vanish.

1941

Ghostly Firestarters in the Mid-West

Human beings are not the only things that sometimes burst into flames for no apparent reason. Invisible pyromaniacs or fire spooks which provoke the spontaneous combustion of inanimate objects have struck on many occasions during the present century. Of these, two examples from the continent of North America which occurred during 1941 are among the best documented.

During early July William Hackler, the owner of a farm near Odon, Indiana, was awoken one night by the smell of burning. Hackler checked the house thoroughly but, finding nothing amiss, decided it must be his imagination and returned to bed. Nothing further happened for several days until early one morning, suddenly and inexplicably, several fires began to break out all over the house.

Since the house had never been wired for electricity and there were no naked flames in either the kitchen or the hearth Mr Hackler was dumbfounded. Yet when he alerted both the local fire service and the county police the officers from both departments bore witness to his amazing testimony. An insurance company report filed by one of their own representatives who visited the farm commented that some fires were so strange as to tax the belief of the most credulous person. For example, a calendar on the wall went up in a puff of smoke. Another fire started in a pair of overalls hung on a door. A book taken from a drawer was found to be burning inside, though the cover of the volume was in perfect condition. As the strange fires continued to break out for no apparent reason during the following weeks the problem got out of hand. William Hackler, driven to despair by his fiery visitor, decided to demolish the building.

An almost parallel story to the bizarre tale related above occurred in December of the same year at the Dominion Golf and Country Club near Windsor, Ontario. In the Canadian outbreaks the fires were even smaller and more localised. Pieces of paper, tablecloths, curtains and towels were all found bursting spontaneously into flames. As the manager tried to find the number of the local fire brigade the telephone directory turned to ashes in his hands.

In all forty-three fires were separately noted and put out after causing minor damage. Perhaps even more incredibly, tiny dancing blue flames which left no burn marks were subsequently seen running up and down highly combustible material such as curtains and tablecloths without igniting them.

The phenomenon of spontaneous combustion in inanimate objects has continued to become manifest throughout the present century. On 7 August 1948 at another farm, this time south of Macomb, Illinois, mysterious brown scorch marks were found smouldering on the walls and ceilings of the house every night for seven days. The local fire chief, Fred Wilson, confirmed that over 200 fires had broken out in total only to be extinguished. But by 14 August there were too many to control and the cottage was destroyed, along with two barns and various outhouses. A similarly plagued family were the Van Reenans of Plettenberg Bay, South Africa, who fell victim to an estimated one hundred fires which broke out in a three-month period beginning on 5 May 1975. Among the affected items were carpets, toys, curtains, chairs and bedspreads as well as the family's two Bibles, yet curiously their home's wooden structure remained unaffected.

Some fire spooks have even gone further, terrorising not simply one home but a whole community. In the summer of 1983 the West Virginia coal town of Warncliff suffered a number of mysterious incidents in which houses were burned to the ground after flames were found shooting out of electrical sockets. However, these were not simply standard electrical fires, for the phenomenon continued even when the mains power was disconnected. No natural solution was offered for the Warncliff outbreaks, nor did the fires appear to be the work of an arsonist. Even more recently, in 1990, the mountain village of San Gottardo situated above Vicenza in northern Italy became the target for a phantom pyromaniac. Televisions, a car, an armchair and a plastic canopy were among the items which burst into flames in houses on the narrow winding lane of Via Calora. A number of fuseboxes blew up but visiting electricians could find no fault. Observing the phenomenon from outside, many thought the village must be affected by mass hysteria. However, when the fires continued, including blazes within the homes of both of San Gottardo's mayors, others suspected that a supernatural force might be at work. At the same time dozens of people began to complain of headaches, sickness, stomach pains and skin inflammations, all of which doctors found themselves unable to successfully treat.

In the event all these effects – both the fires and the mystery ailments – ended as swiftly as they had begun, in April 1990, leaving no one any the wiser about their origin.

1942

The Great Los Angeles UFO Raid

On the night of 25 February 1942, less than three months after America was dragged unwillingly into the Second World War, a large formation of unidentified objects appeared over the west coast city of Los Angeles. Suspecting this might be the beginning of a Pearl Harbor-style surprise attack by the Japanese, the city's air defences lost no time in opening up. Over a twenty-minute period some 1,500 anti-aircraft rounds were fired at the objects, which were hit many times. Yet, incredibly, none were brought down, although many homes and public buildings were severely damaged by unexploded shells and a total of six civilians lost their lives, to falling ordnance.

The next day was one of near-total confusion. By morning it had become clear that there was no Japanese invasion fleet lying offshore and eye-witness accounts of California residents suggested that in any case what had appeared in the skies the previous night had not been conventional enemy aircraft. According to these witnesses, one large round object remained stationary at an altitude of roughly 1,000 feet while anti-aircraft shells burst around and against it. One journalist working for the Los Angeles *Herald Express* was quite certain that he saw many shells explode directly in the middle of the craft without apparent effect. The strange object, which afterwards proceeded at a leisurely pace over the coastal communities between Santa Monica and Long Beach, had eventually disappeared from view, moving back out to sea. Although its speed was never more than slow, few who had seen it believed it to be a dirigible (which would in any case have been blown to pieces by the first direct hit it received). So what exactly was this large object and the smaller ones which had accompanied it? All across the city of Los Angeles people were asking the same question.

Understandably, high-ranking military officers were embarrassed and confused by the appearance of these objects and the all-too-obvious inability of their gunners to shoot them down. Having pondered on the various possibilities and drawing a blank every time they knew it was going to be difficult to offer the American people reassurance. So they decided to kill the story. The following month the US Navy secretary John Knox announced that in fact there had been no unidentified planes above the west coast on 26 February and that the barrage of anti-aircraft fire had been triggered by a false alarm. No doubt mindful of the national interest in those difficult times, the Washington press corps accepted the explanation without question.

In California it was a rather different story, however. Among residents of Los Angeles the announcement served only to incense public opinion and the local media lost no time in condemning it as a piece of crude and unconvincing war propaganda. Yet the same journalists found their attempts to probe deeper into the origins of the mysterious air-raid-that-never-was were consistently frustrated. As an editorial in the *Long Beach Independent* commented at the time: 'There is a mysterious reticence about the whole affair and it appears that some form of censorship is trying to halt discussion of the matter.' We can now say for certain that the *Independent* was correct in its assessment. A hitherto secret memorandum was released in 1974 under the provisions of the US Freedom of Information Act. Written by General George C. Marshall, US chief of staff to President Franklin D. Roosevelt and dated 26 February 1942, it makes it clear that unidentified objects had definitely been sighted and fired upon during the previous night, though the Department of Defense were at a loss to explain the nature and origin of the airborne vehicles.

General George C. Marshall's memorandum was to be a watershed in the secret history of the twentieth century, since it marked the beginning of official attempts to hide evidence of UFO activity in the skies above our planet.

It is a policy that has continued to this day, with governments around the world routinely restricting the flow of information to the general public and steadfastly denying that they are doing so.

1943

Incorruptibility and Other Mystical Phenomena

Whether or not the human spirit survives death is open to endless speculation but we can say with absolute certainty that the human body perishes. Or can we? Medical science has conclusively shown that following the onset of physical death the body rapidly deteriorates when exposed to atmospheric biological agents. Depending on the particular circumstances, this natural process of decomposition will take either several months or a few years to reduce a human corpse to a skeleton. However, not every body has decayed in this way. Though it seems improbable (and entirely beyond the ability of science to explain) some human corpses – usually those of venerated religious persons – remain almost totally uncorrupted long after their burial. Although the phenomenon is not confined purely to Roman Catholic holy men and women, these provide us with the most convincing samples on record, probably because of that religion's custom of exhuming saints.

One of the best-attested cases of bodily incorruptibility was that of St Catherine Laboure, a Frenchwoman who died in Paris in 1876. Buried in a triple coffin in a chapel crypt, St Catherine's corpse lay undisturbed for sixty-seven years until it was exhumed on 21 March 1943 in preparation for her beatification. A stunned surgeon who witnessed the exhumation reported how the woman's arms and legs were perfectly supple with the muscles preserved so well that she might have died only the previous day. Her skin was intact, the hair remaining attached to the scalp. The eyes remained in the orbit, their bluish-grey colour still evident, and a surgical analysis of the saint's internal organs showed them to be in near-pristine condition.

The French female saint is just one of many Christian religious figures to have been exhumed during the present century and found to be undiminished. Others include the Blessed Maria Assunta Paulota, St Jean Vianney, the Blessed Paula Frassinetti and St Bernadette Soubirous (the visionary of Lourdes). St Charbal Maklouf, whose remains are kept at the monastery of St Maro Annaya, Lebanon, is perhaps the most remarkable of all. When St Charbal died a miraculous phenomenon including a bright light surrounded his tomb for forty-eight days following his burial in 1899. Upon his first exhumation in 1937 the saint was found to be perfectly preserved despite frequent heavy rains which had left the body floating in mud.

The corpse was reburied and remained unseen for twenty-three years until 1950, when pilgrims to St Charbal's shrine noticed liquid seeping from the tomb. Upon a second exhumation the saint's body was again found to be incorrupt, flexible and lifelike, though its garments were heavily stained with blood. A further oddity which had never been satisfactorily accounted for was that the corpse seemed to be exuding a viscous, oily substance in copious quantities. This strange miraculous flow has continued ever since and upon each annual exhumation the same mysterious fluid is found to be three inches deep in the saint's coffin. Some believe it has healing properties.

For those who are atheists – indeed for all rationally minded people – stories such as those described above make difficult reading. Claimed to be unequivocal proof of God's existence by some, and ridiculed as naïve delusions by others, the physical phenomena of mysticism present us with some of the most incontrovertible evidence that very strange powers are working through the universe, powers of which we know very little. Without question the existence of perfectly preserved bodies is now an established fact. And since such examples cannot be contained within the accepted physical laws of the known universe we must necessarily look outside those laws for an explanation.

There are plenty of other miraculous happenings that are no less baffling. Every year for a period of twenty-four hours dried blood in a phial held within a cathedral in Naples liquefies into a fresh red substance, believed by Catholics to be the blood of St Janarius, Bishop of Benevitto, who was beheaded by the Romans in AD 305. The transformation from solid into liquid has been witnessed and confirmed by doctors and scientists, as well as adherents of the Catholic faith. Equally hard to explain are the numerous instances where religious images and icons such as crucifixes and Madonnas weep or bleed. Although some of these examples have been blamed on hoaxing, it has now been proven beyond question that others are genuine.

On 29 August 1953 a pregnant woman named Antonietta Januso living in Syracuse, Sicily, noticed that a plaster statue of the Virgin and Child was weeping. News of the miracle spread rapidly and led to an outbreak of religious hysteria across the island. The local church authorities, somewhat embarrassed by the publicity surrounding the story, decided to check its veracity. The truth was that they simply did not believe the woman's story, but when samples of the tears were analysed and found to be indistinguishable from real human tears, the Church officially recognised the miracle and erected a shrine where the statue is venerated by pilgrims to this day.

Since weeping plastic dolls are now mass-produced in many Western countries it is clearly not beyond the wit of man to fake such a 'miracle'. Nevertheless, it would be much harder to effect such a hoax using real human tears and certainly the fraud theory becomes inconceivable when an icon weeps over a period of many years, as is often the case. One would imagine that bleeding images are even harder to fake, yet there is no shortage of these either. In January 1971 a lawyer living in Maropati, Italy, found that a framed painting of the Madonna which he kept over his bed was dripping blood. The red liquid clearly came from behind the picture's glass cover and emanated from the Madonna's eyes as well as the hands and feet of two saints kneeling beside her. To the lawyer's amazement the flow did not simply run down the wall to the floor but formed crosses or haemeographs (blood pictures) on the white plaster above the bed. In the Italian case the actuality of the phenomenon was well attested and police forensic scientists were able to confirm that the red substance was indeed human blood. In this instance a hoax would seem out of the question, for the painting continued to seep blood even when sealed in a safe at police headquarters.

Apparent miracles of this type are so numerous that one could easily write a whole book on this subject alone. Since inanimate objects cannot conceivably weep or bleed it goes without saying that the origin of the phenomena must be supernatural. Perhaps through these simple means God is proving His existence. Yet one cannot help but wonder why the Supreme Being would choose such a crude method to make a point. Clearly something very strange is happening, but is it really the work of the Divine?

1944

Proof Positive?

Although millions of ghosts are reportedly seen in every decade the majority of accounts remain highly suspect. Natural explanations have often proved childishly easy to construct. A vibration from passing traffic closing a door; a draught rattling the pages of an open book; an old house creaking as it settles due to the fall in temperature in the evening. Without doubt the phantoms some witnesses claim to see are truly, as the saying goes, 'all in the mind'. Without question some hoaxers have made up stories for motives of profit or mischief.

Yet there are many stories which cannot be accounted for so easily. For every event which can be put down to a person misidentifying a combination of mundane circumstances, there is another which appears to indicate the genuine presence of discarnate forces. Even if we exclude every tale told by children, persons of a nervous or hysterical disposition or those who wish to claim psychic powers, we are still left with a hardened kernel of inexplicable cases that will not go away. So are these really the returning souls of dead people?

One category of spirit which goes a long way towards building a convincing case for the reality of human survival after death is where visions have returned to impart some piece of specific evidence for their continued existence to friends or acquaintances – evidence of which the percipient had no prior knowledge.

Such an example was the return of Owen Harrison, a young British expatriate living in South Africa who travelled to Europe to fight for his old country during the Second World War and lost his mortal life in the Italian campaign of 1944. Though his immediate family had long since moved to Africa it was in the Kent home of a Mrs Feakes, his English aunt, that Harrison's spirit appeared one evening shrouded in a golden mist. He spoke just once and then only two words, 'tell Mum', before disappearing. Mrs Feakes was too upset to tell anyone, however, and even began to doubt her own sanity. But Owen's ghost was persistent, appearing again a few days later to make the same request and also mentioning this time the name of a girl, 'Helen'. Before he vanished he showed his aunt an exotic blue flower of a type she had never seen. It would, he said, be a sign which his mother would understand. After this second manifestation Mrs Feakes at last wrote to her sister in South Africa describing the uncanny encounter in detail. The reply she received persuaded her that the vision of her nephew had not been a product of her imagination. For it transpired from Mrs Harrison's reply that the blue flower was a rare protected orchid which her son Owen had picked illegally from Table Mountain on his last period of leave. To avoid the possibility of being fined he had shown it only to his mother and sister. If anything the name Helen was an even more conclusive piece of evidence, for although no one in his family had been aware of it at the time, investigations subsequently revealed that the youth had been secretly conducting a courtship with a girl of that name and a quantity of love letters and poems dedicated to her were found. Thus for the grieving relatives of the dead soldier the case against death was proven beyond doubt.

Ghostly encounters of this type are particularly interesting to psychical researchers because the information imparted is unknown to those who have been chosen to receive it. The fact that Mrs Feakes was unaware of the relevance of Owen Harrison's message, and that parts of it were previously unknown also to Mrs Harrison, makes it doubly convincing and puts paid to the possibility that the apparition was created through a telepathic link between the woman and her sister.

Similarly impressive evidence for proof of survival has emerged from seance rooms. Among those who doubt whether channelling is possible are the investigators who argue that so-called guides are simply fragments of the medium's own subconscious mind. As a psychological theory it certainly has its attractions since it has been conclusively proved that the human mind can create new identities. However, this explanation of a spiritualistic phenomenon does not begin to account for those numerous instances where mediums gain access to information of which they themselves could have had no knowledge.

Typical is the communication given to Englishwoman Mrs Elizabeth Dawson-Smith in 1921, through the mediumship of Gladys Leonard. The returning spirit in this case was Mrs Dawson-Smith's son, who had been killed a year before while still a young man. The message concerned an old purse her son had hidden which contained a receipt for a large sum of money previously paid to a debt-clearing office in Germany. Mrs Dawson-Smith knew of the transaction but had searched in vain for the piece of paper. When she found it in the place that Gladys Leonard had indicated she had little choice but to believe wholeheartedly that it was her son who had given the message, for he had been the only person who knew of its whereabouts.

Another example uncovered by Dutchman Nils Jacobsen and included in his book *Life Without Death* serves to prove how difficult such enigmas are to account for within a rationalist framework. In 1928 Jacobsen's uncle was knocked down by a lorry. His head was smashed against a brick wall and he died several days later in hospital without ever regaining consciousness. Jacobsen's family had always assumed that the fractured skull had been the cause of death, until many years afterwards, when a mediumistic message was received which offered a contradictory version of events. After describing accurately the circumstances of the road accident itself, the returning soul of the author's uncle explained that he had really died of a condition which 'came from the bones'. It seemed unlikely until Nils Jacobsen checked the post-mortem report. The hospital records showed that his uncle had died not as a result of brain damage but from an embolism originating from a blood clot in his thigh bone – lower-bone thrombosis.

As Jacobsen wrote, it was a significant factor of which none of his family was aware, let alone the medium. Personally, he became convinced from that moment on that the human personality was not annihilated by physical death.

1945

Terror in the Triangle

Since Charles Berlitz published his sensational book about the Bermuda Triangle in the mid-1970s an avalanche of paperbacks, periodicals, magazine articles and television documentaries has appeared on the subject. Sceptics continue to claim that there is no mystery at all, since the number of ships and planes lost in the area is no higher than one might expect, in view of the area's natural hazards. Everyone is entitled to his own point of view, yet even the most steadfast debunkers are unable to deny that strange events have unquestionably taken place in the waters between Florida, Bermuda and the Sargasso Sea. For one thing too many disappearances of boats and aircraft have occurred in fine weather and after radio messages were received to indicate that all was well on board. Odder still, typical triangle vanishings have often left no wreckage, lifeboats, lifejackets or even oil slicks in the vicinity of the vessel or plane's last-known position. Like it or not, there are questions here that have yet to be answered.

Of all the mysteries to have occurred in the Triangle none is stranger than the disappearance of Flight 19, a group of naval training craft which vanished during a routine exercise just after the Second World War had ended.

At two o'clock on the afternoon of 5 December 1945 five Gruman Avenger torpedo bombers took off from Fort Lauderdale Naval Station, Florida. Each plane, carrying a crew of three, had been given the usual pre-flight checks and had refuelled before leaving for what was meant to be a strictly unhazardous mission to practise torpedo runs. As the ground crew watched the formation fly up and away over the blue Atlantic Ocean no one could have guessed that their colleagues would never return. To begin with Flight 19 proceeded normally along its scheduled route, parallel with the Florida coastline. For a while everything seemed OK, yet at 3.45 pm the operator at Fort Lauderdale tower began to receive a series of astonishing messages from the training mission's flight leader, Lieutenant Charles Taylor. In a voice which portrayed both fear and amazement the group's commander indicated that his instruments were going crazy – indeed, not only his, but the controls of all the planes were malfunctioning simultaneously.

'What is your position?' asked the radio operator.

Taylor could not say. 'Everything,' he yelled, 'seems wrong. We are lost. Even the sea isn't right.'

Alarmed by this incomprehensible turn of events the radio operators at Fort Lauderdale continued to ask their officer to verify his position, yet as the minutes ticked by Taylor's voice became more disturbed and confused, and his messages made even less sense than before. According to one version of events the last words he uttered sounded like a warning: 'Don't come after us, for God's sake . . .' then silence. Yet come after him they did. Following the loss of radio contact a Martin Mariner flying boat was sent out towards the area where the base commander estimated Flight 19's probable position to be. The Navy knew that whatever else might have befallen these men, their planes would also soon be running out of fuel and would have to ditch in the sea. However, the rescuers were themselves about to become the Triangle's next victims. As the flying boat reached the stretch of ocean designated as the search area, it disappeared from radar screens, vanishing into oblivion along with its crew of thirteen.

For the US Navy the loss of six planes in the space of as many hours represented an unprecedented peacetime disaster. An enquiry's report into the events of 5 December ran to some 400 pages. The official document took the line that Flight 19 had fallen into the sea following an unlucky coincidence of a number of chance factors: sudden bad weather, electrical interference and pilot error. It also concluded that flight leader Lieutenant Charles Taylor must have panicked, thus compounding the situation and destroying the nerve of his young and relatively inexperienced men. As for the loss of the Mariner flying boat, it was assumed that a mid-air explosion had claimed it, though no evidence was ever produced to support this hypothesis.

The Navy's official enquiry satisfied few people, however, and certainly failed to convince those writers who studied the numerous reports of peculiar electro-magnetic anomalies in the area. To put it simply, there were many questions which the Navy chiefs had failed to address. Why, for instance, could Lieutenant Taylor simply not have followed the Florida coastline when it should have been clearly visible? Why had no sign of wreckage or bodies been found despite the extensive search that followed the disaster? What happened to make Taylor and his men cease radio contact so suddenly? Since 1945 the loss of Flight 19 and the search and rescue plane that went after it has entered into Triangle folklore and a succession of authors have put forward their own pet theories: UFOs, supernatural evil, time-warps and psychic whirlpools to name but a few. Hollywood director Steven Spielberg even paid homage to the subject by including Flight 19's disappearance in his film *Close Encounters of the*

Third Kind. Yet despite the continued interest no one seemed any nearer to solving the enigma.

Then, on 17 May 1991, it seemed that a dramatic clue to the mystery had at last been uncovered when a salvage team hunting for treasure off Florida discovered the wreckage of five planes in 750 feet of water just 10 miles from the coast. Although the last position of the Avengers had never been determined, the possibility that five other wrecks could be so close together seemed unlikely. At once the tales of 'vile vortices' and other paranormal horrors began to fade.

Yet two weeks later the full truth became clear when a group of Hawaiian-based salvage consultants identified the 'planes' as the remains of a Second World War floating target range used for low-altitude torpedo bombing.

And so today the final resting-place of Flight 19 remains unknown. We are no closer to discovering the real fate of the American airmen who vanished out of the Atlantic skies on 5 December 1945, nor are we any wiser as to the extraordinary force that destroyed them.

1946

Unwelcome Visitors

Poltergeists – those impish spirits of paranormal mayhem – usually inhabit a house for only a short period of time and cause relatively little damage or misery. In nine cases out of ten their bizarre pranks are clearly designed to infuriate and exasperate the human occupants rather than harm them. But unfortunately not all poltergeists have followed this mischievous pattern. In some instances the activities of the invisible entities have been truly malevolent.

In June 1946 a German refugee family called Schrey settled in a small apartment in the Bavarian village of Lauter. Although they had no children themselves the Schreys had during the previous year adopted two girls whose parents had been killed in the Allied bombing campaign which characterised the last months of the Second World War. The orphans settled in well until, soon after their relocation to Lauter, the Schreys noticed that the personality of the older stepdaughter, Edith, seemed to be changing in the most alarming fashion.

Once placid and shy, Edith became unruly and even spiteful, throwing tantrums of such violence that her adoptive parents became concerned for her sanity. Yet it soon became clear that the girl's personality change had a supernatural origin. As summer wore on into autumn the child would be found in a trance-like state for days on end, her strange moods coinciding with the anomalous appearance in various parts of the household of enormous piles of human excrement and pools of urine which seemed to materialise literally out of thin air. Though at first the Schreys had assumed that their daughters were responsible, the persistent appearance and sheer volume of the foul liquids and substances ruled out a natural cause.

Things turned from bad to worse when the Schreys' younger child, Irma, began to fall into a same trance-like lethargy as her adopted sister. During these times various household items including pens, razor blades and even heavy iron files were found broken into fragments for no apparent reason. Food, including tomatoes and other vegetables, came flying from within closed larders and a typewriter owned by the girls' adoptive mother, Maria Schrey, began to type long messages which were either indecipherable or obscene in content. This last phenomenon continued even after the machine was locked inside its case.

Disorder turned to violence when the girls found themselves being hacked at by an invisible instrument which seemed to be a pair of blunt scissors.

Their long braids fell to the ground leaving their scalps bloody and raw, and after one particularly vicious assault young Irma was hospitalised. When doctors learned the full story the Schreys' case was passed on to Professor Hans Bender, a parapsychologist and founder of Freiburg University's institute for border areas of psychology and mental hygiene. Bender visited their home to interview the family. He came away convinced that they were victims of a genuine poltergeist and although he had no way of helping the unfortunate family directly, he told them that he believed their ordeal would end when the girls reached the age of puberty.

Sure enough Bender was proved correct. As the girls grew out of adolescence the disturbances within their home diminished over a period of time and eventually ceased altogether after the eldest one reached the age of sixteen.

Professor Bender continued to study the phenomenon of poltergeists for over forty years. In almost every case he found that the two commonest classes of manifestation reported were percussive sounds – knockings, rappings, thuds, crashes, bangs – and the tilting, displacement, levitation or other movement of material objects. More often than not these two classes of happenings coincided. When objects changed position their movement could be either too quick for the eye to follow or unnaturally slow. Sometimes considerable movement might take place within a room without the sort of resultant damage that might be expected. Bender even found instances where fragile objects including glass, fine china or crystal would be hurled with great force against walls and yet remained intact. At the same time instances of crockery being thrown and subsequently broken were found to be particularly common, a fact which suggested to the researcher that the intelligence behind these disturbances might actually be enjoying the chaos it was causing.

But although the activities of poltergeists often cause panic among the households they invade it was not until several decades later that Professor Bender came face to face with another spirit as vicious as the one which had menaced the Schrey family of Lauter. In November 1980 doctors at the Freiburg institute were alerted to the plight of a young Spanish-born housewife named Carla who was living in Mulhouse, eastern France. Having become the focus of increasingly frightening poltergeist activity the unfortunate woman found herself subjected to a series of brutal attacks culminating in a criss-cross network of deep cuts which opened up involuntarily on her shoulders and thighs. Carla also regularly suffered the sensation of being punched savagely in the stomach.

Although French doctors had originally believed that the woman's injuries were hysterically self-induced, Professor Bender and his colleagues soon became convinced that the reported phenomenon was real. In December an investigation team not only witnessed marks appearing spontaneously on Carla's skin but saw for themselves other anomalous activities at the same time. Moreover, during their stay in the house the German parapsychologists discovered that their equipment was regularly tampered with and their films were mysteriously ruined. Thermometers recorded a temperature of 80 degrees Fahrenheit in certain rooms within the house in the middle of the night when the heating was switched off and the outside winter temperature had fallen to 20 degrees below zero. On a separate occasion the same piece of sophisticated equipment set up to monitor the temperature over a seventy-two-hour period revealed not only enormous fluctuations but also broken horizontal lines on the print-out that were technically impossible to replicate.

Although formerly an adherent of the recurrent spontaneous psychokinesis theory which holds poltergeist outbreaks to be the result of psychical energy releases from the mind of the human agent at the focus of the disturbances, Professor Bender came to believe that some form of autonomous invisible force had taken up residence in Carla's home. So, together with his colleagues, Bender set aside his parascientific preconceptions and tried to make contact with the ghost through glass-rolling, a variation of the ouija board technique. Soon contact was made with the entity, which called itself Henry. It then actually appeared, usually as a somewhat menacing apparition slipping in and out of sight through walls and closed doors.

Unfortunately the phantom's identification in no way assisted in persuading it to leave. In April 1981 Carla and her husband Thierry gave up the struggle and moved away, leaving the house empty. Empty, that is, apart from its uninvited guest.

1947

The Roswell Incident

Among the most controversial aspects of the UFO enigma is the allegation that some saucers have crashed and been recovered under conditions of great secrecy. The claims have regularly been dismissed by military figures, yet in the past few years a steady flow of new information has emerged which suggests that there really might be a factual basis for several of these rumoured events. At least one crash retrieval now seems indisputable.

On the evening of 2 July 1947 a bright disc-shaped object was seen flying low over New Mexico. The next day a quantity of highly unusual wreckage was found by a rancher named William Brazel while he was out riding with his son on their property at Roswell. The ranch was situated some 70 miles north of the original UFO sighting, but in the general direction of the apparent flightpath of the alien vehicle. Sensing that the wreckage was something other than a conventional aircraft, Brazel lost no time in informing the authorities. The local sheriff passed on the news to the USAF, and within hours an investigation team arrived at the scene from the 509th Bomb Group Intelligence Office. Immediately a blanket of secrecy was drawn over the discovery, and the debris was meticulously cleared up and transferred to Wright Field AFB at Dayton, Ohio. No non-Army personnel were allowed anywhere near the B-29 upon which the wreckage was carried. Air Force ground crews who got a glimpse of the plane's special cargo were ordered to say nothing to the press and an official statement was released explaining that the mysterious wreckage discovered on land close to Roswell had been identified as the remains of one of the Air Force's new type of weather balloons, together with its attached tinfoil radar target. William Brazel, the rancher who had found the crashed object, was taken in for questioning and held incommunicado for a whole week until newspaper speculation died down, and then released without explanation or apology. When a story hinting that a saucer had been retrieved was leaked by press wire from Albuquerque, the Air Force stepped in to restrain a radio station from broadcasting it.

Almost half a century after the alleged Roswell crash many people find it impossible that an event of such earth-shattering importance could have been covered up so successfully. Yet supporting evidence continues to accumulate and the Roswell incident of July 1947 has become one of the best-documented and most thoroughly researched in UFO history. During the last fifteen years two American authors, Standon Freidman and William Moore, have contacted more than 160 witnesses who were directly or indirectly associated with the New Mexico recovery, including air crew members who transported the wreckage.

Of the various testimonies received easily the most impressive was that of Major Jesse Marcel, the intelligence officer who was in charge of the initial recovery operation. Completely refuting the Air Force's balloon explanation, Marcel stated that the material he handled was 'like nothing on earth'. One piece of metal foil was so durable that it could not be dented with a 16-pound sledgehammer, despite its remarkable lightness. Marcel's testimony cannot be easily dismissed since he was a Second World War veteran of the strategic bombing campaign and later promoted to lieutenant colonel following his assignment to the Air Force's special weapons programme. Moreover, his description of the alien wreckage closely resembled not only those of other witnesses like rancher William Brazel but also matches details that have trickled out concerning other saucer retrievals which have purportedly occurred since. In the United States these incidents have taken place at the following locations: Paradise Valley, Arizona, 1947; Aztec, New Mexico, 1948; Kingham, Arizona, 1953; and New Mexico, 1962. Additional cases have been reported from countries as far apart as France, Germany, Puerto Rico, South Africa, Australia, the former Soviet Union and Spitzbergen (Arctic Ocean). If we choose to reject out of hand the evidence surrounding the Roswell incident and these other numerous examples as having no factual basis, we must at the same time ask ourselves why it is that governments around the world have taken so much care to hide them. In March 1975 US senator Barry Goldwater was refused access to visit Wright-Patterson Air Base (formerly Wright Field) to examine the crashed debris from the Roswell incident of July 1947. Having questioned why his request was denied Senator Goldwater was apparently told that the matter could not be discussed with a member of the public even though that person was a senior elected official. The Roswell incident, together with all evidence of crashed saucer retrievals, was a matter that has remained classified at a level above top secret.

Since that time more and more details have gradually leaked out, all pointing towards a top-level blanket of secrecy. In the last few years before his death in July 1986 Professor Robert Saurbacher, an American physicist who occupied a high-level post at the Department of Defense during the 1950s, broke his oath of silence and described in graphic detail how the US government had recovered and still possessed the remains of several crashed extra-terrestrial spacecraft. Though not directly involved in the UFO recovery project, Saurbacher had seen the retrieved materials at first hand. He described the metallic hull of the craft to be extremely light and very tough, while the instrument panels and other control systems within were also made of a thin, foil-like substance. Yet laboratory studies undertaken by USAF scientists had proved that these same substances could withstand the tremendous deceleration and acceleration pressures associated with space flight. Knowledge of the existence of these craft was, Saurbacher insisted, restricted to a small group of individuals in the politico-military-security establishment. In his own words it was the most highly classified subject in the United States government, rating even higher than the H-Bomb.

Professor Saurbacher's claims were ridiculed by government agencies and there is evidence to suggest that some rather unsubtle measures were taken to curtail his public utterances. Most people felt that his claims were too fantastic to be taken seriously, yet others, recognising that Saurbacher was not the sort of man to be given to wild exaggerations or fanciful imaginings, believed him. Why would a man who had enjoyed a richly successful scientific, academic and business career choose to tarnish his own reputation by fabricating such a bizarre tale? these people asked. The question had no answer, unless of course the story was true.

Which of course it is.

1948

Lieutenant Mantell's Last Mission

Following civilian pilot Kenneth Arnold's famous flying saucer sighting of June 1947 many top-ranking officers in the US Air Force began to wonder whether the alien presence then emerging above American skies would one day prove hostile. They did not have long to wait to find out.

At around one o'clock on the afternoon of 7 January 1948 a control tower duty officer at Godman Field Air Base, Kentucky, received a telephone call from the chief of state highway patrol. The police officer wished to clarify the veracity of certain reports that had been coming in all morning of a huge glowing object shaped like a saucer measuring over 500 feet in diameter. Could Godman confirm it was one of theirs? The duty officer was not amused and curtly pointed out that a craft of such prodigious size was a physical impossibility. He suggested that it was most probably the sun that motorists were seeing, or some bizarre anomaly of light refraction, and promptly hung up. However, the same man changed his mind a few minutes later when an urgent message verifying the extraordinary aerial phenomenon was received from Army personnel guarding the nearby federal gold reserve at Fort Knox. A massive disc, unlike anything they had ever seen, was presently hovering over the area, they reported. The menace was now taken seriously and the Godman base commander, Colonel Guy Fix, ordered a flight of Mustang P-51 fighters to be scrambled. Within minutes they were in the air and had made visual contact with the UFO, a silvery metal disc of tremendous size, according to the radio commentary of flight leader Thomas Mantell, a Second World War veteran.

As the fighters closed on the object, which was hovering at a height estimated to be some 22,000 feet, other pilots corroborated Mantell's description. 'It appears to be a metallic object . . . tremendous in size . . . directly ahead and slightly above . . . I can see rows of windows . . . it's got a ring and a dome . . .' Listening in the control tower Colonel Fix and his fellow officers were incredulous. Yet their amazement soon turned to horror. With the Mustangs now only half a mile from their target, the flying monstrosity began to climb, demonstrating a manoeuvrability hard to believe. Lieutenant Mantell led his men in chase but just as they seemed to be gaining upon it something suddenly went wrong. Mantell's fighter banked steeply and disappeared from view behind a cloud; simultaneously his radio went dead.

The recovery of the flight leader's plane began that afternoon. Wreckage was scattered over an area of 2 miles, strongly suggesting the likelihood of a mid-air explosion. According to USAF sources Mantell's body was also found though no civilians – not even the dead airman's parents – were allowed to see it. The three other pilots were debriefed and instructed to stay silent. An official explanation was issued the following day stating that Lieutenant Thomas Mantell had unfortunately been killed 'while trying to follow the planet Venus'. It was felt most likely that he had flown too high and fainted through lack of oxygen. Earlier stories of a flying saucer were, said the Air Force spokesman, entirely without foundation and were probably the result of a similar misidentification of the distant planet.

For a number of people the official explanation defied logic. Too many civilians had witnessed the UFO's slow passage over Kentucky that morning and knew that the object they saw was most definitely not Venus. Others found it hard to believe that an experienced pilot, a veteran of the Pacific War, could possibly make such an elementary mistake. And what of the other pilots – why weren't they allowed to state their opinions? The widespread increase in public interest in UFOs across America made it difficult for the Air Force to blame the death of one of their men on such a flimsy story. So a week later they changed it, announcing that the object sighted above Fort Knox had now been 'categorically identified' as a Skyhook reconnaissance balloon, the silvery surface of which reflected sunlight.

With the passage of years, we can now say for certain that neither of these natural explanations was true, nor were they believed by the Air Force at the time. In a now declassified memorandum to the Air Technical Intelligence Centre, General N.F. Twining of Strategic Air Command described flying saucers as being 'interplanetary craft' and confirmed the recent wave of sightings as 'undoubtedly real'. The report was written in the autumn of 1948. Other correspondence written the same year, this time to the supreme commander of the Air Force, Brigadier General George Schlugan, states the case even more categorically: 'It is the position of this command that so-called flying disc phenomena [are] something real and not visionary . . . operating characteristics such as the extreme rates of climb; manoeuvrability and evasive action taken when contacted by human craft lend belief to the possibility that the objects are controlled . . .'

General Twining suggested that all information relating to the UFO phenomenon be made public. His advice was ignored. Instead of telling the American people the truth the US government and its military establishment were to classify sightings as Grade-A secrets and used both the FBI and the CIA to systematically suppress evidence and offer instead transparently artificial explanations for genuine sightings. Swamp gas, conventional aircraft, optical effects, smoke from factory chimneys, reflected starlight, parachutes, satellites, missiles, fireflies, shooting stars, meteorological balloons and the perennial favourite – mass hysteria – were rolled out one by one in an effort to debunk the phenomenon. Meanwhile, the list of dead pilots and missing planes grew longer. Thomas Mantell may have been the first American airman to lose his life after UFO contact, but he was not to be the last.

1949

Halfway to Heaven

It is sometimes said that no one can truly know what the moment of death will be like for no one returns to tell the tale. In fact this is not quite true.

In November 1949 Edmund Wilbourne, a young Englishman suffering from pleurisy, was admitted to Crumpsall Hospital, Manchester. He was already in a critical condition when he arrived, and hopes of Wilbourne's recovery quickly faded. He passed away the same night – or so the doctors treating him thought. In fact, unbeknown to the hospital staff, Wilbourne was still very much alive: although his bodily functions appeared to have ceased his consciousness had simply left his body. He was to remain in this state for some time. Floating peacefully above his inert physical form, the young man watched with detached curiosity as nurses prepared his corpse for the mortuary, noting with distaste and surprise how the body's face was shaved by a nurse using a cut-throat razor, and unaware that this was standard practice in hospitals. Although Wilbourne could not make sense of his out-of-body condition he felt no particular fear either.

Hospital records showed that the Englishman must have remained in this extraordinary state between life and death for several hours. In fact it was only after his corpse had been laid out in the hospital mortuary that he suddenly found himself return without warning to normal consciousness. Not surprisingly, the mortuary attendant fell into a faint when the 'dead' Wilbourne sat up with a start and called for help. In the weeks that followed the Englishman made a full recovery and is still alive today. He keeps his death certificate framed on his wall to prove he did not dream the whole thing.

To many people the story related above may seem too incredible to be taken seriously. Yet unless we choose to call Wilbourne a liar or charge the doctors treating him with incompetence, the bizarre truth seems to be that he really did die for over two hours in the year 1949.

Yet Edmund Wilbourne's memories of dying are far from unique. Similar near-death experiences (NDEs) have been reported to doctors across the world with sufficient persistence to convince paranormal investigators that these stories are neither dreams nor illusions. Indeed, their sheer consistency would appear to bear out the probability that all of us are likely to undergo a similar experience at the moment of ultimate crisis. As medical science progresses, bringing with it more sophisticated techniques of resuscitation, the number of people who are returning to life is on the increase and some doctors have gone out of their way to study the growing body of evidence.

In 1976 a Californian psychiatrist named Raymond Moody published a book entitled *Life After Life* which documented in particularly striking detail the recollections of over one hundred people who had narrowly survived temporary death following accidents or while under the surgeon's knife. Through his research Moody discovered that almost all near-death experiencers had vivid recollections of leaving their body; and since these descriptions had much in common he formed the opinion that the experience of dying remained profoundly similar for all human beings. In his introduction to *Life After Life* the psychiatrist constructed what he considered to be an archetypal dying experience based on the fifteen common elements most frequently reported.

According to Moody, the model NDE would begin when the subject notices an uncomfortable buzzing sound and is transported rapidly down a long, dark tunnel. Following this process the subject's consciousness finds itself outside the physical body, yet in the immediate physical vicinity, almost always floating several feet above his or her corpse. The disembodied viewer is then presented with visions of spirits known to them, people who have gone before them into the realm of death. After this the experiencer usually senses an indefinable feeling of love emanating from these surroundings, a feeling followed by another vision, this time of a Being of Light (variously described) which seems to be a higher spiritual entity sent to guide him or her – telepathically – towards a consideration of his achievements and failures during his earthly existence. A panoramic, instantaneous life-review playback then appears before the near-dead person's eyes. Following the life review many other events may occur, but always the subjects reach a point in which they are asked to cross some form of symbolic barrier or point of no return. Instinctively the astral traveller becomes aware that the time is not right and realises that he or she must return to earthly life. Often disappointed at having to leave this world of beauty, love and happiness, the near-death experiencer will then find him or herself conscious once more within his or her own physical body.

Moody stresses in his introduction to *Life After Life* that no two NDEs are identical, nor have any that he has discovered incorporated every single one of the elements described above. Furthermore, there is no one element which would appear to be absolutely universal to all experiences, though some people

– usually those who have been pronounced clinically dead for a long period of time – recalled particularly vivid memories which came close to the model. As a general rule people who went deeper into the other world were always those who had been 'dead' for longer; those who simply reported leaving their bodies were patients whose life functions had failed for a period of less than two minutes.

Raymond Moody's research was too controversial for most doctors to accept but in subsequent years other American experts following in his footsteps and publishing their own analyses of near-death experiences invariably tended to buttress the Californian's conclusion. Moreover, these psychologists were quick to point out that the modern-day memories of close-call survival corresponded closely to descriptions of the dying experience contained in such ancient texts as the Tibetan Book of the Dead.

Today, in the last decade of the last century of the present millennium, many people continue to view death as a final extinction, complete termination, the ultimate end. But they may be wrong. If we are to lend any credibility whatsoever to the stories of people like Edmund Wilbourne then it would seem certain that some part of ourself – consciousness, mind, soul or whatever – is not snuffed out when the vital functions of the body cease to operate.

1950

The Legendary Ogopogo

The retreat of the last Ice Age left Canada sprinkled with nearly 100,000 lakes and so it comes as little surprise that the world's second-largest country has more lake-monster legends than any other. During the twentieth century reports have come in from literally dozens of Canadian lakes and waterways, all of which indicate the likely presence of long-necked plesiosaur-type creatures among the native fauna of the north American continent.

There is, for example, the Turtle Lake monster of Saskatchewan, first sighted in 1924, and the long black beast of Lake Poningamook, which was first glimpsed the previous year. Manipogo, a creature which haunts Lakes Manitoba and Winnipegogis, which are joined by the Crane Narrows, remained shy of men until the late 1930s and gained serious attention only when it arose straight out of the water before a large group of picnickers at a lakeside location in Manitoba Park in 1960. Described as having a flat, snake-like head, a dark skin and three huge humps, the creature's image was captured in both still photographs and on cine film. 'Champ', the creature which reportedly inhabits Lake Champlain, which runs down from Canada through Vermont and New

York State, has been seen so regularly during the past hundred years that some people have quite seriously attempted to have him put on the United States endangered species list, while 'Caddy', the sea-serpent which apparently resides off the British Columbia coast, has if anything been even more regularly sighted.

Yet none of these reptiles is nearly so famous as the one which reputedly haunts Lake Okanagan in British Columbia, a prodigious body of water which covers an area of some 127 square miles.

Before the incursions of the first white settlers a hundred years ago the Shushwap Indian tribes who made their camps on the banks of the lake worshipped Naitaka, a monster spirit they believed lived in the dark, forbidding depths. According to one story handed down through generations, a visiting chief ignored warnings about the monster and was eaten along with his family when he attempted to cross the lake in a canoe.

Other stories about Naitaka were depicted in crude drawings on stones. They show an animal with a long neck, thick body and four flippers, features reminiscent of the Loch Ness monster and many other lake-serpents around the world. Indian superstitions regarding the Okanagan monster seem to have been quickly transferred to the early white settlers, though the animal's original name was to be replaced by Ogopogo, borrowed from a popular London music-hall song. There was no shortage of sightings in the late nineteenth and early twentieth centuries, and in 1914 the rotting carcass of a strange animal was found washed up on one of the lake's beaches.

However, it was not until a rush of sightings came in 1950 that the majority of Canadians began to take the legend seriously. On 2 July a 'swimming dinosaur' was seen by one Mrs Kray together with a Montreal family named Watson with whom she was cruising off Kelowna. Mrs Kray later described the creature as having a 'long, sinuous body 30 feet in length, consisting of about five undulations apparently separated from each other by about a 2-foot space, in which that part of the undulations would have been under water'. After drifting north for several minutes the animal moved swiftly off across the lake in the opposite direction, apparently chasing a shoal of fish, and leaving a large wake behind it.

As is always the case with lake-monster reports, men of conventional wisdom moved quickly to suggest safe, natural explanations. The Federation of British Columbia Naturalists pronounced their personal belief that an optical illusion caused by 'a freak wave movement across flat water under special lighting conditions' had led witnesses to misidentify large shadows as moving underwater creatures. The convoluted explanation convinced few Canadians and the average sceptics felt more inclined to believe a less charitable scenario: that the purported witnesses had simply faked their encounter. However, as it turned out these early sightings were to be just the start of an enduring mystery.

That same month Mrs E.A. Campbell watched a similar creature from the lawn of her Kelowna house. According to her description it came up three times and then submerged and disappeared. Several weeks later, on 12 August, the Rev. W.S. Bean, rector of the Anglican church at Penticton, saw Ogopogo emerge out of a terrific disturbance in the water and move off, leaving a great wake. This sighting took place in the waters off Naramata, and a month afterwards, again near Naramata, Mr Bruce Miller and his wife saw the monster while driving along the lakeshore road. Pulling up to watch its progress they described it afterwards as having a lithe, sinewy neck with a coiled back. Though this was the last reported sighting of the creature during 1950, the owner of a mobile home site at Sunny Beach added fuel to the story when he claimed to have found Ogopogo's track on the shore nearby. Although there was no way of positively linking the tracks to the creature it was fairly obvious that they had not been made by any recognised animal.

Since that extraordinary summer of 1950, Ogopogo mania has shown no sign of letting up. Researcher Arlene Gaal, who has been investigating sightings since the mid-1960s, has now recorded over 200 separate accounts. More importantly, during the same period she has also helped to publicise cine films and still photographs taken from the lakeshore which seem to conclusively show large animate objects moving in a serpent-like fashion. In August 1968, for instance, tourist Art Folden captured an anomalous reptile in his telephoto lens while standing on Highway 97, a vantage-point which offered an excellent view of the water surface. Folden's 8-millimetre home movie footage shows a large submerged object some 300 yards from the shore. A line of pine trees in the foreground serves to give the picture definition and allows for an accurate assessment of the length of the creature from tip to tail (estimated 60 feet), thick girth (tapering at both ends) and rapid speed. When Arlene Gaal saw the film for herself she arranged for it to be analysed by photographic experts and compared to a surveyor's drawing of the site's layout. The experts accepted the film as authentic and Gaal understandably claimed that it proved once and for all that an unusual lifeform was present in Lake Okanagan.

Further evidence that Canadian lake-monsters were neither hoaxes nor hallucinations came in 1977, when a three-man team of divers using sophisticated sonar equipment tracked a 25-foot-long trace for ten days in Lake Poningamook. Automatic cameras caught a glimpse of the murky black shape as it passed beneath their boat but unfortunately none of the still photographs taken proved clear enough for a positive identification to be made. Taken individually, no single sighting can be said to offer concrete proof of the existence of these creatures. Yet, as with so many phenomena, the sheer number of eye-witness reports is immensely impressive. Unless we doubt the eyesight and honesty of literally hundreds of Canadian citizens then we must surely admit that something very strange is present in Lake Okanagan and many other large bodies of water in Canada.

Finally there is an interesting geographical link which should not be overlooked. For it can hardly be coincidence that the concentration of long-necked-monster sightings in Canada – around isothermic lines 10 degrees centigrade – corresponds with sightings from other parts of the Northern Hemisphere. Without doubt the distribution of these creatures follows a definite pattern and a line can be drawn joining Canada, Ireland, Scotland, Norway, Sweden, Finland and parts of the former USSR where one finds lake monsters. As one cryptozoologist, Dr Bernard Heuvelmans, suggested, 'One could hardly wish for a better circumstantial evidence of their existence.'

1951

Spectral Battles in Britain and France

The supernatural history of the British Isles has been characterised by the occasional appearance of phantom armies marching to, retreating from or actually engaged in the very same battles they fought centuries before while still living mortals. If, as some parapsychologists believe, strong emotions can make the appearance of ghostly activity more likely, then battlefields provide some of the most promising territory for ghost-hunters. Yet in fact most of these examples appear to reflect a former place memory, a visual-sound after-image imprinted in the etheric substance, rather than the activities of true haunting phantoms. Instead of witnessing the movements of ultraphysical entities or earth-bound souls, percipients to these strange tableaux would seem to be glimpsing the original events replayed all over again. Whether the observers have stepped back in time or those engaged in the conflict have moved forward is a matter for speculation. In all probability neither scenario is accurate – at least not in any way that present minds can comprehend. All we can truly be certain of is that such events do seem to happen.

Prior to the beginning of the present century numerous reports were made throughout the United Kingdom of ghostly armies appearing to re-fight ancient wars. Of these by far the most famous were the manifestations which followed the English Civil War battle of Edge Hill, which was fought on 23 October 1642 on the plains near Kineton in Warwickshire. So many stories were heard of a phantom battle being replayed in the months that followed this clash that King Charles sent several representatives to the scene to verify the peculiar tales. The King's officers witnessed the scene for themselves and recognised many of the friends they had lost. Though less celebrated, several other battlefields marking key events in Britain's bloody history have been visited by apparitions. These include Sedgemoor, Somerset; Culloden in the Scottish Highlands and Naseby in Northamptonshire. In this last case the conflict was replayed annually in the sky above the battlefield for about a century after the actual event in 1645.

During the eighteenth and nineteenth centuries there was no shortage of further reports of phantom armies re-fighting age-old battles. Those most frequently sighted by the largest numbers of witnesses include a vast army of men and followers seen marching near Inveraray in the Strathclyde region of Scotland; a troop of cavalry with carriages and infantry support seen several times on Souther Fell in the Welsh district of Cumbria, and a fleet of Viking longboats which, in phantasm form, attacked and slaughtered a group of ghostly monks standing on the shore of the Isle of Iona. Though the real date of this last incident cannot be known for certain, it would seem likely to reflect a rerun of a massacre which is thought to have taken place some time around the end of the tenth century.

Although belief in the existence of ghosts was stronger in former centuries we should not allow our modern preconceptions and prejudices about our ancestors to blind us to the fact that these phantasmagoric events probably took place very much as contemporary records described. Certainly such reports have persistently been made during our present century. While driving home in the early hours of the morning to her home in Letham, Tayside, Mrs Elizabeth Smith narrowly avoided a serious accident when her car skidded on the icy road and landed in a ditch. Forced to abandon it and walk the remaining eight miles to her home, Mrs Smith was dumbfounded to see a group of people carrying flaming torches walking towards her. They took no notice of the woman but instead searched intently around, apparently looking for their dead. As Mrs Smith continued to watch she could see bodies on the ground being turned over and examined. She estimated that the phantom scene lasted for some twelve minutes in total, during which time she could clearly make out the appearance of the people. Afterwards, speaking to investigators about her experience, she described the men's dress as being Saxon or earlier. In fact historians established from her description that she had seen Pictish warriors. It was their guess that the scene she had witnessed was the aftermath of the battle of Nachanesmere, which had taken place in AD 685.

Mrs Smith's sighting took place during the early winter of the year 1951. The woman from Tayside was simply one of many twentieth-century Britons who have suddenly and inexplicably found themselves witness to a re-enactment of their homeland's violent past. Sites which seem to have been most frequently the focus of such happenings include Offham Hill near Lewes in East Sussex, which is the site of a major battle over 700 years ago, Marston Moor in North Yorkshire, the scene of another Civil War battle, and Otterburn in Northumberland, where a battle was fought in August 1388.

Perhaps the most famous twentieth-century example of a phantom battle provides us with a very different case from any of those so far mentioned. Two main features mark it out from the others. First, instead of being a replay of events which took place hundreds or thousands of years earlier, it re-evoked events which occurred only the previous decade. Secondly, and even more intriguingly, nothing untoward was actually seen – only the sounds of the battle were witnessed.

In the early morning hours of 19 August 1942 a large force of Allied troops, consisting mainly of Canadian and British commandos, attacked the German-held port of Dieppe in Normandy, France. Rather than aiming to achieve anything of great strategic importance, the raid was meant to be a full-scale rehearsal for the eventual invasion of Europe two years later. Certainly the Allies learned much from the Dieppe landings, but they paid a terrible price into the bargain. Of the 6,000-plus men who took part almost 4,000 were killed or wounded in a fierce battle that lasted a mere four and a half hours.

Nine years later, two Englishwomen holidaying at Puys, a seaside village a few miles east of Dieppe, were awoken in the middle of the night by the unmistakable sound of heavy gunfire. At about 4 am in the morning the two women distinctly heard men crying in pain as well as distant sounds of shelling and the scream of dive-bombing aircraft. This curious phenomenon lasted for fifty minutes. It was replaced by a brief silence and then a continuation of dive-bombing and explosions at a much greater volume. The women remained awake, listening in amazement to the sounds which they were certain were coming from along the coastline in the direction of the French port. The noise of battle continued to rage uninterrupted until about six o'clock, when all disturbance died away to be replaced by the natural sounds of the waves breaking on the shingle beach outside their hotel. The next morning, 5 August 1951, the women were amazed to find that none of the other hotel residents, nor its French owners, had heard anything unusual. Yet several people living locally had reported similar experiences on summer nights during the previous few years.

When they returned to England the women sent a full account of their experience to the London-based Society for Psychical Research. After looking at British War Office records of the disastrous engagement it became clear to the SPR researchers that the timing of the phenomenon's beginning – about 4 am, according to the two women – corresponded very closely to the first exchanges of fire between Allied assault vessels and German ships moored off the coast on 19 August 1942. Moreover, the dramatic increase in noise which began around five o'clock on the night of 4 August 1951 would seem to have marked the beginning of the bombardment of Dieppe by Allied destroyers and the first wave of RAF bombers delivering their payload on the Germans' defensive lines. Although it would have not been impossible for these two women to have read accounts of the battle for themselves and thereafter concoct the story, the SPR investigators were satisfied that they were telling the truth and rated it almost certain that they had undergone a genuine psychic experience.

Sceptics, as ever, offered a different solution. For those to whom the idea of phantom battles was so much stuff and nonsense it was clear enough that the women had actually heard nothing more than a combination of natural sounds. The crash of the waves breaking on the shingle beach, real aircraft flying on the London to Paris route and a dredger working in the harbour at Dieppe were all proposed as being responsible. The women themselves denied that they could have been deceived by any of these sounds or a combination of them.

Looking back on their experience it is difficult to form a clear judgement one way or the other. We do not know how events might be held in time and space to be replayed at some future date before the eyes and ears of those sensitive enough to tune in to them. It is interesting to note that neither of these women were known to have previously held any interest in the supernatural, or claimed to have had a psychic experience before. They make perfectly credible witnesses. At the same time it is not outside the bounds of possibility that they were simply mistaken by what they heard. What we can say for certain, however, is that we cannot easily discount every alleged sighting of a phantom battle in terms of visual or auditory hallucinations. Unless, that is, we are prepared to reject the value of all human testimony.

1952

The Search for Bridey Murphy

The second half of the twentieth century has seen a startling upsurge in professed belief in reincarnation among Westerners. Opinion-poll figures taken from research conducted in the United Kingdom between 1969 and 1979 show a rise from eighteen per cent to twenty-eight per cent expressing personal belief, while a similar increase over the same decade was recorded in the USA. Belief among those polled under the age of twenty was substantially higher, so it is safe to assume that were the same survey to be conducted today it would show a continuation of the upward curve. In the 1990s it is quite probable that one person in every three on both sides of the Atlantic may have come to accept the idea of rebirth. What makes these statistics so amazing is that comparable surveys from the late 1940s show that fewer than three in every hundred Westerners took reincarnation seriously. So what is behind this enormous shift in the popular consciousness? The answer can be summed up in two words: regression hypnosis. The possibilities opened up by past-life regression hypnosis first came to the attention of the general public with the famous case of Bridget (Bridey) Murphy in 1952. Virginia Tighe, the twenty-nine-year-old wife of a businessman and mother of three from Pueblo, Colorado, recalled her previous life in nineteenth-century Ireland under the hypnotism of Morey Bernstein. An experienced amateur hypnotist of many years' standing, Bernstein had already conducted several past-life regressions before meeting Tighe, but he quickly recognised her as a potential regression superstar after their initial session together revealed a clarity of detail he had never before known.

As has become standard practice with all researchers dealing in past-life hypnosis, Bernstein had first regressed Tighe to childhood and thereafter encouraged her to go back to another place and time before she was born. Answering questions in a rough Irish brogue, complete with slang expressions and colloquialisms which Bernstein did not recognise, the twenty-nine-year old housewife described her earlier childhood vividly. She had, she said, grown up the youngest daughter of a barrister who lived in the Irish city of Cork. Born in 1798, she had lived for sixty-six years before dying after a fall in which she broke her hip. As the sessions progressed Bernstein gradually learned more and more of the girl's background, including all kinds of specifics which would have been hard indeed to make up – names, dates, places, events, shops and businesses which she said had existed in her home city. Even songs, poems and local customs were all described in colourful language. Bridey said that she was married at the age of twenty to Sean Brian Joseph McCarthy, also the child of a court barrister. Thereafter they had moved to Belfast, where McCarthy taught at Queen's University. Although they had been married in a Protestant church in Cork, the couple had apparently chosen to undertake a separate Catholic ceremony at St Teresa's church in Belfast, and the regressed woman was even able to name the priest who had led the service, Father John Joseph Gorman.

Throughout 1952 Bernstein made tape-recordings of each separate session of hypnotism and these extraordinary conversations were serialised in newspapers two years later. They immediately touched a chord in the imagination of the American public and propelled the subject of reincarnation on to the front pages of the Western world's newspapers for the very first time. Bernstein's subsequent book, *The Search for Bridey Murphy*, became an instant bestseller and was eventually published in thirty countries. For most people who read it the most convincing aspects of Bridey's story lay in the numerous ordinary details and the sheer weight of commonplace facts and incidents contained in the endless hours of regression. Believers felt that Bridey really was showing knowledge of things that could have only been known in Ireland, and yet Virginia Tighe's personal history showed without doubt that she had never travelled abroad since her birth in Madison, Wisconsin, and did not seem to have any special associations with Irish people or their culture.

As always, not everybody was so easily convinced. Since Irish official records did not go back beyond the year 1864 – coincidentally the year of Bridey Murphy's claimed death – it proved impossible to corroborate her birth, death or marriage from certificates. Furthermore, some of her memories were found on examination to be factually incorrect and sceptics pointed out that transcripts of her speech while under hypnosis contained glaring examples of twentieth-century American speech mixed in with the old Irish. One newspaper, the *Chicago American*, even went as far as to accuse the Bernstein-Tighe team of deliberately faking the mystery. Having allegedly researched Tighe's background, *Chicago American*'s journalists claimed that she had become friendly with an Irish grandmother named Bridey Corkell who had lived in Chicago at the same time as Tighe. For a while attempts to discredit the purported reincarnation seemed to be working, but when it became clear that Mrs Corkell was herself the mother of one of the editors of the Chicago newspaper the public became less certain. The objectivity of the sceptical journalists was further placed in doubt after it transpired that the *Chicago American* had been unsuccessfully outbid by their rival city newspaper, the *Chicago Daily News*, in an auction for the serial rights to Bernstein's book.

Looking back on the Bridey Murphy affair from the vantage-point of hindsight it is easy to see why the story proved to be such a sensation and why its detractors felt frustrated in their attempts to discredit the rebirth hypothesis. To begin with, many of the woman's trance-induced recollections do appear to contain the undeniable ring of truth. A map of Cork dated 1801 shows the small area of housing known as The Meadows where Bridey supposedly grew up, and anyone who had heard the tapes with their own ears could not help being surprised and impressed by the woman's beguiling accent and the ease with which she conveyed the local colour and everyday life of early nineteenth-century Ireland. Indeed, when Tighe returned to consciousness after the end of each session she was invariably amazed at what she heard on the tape and could not account for the source of the information it contained.

The lack of personal records among the Irish population prior to the year 1864 was irritating to say the least. Nevertheless, specific place names which the American housewife could hardly have been expected to know turned out to be verifiably correct and therefore provided compelling evidence. Among them were details of the nineteenth-century Irish cities she described, including the names of obscure shops in back-street locations. For instance, the cottage in Dooley Road, Belfast, where Bridey allegedly ended her life is known to have existed, as was the family grocer she patronised, Farr and Carrigan.

Four decades after Morey Bernstein regressed his celebrated subject in the small front room of her home in Pueblo, Colorado, the central truth of the matter – and its importance to our understanding of the nature of life and death – remains a matter of great debate. Perhaps it is a case of reincarnation, perhaps not. But in forty years of investigation no one has yet come up with a more convincing mundane explanation for the enigma of Bridey Murphy.

1953

Deadly Encounters

During the early 1950s the potential threat posed by unidentified flying objects was turning to hard reality. By 1953 reports were beginning to come in from civilian pilots suggesting that flying saucers were harassing airliners with increasing frequency. In the skies above America, where the US Air Force was especially vigilant, such activities seemed most prevalent, but in the event the flight which proved to be the first tragedy was lost far away from America's shores.

In March 1953 the pilot of a DC-6 en route from Wake Island in the Pacific to Los Angeles radioed his destination to report that he was being attacked by three glowing balls. Seconds later contact with the plane was lost and the airliner disappeared, along with its twenty passengers and crew of five. Later that spring another DC-6, this time on an international flight, crashed after reporting interference from unidentified lights. Witnesses on the ground confirmed the involvement of UFOs in the disaster. Once more there were no survivors.

By early summer there could be no doubt that the saucer situation had taken a distinctly sinister turn. On 24 June a two-man F-94C jet fighter was scrambled from Otis Base,

Cape Cod, with a mission to investigate a single unidentified radar blip picked up by ground control. As the interceptor closed on its target – a bright light hovering to the east at an altitude of 1,500 feet – Captain James Suggs prepared himself for combat. But the battle was over before it had begun. At the moment Suggs primed his cannon for firing the fighter suffered an immediate and total malfunction. Within seconds the plane was locked into a steep nose-dive and Suggs had barely enough time to eject. His co-pilot, Lieutenant Robert Barkoff, was less fortunate: he was killed instantly as the jet exploded on impact with the earth below. The reason for the breakdown in the fighter's flight systems remained a mystery.

Whatever the cause of the Cape Cod tragedy worse was soon to follow. On 25 November, Lieutenant Felix Moncla and Radar Officer Robert Wilson took off from Kincross Air Base in their F-89 fighter to intercept a saucer spotted by Air Defense Command over the Canadian border. The object, which had appeared on radar screens as one erratically moving blip, turned out to be a large alien craft hovering above Lake Superior at an altitude of 8,000 feet. Moncla's description of the UFO recorded by fellow officers at Kincross turned out to be his last words. Seconds after visual contact was made the impossible seemed to happen. Radar officers stared at their screens as the UFO moved towards the jet at a velocity many times the speed of sound. Within moments the two blips merged into one and the sound of the air crew's voices was replaced by an eerie crackle of static. What became of officers Moncla and Wilson was never discovered. A search of Lake Superior was carried out by joint US and Canadian task forces but revealed nothing. No wreckage or slick of oil was found upon the calm waters to suggest a clue to their fate. Although a mid-air collision seemed the most likely probability, radar controllers at Kincross were unable to shake off the nagging doubt that their fellow Americans might have been space-napped – ensnared in some unimaginable way by creatures whose technology was already known to be far ahead of mankind's.

Whatever the private fears of junior ranks, the top brass quickly took steps to ensure that these incidents received little publicity. Whereas the Otis Base incident had been (by the press at least) blamed on a normal aircraft malfunction, the Air Force line over the Lake Superior disappearances was that the radar controllers had mistaken the UFO for a C-47 flying boat of the Royal Canadian Air Force. When the Canadians disobligingly denied having any C-47 patrols in the vicinity, the Americans changed their story to 'freak atmospheric conditions'.

For a while newspapers accepted these explanations but when the USAF continued to lose planes throughout the next twelve months awkward questions began to be asked. On 1 July 1954 another F-94 sea interceptor, of the same type that was lost in the June of 1953, crashed after encountering a saucer over Griffiths Base, New York State. Although on this occasion the airmen ejected and survived, four civilians on the ground were killed, and naturally enough this last incident prompted many newspapers to hint darkly that certain facts surrounding reports of saucer-related crashes were being covered up. But instead of coming clean with the American public the US government and military establishment decided to redouble their efforts to conceal the truth. In February 1955 a conference was organised in Seattle at which officers from the military's air transport service intelligence division met with the heads of America's major commercial airlines. The single item on the agenda was UFOs – or more specifically the need to control the flow of information regarding them.

The outcome of this secret meeting was the extension of military-style curbs which compelled commercial air crews to maintain strict silence on all UFO sightings. Anyone who did not maintain the level of secrecy required was liable to ten years' imprisonment or a fine of $10,000. Although these draconian regulations provoked a backlash among civilian pilots they remained on the statute books and as a result the flow of UFO information to the press dried up. Only with the declassification of previously secret documents under the United States Freedom of Information Act has it now become clear that the alien presence in the skies above our planet was not only deemed to be both real and proven by the early 1950s, but was also known to be highly dangerous.

1954

Life After Life

In 1954 Jasbir Lal Jat, a three-year-old Indian boy from a poor village near the town of Vehedi, seemingly died of smallpox. After an illness which lasted several days he stopped breathing and his body turned cold. However, the following morning, on the day scheduled for his funeral, Jasbir's body stirred.

But this was only the first miracle of this truly amazing story. For it soon became clear that the boy's personality had entirely changed.

Speaking with a different accent and with mannerisms far in advance of his age, the child now claimed his name to be Sobha Ram Tyagi, the son of a Brahmin family who were, he said, bereaved at precisely the same moment that Jasbir Lal Jat had passed away. It was Sobha Ram's soul which now inhabited the body of the smallpox victim, and not the child of the lower-caste family.

Despite the scorn of all those around him the boy remained firmly convinced of the truth of what he said, refusing to consume food handled by Jasbir's lower-caste family, whom he considered to be unclean. Most people thought the boy had gone mad until one day, by chance, he recognised a passing stranger as Sobha Ram Tyagi's aunt. Sure enough, the woman confirmed that this was so and her version of her nephew Sobha Ram's death from a head injury concurred with the living boy's. More importantly, it became clear that the two children really had expired at precisely the same time on the same day. Eventually Jasbir was taken to the village where he claimed to have lived his former life and was able to greet Sobha Ram Tyagi's relatives by name. They all agreed that the child's description of his old home district was too detailed to be the product of guesswork.

The above-related story from 1954 may sound like a work of fiction but it is not. The Indian enigma comes from the files of Dr Ian Stevenson, an American professor of psychology, who has spent the last forty years of his life gathering evidence of apparent cases of spontaneous past-life memories in children.

In a typical Stevenson case, a toddler starts to tell its parents, and anyone else who will listen, that he or she can remember being someone else. The child's statements concerning its previous life are nearly always accompanied by behaviour which is alien to the child's background but harmonises with elements of the alleged past existence. According to Stevenson, these recollections may increase in intensity between the ages of two and four but are only rarely remembered after the age of five, for reasons which remain unclear. It is a pattern that is repeated irrespective of the child's religious or cultural background.

In many cases children have not only described accurately people, places and customs about which they could have no knowledge; some have even manifested bizarre and alarming signs of their former selves, such as birthmarks corresponding to wounds suffered at the moment of death. Others have shown peculiar psychological traits incompatible with their age; for example, a hunger for adult pleasures such as alcohol, tobacco or sexual intercourse. A few find it hard to acclimatise to their new sexual identities and follow instead the dress and habits of the opposite gender. In such cases it is extremely rare for their personality disorders to be cured through conventional child psychiatry.

One of the most dramatic examples to emerge from the modern era is the case of Reena Gupta, from New Dehli, who was less than two years old when, in 1966, she first told her grandmother she had a *gharada*, a husband, a wicked man who had killed her and now languished in prison for his crime. Reena was not believed, but as she grew up, she never lost the conviction that she had lived and died before. Consequently she would often infuriate her mother when, on shopping expeditions to the market, she would search for familiar faces from the past, hoping that such a recognition might meet with a favourable reaction. Eventually, by chance, a teacher friend of Reena's mother called Vijendra heard a tragic story about a Sikh family which involved the murder of a young wife, Gurdeep Singh, by her husband. Realising that the Sikh family's history closely mirrored events recalled by Reena, Vijendra tracked down the family to their home in another suburb of the Indian capital. There, finding that the dead woman's *gharada* was in prison for the killing, she spoke to the parents of the murdered Gurdeep Singh. Though reluctant at first, the Singhs eventually agreed to meet Reena, who recognised them immediately and without introduction as her own mother and father.

In their astonished presence the little girl recalled many events of her former childhood, including the origin of the unusual nickname by which Gurdeep's younger sister had been known. Subsequently, when she was taken to meet other members of her former family, the girl was able to recognise them too, and several years later, when an adolescent in the 1970s, she even agreed to pose for a photograph with 'her' suspicious and somewhat bemused murderer-husband.

Although many examples of past-life recall arise in Eastern countries they by no means form the majority. In 1981, Romy Crees, a toddler from Des Moines, Iowa, began telling her parents that she was a married man named Joe Williams who had died several years before in a motorcycle accident, leaving a wife, Sheila, and three children. Little Romy pleaded to be allowed to go and see her family who, she said, lived in Charles City, a community some 140 miles away from Des Moines. As devout Catholics and therefore firm disbelievers in reincarnation, Romy's parents were more inclined to think that their child was possessed by the Devil than by the returned spirit of another person. However, when an exorcism failed to remove the impression from the girl's mind the Crees called in a child psychiatrist named Dr Hemendra Bannerjee.

Bannerjee quickly came to realise that his own initial scepticism was unfounded. An expedition to Charles City was arranged during which the toddler was able to correctly identify many locations, even finding her alleged previous home. There, the death of Joe Williams in a motorcycle accident was confirmed by his widow Sheila, along with several other key details of their relationship that could hardly have been guessed by a two-year-old child living 140 miles away.

The parents of Romy Crees were left with little choice but to reluctantly accept that rebirth was the most likely explanation. Like Dr Stevenson Dr Bannerjee has since reviewed his own psychiatric practice to include the possibility of factors stemming from past lives.

Although it challenges many of the basic assumptions that underlie the religious and philosophical concepts of Western society, contemporary reincarnationist research has stood both the test of time and the hostile intellectual onslaught of its professional critics. Whether sceptics like it or not, the fact remains that a considerable number of very young children from virtually every country in the world have recalled past lives and exhibited a knowledge of adult ways which seems impossible to account for naturally. One of Ian Stevenson's subjects, a five-year-old Lebanese boy named Imad Elawor, made fifty-seven verifiable statements about his previous life as tuberculosis victim Ibrahim Bonhanzy. Fifty-one turned out to be, in the researcher's words, 'dead right'.

Unless we accept that the American psychologist and his peers have been consistently and consciously falsifying their records, evidence of such complex cross-referenced correlations cannot be dismissed as the stuff of childhood fantasies or coincidence. Logically, on any objective analysis, we must accept that the phenomenon Ian Stevenson first discovered really is throwing up some quite extraordinary possibilities regarding the nature of human existence.

1955

The Kelly–Hopkinsville Visitations

The first to notice something strange was Billy Ray Taylor, a twenty-one-year-old farmer's son who ventured outside his family's home in Kelly, Kentucky, at around 7 pm to get a drink from a well. Above him he saw a huge shining UFO with an exhaust all the colours of the rainbow descend and land in a dried-up riverbed several hundred yards away. Running back into the farmhouse in a state of high excitement, Billy Ray recounted his story only to find it ridiculed. But the family's mirth was short-lived. For approximately one hour later the Taylors were alerted by the furious barking of their watchdog, and when they opened their front door the animal dashed into the house, obviously terrified. Armed with a 20-gauge shotgun and a 22-calibre rifle two of the men went outside and were confronted by the cause of the alarm: a 4-foot creature with a round, oversized head, large luminous yellow eyes and long talon-tipped arms was making its way across the yard. Though at first frozen with fear and incredulity, the men recovered themselves before the alien was upon them and blasted it with their weapons. The creature somersaulted backwards and scurried away into the cover of the trees, screeching in pain.

The thing was not alone, however. As the men ventured forward they turned to see a similar creature on the roof and this too they felled with their guns. A third alien, spotted perched in a maple tree, was also apparently hit and they saw it running away, wounded, with an awkward lopsided gait. When yet another creature rounded a corner of the house Billy Ray opened up with both barrels at point-blank range. Howling hideously the creature retreated, disappearing into the scrub with the others.

Having expended their ammunition the two men went inside to reload, but, persuaded by their family not to face the strange visitors again, they bolted their doors, doused the lights and simply watched the aliens roaming outside. For a while they were left alone but when it became clear that the creatures were once more trying to gain entry the younger members of the family became hysterical. So finally, at around eleven o'clock, the terrified Taylor menfolk came out blasting once again, covering their women and children, who sprinted to the family's two cars and sped off to the nearest police station at Hopkinsville. Moments later the men followed in a pick-up. Although he had heard nothing remotely like it before the local police chief, Russell Greenwell, saw the family's distress and, knowing them to be the sort of people who would not flee their home without good reason, decided to investigate further.

Yet when the police examined the area around the Taylors' farm they found only bullet holes and no trace of the alleged UFO or the creatures. A bemused Greenwell went back to Hopkinsville to reassure the family that no further danger appeared likely. But the sheriff was wrong. In the early hours of that morning, after the Taylors had returned home, the eldest member of the household, Glennie Lankford, sat up screaming in bed as she saw one of the creatures peering in her bedroom window.

Alerted by her cries, her son Elmer then shot through the window at the creature, which fell backwards to the ground and scuttled away. Thereafter, throughout the remaining hours of darkness, the creatures occasionally reappeared only to be repelled by the Taylors' firearms. At 5.15 am, just before dawn broke, the aliens vanished for good.

For the bewildered Taylor clan this was by no means the end of the story, however. During the next few weeks their farm swarmed with reporters from several states who had heard about the incident. Projected into the spotlight of public attention the family at the centre of the controversy were photographed, interviewed and then held up to ridicule in print. So bad did the humiliation become that before long they began to wonder whether their treatment at the hands of the press was worse than their original encounter with the aliens.

The journalists rejected the Taylors' story out of hand, and the standard line taken was to conjecture why they had had the temerity to waste police time over such an obviously implausible fabrication. Some newspapermen accused the family of trying to make money out of the saucer mania which was currently gripping the American public. Other reporters portrayed them as illiterate hillbillies too feeble-minded to know the difference between a moving ball of tumbleweed and a man from Mars. Several editorials suggested that the whole Taylor clan must have been drunk on moonshine.

Their claims were not helped by the fact that even seasoned ufologists already convinced of the reality of flying saucers found the details of their story impossible to accept. To imagine that creatures from an advanced civilisation might be visiting the earth was one thing, but the possibility that such highly developed aliens would choose to descend upon the home of an ill-educated hillbilly family from Kentucky was quite another.

So what really happened on the night of 21 August? The hoax theory can never be completely discounted, though in fact it should be pointed out that the family from Kelly never received a penny for their story and were hassled by newspapermen and sightseers for months on end. And while it is perfectly true to say that no physical evidence was ever found to indicate a landing – and neither bodies nor traces of alien blood were left behind to corroborate claimed shotgun and rifle hits on aliens – something strange *was* reported to have passed over the vehicle of investigating officers that same night.

In further support of the Taylor story it should be remembered that several comparable reports of non-human entities were to emerge from other parts of the USA during the same year. In March a man driving a truck over a bridge near Branch Hill, Ohio allegedly saw three small figures kneeling by the road. He stopped his vehicle and got out to investigate, whereupon he was rendered unconscious by a flashing beam from a weapon one of the creatures was holding. Interestingly, his recollections of the alien's physical appearance closely matched those made by the family from Kentucky. On 3 July another motorist, Mrs Margaret Simmonds, almost ran over several small figures which were walking across the highway near Stockton, Georgia. As she swerved to avoid them she got a close enough look to be certain that they were neither human nor any mundane species of wildlife. Once again artists' impressions made from Mrs Simmonds' description bear a close resemblance to the entities claimed to have been seen by the Taylors.

The encounters reported by witnesses in Ohio and Georgia may or may not be connected with the siege which took place at Kelly. Since no UFO was actually seen to land it cannot even be established that there was an extra-terrestrial dimension to either of these incidents. But it is surely worth pointing out that the Taylors were not the only Americans who experienced strange visitations during 1955.

Moreover, in assessing the overall credibility of their tale we ought not to forget that in total there were eleven witnesses aged between seven and seventy, including eight adults over twenty, all of whom saw the creatures and described them, consistently, as beings which bore no resemblance to a terrestrial species. Is it really possible that so many could have suffered from hallucination at the same time? It seems improbable to say the least.

As police chief Russell Greenwell later commented: 'Something frightened these people, something beyond their comprehension.' And in the thirty-eight years since the alleged close encounter not one single member of the Kentucky family has retracted their original version of events, even though to do so might have alleviated the public ridicule to which they were collectively subjected.

1956

The Day it Rained Fish

On a clear, hot day in May 1956 live fish fell from the sky on a farm at Chilatchi, near Uniontown, Alabama, USA. Witnesses to the event say that the creatures fell from a single dark cloud which formed through a swirling motion 'as if from nowhere'. As it began to rain over a very small area about 200 feet square so the unusual cloud turned from dark to almost white and three types of fish – catfish, bass and bream – were unleashed from the heavens. Since the fish were alive and flapping about they had clearly not been in the sky for very long, yet none of those who saw it could account for the downpour, which lasted for some fifteen minutes in all. Although the fish were local varieties and a creek teeming with them was to be found just 2 miles away, there had been no whirlwinds or tornados for many weeks so it was hard to imagine how they could have been lifted into the sky and transported the necessary distance. As one witness remarked: 'It seemed to me to be about the strangest thing ever.'

Strange, certainly, but it would be wrong to describe it as the strangest ever. Fish-falls have been noted from just about every corner of the globe. First-hand accounts of these frotskis (falls from the sky) litter the pages of Fortean magazines and even sane and sensible meteorological journals regularly report hailstones of herring, squalls of squid and tornadoes of trout.

During the present century there have been many other examples from the United States, including deluges in Boston, Massachusetts; Thomasville, Alabama; and Witchita, Kansas. On the morning of 19 December 1984 fish fell in particularly large numbers on the Santa Monica Freeway near Cranshaw Boulevard, Los Angeles, causing traffic chaos. The following year, in May 1985, another large quantity of fish fell into the backyard of Hispanic Louis Castorino of Fort Worth, Texas. Castorino admitted afterwards to have been very scared by the experience, which he firmly believed to be of supernatural origin.

Falls of fish are so common in some countries, such as India and Australia, that newspapers there have almost given up mentioning them. One Australian naturalist, Gilbert Whitley, was even able to publish an historical list of no fewer than fifty Antipodean rains of fish in 1972. Whitley's trawl included creek minnows at Cressey, Victoria; shrimps near Singleton, New South Wales; pygmy perch in Hayfield, Victoria; and an unidentified freshwater species which rained on the suburbs of Brisbane.

Though falls in Britain are less common there have still been many reliable reports. August 1914 saw sand eels land in the Hendon area of Sunderland, while the same month in 1948 found one Mr Ian Patey of Hayling Island, Hampshire caught in a herring shower as he walked along a golf course. Crabs and periwinkles are among several varieties of crustacean which have come down during anomalous outbreaks over Britain.

Can such events be understood in any way other than the preternatural? Some believe so. It is the considered opinion of most meteorologists that while fish-falls can no longer be considered a fantasy the explanation for them need not be a paranormal one. Such experts believe that a whirlwind or waterspout sweeps them up from water vacuum-cleaner-like into the sky, carries them a short distance and then drops them. This version of events might possibly explain some examples, yet it should quickly be pointed out that no one has ever witnessed a whirlwind lifting marine creatures in this way. It is even harder to imagine how wind could select only a single species, and it does little to explain why no debris such as sand or plant material is ever dropped with the creatures. Where saltwater species descend there have been no records of the accompanying rainfall being salty, and while the waterspout theory might conceivably account for a fish type which commonly shoals on the surface in nearby waters, it does little to account for examples where fish are dropped many miles from coastlines, or when the species involved is a deepwater variety.

Perhaps the most bizarre of all fish-falls was the gift from heaven which fell into the 16-foot open boat belonging to three fishermen from a tiny Pacific island in the Kiribati group on 4 April 1986. Having been shipwrecked during a storm the three occupants survived for an incredible 119 days adrift before being picked up more than 500 miles away from where their vessel had sunk. During that time they had survived by catching sharks with their bare hands, clubbing them to death and then eating them raw. One night close to the end of their ordeal, in despair and sickened by the repetitive taste of shark meat, the three men were praying for God to grant them a different type of food when to their amazement something suddenly fell into the boat. It turned out to be a rare but delicious blackish fish of a type that never came close to the surface but was known to stay much deeper down. Later, having been rescued, the three men related their extraordinary tale to bemused marine biologists, who confirmed that this particular variety of fish tended to stay below the depth of 600 feet, which neatly ruled out the most obvious possibility – that an over-flying bird had dropped the fish. An answer to a prayer, then? Most people would think twice before evoking the hand of God, but is there really an explanation that makes more sense?

All in all, falls of fish might best be summed up in the words of Winston Churchill – a riddle wrapped up in an enigma.

1957

Sex on a Saucer

Most contact between humans and aliens involves close encounters of the first kind – the sighting of UFOs in the sky. A less common type is the close encounter of the second kind, where landed saucers are seen together with their occupants. Close encounters of the third kind – those examples where human beings claim to have been taken aboard an alien craft – are the least common of all. Yet such examples, while representing only a small minority of all reports, are also the most difficult to account for through mundane speculation. The number of people claiming to have been abducted by aliens has increased dramatically during the past decade and a half, for reasons which remain unclear, but similar tales have been told by contactees for well over thirty years.

On the evening of 14 October 1957 a twenty-three-year-old Brazilian farmer named Antonio Villas Boas saw a peculiar white light hovering low in the corner of the field he was ploughing with his tractor. When he approached the light on foot it began to move away, and despite his several attempts to catch up with it it evaded him.

The following evening the light appeared once again but this time it landed directly in front of Villas Boas' machine.

From close up, Villas Boas realised that the light was illuminating a metallic rotating dome standing on telescopic legs and changing colour from red to green. Sensing danger the Brazilian leaped from his tractor and attempted to escape, but found himself instead dragged back by three small entities wearing tight-fitting grey suits and helmets concealing their faces. He was taken into the machine, and once inside he was forcibly stripped and covered with a clear liquid before being given a form of medical examination.

What occurred next, if it is true, marked a departure from all previous close encounters between humans and aliens. Placed in another room inside the ship the farmer was presented with a naked female alien whom he described later as being 'beautiful, though of a different type from the women I have known'. She had bleached hair reaching halfway down her back, high cheekbones, somewhat pointed features and large, slightly slanted eyes.

Villas Boas later described her body as being exquisite with high and well-separated breasts, a thin waist and a small stomach, wide hips and large thighs. Though she was evidently non-human, the farmer was nevertheless aroused and within moments found himself having sexual intercourse with her, the moment of interplanetary passion being only slightly spoiled by the animal-like grunts which regularly came from her mouth.

When their embrace was at an end the woman pointed at her stomach and then at the sky, leaving the other humanoids to escort her bemused lover off the craft. Reasoning quite correctly that no one would believe him Antonio Villas Boas said nothing about the incident, even to his family or close friends. However, in the next few weeks, when he began to suffer a range of unpleasant physical symptoms (including severe headaches, burning and watering of the eyes, blackouts and the appearance of various lesions on his body), he changed his mind. Relating his incredible tale to doctors at a local hospital, Villas Boas ended up being sent to Rio de Janeiro, where he was examined and interrogated.

The man in charge of the investigation, Dr Alvaro Fontes, concluded that his patient was being completely truthful in his account, adding that the physical symptoms he showed suggested radiation poisoning or exposure to radiation, although their own examinations could not confirm such a possibility beyond doubt.

Due to the bizarre nature of his recollections few people, including the most committed ufologists, found it possible to lend credence to the alleged encounter of Antonio Villas Boas. However, in the last thirty years a number of other abductees have recalled similar stories under regression hypnosis. Medical examinations, especially operations including an extraction of blood, ova or sperm, have become particularly common features of such encounters. There are now several examples where humans claim to have been forced to undergo intercourse with aliens. Though these tales seem outrageous, physical marks on the abductees' bodies often appear to be consistent with their memories.

In other cases female abductees have either suffered nervous breakdowns or lived in continual terror of a repeated experience. Psychological profiles of such women built up by a practising psychiatrist show that their subsequent behaviour corresponds strikingly with that of victims of normal rape: a low self-esteem, a distrust of their bodies, an abhorrence of their own physical sexuality and a hesitancy to trust others are commonplace features. In America, at least three individuals are known to have committed suicide after claimed abductions.

Just what aliens might hope to learn from our civilisation through these crude methods of enforced artificial insemination or ovary-retrieval operations can only be guessed at, but many ufologists are now convinced that UFO occupants are regularly abducting humans in order to carry out some form of cross-fertilisation programme and that the abductees themselves have been the unwilling guinea pigs for extra-terrestrial experiments into genetic manipulation. Could they be right?

There was a time when the abductee phenomenon was discounted by virtually all serious investigators. But those days have long since passed. Following the claimed abduction of the Brazilian farmer over three and a half decades ago too many people have come forward with basically the same tale for us to write off their experiences as being purely subjective fantasies. Like Antonio Villas Boas, they were given no choice but to submit to the will of their captors. Like him they were given no room to protest or refuse to comply. But what is most important on the level of evidence is the fact that their descriptions of the alien beings who violated their bodies correspond closely to that made by the Brazilian in 1957.

For the record, Antonio Villas Boas died recently, maintaining to the very end that his extraordinary story was true.

1958

Phantom Felids in New South Wales

Although most creatures on the earth's land surface had been hunted, caught, dissected and documented well before the beginning of the present century, surprises have occasionally turned up in the years since 1900. The world's largest ape, the mountain gorilla, remained unknown until 1901; the world's most massive lizard, the komodo dragon, was only discovered in 1912. Incredibly, a species of gazelle, the biltis, made its presence known in Kato as recently as 1986. There may very well be more to come. Vast expanses of forest, mountains, desert and polar regions still await man's footsteps and have so far only been mapped from aerial photographs. In such places, the potential for the existence of quite significant discoveries remains high.

However, while accepting the logic of this argument most naturalists are less than willing to face up to the real possibilities, and when odd creatures do turn up in unexpected places they tend to ignore the evidence. In the USA, for instance, you would be hard pressed to find any experts willing to entertain the possibility that crocodiles and alligators might be found living in the colder climates of America's northernmost states, despite the fact that many fully grown specimens of these reptiles have been found there either alive or dead. The very same creatures which you would ordinarily expect to find only in the warm rivers, marshes and swamps of the deep south have during the past century been occasionally sighted, trapped or shot in locations as far apart as California, Colorado, Connecticut, Delaware, Illinois, Indiana, Kansas, Massachusetts, New York, Ohio, Oklahoma and Washington State. How these creatures came to be there in the first place and then to survive at temperatures well below those provided by their natural habitat is a question that remains unanswered.

Of course, since the states in question are landlocked and connected by innumerable waterways, one is led to conjecture that the animals simply swam north. But when out-of-place creatures are found on islands or subcontinents unconnected to areas where they would usually be found the same sort of explanation does not seem sufficient. The phantom felids of Australia provide us with just such an example.

Having no native big cats whatsoever, and having been separated from other continental land masses for the last 50,000,000 years, Australia must seem one of the least likely places on earth where you might expect to find large feline creatures hiding from man. Yet during the latter part of the present century evidence has grown to suggest that big cats of an unrecognised species may very well inhabit the subcontinent. How they have come to be there and why the numerous hunts for them have so far proved unsuccessful remains unclear. Nevertheless, reports have become so frequent that it is simply illogical to question the likelihood that some type of big cat is on the loose.

In the year 1958, the town of Emmaville in New South Wales became the centre of a bizarre series of events and encounters involving very large phantom felids of jet-black colour. Known thereafter as the Emmaville Panther, the phenomenon began to receive widespread media coverage after a Sydney businessman, Wallace E. Lewis, saw the animal at close range that October, describing it as being many times larger and more ferocious than the largest feline native to the subcontinent. The panther's notoriety grew and further appearances coincided with the wholesale slaughter of sheep and other farm livestock, including heavy cows. In just one case 340 of farmer Clive Berry's sheep were massacred by a strange carnivorous animal on his 4,600-acre property at Pretty Gully, west of Uralla. Dismissing altogether the possibility that the culprit was a dingo or domestic dog, Berry pointed out that the manner of the killings bore the hallmarks of an exceptionally large felid. When John Godley, a neighbouring farmer who had also lost sheep, made a plaster cast of the creature's spoor and sent it to the Taronga Park Trust for formal identification, he received a reply saying that it corresponded with that of a tiger. The local community offered large rewards for the creature's capture yet they were never claimed. Meanwhile sightings and alleged cat killings continued in New South Wales throughout the 1960s.

Many reports left little doubt that a very peculiar creature indeed was involved. In 1966, on a farm owned by Samuel Knight 3 miles north of Nowra, a large, black, panther-like animal was cornered by two large guard dogs. Defending itself, it managed to virtually rip its canine assailants apart before escaping into the surrounding bush.

In 1969 several attacks upon tourists close to Emmaville resulted in a widespread systematic search by no less than fifty sharp-shooters with rifles, but nothing was found.

By the beginning of the next decade sightings of panther-like creatures were emerging from other parts of the subcontinent. In September 1972 farmer George Moir of Kulja, Western Australia, found several of his pigs dead with their hearts torn out and their throats ripped open; the following day the same man was amazed to witness a flock of panic-stricken sheep being rounded up sheep-dog style by two large black cats which ran with a canter-like gait. Chased by Moir and local fauna warden Don Noble in their Jeeps, the cats seemed able to easily outpace the motorised vehicles and eventually escaped. George Moir subsequently learned that two neighbouring farmers had lost no fewer than fourteen of their own pigs during the previous week, all killed in the same distinctive, unpleasant style. Throughout that year residents in the area reportedly heard bloodcurdling cries on those nights when the strange nocturnal canine visitors arrived to savage their animals.

These unwelcome callers were sighted by so many inhabitants that they began to receive the same sort of press coverage as the earlier outbreaks in New South Wales. The state's agricultural protection board insisted that the so-called 'Kulja panthers' were probably not felines at all but merely black kangaroo dogs. But although one dog was shot the panther sightings continued, along with the outrages on livestock, and few local people thought much of the official explanation.

During the mid to late 1970s reports of Australian pantheresques intensified dramatically and a series of articles was published, including photographs taken by eye-witnesses, which seemed to prove beyond doubt that large feline creatures with jet-black fur really did exist in the Australian wild. Those farmers who continued to suffer maiming outbreaks came to believe that the creatures had the ability to appear and vanish at will and there were even some reports of panthers walking through walls with phantom-like ease, exploding into thin air with an enormous flash, and showing immunity to bullets. As in earlier decades repeated massive hunts with riflemen produced nothing and Mr James MacKinnon, Minister for Wildlife in the Australian Parliament, was moved to admit that only a phantom creature could conceivably be responsible for the carnage being meted out across certain locations in New South Wales and Western Australia. Some questioned MacKinnon's choice of words, but none could any longer doubt that the menace existed – the all-too-available evidence of slaughtered livestock proved that.

By 1981 journalist David O'Reilly was able to construct a virtually unanswerable case for the existence of the creatures by focusing upon one small area near Perth in Western Australia. O'Reilly's book, *Savage Shadow*, contained numerous reports and eye-witness accounts carefully and painstakingly documented, as well as supplementary data on physical evidence including spoors and fur samples identified as feline, the idiosyncratic droppings of large felid carnivores, and descriptions and photographs of animal kills which bore the unequivocal signs of feline behaviour. The author's book made it perfectly evident that previously sceptical zoologists were no longer prepared to accept the theory that sightings in various locations during the previous two and a half decades were simply the product of urban folklore. Yet neither could the same experts claim to offer a satisfactory solution to the mystery. The possibility that an abnormally large strain of feral domestic cat might have evolved seemed hardly worth considering since it could not have attained a sufficient size to be capable of killing sheep and kangaroos. Another possibility – that the creature could be some form of hitherto unknown native eutherian carnivore – was, if anything, even more unlikely since the beasts had only begun to appear in the second half of the twentieth century. Had they existed before that time they would presumably have been seen much earlier. A third theory, that the creatures were in fact pumas which had escaped from captivity, or were the descendants of creatures which had gained freedom in the past, seemed on the face of it to offer the greatest hope. However, no animals of this type were known to have been held in captivity, let alone reported as missing. And since all livestock moving between Australian states has to be recorded on entry and checked out on departure, the possibility of an escape avoiding official notice was extremely slim.

All in all, given the numerous contradictions which these feline enigmas pose, it is probably unsurprising that so many Australians still prefer to disbelieve stories of big cats roaming their countryside. Numerous investigations have now taken place to track down the creatures using high-tech sound equipment, powerful zoom lens cameras, infrared sights, sophisticated trapping devices, as well as, inevitably, the activities of hunters armed with high-velocity rifles. Still the Australian big cat remains elusive, and none has been caught either alive or dead. Yet despite all the improbabilities, the fact remains that some form of mystery animal does seem to exist in Australia. It just prefers not to be found.

1959

Voices from the Afterlife

One evening in the late summer of 1959 Freidrich Jurgenson, a Swedish film producer, decided to make a tape of birds singing in the garden of his villa at Molvo, near Stockholm. A keen amateur bird-watcher in his spare time, Jurgenson had made similar tapes on many previous occasions. This time, however, the recording came out very differently, for when the Swede played it back he was astonished to find a man's voice mixed in with the natural sounds. Clearly audible, the man appeared to be giving a lecture, ironically on the subject of ornithology; even more curious was the fact that the language spoken was not Swedish but Norwegian.

Since it was certain that no one had been in the garden while the recording had taken place, Freidrich Jurgenson became convinced that the voice must have been superimposed preternaturally. His imagination aroused, he began experimenting with a radio receiver; altering the frequency between conventional wavelengths. After a while, to his amazement, he found he could regularly make out messages mixed in among the background music coming through from the transmissions of terrestrial radio stations.

Although he had to concentrate hard to pick out the

fleeting voices from the general radio traffic that surrounded them his patience was rewarded with positive results on nearly every occasion. To begin with the anomalous voices spoke just single words but soon Jurgenson began receiving whole sentences in which the voices explained about afterlife reality, referring either directly to him or the questions he had asked; and on some occasions even discussing him and the recording situation between themselves.

Finally, in December, the Swede received a message which he knew could only come from someone who had died. Jurgenson's certainty was easy enough to explain: he recognised the voice to be that of his own deceased mother.

Interest turned to obsession and for many months Jurgenson made tapes of these spirit signals. Eventually he had collected over a hundred voices, many of which identified themselves as dead people. He became convinced that he had uncovered a secret of fundamental importance to the human race, yet when he eventually announced the findings of his research they were treated with derision and contempt by most scientists. The Electric Voice Phenomenon, as it subsequently became known, has remained a source of controversy ever since. Some parapsychologists have made outlandish claims on its behalf; others insist that the only baffling thing is that so many otherwise sensible people should consider wasting time on it.

Certainly there are no shortage of renowned figures who claim to have duplicated Jurgenson's recordings. In 1965 Professor Hans Bender, a director at the University of Freiburg, undertook six months of tests which, in his own words, appeared to confirm that 'under differing conditions and circumstances a factory-clean tape would, after being run through a tape-recording head in an otherwise silent environment, be found to contain the imprint of recognisable messages which were not audible to the human ear but registered as visible oscillograph impulses.'

Six years later, in March 1971, a British paranormal writer named Peter Bander persuaded publisher Colin Smythe to undertake a series of EVP tests at the studios of Pye Records in London. Using Jurgenson's diode method Bander had received messages from his own dead mother which voice-pattern analysis had virtually proved to be genuine. Sufficiently intrigued by Bander's story, Smythe arranged for a demonstration, watched by two of Pye's senior recording engineers who guaranteed that no strange signals could enter the recording process.

On 24 March 1971 the session, which lasted only eighteen minutes, took place. Throughout the exercise the diode constantly flickered even though Pye's engineers could hear nothing on their microphones. The playback was a different matter. Over 200 voices had been recorded, twenty-seven of which were intelligible to all in the studio. One witness present, the chairman of Smythe's publishing company, Sir Robert Mayer, even recognised the voice of an old friend, the concert pianist Artur Schnabel. Afterwards Roy Prichet, Pye's chief recording engineer, who had supervised the test, described the voices as 'astounding'. With a bank of four recorders synchronised together and protected by sophisticated instruments to block out freak pick-ups from the high or low frequency transmitters of radio hams, Prichet knew that the possibility of conventional interference was nil. These voices were, he said, 'voices from nowhere'.

Three days later a second experiment was conducted by Smythe at the Enfield laboratories of Belling and Lee using a radio frequency screen laboratory that excludes any form of electro-magnetic radiation. Supervising the procedure this time was Peter Hale, Britain's foremost expert in electronic screen suppression, with the assistance of Professor Ralph Lovelock, a top physicist. Again voices were clearly received.

Hale admitted that they could only have been made in a way that 'cannot be explained in normal physical terms'. Ralph Lovelock concurred. 'They are beyond explanation,' he added.

The investigation process has continued. In 1980 an American research group called Metascience released tapes containing several hours of communications with the dead through the medium of a device they called the Spiricom. Then perhaps the most impressive demonstration of all occurred in January 1983, when a German engineer named Hans Otto Konig demonstrated his so-called 'generator' before a meeting of the German EVP Association in Falder, a suburb of Frankfurt. Unlike other researchers working in the field, Konig had managed to build a machine through which living people could speak directly to spirits and receive audible replies. Even the most sceptical of journalists present at the conference were confounded by the evidence of their own ears. To their amazement several of those present recognised the unmistakable voices of dead friends and relatives and there were contributions from at least two former EVP researchers who had passed on to the next life. Only Hans Otto Konig, who had heard the voices many times before in the seclusion of his own laboratory, remained unmoved by the extraordinary demonstration.

The full impact of EVP research has yet to be felt. The vast majority of the population is entirely unaware that such a phenomenon exists and most mainstream scientists avoid the subject altogether, knowing full well that conclusive proof of EVP would turn their established beliefs upside-down. But the phenomenon will not go away and research continues among enthusiasts on both sides of the Atlantic. The voices first picked up by Fredrick Jurgenson in 1959 may one day convince us all that death itself is a process of transition rather than annihilation.

1960

Monster Sightings on the Emerald Isle

The Irish love a good story and are never happier than when telling a tale of the supernatural. Who, after all, has not heard of those favourites of Irish folklore, the leprechaun and the wailing banshee? Yet the most common of all mysterious creatures to roam the Irish countryside would appear to be neither of these, but a group of strange aquatic creatures variously known as piast, peist or ollpheist. Like the tales of the little people, legends of Irish water-monsters go back a long way. The Fenian cycle of Irish sagas tells of how Lough Berg (the Red Lake) got its name after an incident in which the hero Finn slaughtered a monster which swallowed several of his followers. The seventh-century life of Saint Mochua of Balla describes a similar beast devouring a swimmer who attempted to cross the River Shannon. In yet another story, St Colman of Dromore supposedly saved a girl from a hideous animal which rose up out of Lough Ree.

Throughout the Middle Ages and afterwards there was no shortage of sightings from locations such as Lough Mask, Lough Graney and Lough Bran, a small yet particularly beautiful lake at the source of the River Blackwater. Nevertheless, few educated people in the twentieth century seriously considered the possibility that the depths of Ireland's larger water courses might hide creatures of an unknown species. Even when several people living close to the banks of Lough Ree claimed to have seen a long snake-like creature in the years immediately following the Second World War, most people continued to scoff at such superstitious credulity. However, when the year 1960 saw a series of sightings from credible witnesses even the sceptics began to have second thoughts.

On the evening of 18 May 1960 three priests from Dublin were fishing off Holly Point on Lough Ree. Father Mathew Burke, Father Daniel Murray and Father Richard Quigley had visited the area many times before and knew the lake well. Up until that time they had never considered the stories of monsters to be anything other than colourful tradition and so they were all entirely amazed when on that warm summer evening the still water of the lake was broken by an animal the like of which they had never seen before. Swimming at a distance of some 100 yards away its humped body appeared snake-like, writhing in the form of a loop and its head, which protruded above the surface by some several feet, seemed to be flat like that of a python's, though incredibly huge.

They were not sure of the exact size of the creature as they did not see all of it, though they guessed that the overall length of the two visible sections, the second of which appeared to be a large round, humped body, perhaps propelled by flippers, would probably be over 16 feet. Writing of his experience afterwards one of the priests, Father Burke, described the creature as 'cruising at a very leisurely speed, apparently unconcerned about our presence. We watched it moving along the surface for a period of two or three minutes in a north-easterly direction. It was going towards the shore but submerged gradually and disappeared from view completely.'

The following day the three clergymen spoke to journalists

of their encounter and afterwards submitted a full account of their sighting to the Irish Inland Fisheries Trust. Unlike many previous water-monster reports from Lough Ree and elsewhere, the sighting of 18 May was difficult to ridicule. For a start it was not reasonable to assume that three priests would deliberately perpetrate a hoax, and it seemed equally unlikely that their relatively close call with the animal could have been an optical illusion. In the following weeks sceptical experts did suggest a number of natural alternatives: that the creature was a midget Russian submarine; a line of otters; or three or four large eels, caught on the same hook, whose frantic wriggling and twisting had caused an undulating impression of one large creature swimming through the water. Yet none of these possibilities seemed particularly plausible, and when several other reports of similar sightings came in during the following months it served to add to the growing conviction among many Irish people that there really was something mysterious in the lake.

In August two pike fishermen, Patrick Ganley and Joseph Quigley of Inishturk, caught something unaccountably large in their net which escaped before they could haul it aboard. Ganley remarked afterwards that the creature they had caught must have been as strong as a horse to have broken through such heavy-duty mesh. He also claimed that it had actually towed their boat some 30 or 40 yards in the process. This happened in 60 feet of water out in the middle of Lough Ree about half a mile from where the priests had seen their creature several months before. Following the publication of details of the August incident two English tourists wrote to an Irish newspaper claiming to have also been towed around the lake by their fishing line during a holiday in 1958, and the owner of a cabin cruiser said that his boat had struck a huge moving object in mid-channel at a point where the water was thought to be very deep. In response to this last story the lake was dragged at the spot where the skipper had estimated the incident took place, but nothing was found.

As news of the Lough Ree sightings spread, interest in the phenomenon of Irish water-monsters grew and no doubt partly as a result there were many claims of similar creatures from across the country. A large proportion of these were probably the result of overheated imaginations and the misidentification of logs or other natural objects floating on the surface of rivers and lakes, yet others can only be explained naturally if one chooses to believe that the witnesses were lying. On May Day 1968 a building contractor named James Cooney was driving with his friend Michael McNulty past Glendarry Loch, which is situated on the offshore island of Achill. In their headlights the men saw a peculiar dinosaur-like animal with a long neck like a swan's, cross in front of their van and disappear into thick undergrowth. Approximately six weeks later Gay Denver, a sixteen-year-old trainee carpenter, was cycling home from mass when he saw a similar creature 'humping' up a turf bank near a wood close to Glendarry Loch. Then on the first Sunday in June a Dundalk businessman and two hitch-hikers were among several people who saw a long-necked lizard about 20 feet long on the shore of the same loch.

Sceptics regularly claim that Irish monster stories are probably invented by local people to attract tourists. In the case of Glendarry Loch, which is a reasonably accessible location, there might be some truth in the allegation. However, most of Ireland's supposedly monster-haunted lakes are extremely secluded and few if any tourists would bother making the arduous journey into the remote wilds to find them. Moreover, even if they did they would discover the majority to be uninspiring locations and many hardly bigger than bogland puddles. This last detail opens up a fresh objection to belief in the Irish piast, namely that the lakes many of them reportedly inhabit are too small to conceivably hide or provide food for a large aquatic creature. And perhaps more importantly, where attempts have been made to search these small bodies of water (which can be done quite effectively), nothing has been found.

In 1968 a variety of methods including nets, fish-stunners, skin-divers and even gelignite charges were used to try to trap a 12-foot long hump-backed creature seen by many people in Lough Fadda in Connaught, a lake measuring only 130 yards by 80. Investigations found the fish population in the lough to be normal, but no monster showed itself.

Shortly afterwards the same team of researchers, led by Professor Roy McCall, carried out the process all over again in Lough Nahooin, County Galway, where a huge eel-like creature had shown itself on 22 February of that year to farmer Stephen Coyne. On this occasion echo-sounders and dragging were also used in addition to the techniques employed in Lough Fadda, but once more the search drew a blank. Professor McCall gamely concluded that the animal must have escaped to the sea down a shallow stream, but the hypothesis, like the existence of the creature itself, remained open to considerable doubt.

So what truth really lies behind the ages-old tradition of the Irish water-monster? Logic tells us they cannot really exist; contemporary accounts suggest they might. For those who research the annals of unexplained phenomena it is a familiar choice.

1961

Flight into Oblivion

Since unidentified flying objects were first seen in the skies above our planet there have been numerous instances where terrestrial aircraft, either military or civil, have gone missing or crashed following apparent contact with alien craft. Occasionally these incidents make sensational headline news, but more often they are hidden from public view through media suppression and the plane's loss blamed on mundane causes. Sometimes, however, the effects of alien interference are rather more bizarre than simply the destruction of men and machines. One such example involves the last flight of a Soviet Antonov AN-2P mail plane which took off from Sverdlovsk airfield bound for Kurgan with seven people on board in February 1961. According to a report originating from the Moscow Aviation Institute and corroborated by officials at the Soviet Embassy in London, who were interviewed by the British UFO researcher Derek Mansell in January 1965, the extraordinary details of the encounter were as follows.

The aircraft disappeared from radar screens about 80 to 100 miles from Sverdlovsk, just after the pilot had communicated with ground control to say that he was being followed by a round object. Following unsuccessful attempts to regain communications a search was launched involving helicopters and ground troops, and within hours the aircraft was found in a small clearing in a dense forest. To the amazement of the searchers it was completely intact apart from its crew. Of these men there was no sign. But the plane had not simply landed, for quite evidently there was no way that an Antonov AN-2P could have put down in such a small clearing without hitting the trees on one side or the other. No marks, tyre tracks or footprints were found at the site but a 30-metre wide, clearly defined circle of scorched grass and depressed earth was discovered 100 metres away from the aircraft. Summing up their report, investigators from the Moscow Aviation Institute were unable to offer even the slightest conjecture as to the whereabouts of the seven men who had taken off from Sverdlovsk airfield earlier that fateful day. And since they never turned up, that was the way it stayed.

Despite the routine official denials it is now clear that the crew of the Russian mail plane are among many human fliers to suffer at the hands of alien visitors. Others have had narrow escapes. In November 1979 a charter jet carrying 109 German and Austrian tourists to the Canary Islands was buzzed by two unidentified objects while crossing Spanish airspace. Assistance arrived in the form of two French-built Mirage fighters and the discs flew off after the first burst of their cannons. Having made an unscheduled landing at Valencia, the shaken pilot, Captain Javier Lerdo-Tejeda, described his close encounter to astonished officials. Sanchez Tehran, Spain's Minister for Transport Communications, went on record as admitting the truth behind the bizarre episode.

The passengers and crew of the Spanish charter flight had a lucky escape. Earlier that same year five Arab businessmen travelling aboard a private Lear jet on a trip from Athens to

Jeddah were less fortunate. Just after the pilot had reported a strangely shaped craft flying alongside the jet disappeared from radar screens over the Sahara Desert.

When it was found the plane's fuselage was still intact and there was no sign of fire; yet the men's bodies had been reduced to piles of thin powder. Examining samples of the remains at London's St Thomas's Hospital, osteologist Professor Michael Day was certain that no natural circumstances – neither wild animals nor the desert's extreme temperatures – could have produced the remarkable change in bone structure that he found. In Day's opinion, a force outside the laws of science was responsible.

Yet another probable victim of alien interference was Frederick Valentich, an Australian pilot who vanished on the night of 27 October 1978 while flying his single-engine Cessna 182 from Melbourne to King Island in the Pacific. Valentich had been airborne for only about fifteen minutes when he radioed Melbourne air traffic control to report that he was being followed by four brilliant orange lights. For the next two minutes radar screens at Melbourne recorded the UFOs closing in on and finally merging with the Cessna. As they did so contact with Valentich was lost. The following morning rescue planes scoured the area of the Bass Straits where the Cessna was presumed to have gone down, but nothing was found.

In the weeks following the Cessna's disappearance the Australian Bureau of Air Safety attempted to play down rumours of a UFO link in the mystery, even though six other reports of strange lights over the Bass Straits had been filed that same night. And when one newspaper editor tried to obtain a recording of Valentich's last words he was told that the tape had been erased. What the newspapermen did uncover, however, was that the general area of the Cessna's last reported position had seen more than its fair share of enigmas in the past. As early as 1920 odd lights in the sky had accompanied the loss of the motor cruiser *SS Amelia* as well as the search vessel sent to find her. Reports of strange flying shapes over the Bass Straits persisted during the next three decades, a period which saw the vanishment of no fewer than seventeen aircraft in circumstances uncannily reminiscent of Frederick Valentich's last flight.

The incidents described above may simply represent the tip of a much larger iceberg. Dozens of planes crash or go missing every year and often the reason for their loss remains mysterious. These tragedies may or may not be linked to UFO activity, yet we can say with absolute certainty that where a connection with flying saucers becomes apparent all evidence relating to the incident tends to get buried. During the early 1960s a team of distinguished scientists, astronomers and ex-military officers called NICAP (National Investigations Committee on Aerial Phenomena) published a 184-page review entitled *The UFO Evidence* which not only stated unequivocally that UFOs were dangerous but charged official agencies in the United States with the deliberate falsification of evidence. Shortly afterwards senior USAF officer Captain Edward J. Ruppelt, former chief of the US Air Technical Intelligence Centre, admitted that the CIA had ordered the Air Force to debunk sightings and discredit witnesses following suspicious air crashes. An even more revealing statement came from General Benjamin Chidlaw, former commanding officer of Air Defense Command, who was quoted as follows: 'The US Air Force lost many men and planes trying to intercept them [UFOs].' Chidlaw also revealed that it was the standard practice of the intelligence services to hide details of these incidents.

With the release under the US Freedom of Information Act of more than 40,000 pages of concrete evidence for the existence of the UFO menace, collected by such organisations as the USAF, the CIA and the FBI, there can no longer be any doubt that the US government was simply one among many Western governments suppressing evidence of saucer sightings, harassing witnesses and generally resorting to methods incompatible with a free society in order to maintain a level of secrecy. The official policy of denying the reality of UFOs remains firmly in place today and respectable citizens who find themselves in close proximity to an alien presence may very well end up being accused of deceit, insanity, hallucinations or incompetence. Marriages are still being broken, careers wrecked and reputations ruined. Methods of intimidation would seem to range from the threat of legal action to direct physical violence, depending on the particular official strategy being employed. So far these tactics have usually worked, and the vast majority of people continue to assume that UFOs are either the misidentification of mundane objects such as stars, weather balloons and terrestrial aircraft, or the bizarre imaginings of feeble-minded attention-seekers.

In the meantime, the carnage in our skies continues unabated.

1962

Surrey Pumas and Exmoor Beasts

In a country the size of Britain, which is one of the most densely populated areas of the planet, it is not only hard but virtually impossible to imagine how large wild creatures might roam undetected. But unless we are to dismiss the value of human testimony out of hand, it would appear probable that this startling suggestion is precisely the case.

During the modern era, and particularly since the early years of the 1960s, a prodigious number of sightings have been reported from many parts of the UK – sightings which suggest the existence in the wild of several species of large cats unlike any native British felid. In these somewhat inconsistent accounts, mysterious animals are variously described as pumas, cheetahs, panthers, lionesses, lynxes and so on, and for every reliable report it must be stressed that there are a dozen which stretch credibility beyond the limits of even the most dedicated mysteriologist. Nevertheless, even if we cast a wary eye over these stories it is clear that some element of truth must lie at the bottom of the enigma. And that truth is baffling.

The first wave of British big-cat sightings to excite widespread media attention focused on a long-limbed cheetah-like animal with an upward curling tail, which was seen sitting by the roadside near Shooters Hill, Woolwich, a suburban district of south London, on the night of 18 July 1962. When approached the creature moved off into nearby woods and despite several further sightings and a well-manned police search of the area the following day it evaded all attempts to capture it – on one occasion leaping over the bonnet of a pursuing police car. Unaccountably, the Shooters Hill cheetah was not seen again after 19 July, but four days' later, on the morning of 23 July, mid-Wessex Water Board officials reported seeing a large cat stalking a rabbit near Heathy Park Reservoir in Surrey. It was the first appearance of an animal which was to become infamous as the Surrey Puma.

In the following months, throughout the unusually harsh winter of 1962–63, a variety of strange cat-like animals made nocturnal visits to farms between Crondall and Ewshott on the Hampshire border, killing chickens and leaving farm dogs terrified. Eighteen months later, on 30 August 1964, a 4-hundredweight Friesian bullock was found badly mauled near Cranleigh and the following week a calf's carcass which had apparently been dragged across several fields, was discovered. Pawprints near the animals' bodies suggested the presence of a puma-type felid, though the spoors were in fact over three times larger than those of a fully grown adult puma. It was dubbed the Munstead Monster after a neaby village and the sightings of this prodigious creature which continued throughout the autumn of 1964 bore out its hugeness. The puma pandemonium reached a peak after a dead roe deer was discovered with its neck broken and wounds compatible with the earlier killing at Cranleigh. The police for their part remained sceptical until two of their own officers sighted the beast for themselves by the Thomas Grey Memorial at Stoke Poges on 12 November. As the nights drew in once more the residents of the home counties were terrified by the spine-chilling screams and growls which accompanied the nocturnal activities of this unwanted predator.

Little happened during 1965 but sightings intensified dramatically during the summer of 1966. In one of the most compelling encounters police and several villagers watched a big cat for a full twenty minutes while it killed a rabbit in fields near Worplesdon. Then in early August an ex-police photographer named Ian succeeded in producing a picture of the creature crouching in fields in the same area. For many people, positive proof of the cat's existence was achieved beyond doubt when Victor Manton, curator of Whipsnade Zoo, collected hairs from a barbed-wire fence which were analysed and found to compare closely with the tail tip of a puma. Yet despite several police hunts no animal was ever caught and when the Surrey Constabulary finally terminated their investigations in mid-August 1967, having collected no fewer than 362 listed sightings, many people outside the county still refused to believe that such a creature as the Surrey Puma had ever truly existed.

During the 1970s there was no shortage of mystery cat reports from other parts of the United Kingdom, though in each case these were less concentrated and for that reason less convincing. But then in the 1980s another highly significant case emerged, this time centring on open land between Dartmoor and Exmoor in the English West Country.

The Exmoor Beast, as it became known, first attracted media attention after the unexplained loss of several lambs during the spring of 1982 from Drewstone Farm, South Molton coincided with rumours of a panther-like creature seen in the area. Searches revealed nothing and the sensation died down. But the following year, as the lambing season came round once more, farmers in the area again began to lose lambs at an alarming rate, including no fewer than thirty from Drewstone Farm. Several dogs suspected of the killings were shot but the slaughter continued. Horrified farmers found that the beast killed its victims in an unusual and unpleasant fashion, crushing the lamb's skull and then eviscerating the flesh from the neck downwards, leaving the skeleton virtually untouched. No dog, they knew, would behave in such a way. For their part the police were baffled and by May the losses had become so serious that Royal Marines stationed at Lympstone were brought in along with their infrared searching equipment. At 5.30 am on 4 May a Marine sniper, John Holden, saw a very large and powerful black quadruped crossing a railway line some distance away but it evaded his bullets. The creature was not sighted again and by early July the Army had pulled out, admitting defeat and bewildered at the predator's almost supernatural behaviour.

During the following years reports of phantom feline activity on the high grasslands of Dartmoor and Exmoor diminished markedly. At the same time the discovery of several canine-type killings of sheep and deer throughout the region predictably led sceptics to claim that a pack of large dogs had been responsible for the original outrages all along. Yet the beast was to return. In January 1987 nine enormous pawprints were discovered near Bideford by researcher Trevor Beer. This area became the focus of sightings two months later, and on August Bank Holiday a large, dark cat of an obviously non-British species was actually photographed by Beer and three other witnesses. One of the shots was subsequently shown in a BBC wildlife report, and for many this fresh evidence seemed to show conclusively that a mystery felid did exist. But if so where had it come from?

Among those who take the stories of mysterious cats in Britain seriously there have been many natural theories. Some zoologists contend that the beasts must be unusually large hybrids bred from a combination of feral domestics and the natural British wild cat. Others prefer to believe that sightings involve specimens of various foreign species which have somehow escaped from captivity in zoos, private collections, circuses and so on. Although on the face of it this second theory would seem to provide the most logical answer, the concentrated outbreaks of sightings have not followed reported losses of such creatures. Many experts continue to insist that apparently inexplicable killings of large numbers of lambs in spring are actually the responsibility of large dogs rather than phantom felines, yet this explanation in no way accounts for the numerous sightings of Pantheresque creatures that coincided with the deaths to a remarkable degree. When considering the phenomenon as a whole the importance of this last point can scarcely be overestimated.

In Surrey the many hundreds of reports of pumas in the mid-1960s were eventually thought by police to be the result of hallucination, hysteria or mistaken identification, despite the reliability of witnesses and the frequent presence of physical evidence such as droppings, tracks and the butchered half-eaten carcasses of farm stock and wild deer. Even among those who do accept the evidence many continue to prefer the traditional explanation of big-cat reports – that the puma or panther escaped from captivity – despite the absence of recorded losses from these sources. But the blunt truth is that no natural explanation comes close to fitting the facts, either in Surrey or in Devon. Mad dogs cannot have caused the variety of mutilations found on carcasses in the home counties – indeed no known animal could. Nor is it reasonable that a single beast could cover the considerable distances between attacks that took place on the same night in Devon, attacks which occurred simultaneously over a wide area of Exmoor and Dartmoor. While it is just about possible, though unlikely, that some big cats of the type regularly sighted across Britain might have escaped unrecorded from private game collections, it is frankly inconceivable that they could have lived unnoticed in the British countryside for very long. In any case, not once have the massive armed searches produced a single predator, dead or alive. All in all, the fact remains that the sheer oddity of the reported attacks on livestock and the uncanny ability of these feline creatures to appear and disappear at will point strongly towards a conclusion that they derive their existence from a dimension outside our physical universe.

1963

History Repeats Itself

Few would disagree that coincidence provides an endlessly fascinating topic of conversation. Everyone has their own bizarre experience to relate and even the most trivial of examples can sometimes make us stop and wonder whether some unknown force is at work behind the scenes of our everyday lives. Even so, most modern-thinking Westerners would, if pressed on the matter, scoff at the idea that chance could itself have a direct influence upon human lives. We live in a world of scientific certainties and materialistic values where the invisible, super-normal forces of unreason have no place. Yet as we have clearly seen some coincidences, particularly those of the sinister kind, involve a series of chance connections so remarkable that we are offered little alternative but to accept the startling probability that the physical universe as we know it is subject to an underlying pattern or framework which is beyond our comprehension.

Usually such a sequence of events surrounds accidental deaths. But curiously even some murders seem to have the most peculiar links. The most famous political assassination of the twentieth century provides perhaps the most striking example one could hope to find. The links surrounding the lives and deaths of both victims and gunmen involved in the murders of the American presidents Lincoln and Kennedy stand as a definitive testament to the extent to which coincidence can run on and on and on. For the historian it is their achievements in office which make the deaths of these two American statesmen momentous; for the student of the inexplicable the relevant details concern their last moments on earth.

Abraham Lincoln, emancipator of the slaves and leader of the union, was shot in the back of the head at point-blank range while watching a play in Ford's Theatre, Washington DC. His killer, John Wilkes Booth, used a pistol for his crime, which took place in 1865, a few days after the end of the American Civil War. John F. Kennedy, Democratic president and champion of civil rights legislation, was shot in the head while travelling by motorcade along a Dallas thoroughfare. His murderer, Lee Harvey Oswald, chose a high-powered rifle with a telescopic sight as his weapon. The date, as everyone knows, was November 1963. So what are the supposedly strange connections between the two crimes? Both took place on a Friday, but that is a minor coincidence, as is the fact that both assassins were southerners.

Of much greater interest is the birthday of the two killers, for Lee Harvey Oswald was born exactly one hundred years after Lincoln's killer. This century time-span, a small point in itself, recurs with ominous regularity in the life histories of other men involved in the drama. It is interesting to note, for example, that John Kennedy was elected to congressional office exactly one hundred years after his illustrious predecessor and that their respective elections to the office of president also shared the same century-wide margin. Both Lincoln and Kennedy were succeeded by southerners named Johnson and the birth-dates of each vice-president are also separated by exactly one century: Andrew Johnson was born in 1808; Lyndon Johnson in 1908.

There were further coincidences of name apparent in the murders. JFK's personal private secretary's surname was Lincoln; Abe Lincoln's secretary had the Christian name John. Lincoln died in Ford's Theatre in Washington while Kennedy was riding in a Ford-manufactured automobile on the day of his eclipse. Ironically enough, the limousine in which the president rode along with his wife Jackie was a Lincoln Continental. Perhaps we might be forgiven for not redefining our view of the universe on this evidence alone, but this is not the end of the eerie parallels between the two events. It is well recalled that neither Booth nor Oswald lived to stand trial; what is less well known is the similarity between the way each man attempted to escape justice. Booth, having committed his terrible deed in the theatre, escaped eventually to meet his death in a warehouse. Oswald, on the other hand, having aimed his deadly salvo from a warehouse window, ran to a theatre before being captured.

Perhaps the most intriguing of all the many presidential parallels concerned the first public proposals for Lincoln's nomination. In a letter printed in the *Cincinnati Gazette* on 6 November 1858 came a call for Lincoln to run for president alongside a long-since-forgotten vice-presidential running-mate, then secretary to the Navy. The secretary's name? John Kennedy.

In the early 1950s two of the most respected minds of our century, Nobel Prize-winning Wolfgang Pauli and the distinguished psychologist Carl Gustav Jung, joined forces to produce an all-embracing concept of coincidence which they labelled synchronicity. To these men apparently eccentric correlations of time, place or circumstance were evidence of a single force-field which lies ever-present beneath the substrata of our daily lives, trying to impose its own form of discipline on the general confusion of everyday events. Such a force, if it were to exist, might very well go some way towards explaining the bizarre links between the Lincoln and Kennedy assassinations. It might also place in perspective the jinx which seems to follow America's foremost political family.

When one talks of the Kennedy curse one naturally thinks of the shootings of Jack and Bobby. But even more odd is the apparent link to modes of travel. The president's elder brother and sister both died in mid-air plane explosions in the 1940s, and of course JFK himself died while travelling. His younger brother Edward nearly died in another crash in which several Democratic party workers were killed; Edward again had a brush with death when his car plunged from the Chappaquiddick Bridge, drowning his companion, Mary-Jo Kopechne, badly damaging his reputation in the process. In 1969, while running for the Democratic nomination, Bobby Kennedy talked of his family's misfortunes being a tangible reality: 'Good luck is something you make and bad luck is something you endure,' he said. Two weeks later Bobby was shot dead. Although in his case the killing did not involve powered motion, the family's travel jinx returned with a vengeance only days later when the train carrying the statesman's coffin hit some mourners, cutting one man in half.

During the 1970s the next generation of Kennedys was plagued by drug addiction, scandal or severe ill health; there were also a number of automobile accidents. In one of these Pam Kelly, a granddaughter of family patriarch Joseph Kennedy, was paralysed for life. In another, a car driven by Bobby Kennedy Jr ran down and killed a Mexican peasant boy on a trip to Central America. In 1976 David, another son of the deceased Bobby Kennedy Sr, was stabbed by a black drug-dealer in the public toilet of a railway station. He survived, but two years later he was found dead in a Palm Beach motel room while on a touring holiday in Florida.

The jinx (some people would prefer to call it a curse) that has dogged the Kennedy clan during the last half-century shows no sign of letting up and one can only feel pity for those who bear the name. Since much doubt now surrounds Lee Harvey Oswald's part in President Kennedy's assassination it may very well be that no true synchronism surrounds the two killings. Yet even if Oswald played no part in the 1963 tragedy, how extraordinary it is that fate should have chosen as the scapegoat for the crime a man who so perfectly fitted the historic role.

1964

Water, Water Everywhere

Sometimes a paranormal occurrence can be so weird that those caught up in the seemingly impossible drama almost go out of their minds in an attempt to make sense of that which cannot be explained. When such an event takes place in one's own home it is even harder to come to terms with it.

On one late October day in 1964 the Martin family of Methuen, Massachusetts noticed a damp patch appearing on the wall of their lounge. The Martins were puzzled because the weather was evidently too mild for pipes to freeze and burst. It was not until the next day, when the dampness turned into a veritable flood, that they began to realise that something genuinely strange was going on. Mr Francis Martin was watching an American football game when all of a sudden he heard a popping noise. The sound was followed by a sudden spout of water bursting from the damp part of the wall. Thereafter many other odd fountains of water began to flow from many parts of the room's wall and ceiling. The bizarre showers lasted twenty seconds and occurred roughly every twenty minutes. Eventually, so great was the amount of water sloshing about their floors that the family was forced to move into the home of Mrs Martin's mother several miles away. This, however, was to prove no solution, for to the family's horror the water gremlin pursued them, and in no time at all every room in their new refuge was similarly drenched. When the local water department were asked to investigate both houses were thoroughly checked for leaky pipes. None were found.

It was clear enough to the Martins that some people would choose to simply disbelieve their story rather than to puzzle over it. But after water department officials saw for themselves the anomalous huge jets of water continually bursting through dry plaster walls no one in authority was going to call them liars. Even when the mains water supply was turned off at an outside source and the pipes inside the house were drained there was no lessening of the spouts, gushes and floods which besieged the unfortunate Martins.

Frank Martin took his family back to their home in Methuen. Again the water gremlin followed, although its activities were less pronounced, and after several more weeks the anomalous appearances finally ceased altogether.

Although the aqueous spirit which invaded the home of the New England family in 1964 never threatened any form of physical danger, one can easily imagine how frayed the Martins' nerves must have been. The discomfort of finding themselves at the centre of such an impossible sequence of events was made worse by the total failure of the so-called experts to account for the mystery. But of course this was only to be expected: there was simply no way that gallons of water could continually jet from dry plaster walls from any natural source. Quite clearly the aqueous phenomenon was preternatural in origin and therefore beyond the capacity of the local water department to investigate.

Although we have yet to understand how or why such bizarre flows and oozings become manifest, a trawl through the various paranormal events of the twentieth century will uncover plenty of other examples involving a wide variety of liquids. In August 1985 Jean-Marc Belmer, a lorry driver aged thirty, and his wife Lucy redecorated their home in St Quentin, Picardy, France. The following January tiny red droplets began to appear all over the walls and carpets of the Belmers' living room. The phenomenon stopped after a day but around the beginning of February the spots reappeared once more in increasing numbers. The couple became afraid, and when one morning they woke up to find their own pillows and bedspreads covered in the same red stains, they abandoned their home and went to Jean-Marc's parents. The next week police forensic scientists who were called in to investigate the goings-on were astonished to find the whole house literally drenched in a congealed substance that they quickly recognised as blood. Subsequent analysis proved that it was human blood, but since no victim was discovered to provide a readily available source the police investigation never reached any conclusion.

Two years later, in September 1987, another house of blood hit newspaper headlines, this time across America. Minnie Clyde Winston, a seventy-year-old resident of Fountain Drive, Atlanta, Georgia, was woken at 11.30 pm by a noise which she assumed at first to be a running tap. Instead upon investigation she found blood spurting like a sprinkler from walls and ceilings in the kitchen, living room, bedroom, hall and basement. Along with her husband William, Mrs Winston had been living in the six-roomed brick house for more than twenty years before the curious happenings began, and could confirm that the place had no reputation for being haunted. Neither had the former owners reported any untoward goings-on in the past.

Perhaps the strangest of all anomalous flows is provided by an example from much earlier in the century. In August 1919 crude black oil began to seep from the walls and ceilings of

Swanton Novers Rectory in Norfolk, England. At first it was assumed that the house must have been standing over a natural oil well, but when the thick, black liquid eventually gave way to a less viscous substance which was quickly identified as refined gasoline, the search for a natural explanation was abandoned. Heavy showers of various liquids, including salt water, methylated spirits and sandalwood oil, followed during the next few weeks and as the variety widened so the rate of flow increased.

One official who went to investigate claimed to have caught two gallons of liquid in four hours by leaving a bucket under just one of the many outpourings. As the situation got out of control the rectory's occupant, the Rev. Hugh Guy, was obliged to move his furnishings to another house. For a while the rectory remained empty but by the beginning of the following year the curious flows had dried up, never to be repeated.

1965

The Man Who Took Snapshots with His Mind

Throughout the last forty years there have been many convincing demonstrations of psychokinesis – the ability of the human mind to affect physical matter. Spoons, keys, coins and many other varieties of metal objects have been bent, scrunched, or split in two through the influence of PK. Broken clocks, music boxes and all manner of defective mechanical appliances have been made to work through the application of psychic energy. Physical objects, including sometimes very heavy pieces of furniture, have been seen to move or even rise into the air under the watchful gaze of a telekinetic adept. Yet surely the most bizarre of all the strange powers of the human mind was that demonstrated on many occasions by the American 'thoughtographer' Ted Serios during a four-year period which began in 1965.

A former US Marine and a part-time bellhop at the Chicago Hilton Hotel, Serios seemed an unlikely candidate for supernatural powers. Indeed, by his own admission he was more interested in his regular intake of beer and cigarettes than he was in proving or disproving the existence of mind over matter, reproducing his remarkable powers only as a party piece. But after some persuasion he gave up his sideshows and allowed himself to be scientifically monitored while he produced his highly idiosyncratic paranormal trick: producing thought-images upon virgin photographic film. In the laboratory of Dr Jule Eisenbud of Denver, Colorado, Serios would point a camera at his face and produce, by sheer thought, picture after picture of distant objects that he was holding in his mind. Many of these turned out to be, for ease of recognition more than anything else, familiar sights or famous buildings in Europe. In practice the technique was childishly simple; but the mental energy Serios employed has baffled scientists ever since.

Even those who began by being sceptical soon had to admit that a genuine mystery had been uncovered. Since the experiments were conducted using a Polaroid Instamatic camera which not only produced photographs at the touch of a button but also eliminated any suspicion of trickery at the dark-room stage, the fact that anomalous images really were appearing could hardly be disputed. The photographs which emerged were sometimes of locations of scenes only too well known, such as the Piazza San Marco in Venice or London's Westminster Abbey. At other times, when Serios failed to achieve his mental target, the photographs would come out completely black or white, as if they had been pointed at either a totally unlit room or towards a bright light. Only rarely was a natural image produced – close-ups of Ted Serios' own face contorted into a grotesque image of intense concentration.

Not all the sessions took place in Dr Eisenbud's laboratory. His subject's thoughtographic powers were also demonstrated in front of live audiences in lecture theatres and television studios. In these cases cameras provided by the visitors themselves would be made ready and loaded with film, then sealed and marked against possible fraud. Investigators would then choose a specific target for him, usually a well-known landmark. In nine out of ten cases the finished product was startlingly accurate, though some photographs showed scenes quite unconnected with the target yet containing an uncanny link. For example, the thoughtographer once produced a whole series of pictures of a store front which he had never seen. Subsequent investigations tracked it down to Central City, Colorado, though the establishment's name in Serios' picture, The Old Gold Store, had long since been changed to The Old Wells Fargo Express Office. Extraordinarily, pictures which Serios subsequently thoughtographed of the same subject contained a sequence of letters which incorporated both names. On another occasion the same year the psychic thoughtographed part of a building which he did not recognise but which was later identified as a hangar belonging to the air division of the Royal Canadian Mounted Police. In this picture the word 'Canadian' was misspelled, though the same sign on the actual building was spelled correctly.

For those people who chose not to believe in the thoughtographer's amazing feats the easiest explanation was that Serios was cheating, producing pictures through sleight of hand rather than paranormal powers. In 1966, after Serios had appeared on television astonishing millions of viewers across America, a team of investigators from the magazine *Popular Photography* claimed to have achieved similar results using a tiny optical device which, when positioned with a microfilm photograph and held in front of the camera, produced a passable imitation of a Serios thoughtograph. However, even the sceptics were forced to admit that such a technique could only work when an ordinary source for the picture – a postcard, still photograph or book illustration – was already available. This was evidently not the case in most of Serios' thought-induced examples. Moreover, Serios had always been only too willing to allow himself to be searched before the beginning of each session and never once was it established that sleight of hand had been used.

Had Ted Serios been able to continue his strange career of thoughtography for very long there can be little doubt that his psychic achievements would eventually have come to stand as a definitive testimony of the unexplained powers of the human mind. Unfortunately, however, his growing fame proved to be no compensation for his lack of freedom and he consumed ever-growing amounts of alcohol. Throughout 1967 Serios' behaviour grew ever more erratic and domineering and he verbally attacked anyone who doubted his unique abilities. Even Dr Jule Eisenbud, who had become a personal friend, wasn't able to control his wayward subject and the thoughtography experiments were regularly interrupted by Serios' infuriating habit of going absent without leave. Parascience was the real loser, because as the psychic's consumption of alcohol increased, so his powers of thoughtography diminished. All Ted Serios can produce today is a snapshot of his own face and his last successful print, made over twenty years ago, was entirely appropriate: it shows a pair of drawn curtains.

1966

UFOs and Power Failures

One of the most frequently reported effects of low-flying UFOs is their regular coincidence with electrical malfunctions on the ground. In the vicinity of hovering alien craft motor vehicles are prone to cut out and street lighting is regularly extinguished; sometimes whole blocks can be blacked out.

The year 1966 saw one of the most significant cases when, during the spring, an underground USAF command control centre at an intercontinental ballistic missile base in Great Falls, Montana found itself subject to an entire loss of electrical power immediately after personnel above ground reported seeing three UFOs land near the perimeter of the base. Missile crews housed in the base control centre looked at each other in amazement when their instrument panels indicated a fault affecting ten missiles simultaneously. In fact the guidance and control systems had suffered a total loss of power. This meant that in effect the missiles were unlaunchable and that a major part of the United States nuclear arsenal was being temporarily rendered impotent by alien interference. Only after the UFOs departed did the situation at the Montana launch base return to normal.

Naturally enough, the Pentagon was reluctant to make public such a disconcerting event and ordered their men never to speak of the incident. Only with the release of previous classified documents under the provisions of the American Freedom of Information Act has the whole 1966 incident at Great Falls now become known. Declassification of other documents would seem to indicate that the above-related story was simply the first in a string of similar incursions by alien vehicles over strategic air command bases during the 1960s, including several others housing land-based strategic nuclear missiles in the mid-west. For instance, it seems that a near identical incident probably occurred during the week of 20 March 1967, when a radar at Maelstrom AFB, Montana confirmed the presence of a UFO hovering close by at the same time as the base's entire missile systems became inoperative.

More recently still, a number of low-level intrusions by unidentified flying objects close to the nuclear weapon storage areas at Kirkland AFB, New Mexico in the summer of 1980, coincided with both radar jammings and blackouts rendering scanner radar inoperative.

According to a leaked Air Force office of special investigation memorandum, sophisticated radio-frequency monitors determined by vector analysis that the jamming interference was being sent from an area around the Manzano weapon storage area close to Coyote Canyon. At this precise time on 13 August 1980 three USAF security policemen on duty within the weapon storage area reported seeing an unidentified light travelling over Coyote Canyon before descending to earth. Security guards approached the landing craft, which they described as a metallic disc. However, before they could reach it the vehicle took off in a vertical direction and at a tremendous speed.

Worrying though these incursions must have been to the

United States armed services, the Pentagon's top brass might have taken comfort in the fact that their own mainland defences had not been especially persecuted by the presence of alien forces. In the small hours of 1 July 1977 the giant NATO base at Aviano in north-eastern Italy was buzzed by a peculiarly large bright light which eventually came to rest in mid-air, hovering some 100 metres above the camp. Witnessed by many military personnel, it was described afterwards as resembling a spinning top revolving on its axis, with a domed upper section. Changing colours alternately, white, green and red, the object remained over the base for roughly one hour, during which time there was a massive power blackout over a radius of roughly 5 miles.

On 12 September 1979 it was the turn of a Chinese military base situated between Xuginglong and Huaihua in the Hunan Province to suffer a power loss. The bright disc appeared overhead and emitted a vertical stream of white rays for less than sixty seconds, but it was only after a further period of fifteen minutes that the base and a large surrounding area of civilian habitation regained their normal electrical supply.

1 June 1982 saw the appearance of two similarly shaped UFOs hovering above a cosmodrome at Baikonur in the Soviet Union. In this incident not only was the establishment's entire power supply cut off but severe damage was meted out to the mechanical fabric of the base. Engineers investigating the scene the following day found that rocket-support towers had been buckled and welded sections of gantries attached to rocket fuselages had come apart altogether, while in a nearby housing complex thousands of panes of glass had been shattered, causing laceration injuries to a number of residents. As a consequence of this encounter it would appear that the entire Soviet cosmodrome was put out of action for two weeks.

With the growing evidence that UFOs have the ability to either drain off or knock out electrical power supplies through some unknown means (whether deliberately or by accident is still not clear), many ufologists, including some of the more eminent former representatives of government agencies, have speculated that widespread power failures elsewhere might have been caused in a similar fashion. During congressional hearings before the House Committee on Science and Astronautics in July 1968, Dr James MacDonald, an atmospheric physicist with an established track record of involvement with NASA, voiced his own personal hunch that the great north-east American blackout of 9 November 1965 might have been linked to the extraordinarily high number of reports of UFOs which came in from all over New England in the midst of the power failure. In MacDonald's opinion the disturbing series of coincidences 'warrant much more attention than they have so far received'.

The year 1965 was a bumper one for UFO sightings across north America. In Britain, 1981 was a comparable year. It may or may not be coincidence, then, that 5 August 1981 saw the largest UK power failure for over twenty years, causing chaos in much of southern England and Wales. In an unprecedented occurrence two power lines failed within minutes of each other in separate and – officially – unrelated incidents. Electrical engineers from the English Central Electricity Generating Board were baffled and an official spokesman was forced to admit to the British people the following day at a press conference that the CEGB had never known anything like it before. In their representative's own words, the chances of two power lines failing in such a short period of time was 'impossible'. Moreover, even after the event the company had no idea what had caused the failure. Since their grid was working well below capacity, with many factories closed for the summer holiday and domestic consumption well below average owing to the warm weather and light evenings, a surge in demand could not have overloaded the system. Nevertheless, something had interfered with the electricity supply and as a result people living in the home counties of Kent, Surrey, Berkshire, Hampshire, parts of Gloucestershire, the whole of the West Country and most of south Wales were left without power for over two hours. While it cannot be stated with absolute certainty that UFOs were directly responsible for the blackouts, it is significant to recall that the majority of sightings reported in the seven days prior to 5 August came from the very same areas which were affected and that the previous night of 4 August had seen the coincidence of several UFO reports in Holland, where two power lines had failed simultaneously, plunging a large part of that country into unexpected darkness as well.

Although we still do not know why or how UFOs affect main electricity supplies the causal link is now established beyond reasonable doubt. This fact is significant because it virtually proves the objective reality of the phenomenon. Mass hysteria, hoaxes or hallucinations could hardly be held responsible for the power blackouts.

1967

A Gruesome Harvest

On 9 September 1967 the UFO situation in America took an unexpected and somewhat gruesome turn. A rancher living near Alamosa in the San Luis Valley of southern Colorado was horrified one morning to find his favourite three-year-old colt, Lady, in a frightful condition. Not only had the animal been killed but its entire head was stripped clean of all flesh and muscle, and its brains, organs and spine were missing. Incredibly, there was little sign of blood at the scene and no footprints or fresh tyre tracks were evident in the general vicinity. What *was* found, however, was far more disturbing. Fifteen circular exhaust marks seemed to have been blasted into the earth close to Lady's corpse together with a 3-foot circle of six holes in the ground, each roughly 4 inches across and 4 inches deep. When called to investigate, the forest service ranger had the wit to check the area with a Geiger counter and recorded indisputable evidence of radiation, both around the exhaust marks and upon the mutilated horse's carcass.

Although the death of one animal was hardly of earth-shattering importance the bizarre nature of its demise made headline news and the authorities quickly moved to investigate the affair. Ten days after the discovery Lady's remains were examined by Dr John Altshuler, assistant clinical professor of medicine and pathology at the University of Colorado Health Science Centre. Altshuler was profoundly shocked by the injuries, not because of their viciousness, but because they appeared to have been made in a way which he could not possibly explain. All cuts upon the beast's body had been made with clean incisions and there was a patch of darkened colour suggesting that the flesh had been opened and cauterised by some form of expert surgical heat beam technique. (Although such surgical laser technology now exists, there was nothing of the kind available in 1967). Most disturbing of all to Altshuler, however, was the inexplicable absence of blood. As he was later to write, 'Whoever did the cutting managed to remove the horse's heart, lungs and thyroid, leaving its entire mediasternum completely dry.' How this could have been achieved was beyond the pathologist's imagination.

Although the Alamosa case was the first to attract nationwide media attention in the USA, much evidence has now emerged to suggest that Lady's death had been preceded by a substantial number of earlier American mutilation cases. What is beyond all doubt is that several thousand comparable examples have been reported since. About ninety per cent of these instances involve cattle, yet horses, sheep, goats and other animals, including some domestic species – most notably dogs – have been found inexplicably mutilated. In the majority of cases sex organs have been removed from the animals, usually extracted with immaculate precision, leaving no sign of blood. Although there have been a number of non-alien explanations for these outrages, including the activities of predators and ritual sacrifices of satanic cults, a UFO link is now virtually beyond dispute.

In February 1968 officers from Project Blue Book, the

USAF's own UFO information-gathering body, investigated the claims of a farmer who lived about 30 miles north of Kansas City, Missouri. The man, who is unnamed in the Project Blue Book files, apparently saw an illuminated object which he estimated to be at least 100 feet in diameter, hovering about 20 to 25 feet off the ground. The appearance of the object, which took place at approximately 3.20 am, was followed by the discovery the next morning of the inexplicable loss of a number of the farmer's herd.

Seven years later, in early 1975, a Coryell County deputy sheriff investigated the mutilation of a calf near Copperas Cove, Texas following a spate of UFO reports over the area. Law officers discovered that sex organs had been removed bloodlessly from a number of cows and that in all cases peculiar markings were found near the carcasses, consisting of concentric circles pressed deep into the hard ground.

The following year Gabriel Valdez of the New Mexico State Police noticed similar ground traces on land at the ranch owned by Manuel Gomez near Dulce, New Mexico. In this case the mutilation involved a three-year-old black white-faced cow which had had its left ear, tongue, udders and rectum removed by what appeared to be a sharp, precise instrument. Anomalous markings found near the animal included several triangular-shaped tripod tracks and a round area of scorched grass close to where the animal's carcass lay. Tests confirmed that radiation levels around the area were more than twice the normal background reading. Another bizarre mutilation which took place at the same ranch two years later involved the discovery of a dead Hereford Charolais bull on 24 April 1978. An analysis of this incident suggested that the animal's rectum and sex organs had been removed by sharp, precise instruments and that the animal's cause of death was almost certainly the application of an extremely high dose of radiation.

Understandably, farmers across America grew increasingly angry at these attacks upon their livestock. But they are helpless and during the course of the past twenty-five years the phenomenon has grown more and more widespread, recent examples being reported from the states of Nebraska, Arkansas, Montana, Wyoming, Idaho and New Mexico.

It is now perfectly evident to all but the most die-hard sceptic of UFOs that alien visitors are engaged on a programme of genetic experimentation with certain mammalian species on earth. Precisely why is much less clear.

1968

Submarines That Failed to Surface

During the first half of this century submarine travel was a decidedly risky business. Prior to the outbreak of hostilities in 1939 submarine vessels had been lost through accident or malfunction in every year since their invention, and even leaving aside those known to have been sunk by enemy action, over a hundred more vessels went missing during the Second World War. During the last fifty years, however, submersible technology has improved greatly and as a result only two dozen vessels have been lost in the years since 1945. That is the good news. The bad news is that several of these more recent submarine disasters seem to have come about through the involvement of forces beyond the understanding of mankind – alien forces lurking beneath the ocean's surface.

The year 1968 provides us with three of the clearest possible examples. Launched in December 1959, the *USS Scorpion* was a 3,000-ton submersible leviathan powered by a water-cooled nuclear reactor. A source of pride to the US Navy, the ship functioned flawlessly on her naval exercises and was reckoned to be one of the most reliable of all the Navy's underwater vessels. In February 1967, after eight years' service, the *Scorpion* was refitted in a Norfolk naval shipyard and afterwards successfully completed a number of post-overhaul sea trials before joining the US Mediterranean fleet in March 1968.

She remained on active duty until May, when together with her crew of ninety-nine, she set out on a return journey to Norfolk. The trip should have been routine, but when on 25 May, while passing a position 250 miles west of the Azores, the *Scorpion* transmitted a standard progress signal, it turned out to be the last contact she ever made. During the following days all efforts to establish radio contact with the sub provoked no response.

At first it was assumed that a technical hitch rather than a disaster might be to blame, but when at length the *Scorpion* failed to show up at Norfolk she was reported overdue and an intensive search began. Hopes faded in the weeks that followed when no trace of her was found. She was officially declared lost with all hands in late June.

Following the official announcement of the ship's loss, speculation among the American press focused upon rumours that the US Navy possessed tapes which contained unreleased verbal messages from the *Scorpion*, communications to the effect that, shortly prior to its disappearance, the sub had been chasing an anomalous target which was travelling at a speed well beyond the capacity of any terrestrial ship.

The Navy refused to comment on the rumours while at the same time attempting to scotch talk of a Russian involvement in the tragedy. When in August 1966 the search ship *Mizar* claimed to have photographed and positively identified the *Scorpion*'s crashed hull lying on the sea bed at a depth of 10,000 feet at a position 400 miles west of the Azores, the Navy refused to comment on the claim or to confirm or deny that they had previously discovered the ship's last resting-place. Press speculation was further fuelled when at the subsequent court of enquiry several sections of the Navy's findings were labelled classified and never released, clearly indicating that public debate over the matter was not welcomed by the Pentagon. At the end of the hearings no firm conclusions were reached as to the reason for the ship's untimely demise, though the Navy itself let it be known that it was content to conclude that a combination of human error and mechanical malfunction was probably responsible for the tragedy. Any suggestion of alien interference and the anomalous sonar trace that had been purportedly recorded in a final message from the submarine was quashed.

Had the last voyage of the *USS Scorpion* been the only peculiar story to emerge from the year 1968 it might still be worthy of inclusion in any book about the century's great mysteries. But in fact the American vessel had become the third sub to disappear in almost identical circumstances – the other two had been lost within the space of 48 hours earlier the same year.

On the afternoon of 26 January 1968 the Israeli submarine *Dakkar*, manned by a crew of sixty-five, radioed her home base and destination at Haifa to report that she was on schedule for a safe and prompt arrival. The vessel had successfully undergone a complete rebuilding and modification operation at the English port of Portsmouth and was returning to Israel via the Mediterranean. In the event the *Dakkar* never arrived and that message proved to be her last contact. A search involving thirty ships and dozens of aircraft from five nations found nothing and an Israeli naval court of enquiry failed to reach any conclusion as to the reasons for the ship's loss. Yet at roughly midnight on the night of 26 January a Greek Cypriot fishing vessel working some forty miles north-east of the *Dakkar*'s last reported position claimed to have seen a large, glowing, oval object gliding silently underwater off their starboard bow. Certain that this was no normal submarine or some enormous marine creature, the fishermen became firmly convinced that the vision they had seen was in some way connected with the loss of the Israeli sub, whose fate they only learned about later.

The disappearance of the *Dakkar* with all hands was just the first half of a remarkable double tragedy which – unless one accepts the probability of alien interference – makes little sense even today. For at almost precisely the same time, elsewhere in the Mediterranean, 1,000 miles to the west, the French submarine *Minerva* was about to disappear while taking part in a combat exercise.

The vessel was just 40 feet below the surface when at 8 am on 27 January she radioed a French Air Force plane circling overhead to say that she was going down deeper to check out a strange sonar trace which had appeared to be following her for some minutes. From the 190-foot Daphne-class French submersible no more was heard. Along with her crew of fifty-nine she was listed as missing, presumed sunk in water with a depth of 8,000 feet. Of the peculiar sonar trace which she was investigating little more was said.

The loss of two submarines without apparent cause in the space of less than forty-eight hours stretches the possibility of coincidence beyond its limits. That there might be a causal link between the two disasters and the sinking of the *USS Scorpion* crossed the minds of many of those in the nautical fraternity. Given the circumstantial evidence, the idea of a link was perfectly logical – the only problem was that the connection appeared to involve something extremely unsettling: interference by unknown forces; forces which, officially at least, the world's governments and military organisations still choose not to recognise.

1969

Phone Calls from the Dead

The idea that ghosts can and sometimes do make telephone calls seems on the face of it to be just about the silliest thing you are ever likely to hear. Yet unless an awful lot of people are telling lies, or are having the most extraordinary tricks played upon them, this bizarre possibility must be taken seriously.

In 1969 the rock musician Karl Uphoff received just such a phantom call from his grandmother, who had passed away two days earlier. Uphoff was eighteen years old at the time of his grandmother's death and throughout his childhood there had always been a special bond between them. When during the boy's teenage years his grandmother grew very deaf, she developed the habit of calling him at his friends' homes, dialling each number one by one and repeating the same phrase loudly: 'Is Karl there? Tell him to come home now.' Eccentrically, she would repeat the message a few times without waiting for a reply (which in any case she could not hear), and proceed to the next number on her list. At first, perturbed by this abrupt behaviour, the parents of Karl's friends would sometimes remonstrate with him, but when the situation was explained they tended to treat the whole thing as a joke.

Though they had remained close until the end of her life Karl Uphoff never imagined that his grandmother would seek to contact him after her death. The youth himself had no special interest in spiritualism, nor had any member of his family ever attended a seance. Nevertheless, it seems clear that the dead woman was determined to make her personal survival of death known to her favourite grandson and chose as her channel the standard telecommunication network rather than a clairvoyant. Just two days after his relative's death Karl decided to pay an impromptu visit to the home of a friend named Peter D'Alessio who lived with his parents in Montclair, New Jersey. It was late in the afternoon and the boys were talking in the basement when the phone rang upstairs. Both could hear Mrs D'Alessio's voice becoming somewhat impatient. Moments later she shouted down the stairs for Karl to come up. 'There's an old woman on the phone,' she yelled, 'she says she's your grandmother and needs you. She keeps saying it over and over. Can you speak to her? I can't seem to make her understand.' Trembling with the conflicting emotions of fear and excitement, Karl Uphoff dashed upstairs to grab the receiver but by the time he reached the phone the caller had gone.

Later that night, having returned home, Karl received a whole series of phone calls. On each occasion the call was cut off the moment he picked up the receiver. Though neither his parents nor the D'Alessio family could come to believe that the dead woman had really made contact through such a mundane medium as a conventional telephone, Uphoff himself remained certain in his own mind that the calls were not a hoax.

Were the future rock musician's story an isolated one then it would be extremely hard to take it seriously. Yet the twentieth century has seen too many similar examples for the ideas of phantom phone calls to be dismissed as figments of a bereaved person's imagination. During the year 1971, for example, two sisters named MacConnell from Tucson, Arizona spoke for over thirty minutes to an old friend, Mrs Enid Johnson, several hours after she had died in the Handmaker Jewish Nursing Home in New York. It was only later that the two women realised they had been talking to somebody who had passed away. Six years later, in 1977, a girl named Mary Meredith got a call to her Oklahoma home from her cousin Shirley who was living in Kentucky. This event was in itself unsurprising since the two often communicated by phone. The difference on this occasion was that Mary Meredith had only minutes before opened a letter describing her cousin's sudden and unexpected death.

Yet another example of a ghost demonstrating its survival via the medium of a telephone was the curious case of Christopher Evans. In October 1987, Evans was killed instantly when a pilotless jet plane crashed into the Ramada Inn Hotel in Indianapolis, Indiana where he was working as a receptionist on the front desk. Residents all over the city were quickly alerted to the disaster, both by the sound of the crash and by the heavy pall of smoke which rose above the skyline. When Evans' parents heard a newsflash on the local radio station indicating that it was the Ramada Inn Hotel that had been hit, they naturally feared for their son's safety. Almost immediately these fears were allayed when the phone rang and they heard Christopher's familiar voice on the other end telling them not to worry. But when their son did not return home the Evans' concern grew once more and sure enough, as they reached the hotel, now a scene of total devastation, they found Christopher's body laid out and covered with a white sheet. He had been discovered crushed and burned almost beyond recognition, and rescuers confirmed that he had almost certainly been killed instantly, buried under the flaming debris at the moment of the plane's impact.

There was no feasible way that Christopher Evans could have made the phone call and stated the message so clearly heard by his parents. Was he all right? Perhaps, but not in his earthly body.

1970

Sasquatch Sightings in Washington

In the late afternoon of 19 August 1970 Mrs Louise Baxter of Skamania, Washington, was driving in the vicinity of the Beacon Rock trailer park when her car suffered a flat tyre. Mrs Baxter had just finished changing the wheel when, and without quite knowing why, she was suddenly overcome with a peculiar sensation of being watched. Her hunch was correct, though her observer was rather different from what she had anticipated. Looking towards the wooded area beside the road she was dumbfounded to see the massive face of a coconut-brown, shaggy, dirty-looking creature with a row of large square, white teeth and big, wide ape-like nostrils. As one might expect the woman screamed in terror, jumped in the car and drove off in a flustered panic. She looked back in her rear-view mirror just once to see that the creature had moved into the road and was standing erect at a full height which she estimated afterwards to be about 10 feet. 'It was quite simply enormous,' she later recalled. 'A huge great ape-like thing. Definitely a bigfoot.'

Frightening though it must have been for Mrs Baxter, the encounter she described was not particularly unusual for residents of Washington. For throughout this century and before there have been countless reports of a creature which seems to be the world's most elusive primate, the so-called bigfoot or sasquatch, a man-beast which is believed by many cryptozoologists to inhabit the dense forests of the Pacific north-west. These huge hairy ape-like figures, standing far taller than a man and weighing well over 400 pounds, may, like the abominable snowman of the Himalayas, be a throwback to prehistoric times. Or they may be something very different. Ghosts perhaps, or alien creatures. Orthodox anthropologists tend to dismiss the sightings as the product of urban folklore, yet their regular appearances during modern times in various locations in more than a dozen states across north America and Canada makes it hard not to believe that such throwback creatures really may have survived in the great, remote forest regions which are their habitat.

Compelling evidence is to be found in the numerous footprints that have been discovered, photographed and cast in plaster during the past century. Though some of these alleged bigfoot spoors are undoubtedly the work of hoaxers, fraud cannot be held up as a general interpretation for all the anomalous tracks. For one thing, trails of over 3,000 footprints have now been found, sometimes covering distances of several miles and appearing in the most remote spots. That anyone should have taken the trouble to engage in the time-consuming exercise of falsely creating such trails is beyond belief.

During the past two decades sasquatch footprints have been subjected to careful examination in several of America's most famous state universities as well as laboratories in Canada. It has been found that typical adult prints tend to be up to 16 inches long by 7 inches wide, and reflect absence of a notable foot arch. Meanwhile, the distinct double ball common to all these finds indicates an evolutionary adaptation designed to take considerable weight. Correspondingly, the depth of foot impressions suggests a bipedal animal with the bulk of over 300 pounds and in some cases very much more. The lack of marks which show the likely presence of claws rules out the possibility that bigfoot prints are made by bears, while other anatomical details (such as evidence of dermal ridges on the soles of the feet along with sweat pores and wear patterns) would be almost impossible to duplicate artificially, once again lessening the likelihood of hoax.

For decades bigfoot encounters like the one described by Mrs Baxter were treated with incredulity by the majority of American zoologists, despite the supporting evidence of tracks. Yet the derision of the sceptics was jolted somewhat in 1967 when a hunter named Roger Patterson took a brief but apparently conclusive film of a fully grown female bigfoot ambling along by a shallow river bed at Bluff Creek, northern California. The position of fallen logs in the film's foreground made it easy to accurately estimate the creature's height and physical dimensions. Careful analysis of the film undertaken by experts in biophysical departments at universities in London, New York and Moscow suggested that the creature captured on film was about 6 foot 5 inches high, with shoulder and hip widths well beyond the human range and a stride above 1 metre – too long for a man. Although it was not beyond the realms of possibility that the creature in the footage might in reality be a tall, heavily set man wearing padding and a monkey suit, the experts readily accepted that a human hoaxer would have found it extremely difficult to imitate the free-striding, arm-swinging movements seen in the film had he been so encumbered. Indeed, according to three senior Russian scientists who examined the film in Moscow, the gait of the creature showed 'the natural movement without signs of encumbrance one would expect in an imitation'. Distinctive features of its appearance – its flat face, receding forehead and prominent brow ridge, virtual absence of neck and a walk with slightly bent legs – all suggested that the closest known relative to the north American sasquatch was the pithecanthropus erectus, an ape-like creature thought to have become extinct several million years before.

Whatever else the thing captured on film near Bluff Creek might be it clearly does not show an animal shaped remotely like a bear. This is an important element in its favour, for it tends to weaken the most commonly voiced objection of sceptics: namely that percipients to bigfoot sightings are actually misidentifying one of the more common natural species of north America – grizzlies. In reality this explanation for the regular sasquatch sightings is nothing more than an insult to the eyesight and the intelligence of the average American witness.

As the twentieth century draws to a close those who believe in the existence of America's very own native wild man of the woods point to the growing evidence and ever increasing number of sightings in states as far apart as Florida, Tennessee, Michigan, Alabama, North Carolina, Iowa, Washington and the huge expanse of the great north-west where the legend of the sasquatch originated among the Indians. Sceptics point out (not unreasonably) that since no bones, skin or bodies have been found the evidence remains very thin.

Without question the jury is still out on this particular mystery, but given the fact that bigfoot reports now number many thousands and that genuinely odd footprints have been found in equally prodigious numbers, I for one am content to believe that a giant bipedal primate really does inhabit the forests of the Pacific north-west.

1971

The Belmez Faces

In a famous interview given to the *Scientific American* in 1920, inventor Thomas Alva Edison set out the logical argument for believing that contact with the dead was possible in the following terms: 'If our personality survives, then it is strictly logical and scientific to assume that it retains memory, intellect and other faculties and knowledge . . . therefore, if personality exists after what we call death, it is reasonable to conclude that those who leave this earth and survive would like to communicate the fact with those they left here.'

One of the foremost scientific geniuses of the modern era, Edison never achieved his ambition to create a mechanism subtle enough to capture the vibrations of the spirit realms, yet he was surely right in his assumption that the dead wish to show that they remain alive. Over the past century they have chosen a variety of ways to do so, mostly on a mental level through mediumship and spectral incursions, but on other occasions through a direct imprint on the physical world. These latter examples are among the most startling.

On a warm, sunny morning in August 1971 Señora Maria Gomez Pereira, a resident of Belmez de la Morelada, a village near Cordoba in southern Spain, awoke to find that a peculiar portrait of a human face had appeared overnight on the tiles of her kitchen floor. Although the sight of the face did not particularly frighten her, Señora Pereira became alarmed when sightseers arrived in large numbers to view the manifestation. So she decided to get rid of it. After scrubbing with detergent failed to remove the image she told her son Miguel to break up the floor with a pick-axe and lay a new surface. The renovation was duly carried out but the Pereiras' lives had only just returned to normal when new and even more clearly defined faces began to spontaneously appear in the fresh cement. Among these was that of a middle-aged man whose identity was recognised by elderly residents of Belmez as being that of a villager who had died many years before. They were certain that his body had been laid to rest in a long since disused cemetery upon which Señora Pereira's home now stood.

Inevitably, the Belmez phenomenon drew the interest of the parascientific community. One expert, German de Argumosa, analysed the concrete and confirmed the absence of any known pigment or dyeing agent; only a paranormal explanation seemed possible, he concluded. In November 1971 the visages were carefully cut from the floor and mounted behind glass. Following their removal the floor was excavated and several metres down some human bones were found, reinforcing the probability that the house had been built on the site of a graveyard. Moreover, old photographs appeared to lend credence to the views of local people that it was the faces of those buried in the graveyard which were now imprinted on the Pereiras' kitchen floor. From that moment on, no one in Belmez doubted the existence of the hereafter.

When anomalous images of human faces suddenly reveal themselves in unexpected places it is hardly surprising that they are held to be miraculous or evidential of the spirit's survival of death. The year 1897 saw the death in Wales of

John Vaughan, dean of Llandaff Cathedral. Two weeks after Vaughan's body was laid to rest a damp spot on the west wall of the cathedral where his funeral service had taken place formed itself into a likeness of the man's face and his initials J.V. could be clearly seen below.

According to contemporary records, the Welsh oddity remained evident for only a few days but a much longer-lasting phenomenon appeared in Christchurch Cathedral, Oxford, England, just over two decades later. It was in the summer of 1923 that the distinct profile of a well-known Victorian Oxford cleric, Dean Henry Liddell, became visible on the white plaster wall next to a tablet that had been erected to his memory following his death in 1898. According to one man who knew him the portrait showed a 'faithful and unmistakable likeness' which was just as 'it might have been drawn by the hand of a master artist'. By 1926 an investigator apparently discovered other faces near to that of the late dean and was informed that several others had appeared over the previous century in various parts of the building. Why Christchurch Cathedral should be especially blessed with the capacity to create such imprinted visages is unclear, yet relatives of the dean seemed to connect the appearance of his portrait with a family marriage which had only just previously taken place in the cathedral, thereby ending a long-lasting rift within the Liddell clan.

Whatever caused the Oxford manifestation it proved to be a much more permanent feature than the earlier image of the Welsh dean. In 1931 Dean Liddell's face was still 'beautifully clear', according to Mrs Hewat McKenzie, president of the British Society for Psychical Research. It was still there the following year when a new altar was built across the wall, completely concealing it. Whether the portrait remains today no one can say.

1972

The Airmen Who Refused to Die

When an individual witness claims to see a ghost it is possible that he or she may be hallucinating. When the same ghost is seen by several witnesses the chance of this possibility is greatly reduced. When dozens of witnesses see the same ghost it disappears altogether.

On the night of 29 December 1972 an L-1011 Eastern Airlines Tristar jet liner bound for Miami plunged into the swamps of the Florida Everglades, killing 101 passengers and crew. Two weeks earlier, a stewardess who regularly worked on the New York to Miami shuttle route had told colleagues how, during her leave period in late November, she had been awoken one night with a sudden visual impression of an L-1011 plane approaching Miami over the Everglades at night, before crashing into the black waters below. Throughout the vision – which lasted only a few seconds – she could clearly hear the screams of the injured and drowning passengers.

Naturally, the stewardess was extremely upset and came to feel that very soon a flight along the shuttle route would turn out to be her last. Indeed, when telling companions of her nightmare she claimed to be certain that the horrible event would take place close to New Year – only one month away.

Although flight crews tend to become used to the daily hazards of flying there remains the vague fear at the back of their minds that something will one day go wrong. Knowing this, cabin staff tended to attribute their colleague's reaction to nervous fatigue rather than a genuine prevision. Together they counselled her, pointing out that whilst some dreams might come true, the vast majority do not. And so the doomwatcher, whose identity has never been released from the American Society for Psychical Research files, returned to her normal role, desperately hoping that nothing would happen. Several trips passed without incident until, on 29 December, when the stewardess was assigned to Flight 401, she suddenly felt a renewed sensation of doom. To her relief she was unexpectedly pulled off duty in a last-minute switch of personnel. And so, when the plane crashed that night in the Florida Everglades on its approach run to Miami, the one person who had foreseen the disaster was not among the victims.

If this were the only mystery surrounding the American airliner crash then it would still be worthy of inclusion in such a book as this. Yet extraordinarily, an even more bizarre series of events was to follow. During the spring of 1973 strange tales began to spread among Eastern Airlines air crews. According to these stories spectral figures wearing the unmistakable uniforms of flying officers would materialise inside the cockpits of Tristars operating the same route as the doomed aircraft. Executives of Eastern Airlines, fearing adverse publicity from these ghostly goings-on, instructed flight crews to keep their experiences to themselves, but rumours of the skyborne manifestations gradually spread despite the boardroom orders.

Eventually the press were alerted and the company's senior

officials had little choice but to take the phenomenon seriously. They started to interview employees who claimed to be eye-witnesses. Those who had seen the apparitions described them as wholly lifelike, three-dimensional, solid forms which never spoke but which sat stone-faced in the pilot's seat on the aircrafts' flight deck. In all cases the phantoms were identified as Captain Robert Loft and Flight Engineer Don Repo, two men who had lost their lives on Flight 401. The identifications were even confirmed by passengers who matched their own sightings with company photographs of the two men. Nothing could convince any of these witnesses that they were hallucinating. As far as they were concerned the ghosts were there no matter who called them liars.

Understandably enough, the attitude of those on the ground was somewhat different. It was hard enough to believe stories of ghosts haunting ancient castles and lonely graveyards: to accept that spectres could appear 6 miles high in the air-conditioned comfort of a modern aircraft's flight deck seemed beyond the realms of possibility. One person who did become convinced of the story's truth, however, was the journalist and writer John G. Fuller, whose investigation into the phenomenon was eventually published in a bestselling book entitled *The Ghosts of Flight 401*. Although perfectly aware that urban myths had a habit of growing into accepted fact, Fuller was intrigued by the consistency of the reported ghost sightings. They never shifted from Eastern Airlines or the L-1011 Tristar airliner so frequently used by the company. Researching the alleged manifestations further, Fuller then realised something which had escaped the notice of other investigators: the apparitions were not appearing exclusively on aircraft operating the same flightpath as the crashed plane; they were manifesting most frequently on those Tristars which had been serviced with spare parts salvaged from the wreckage of Flight 401. The writer concluded that some element of psychic energy had also been transferred – the lifeforce of two human beings.

Assisted by three Eastern Airlines pilots who were themselves spiritualists by faith and gifted mediums into the bargain, plus a federal aviation agency technical officer who had known both Loft and Repo in life, Fuller set up a seance designed to make contact with the dead duo. In his book he explains how the seance helped the two men, who were both atheists, to comprehend their death state and travel onwards towards the higher planes of existence, those other worlds to which spiritualists believe all humans are meant to ascend following physical death. According to Fuller's account the ghosts of Loft and Repo ceased to be seen aboard the Tristars as soon as they realised that there was a better place waiting for them.

For their part, Eastern Airlines ordered the removal and destruction of the elevators, radios, fans, seats, panels and other equipment that had been salvaged from the crashed plane. Company records show that after the last recycled part had been removed from their fleet of Tristars there were no reports of further manifestations.

1973

The Village that Lived in Fear

As we have already seen in our review of 1919 there have been plenty of occasions where concentrated hate allied to the application of magical ritual has acted as a lethal psychic spear. While few doctors will claim to believe in the power of spells or hexes many psychologists admit that the very fear of a curse may in itself bring about the physical deterioration which could lead to death. The chance of a person literally dying of fright is of course greatly increased in closed societies where belief in curses is widespread. If one inhabits the Australian outback, the voodoo-ridden island of Haiti, or lives among the wandering communities of gypsies across Europe and Asia, then one is much more likely to suffer the malign effect of a curse than, say, the average Westerner, who might treat the subject of maleficence with contempt. Undoubtedly this neat psychological theory has convinced many Western people that supernatural curses are a myth. But does it account for all examples?

Psychosomatic illnesses have been proved to exist and anyone who has studied the powers of certain gifted individuals should not doubt the ability of the human mind to control bodily processes to a remarkable degree. But the hypothesis falls down as an all-embracing explanation for the apparent success of curses. Some cursed individuals are firm disbelievers in the supernatural, yet die nonetheless. Others have fallen victim even though they have been unaware all along that they have become the subject of a curse. By far the most serious drawback of the psychological theory, however, is that not all curses kill their victim through illness. Where lives have been brought to an end by accident or other form of violent death, the 'fear of death' explanation cannot be held to have played a part.

Two particularly spectacular examples of this type of curse were made in a fit of rage by a couple of the century's less endearing black magicians. Britain's most notorious witch was Aleister Crowley, the so-called Great Beast who claimed to have sold his soul to the Devil at the age of fourteen. Reviled by popular newspapers in the 1920s and 1930s as the most evil man alive, Crowley was in reality a ludicrous figure whose pretended excesses were usually too incredible to be taken seriously. But even so Crowley did have some genuine powers, cursing several people with apparent success. One of his victims was a young general practitioner, William Brown Thompson, who had angered the ageing witch by refusing to prescribe him morphia to feed his addiction. In return Crowley laid a curse upon his physician, promising that he would take the doctor with him the day he died. Sure enough, when Aleister Crowley descended to hell on the first day of December 1947 Thompson suffered a fatal head injury.

Another twentieth-century satanist with the dark gift of prophecy was American Anton Le Vay. Le Vay, who was employed as a technical adviser on the film *Rosemary's Baby*, established in the mid-sixties a bizarre religious sect dedicated to the worship of the Antichrist. Soon after the group was set up the actress Jayne Mansfield became interested in the cult. To begin with Le Vay was delighted with the publicity Mansfield afforded him, but things soon turned sour. After they quarrelled violently, Le Vay cursed his star disciple, reportedly drawing a red line across the throat of her portrait. A fortnight later the actress was killed in an accident on a Los Angeles highway. When her body was cut from the wreckage she was found to have been decapitated.

Usually maleficence involves a one-to-one relationship between sender and receiver. Yet surely the strangest of all curse stories to emerge during recent years involved an entire community and the loathing of a nation. The evil spell which descended upon the Lincolnshire seal-hunting village of Fosdyke for a year-long period during 1973–74 accounted for the deaths of some fifteen people and would seem to have been activated by a form of collective hatred directed towards the inhabitants of the village rather than by one specific individual source.

The trigger for the curse was a television film made about the small community and broadcast on British television in April 1973. In the film, a documentary about seal-hunting, interviews with local men were interspersed with some particularly unpleasant shots of seals being battered to death. One Fosdyke villager, Len Lineham, described in graphic detail how, along with other local fishermen, he had caught and clubbed over 300 baby seals the previous year. The British are a nation of animal-lovers and predictably a storm of protest followed the screening of the programme. While thousands wrote to the television company to complain dozens more wrote poison-pen letters to individual members of the Fosdyke fishing community. Significantly, among these were several death threats and curses. Such was the sustained level of anger engendered by the documentary that the Lincolnshire villagers began to feel as if they had become the collective subject of a national hex. For sixty-year-old Len Lineham the pressure soon became unbearable. Nine days after the film was shown he shot himself in the head.

If the villagers of Fosdyke hoped that the curse would be lifted by Lineham's death they were very much mistaken. Instead his suicide was to be the beginning of a macabre series of events in the locality. Three weeks after Lineham took his life, his grandson was killed in a road accident and a day later his niece choked to death. Other deaths in the community followed within months. Two more men were killed in road crashes and a further seven expired in as many weeks from supposedly natural causes. Most mysterious of all was the drowning of thirty-year-old Colin Runnals, a Fosdyke seal-hunter whose body was found floating face-down in a shallow dyke. Runnels was known to be an excellent swimmer.

As an atmosphere of hysteria began to haunt the fenland village religious help was sought to lift the spell. Canon Henry Cooper, then chaplain to the Archbishop of Canterbury, visited Fosdyke to reassure the villagers that the powers of evil could not finally prevail against the greater power of God. Even so, further deaths continued to dog the hapless seal fishermen until the curse ran its full course precisely a year and one day after the television programme was shown. Today the residents of Fosdyke once more sleep easily in their beds. But none who lived through it will forget those terrible 366 days when they found themselves the focus of a nation's anger.

1974

A TV Prophet and Other Doomwatchers

For Mrs Lesley Brennan, an English housewife from Grimsby, Lincolnshire, 1 June 1974 began like any other normal Saturday. Having returned from her morning shopping she made herself a light lunch and settled down in front of the television to watch her favourite sport of wrestling. Instead of the normal programme, however, the screen contained pictures of fiery devastation, while the news reporter's voice described in graphic detail how a large chemical plant at Flixborough had exploded that morning, killing and injuring dozens of workers. Since Flixborough was only twenty miles away from her home town it was natural that Mrs Brennan should mention the disaster to two friends, Janice and Peter East, who visited her early that afternoon. Neither had seen the newsflash and they were understandably dismayed.

Mrs Brennan's friends stayed for tea, and together that evening all three watched the early-evening broadcast which contained once again the scenes of flaming horror; twenty-four people were dead and over a hundred buildings in the surrounding area had been damaged. All this Mrs Brennan and the Easts expected to hear. Yet to their astonishment the newsreader now said that the Flixborough disaster had occurred late that afternoon, several hours after Janice and Peter East were told of the tragedy by Mrs Brennan. A phone call to the television company confirmed that the series of explosions at the plant had begun at ten minutes to five and that no special midday bulletin had been screened.

The nature of the Englishwoman's foresight – through the medium of television – is highly unusual, since usually the gift of prevision manifests itself through dreams or waking visions. But its significance to the avid mysteriologist lies in the fact that she told other individuals of her premonition before the tragedy had actually taken place, thus ruling out the possibility that she was a hindsight prophet, making claims of foresight which she did not actually possess.

Undoubtedly some claimed premonitions are exactly this: stories based on the imaginings of those eager to be thought of as psychic. It should not be suggested, however, that the claims of many doomwatchers are simply lies. Most are genuinely unwilling observers of events beyond their understanding and control, horrified onlookers who not only see but actually share the pain, anguish and grief of the victim caught up in the visionary moments of disaster and mass destruction. Such disaster premonitions, whether they occur in a dream or waking state, are brief, spontaneous psychic glimpses which take place without warning and for no apparent reason.

For those who may have absolutely no connection with the real event itself they are almost always unwanted. The fear of ridicule is common among doomwatchers, and just as many people who see ghosts or UFOs decide to keep silent in case they are thought of as mad. So many witnesses to premonitions prefer to keep their experiences to themselves or else tell only those they completely trust.

There are, of course, exceptions to this rule. In 1979 David Booth of Cincinnati dreamed for seven consecutive nights that a DC-10 airliner had crashed at an American airport. Booth took his prevision so seriously that he pestered the various US airlines until at last he got someone to listen. He was interviewed by Paul Williams, an official of the Federal Aviation Association. Initially wary, Williams was impressed by the clarity of detail in Booth's mental impressions. He also became convinced of the man's integrity. However, since neither Williams nor his superiors could think of any practical way to avert the predicted outcome – short of grounding all American-based DC-10s – they simply did nothing and prayed that it would not happen.

Booth went away unsatisfied and continued to experience his nightmare. Three days after his conversation with Williams the vision was tragically fulfilled when a Pan-Am jet crashed in flames at Chicago Airport. In all there were 270 fatalities, making it the worst death toll in US aviation history. Seeing pictures of the stricken airliner, American Airlines Flight 191, David Booth knew for certain that it was the same one he had seen in his vision. Horrified though he was, his ordeal was over and his dream never returned.

Though most doomwatchers experience a prevision only once some have proved so prolific that they have even made a living out of it. Until he exploited his gift of predicting the future American hairdresser Joseph Delouise was like any other member of the public. But during the 1960s he proved on several occasions that his mind was a reliable psychic antenna for future tragedies. On 25 November 1967 Delouise appeared on television describing how he had dreamed of the collapse of a bridge. Three weeks later, on 16 December, the Silver Bridge across the Ohio River at Point Pleasant, West Virginia, collapsed due to undiscovered structural weaknesses. Forty-six people died. Less than two months later, on 8 January 1968, Delouise predicted that the spring would see major riots in his home city of Chicago. On 7 April the governor of Illinois was forced to order 5,000 federal troops to quell the civil disturbances which had engulfed the state capital. On 15 December of the same year Delouise predicted that during the following twelve months a major politician would be involved in an accident leading to a woman's death by drowning. On 18 July 1969 Mary-Jo Kopechne died after Senator Edward Kennedy's car fell from a bridge at Chappa-quiddick.

By far the most astonishing prediction of all was Delouise's claim on US television on 21 May 1969 that before the end of the year an aircraft tragedy would kill seventy-nine people and that the number 330 would in some way be involved. At 3.30 pm on 9 September, an Allegheny Airlines DC-9 collided with a private plane near Indianapolis. Seventy-eight passengers and crew aboard the airliner were instantly killed, and the demise of the light aircraft's pilot brought the total death toll for the accident to seventy-nine, just as Delouise had predicted four months earlier.

1975

Unlucky for Some?

Most people believe that mankind has been given free will and that we all start with a blank page the day we are born. Others, especially those who adhere to the concepts of fate and destiny, believe that our futures are mapped out for us in some hidden way and that our journey through life (and our meeting with eventual death) is predestined by some higher authority.

Strange synchronistic links which surround famous events like the assassinations of American Presidents Lincoln and Kennedy lend credence to the second possibility. Perhaps these occurrences are more widespread than we imagine: the many examples I have uncovered during my research seem to show that truly grim coincidences occur rather more frequently than is generally assumed and remain unnoticed simply because the individuals involved are less well known. Indeed, it would sometimes appear that fate enters our lives clothed in the form of a macabre cosmic joker intent on making sad fools of its human victims.

Several incidents which emerged in 1975 serve to prove the point. On 21 July 1975 an English local newspaper, the *Liverpool Echo*, described how two brothers from Merseyside had been killed in separate accidents a year apart. Entitled 'The Cruellest Twist of Fate', the article began by describing how the two men, both in their twenties, had been killed while riding mopeds in the same street; in each case the other vehicle involved in the fatal collision was the same taxi driven by the same driver and – most amazingly of all – whilst he was carrying the same fare-paying passenger en route to the same destination on each occasion. This last detail seemed especially strange since that particular passenger was not a regular cab-user and had not travelled along the road in between the two crashes. Finally, to complete the oddity, the *Echo* reported that both brothers had met their respective demises at approximately the same time of the day, and on precisely the same date, exactly twelve months apart.

Another strange story involving the deaths of two English brothers to emerge that year concerned John and Arthur Mowforth, who were twins. It is well known that sets of twins, particularly identical ones formed from the same egg, often share remarkable physical and psychological similarities. It has even been shown that twins can sometimes, if separated from birth, go on to lead lives which parallel each other in almost every important respect. Doctors and psychologists would frown, however, at the suggestion that twins are bound to become ill at the same time and I have never read of any medical specialist who believes that twins are bound to die at the same time as each other. Yet in the case of John and Arthur Mowforth, who both expired in the late evening of 22 May 1975 aged fifty-six years, this is exactly what happened.

At approximately seven o'clock in the evening John Mowforth began to complain of severe chest pains and was rushed to the local hospital near his home in Bristol. Meanwhile, some 80 miles away in Windsor, Arthur Mowforth, who was quite unaware of his brother's condition, suddenly collapsed without saying a word. Each man died in hospital that night within the space of a few minutes of each other, knowing nothing of the fate of the other.

Since both the examples described above involve the correlation of just two incidents it remains conceivable that the spectacular coincidences can be explained by the statistician's old standby, the law of probability. But where these sinister tapestries of doom run to a much greater length the likelihood that mere chance is responsible gradually fades. The film *The Omen*, which dealt with the coming of the AntiChrist, was also made in 1975. Although it went on to become a box-office blockbuster when it was released the following year, *The Omen*'s production was positively plagued by odd accidents, illnesses and death. The author of the original script, David Seltzer, narrowly escaped death when the passenger plane in which he was flying was struck by lightning. Meanwhile, on the same night, Gregory Peck, the film's star, suffered an identical experience on a separate flight. Director Dick Donner was knocked down and seriously hurt in an automobile accident on location, while chief special-effects man John Richardson was injured in another car accident in which his passenger was killed. In the worst incident of all, two stuntmen were badly savaged and a keeper killed when lions ran berserk during filming at a wildlife park. By the time the movie was completed the majority of the cast and crew were reportedly convinced that their string of misfortunes could be blamed on the film's subject matter. John Richardson, the special-effects expert who had narrowly survived a car crash, felt particularly certain, since his accident had taken place outside a small Dutch town called Ommen.

Evidence of an underlying force active beneath the everyday events of human existence? Or just plain bad luck? I leave the reader to make up his or her own mind.

1976

Pterodactyls Over Texas

The last dinosaurs were supposed to have died out 65,000,000 years ago, yet every so often a story will emerge from some far-flung corner of the globe which offers the tantalising possibility that some may have survived. The vast bulk of these sightings involve lake-monsters or sea-going reptiles. The Loch Ness monster, Ogopogo and Japan's famous Issie are thought to closely resemble the plesiosaur, a long-necked marine animal supposedly extinct for 70,000,000 years, while Champ, the monster which haunts Lake Champlain in Canada and the USA, has been tentatively 'identified' by cryptozoologists as a zooglodon, a snake-like primitive whale supposedly extinct for a mere 20,000,000 years. Since each of these creatures has been making regular appearances throughout the present century to (taken collectively) thousands of witnesses, one would need to be an extremely hardened sceptic to rule out the idea of dinosaur survival altogether.

The appearance of non-marine species is far less common and the survival of such creatures seems far-fetched to say the least. Mokole Mbembe, the brontosaurus-type creature which is reportedly a denizen of the Likouala Swamps in the People's

Republic of the Congo, is one of a number of central African legendary dinosaurs whose factual existence remains unproven. Hunted by Captain Freiherr von Stein du Lausnitz, who led an expedition to the Likouala district in 1913, and many decades later by an American team led by Dr Roy Mackal and James Powell, Mokole Mbembe has proven elusive, yet so vast is the thick jungle area of its natural habitat that the existence of an unknown creature there remains an even bet.

Easily the most controversial idea of all is that flying reptiles of the pterodactyl family may presently be living in north America. This theory seems so ridiculous that one supposes that any sane person would reject it out of hand. Yet so many have been the reports of such creatures and so compelling is the testimony of the witnesses that once again we are faced with a situation in which reality seems to have taken a step, quite literally, beyond the impossible.

During the first two months of 1976 something strange and hideous invaded the Rio Grande Valley. First to notice the oddity was Joe Suarez, a rancher who found several of his goats ripped to pieces in a corral behind his house in Raymondville. There were no footprints around the bodies and police who investigated the scene could not explain how the animals had been killed. What was more, the one clue they did have made no sense. On the night the attack had taken place Joe Suarez himself had been awoken by the eerie sound of flapping wings rising above his house. He was certain that whatever had made the noise was bigger than any local species of buzzard. Indeed, from the rancher's description police got the impression that the creature must have been of literally gigantic proportions. Understandably, the law officers considered the mystery of the dead goats to be enough for one day and simply reassured Mr Suarez that whatever had made the noise was unlikely to come back. But come back it did, and with a vengeance. Several days later, on

14 January, Armando Grimaldo was sitting smoking a cigarette in the backyard of his mother-in-law's house on the north side of Raymondville when a creature he described as looking like 'something out of hell' descended upon him. With a wing-spread of some 10 to 12 feet, a leathery, blackish-brown skin, a long-toothed beak and terrifying huge, red eyes the flying creature ripped and tore at Grimaldo with its claws, attempting to drag him into the air. When other people inside were alerted by Grimaldo's hysterical screeching they rushed outside just in time to see the creature fly off into the night. Badly lacerated and in a state of shock, the injured man was taken to the local Wallacey County Hospital.

Like so many people who encounter the inexplicable Armando Grimaldo and his family found themselves subject to hostility and derision from the majority of Texans, who simply disbelieved their story. But as the weeks went by more sightings were to follow. On 31 January something huge slammed into Alverico Guajardo's trailer in nearby Brownsville. When Mr Guajardo went outside to see what had happened he was confronted by a sight which he later described as being like something from another planet. A long-beaked creature with featherless bat-like wings was hopping forward towards him making a horrible, croaking noise in its throat. Guajardo fled back inside his trailer and watched through a window as the creature took off and disappeared into the darkness.

The following month saw no more sightings, until on 24 February three schoolteachers driving to work near San Antonio witnessed the slow flight overhead of a huge reptile with a 15- to 20-foot wing-span. Talking afterwards of their experience, one of the teachers, Patricia Bryant, told how she could see the skeleton of the creature through its skin-covered wings, which it seemed to be using to glide rather than flap in the usual way. The three teachers later studied some illustrations of dinosaurs in an encyclopaedia and recognised the creature they had seen as a pteranodon, a kind of flying lizard which had not existed for 150,000,000 years.

The schoolteachers were not the only Texans to see the creature on 24 February. Other motorists also made reports, saying that the dinosaur flew so low that when it swooped at the cars its shadow covered the entire road. Elsewhere rangers claimed to have seen a similar horror circling a herd of cattle in the distance. Yet enigmatically, just as the story was gaining credibility, the winged reptile scare of 1976 ended. The creature was not to be seen again until six years later when, on the afternoon of 14 September 1982, ambulance driver James Thompson had a close-up view of it as it flew over Highway 100 near Los Fresnon, close to the Texas–Mexico border. Describing the vision to reporters from the local newspaper, *Valley Morning Star*, Thompson said the animal had a hide covering of a rough greyish texture and was entirely without feathers. With a body some 10 feet long and a wing-span of 15 to 16 feet, it had a hump on the back of its head, almost no neck and a pouch near its throat. In the interview Thompson specifically referred to the creature as being pterodactyl-like.

Should such stories as these be taken seriously? The logical answer should of course be no, but then that goes not one inch towards explaining why they keep cropping up. Given the details contained in the descriptions made by James Thompson or Patricia Bryant, one can hardly blame these stories on the misidentifications of microlight aircraft or birds of a larger natural species. Nor is it easy to imagine why such people would make up something like this. Yet if flying dinosaurs really do exist in the north American continent why are they not seen far more frequently? The most infuriating aspect of this type of mystery is that, whichever way one approaches it, one is confronted by a fresh set of seemingly insurmountable contradictions.

In 1977, following the first wave of pterodactyl sightings over Texas, the International Society of Cryptozoology, an organisation that investigates reports of unknown or allegedly extinct animals, proclaimed its own belief that such creatures might have survived undiscovered in the higher reaches of Mexico's Sierra Madre Oriental, a mountainous area 200 miles east of the Rio Grande Valley and one of the least-explored regions of north America. Certainly huge creatures of the flying lizard type did once exist in what is now the Lone Star state. As recently as 1972 the skeletal remains of an enormous pterodactyl with a 50-foot wing-span were unearthed from rock in the Big Bend National Park. But even having proven that simple fact, it is a very much larger leap of faith to accept that these animals might have remained alive to the present day undetected apart from a couple of dozen sightings during the past twenty years.

Without doubt this is one enigma where the sceptics can fairly claim to hold the upper hand. And until the day comes when a flying lizard is either shot out of the sky or captured alive, I am sure things will remain that way.

1977

The Mysterious Morgawr

Living as they do on an island it is perhaps unsurprising that so many British people seem to report sightings of sea-monsters. Researcher Bernard Heuvelmans, who has recorded details of sea-serpent sightings trawled from articles in newspapers and magazines throughout the world, has discovered that two-thirds of those reported prior to 1900 come from British sources. During the twentieth century similar sightings have continued to come in from coastal waters off every shore around the British Isles. But while each region may have its own tales to tell, by far the greatest concentration come from the south-west peninsula of England, and more particularly from the country's most extreme county, Cornwall. For decades such tales were put down to the fanciful imaginings of local folk whose myths and legends of the sea had long been colourful. Yet during the last two decades persistent sightings of one particular creature known as Morgawr (a name derived from the ancient Cornish language, meaning 'sea-giant') have led some researchers to seriously consider the possibility of a strange creature inhabiting the waters off the English west coast.

The spate of Morgawr reports appears to have started in

September 1975, when two Falmouth women, Mrs Scott and Mrs Riley, watched a long-necked, hump-backed creature with stumpy horns and bristles down its back struggling with a large conger eel in its jaws at a location off Pendennis Point. But it was two years later, in 1977, that the sightings really took off. In January a dentist name Duncan Viner saw a long-necked creature which he estimated to have a total length of 40 feet swimming in the seas off Rosemullion Head. The same afternoon a similar creature was sighted by fishermen in the mouth of the Helford River. Four months later, in mid-May, two bankers from London who were fishing on rocks near Parsons Beach watched a similarly sized hump-backed animal surface in the sea at a distance about 100 yards away. According to the witnesses, it was visible for about ten seconds and looked straight at them before submerging. Then in June 1977 the head and neck of Morgawr startled the crew of a small inshore fishing boat in seas off the rocky expanse of Lizard Point, the extreme southern-most tip of the British mainland. One of the witnesses, George Vinnecombe, who had been fishing in Cornish waters for over forty years and was familiar with all the larger species of marine animal native to them, including whales, had no idea what it was. The leathery, black, shiny skin of its three-humped back, which he reckoned to be about 20 feet long, was clearly visible above the surface of the water, which led him to estimate that its bulky body must have weighed several tons. Yet the creature's head, when it rose 1 metre out of the water, was slim and held a head not unlike that of a seal's, though with proportionately larger eyes.

Encounters such as these, including detailed descriptions by experienced seamen, are far more convincing than the vague, inconsistent and often far-fetched tales of earlier decades. By mid-summer, with the talk on the Cornish quaysides all focusing on the same subject, and with dozens of new reports coming in every week from holidaymakers, the editor of the magazine *Cornish Life*, Dave Clarke, decided to undertake a personal investigation of the mystery. One of the more bizarre eye-witnesses he talked to was a local character named Anthony 'Doc' Sheils, a self-professed wizard, who claimed the ability to call up Morgawr from the depths through the casting of an ancient magic spell. Clarke, though highly sceptical of Sheils' claim, was sufficiently intrigued to accompany the self-styled wizard to Parsons Beach at the mouth of the Helford River, the scene of a recent sighting. There Sheils made several incantations and waved his arms about while the journalist took photographs. Throughout the ceremony nothing unusual appeared, yet just as they were about to leave both men noticed a small head sticking out of the water about 90 metres from the shore. Clarke at first thought it was a seal, yet as it swam closer he began to realise that the neck was much longer than he had first thought, reaching down to a body of considerable bulk which he estimated to be some 18 metres long. Both men took a number of photographs of the creature before it submerged, although in his excitement the newspaperman had managed to jam his wind-on mechanism. 'Doc' Sheils' Rolleiflex proved a more reliable model and several frames were subsequently blown up to reveal the distinct image of Morgawr's head and neck.

These were not the only photographs of the creature to appear during 1977. In the early autumn another local newspaper, the curiously named *Falmouth Packet*, carried excellent snaps of a sea-giant which had chased a local trawler in the Penryn River. The sighting – unfortunately for the witnesses, who earnestly wished to be believed – had taken place several months earlier on 1 April. But it seemed that something unusual *was* in the water, for a similarly humped animal was spotted by the crew of a tanker mooring a few miles away at Coast Lines Wharf the same day.

As the sightings accumulated natural explanations for the mystery were put forward, including floating tree trunks, floating mats of kelp, upturned boats, small whales, dolphins, low-flying formations of seabirds and giant jellyfish. The favourite, however, as in all similar cases, was that it was a hoax perpetrated by the unscrupulous and pounced upon avidly by the credulous. Yet the descriptions of Morgawr drawn from 1977 echo other interesting though rather more sporadic sightings made in Cornish waters in earlier times. In 1876, for example, a sea-serpent was actually caught alive in Gerrans Bay to the east of Falmouth and taken ashore for exhibition before being cast again into the sea. Fifty years later two fishermen trawling 3 miles south of Falmouth caught an equally extraordinary animal in their nets before it escaped, while in 1933 an unidentified carcass seems to have briefly appeared on Praa Sands in Mount's Bay. Since all the witnesses to these events saw the creatures at close range, either alive or dead, it is difficult not to reach the conclusion that something genuinely mysterious lives in Cornish coastal waters.

There have been at least two sightings of Morgawr during the 1980s. On 20 February 1980, an undergraduate from London named Geoff Watson sighted an object some way from the shore near Helford Passage and managed to take some still photographs using a telephoto lens. Watson, who it must be said was something of an enthusiast for monster mysteries, was convinced that he had seen an animate, long-humped creature, but when his films were processed his shots were found to be too indistinct to prove useful as evidence.

Five years later Morgawr was seen again, this time by Sheila Bird, a writer and local historian, together with her brother, scientist Eric Bird, who was on a visit from Australia at the time. The pair were relaxing on a clifftop west of

Porthscatho on 10 July 1985 when suddenly, in the water below quite close to the shore, a large grey creature with a distinctive long neck and huge hump broke through the waves. Estimating the creature's total length to be slightly over 20 feet both witnesses watched in awe as it slowly and gracefully paddled through the water in full view of them before submerging once again. For Sheila Bird, a writer on local matters who had long been sceptical of Morgawr stories, it proved to be a revolutionary experience. Never again did she doubt the ancient legends of the Cornish sea-giant.

1978

Nightmare in the Caucasus

For the greater part of the present century ball lightning has been a subject most scientists preferred to avoid. Since there was no conceivable way in which electro-magnetic energy could be confined within a spherical shape and move about unhindered, physicists rejected reports as unreliable. But now, since hundreds of reports have been made around the world during the past thirty years – including a good many by scientists themselves – it is no longer possible to deny the existence of this mysterious and sometimes frightening phenomenon. Usually seen as luminous spheres of roughly 15 inches in diameter, these high-energy balls of light can be coloured either yellow, red, bluish-white or green. They sometimes make a hissing or buzzing noise and upon their disappearance or explosion tend to leave behind the unmistakable smell of sulphur. Although in the popular imagination their occurrence is usually associated with thunderstorms, confusion over their origin is compounded by the fact they have been known to become manifest in periods of clear weather.

Most bizarre of all, however, and most troubling to the minds of traditional scientists, is the fact that these peculiar light forms have occasionally behaved in a way which suggests direction by some intelligence. According to paranormal investigator Vincent H. Gaddis, writing in his book *Mysterious Fires and Lights*, 'They display an independent will and curiosity, circling objects and human beings, entering and exploring houses . . . they exhibit either in an intelligence or controlled by intelligence . . . after brief visits they must return to their invisible natural habitat and so their temporary vehicles explode or fade away.' Gaddis is perfectly correct to describe lightning balls as probably having an independent will. What he failed to mention, however, was that their will is sometimes malevolent.

Of all twentieth-century sightings of ball lightning few could have been as frightening as a reported attack on a party of climbers which took place high up in the Soviet Union's Caucasus mountain range on the night of 17 August 1978. Having pitched camp at an altitude of 12,000 feet the five-man team was awoken by the sudden appearance of a glowing object in their tent. One of their number, Victor Kavunenko, described the ordeal which followed: 'I woke up with the feeling that a stranger had made his way into our tent. Looking up, I saw a bright yellow blob disappear inside Oleg Korovin's sleeping bag. He screamed in pain. The ball jumped out and proceeded to circle over the other bags, now hiding in one, now in another. When it burned a hole in mine I felt an unbearable pain, as if I were being burned by a welding machine, and blacked out.' Moments later, when Kavunenko regained consciousness, the blob was still in the tent, proceeding to burn each man in turn, 'methodically observing a pattern known only to itself', according to the Russian climber. As it entered the sleeping bags of the men there were screams of agony but the light sphere ignored their pain, repeating the pattern of attack again and again. By the time it disappeared from whence it had come one of their number, Oleg Korovin, was dead and the others were all seriously hurt. The survivors were flown by helicopter to hospital, where their injuries were found to be far worse than normal burns. Pieces of muscle had been seared right down to the bone as if they had been subjected to contact with a welding torch. Soviet doctors had never seen anything like it.

The testimony of the four surviving Russian climbers is as bewildering as it is disturbing. Although no one yet knows how or why ball lightning appears (antimatter, plasma energy and nuclear fission have all been put forward as a possible energy source), most experts would still insist that it is a terrestrial phenomenon caused by an atmospheric anomaly and therefore lacks the capacity for intelligent action. Yet the homicidal behaviour exhibited by the circular light form that entered the Russian mountaineers' tent is not the only modern instance of ball lightning apparently deliberately causing death or destruction. In 1953 a fireball came to rest beside a 30-foot-high water tank in Tucumari, New Mexico, causing it to collapse; a number of houses were demolished and four people killed. In July 1958 several fireballs fell from an overcast sky on to the remote Lappland community of Parajaevarra, fatally burning one man and seriously injuring several others. More recently, on 7 July 1977, two large luminous globes descended upon the audience of an outdoor cinema in Fujian Province, China, killing two children and causing a panic stampede in which more than 200 were injured. And finally, in an incident which took place in Kuala Lumpur, Malaysia in 1980, a row of houses in the Port Kuang district were gutted by fire following the appearance of a glowing red light form which chased residents and ignited their clothes.

None of the incidents related above took place during a thunderstorm.

1979

Phantom Hitch-Hikers

The persistent haunting of stretches of road by ghosts who met an early death in road traffic accidents would seem to provide some of the most compelling evidence for the survival of the human spirit beyond death. Such occurrences seem to fall into two groups. First there is the phantom road accident variety in which a real car collides with a figure and the poor driver, who invariably thinks he has hit a live person, gets out of his car to find no sign of a body. The second type involves stories which have come to be called the phantom hitch-hiker syndrome, in which the ghost actually hails someone's car, gets in, perhaps engages in friendly conversation, and then suddenly vanishes. Although it is widely assumed that such stories are simply apocryphal and have attained the status of the proverbial urban legend, it is apparent to those who have studied these examples closely that many of the witnesses have undergone genuine experiences.

The story of English motorist Roy Fulton is typical. Returning from a pub darts match on 12 October 1979, Fulton, who had drunk only two pints of lager during the evening, picked up a young male who was thumbing a lift on a deserted road near Dunstable in Bedfordshire. It was roughly nine o'clock, dark and growing steadily foggy when the driver first encountered the youth, half a mile after passing through the small village of Stanbridge. The stranger on the road looked real enough in the headlights; he was later described by Fulton as being roughly nineteen years old with dark, longish hair. The driver even remembered what he wore – a dark-blue round-necked jumper over a white shirt. Once he was in the passenger seat Fulton asked where he was heading. He said nothing, smiled slightly and simply pointed ahead. The two men drove on in silence for several miles until they had almost reached the next town, Totternhoe, at which point Fulton offered his uncommunicative passenger a cigarette. It was not accepted – the youth had disappeared. Minutes later the shaken motorist was relating his story to stupefied customers in a nearby pub.

Although there have been no reports of Roy Fulton's experience having been endured by other motorists passing along the same Bedfordshire road his personal integrity has impressed many a paranormal researcher who has looked into his bizarre case. Moreover, in telling his own peculiar tale, Fulton was only echoing the stories of other motorists who have picked up phantom figures while driving alone at night along other lonely, dark, unlit carriageways. Many of these so-called phantom hitch-hikers have been seen over a number of years by more than one witness, reinforcing the likelihood of their objective reality. In such cases the amazed driver invariably finds that a person answering to the description of his passenger had been killed several years earlier in a fatal road crash.

A typical 'repeater' case caused considerable interest in South Africa during the summer of 1978. On the night of 10 April that year South African motorcyclist Dawie Van Jaarsveld picked up a girl on a highway near the town of Uniondale. Ten miles on, when he stopped to pick up some petrol, he found his passenger gone and the crash helmet he had given her to wear strapped to the seat. When he went to the police they confirmed that an identical report had been received two years before from a motorist named Anton Le Grange. Subsequent enquiries by paranormal researcher Cynthia Hind identified the ghost as one Maria Roux, killed in an accident on 12 April 1968 at the spot where both Van Jaarsveld and Le Grange had met her. A photograph of Roux was recognised by both men. Reports from the past decade suggests that the woman's ghost has continued to appear at the same location, always around the anniversary of her death and invariably to young men travelling alone.

Often a particular stretch of road becomes the focus for so many similar experiences that it soon earns a reputation for being haunted. Once again in Britain, a particularly notable location is Bluebell Hill on the A229 south of Chatham in Kent. Reports of paranormal events along this stretch of carriageway seem to have begun in 1968 and have included both variants on the central theme – the ghostly accident that never was and the phantom hitch-hiker syndrome. These events seemed to have been triggered by a specific incident in which a child bridesmaid was killed in a car crash at the foot of a hill in 1965. The young girl has since been seen flagging down cars and asking for a lift on a number of occasions. One witness to the event, Maurice Goodenough, was driving on a hill after midnight on 13 July 1974 when the bridesmaid appeared in his headlights and disappeared beneath his wheels. Horrified, Mr Goodenough got out and found the child, her forehead bleeding badly, lying in the road in a crumpled heap. He covered her with a blanket and carried her to the pavement before driving to the nearest police station, in Rochester, to alert the authorities. But when the police arrived at the scene the victim had disappeared, leaving only the blanket and no trace of blood or anything else to suggest an accident had taken place. The mystery was never solved.

Yet another English location favoured by an especially persistent phantom is the stretch of the A38 which passes close to Wellington in Somerset. Although he has been seen by more than one witness, most notably the ghostly hitcher was picked up by a lorry driver named Harold Unsworth on several occasions in 1958 before the human witness even suspected that there was anything strange about his passenger. The first encounter took place in the early hours of a wet morning in late April. Mr Unsworth picked up a middle-aged man wearing a light raincoat who was standing thumbing a lift near the Blackbird Inn, a mile west of Hetherton Grange. Unlike Roy Fulton's ghostly companion, Unsworth's passenger spoke freely and got out with a salutation of thanks at his indicated destination. When Mr Unsworth came across the same man once more wandering along the same stretch of road he picked him up again. A similar incident happened again the following month. On each of these occasions Harold Unsworth noticed nothing about his companion's behaviour which led him to suspect that the man sitting beside him was anything other than physically real. But a fourth encounter, which took place in November, finally enlightened him to the bizarre truth.

This time, instead of simply getting in as usual, the man asked him to wait a few moments while he collected some luggage. Mr Unsworth stayed put for twenty minutes but there was no further sign of his prospective passenger so he gave up and drove off. However, several miles down the road the lorry driver was amazed to see the same man waving a torch at him and evidently attempting to flag him down. As there had been no other traffic travelling in the same direction along the A38 since he had last seen the man Mr Unsworth could not comprehend how the man could have reached this new spot. He also began to feel – though he could not adequately explain how – that there was something very strange indeed about his former passenger.

So, forsaking his usual charity, Mr Unsworth decided not to stop. When he saw this the figure at the roadside threw himself in front of the lorry. Unsworth braked sharply and got out, only to find that there had been no accident. Instead, 30 yards or so behind him, the familiar figure stood in the road shaking his fist and shouting angrily about the driver's refusal to pick him up. Moments later the man vanished – literally into thin air.

It is not hard to understand why so many rationalists find these tales so difficult to take seriously. It is certainly easier and more comforting to believe that these drivers imagined the whole thing during periods of extreme tiredness or under the influence of alcohol. Nevertheless, these are not isolated examples. Tales of phantom hitch-hikers are now too numerous to ignore and it can hardly be coincidence that encounters follow a characteristically similar pattern. Clearly some of the tales may be no more than legends and others may have been embellished to such a degree that they bear little relation to the original incident. But the fact that most phantom hitch-hikers are seen over a number of years by more than one witness remains the strongest possible evidence for their objective reality. Self-engendered hallucinations or genuine psychic experiences? As yet we are not in a position to judge. But one thing remains clear: reports of haunting ghosts remain as common today as at any time in the past.

1980

An Alien Liaison?

Among people who have studied UFOs there are many (myself included) who also believe that governments around this planet have been carefully limiting public access to factual evidence for the objective reality of a phenomenon. A second, even more dramatic conspiracy theory – to which I have alluded in my review of 1947 – is that several governments, most notably that of the United States, have retrieved hard evidence of UFOs in the form of crashed saucers and dead aliens. But there are some ufologists who have seriously come around to believing an even more bizarre possibility, namely that humanity has now successfully made contact with extra-terrestrial beings and has already benefited from knowledge from their advanced technology.

So far this extraordinary idea has been given little credence within mainstream UFO research circles and is ignored entirely outside them. Where former members of the political and military establishment – including NASA scientists, retired CIA agents, ex-military personnel and other individuals who have had access to classified information through their earlier occupations – have come forward to corroborate this startling suggestion they have been quickly and effectively rubbished by the media. But while few believe the rumours there have been several sightings of UFOs flying at a low level in apparent formation with obviously human craft, sightings which tend to back up this most amazing of all conspiracy theories. One such encounter took place in America in 1980, and for those involved it was an experience they would live to regret.

At roughly 9 pm on the night of 29 December, two middle-aged women were driving along a lonely desert road near Huffman, a suburb of Houston, Texas. Betty Cash, fifty-one years of age, and her friend Vickie Landrum were driving towards Dayton, where they were meeting friends for dinner. Also in the car was Mrs Landrum's seven-year-old grandson, and it was he who first noticed a light gliding low over the pine trees towards the path of their vehicle. As it came closer the light could be more clearly seen as a brilliant diamond-shaped object with flames shooting out from its underbelly. Mrs Cash, who was driving, stopped the car and got out to watch, while Mrs Landrum, extremely fearful, stayed inside to comfort her grandson, who was by now crying hysterically. According to Mrs Cash's later testimony the object emitted a pulsing noise and she remembered that she could feel intense heat coming from it even though it was never closer than 50 metres away. After hovering above them for a few minutes the diamond began to glide silently away, yet instead of disappearing from sight it continued to follow the line of the road upon which the witnesses were travelling. Rather than turn back they decided to follow it, albeit keeping a healthy distance behind.

What purportedly happened next is the part of the Cash–Landrum story which differentiates their close encounter from virtually all others and has proved baffling for most ufologists. For, according to both women and the boy, the glowing object was soon afterwards joined by a large number of helicopters of obviously human design (they were later identified by Cash as double-rotor CH-47 Chinooks) which surrounded and appeared to accompany the UFO in a protective fashion on its journey. This astonishing formation remained visible for some time, so slow was the progress of the object and its escorting military choppers. Indeed, the women claimed to have stopped on three further occasions to get out and view the craft as it gradually disappeared towards the horizon. The party arrived at their destination at 9.50 pm and lost no time in telling their friends and families of the evening's curious events.

This was, however, by no means the end of their story. Within hours of the bizarre close encounter Betty Cash began to feel nauseous, a condition which coincided with the onset of a blinding headache. By daybreak her two other companions on the journey were similarly afflicted and doctors called to treat them recorded that the witnesses' bodies exhibited burn-like blisters and peculiar nodules on their heads and scalps that burst, seeping clear fluid. Betty Cash, who had been out of the car for the longest period when the object was at its closest, was by far the worst affected. Her eyes swelled up, she was temporarily blinded and suffered for many weeks from extreme bouts of vomiting and diarrhoea. She was admitted as a burns victim to Parkway General Hospital, Houston, where her condition proved beyond the diagnosis of a skin specialist, and when she discharged herself in early February (having by then run up a medical bill of more than $10,000) her health had not improved in the slightest. As time wore on things got worse for both the women involved in the sighting and each lost a large quantity of hair, which simply fell out. More seriously, during that spring Betty Cash developed breast cancer necessitating a mastectomy.

The appalling after-effects of their close-up sighting were, in the opinion of the women involved, obviously the result of a dangerous dose of radiation, and although the truth or otherwise of the matter is unlikely ever to be proven their claims certainly seem to fall within the bounds of possibility. Interestingly, both Mrs Cash and Mrs Landrum were in no doubt that the craft was either American in origin or over-flying American airspace with the consent of the US military, and Cash went as far as to sue the US government for $20,000,000 in damages for her horrific injuries. The case was lost on the predictable grounds that no object meeting the witness's description was owned, operated or currently under planned construction by any branch of the US military. These facts as stated in court might very well be the case, yet given the certainty of the women who saw the amazing scene in the skies above Texas and in the light of their undeniable suffering, many continue to believe that the strange liaison really had taken place on that December night in 1980.

1981

Giant Hailstones

In the first week of June 1981, a ninety-five-year-old Englishwoman named Mrs Mary Nickson of Wirral, Cheshire was sweeping her front bedroom carpet when she heard a terrifying crash and found plaster raining down on her. When she had recovered herself she saw the cause of the mayhem: on the floor was a football-sized chunk of ice surrounded by several smaller fragments. Clearly the ice-mass had fallen from a great height, tearing through the roof and ceiling and ending up in the position where it now lay. Had the pensioner been standing a few feet to her left she would undoubtedly have been killed. Almost three weeks later, on 24 June, a similarly sized block of ice fell upon a house in Stembridge Road, Anerley, Kent, smashing a two-foot-wide hole in the roof. The missile just missed five-year-old Joe Wells, who was asleep in his bedroom. Though it shattered into smaller fragments the largest of these was recovered by the householders and found to weigh 11 pounds 9 ounces.

Six weeks on and it was the turn of Englishman Stephen Puckering to have a close call with a single lump of falling ice. In Puckering's case it was too close for comfort. While windsurfing on holiday in the south of France at Lac de St

Cassien near Cannes, he was badly stunned after being struck on the head by a tennis ball-sized lump of ice which fell out of the clear, hot sky. Though he was partially blinded, things could have been much worse. On 28 September a far more massive block of ice hurtled down upon the home of the Pearce family of Yateley, Hampshire, causing considerable damage, and just eleven days later another anomalous ice-fall was noted in the Fleet district of the same county, an area several miles to the south. Finally, the largest ice-bomb of all fell upon the annexe of a farmhouse owned by Michael Mogridge of Dorset on 15 October. Not only did this huge mass – estimated later to have weighed several hundredweight – virtually destroy the annexe's slate roof, it snapped in two some heavy wooden support beams in its descent.

Just why the year 1981 should have seen such a plethora of anomalous falls of ice over Britain and France is hard to explain, but the phenomenon itself is not particularly rare. Moreover, the usual explanations offered for these rather frightening occurrences – that the ice-blocks have fallen from a plane – should be treated with caution by mysteriologists. At high altitudes fresh water can certainly form on the fuselage of an aircraft and thereafter fall off when the plane enters warmer air. There have also been cases in which disinfectant and other waste matter has leaked from aeroplane toilets and frozen in the same way.

However, not all ice-bombs are composed of sewage and many have fallen to earth in places well away from jet-liner routes. Indeed, some of the largest single ice-bombs on record have come from the era which predated the development of powered flight. For instance, on 14 August 1849 the London *Times* reported in detail the fall of a large ice-mass weighing over half a ton upon grassland near Ord on the Isle of Skye in Scotland. A block which was reckoned to be over 20 feet in circumference and of a proportionate thickness came down after one single tremendous peal of thunder. Examinations showed it to be entirely transparent and composed of diamond-shaped crystals from 1 to 3 inches long.

An alternative theory which holds that huge blocks of ice which appear out of the blue might be extra-terrestrial in origin, ice meteorites in other words, is scarcely more credible. Almost certainly such celestial visitors would melt during their descent to earth, or at least be extremely hot on the outside when they impacted. At the time of writing there are no descriptions which would fall into this category.

Given the difficulties in explaining such falls it is not surprising that for many decades in the earlier part of the twentieth century meteorologists dismissed such reports out of hand. However, on 2 April 1973 the fact of their existence was finally proven when a lump of ice weighing over 2 kilogrammes narrowly missed Dr Richard Griffiths as he was walking along a tree-lined road on the outskirts of Manchester, England. As a scientist and part-time weather observer himself, Griffiths was an unimpeachable witness and had the quickness of mind to take the largest fragment home and preserve it in his freezer. He subsequently examined it in a laboratory at the Manchester Institute of Science and Technology, and was able to establish by careful analysis of the material's crystal structure that the object was made up of fifty-one layers of ice separated by thinner layers of trapped air bubbles. It did not seem to resemble any known hailstone and chemical analysis virtually ruled out the possibility that it had fallen from an aircraft. A further set of tests suggested that the ice was probably formed from cloud water, but various experiments to reproduce the effect under laboratory conditions failed to create anything even remotely resembling the anomalous ice-block's peculiar crystal structure.

In the end Dr Griffiths and his fellow scientists at the Manchester Institute were forced to give up any hope of solving the riddle. One scientist summed up their frustration eloquently: 'It's all negatives. Lots of things that it isn't and not a word about what it is. I can't give you an answer. Not even half an answer.'

1982

Human Flame-Throwers

Stephen King's novel *Firestarter* portrays the story of a girl whose mental ability to set objects ablaze becomes her undoing when the CIA decide to acquire her as a weapon. Understandably most people see the tale as a piece of pure fiction, which indeed it is, yet the strange gift described by the bestselling author is real enough.

Early in 1982 a ten-year-old Italian boy named Benedetto Sepino, who lived in the resort of Formia not far from Rome, discovered that he could set objects on fire simply by gazing at them and concentrating hard. First to go up in smoke was a comic Benedetto was reading in a dentist's waiting room. The very next morning his mother awoke to find her son's bedclothes on fire and the unfortunate boy was painfully (though not seriously) burned before he could be woken. Next to go was a plastic object held by his uncle Erasmo, which was followed by all manner of combustible materials. Everywhere young Benedetto went, the heat he generated with his mind was sure to follow. Furniture, fittings and objects smouldered; pages of books were scorched when he touched them with his fingertips. Witnesses even claimed that the boy's hands would themselves begin to glow preternaturally at such moments.

Benedetto Sepino's anguished parents began taking him to doctors and once the scepticism of the medical fraternity was laid to rest by demonstrations of his powers the boy was brought to the attention of some of Italy's top scientists. One suggested that the source of his power was static electricity, though Dr Giovanni Ballesio, dean of physical medicine at Rome University, demurred. Meanwhile, Professor Mario Scunio of the Tivoli Social Medical Centre claimed that tests showed that physically the boy was perfectly normal. For his own part, Benedetto was embarrassed at the attention he was getting for what he knew to be usually involuntary incidents. 'I don't want things to catch fire. But what can I do?' he told a Rome newspaper. 'I look at them, they are on fire and up they go in flames.'

Human flame-throwers may be rare, but the twentieth century is not without other examples. In 1921 a thirteen-year-old boy living in Budapest, Hungary caused fires to break out in rooms when he grew angry, and as he slept flames flickered over him, scorching his pillow. In 1934 another teenager, Anna Monara of Trieste, Italy, manifested crackling blue lights which flashed above her body as she slept. In neither of these cases, as in the case of Benedetto, could the youngsters at the focus of the enigma claim conscious control over the peculiar combustion they generated. However, this might not be a universal trait among fire-starters – at least, not in the opinion of some law courts.

In the same year that Benedetto Sepino discovered his dubious ability a nineteen-year-old Scottish nanny named Carole Compton (coincidentally also working in Italy) found herself in a Naples jail under suspicion of attempting to burn alive her young charges. On several occasions the infants' cots had been discovered engulfed in flames. Compton was labelled a witch by local people and held as an arsonist by the Italian justice system. Yet if eye-witnesses' accounts were to be believed it seems certain that the girl did not deliberately start the fires – at least, not in a natural way – and nor could traces of flammable substances be found by forensic experts. In court Professor Vitolo of Pisa University admitted: 'In all my forty-five years of this sort of investigation I have never seen fires like this before. They were created by an intense source of heat, but not a naked flame.' Compton herself compounded the mystery by refusing to deny the charges and in fact claimed communication with unseen intelligences who she said were actually responsible for the blazes. Although she was found guilty at her subsequent trial, few among the Italian legal system believed it probable that the young Scot was really to blame for the bizarre series of incidents and she was immediately set free.

The Italian enigma has been repeated elsewhere many times, often with tragic results. In 1991 Samantha Piper, a twenty-year-old nursing assistant working in an old people's home in Brentwood, Essex, was convicted of the homicide of an old woman in her care, Mrs Elsie De'ath. Mrs De'ath had been found engulfed in flames one morning by other members of staff. Noting that many fires had been started apparently inexplicably in the past in buildings where Samantha Piper had been present, and taking into account her earlier history of mental illness, the court concluded that she must have deliberately set her patient alight through malice. Yet Piper denied it, and in reaching their verdict the court ignored the fact that more than eight mysterious fires had been found in the Brentwood complex during the previous few months, several of which (as even the prosecuting counsel admitted) could not conceivably have been started by the defendant. Samantha Piper is still behind bars although a question-mark over her guilt remains.

The fire-starter syndrome seems to follow a pattern reminiscent of some poltergeists, in that the disturbances tend to emanate from children, teenagers or young adults. Whether the two phenomena are linked remains to be seen. All that we can say for certain is that they are entirely real.

1983

The Reincarnation Experiments

Since the controversial Bridey Murphy case of 1952 medical experts have been deeply divided as to the relevance of apparent memories of past lives recalled under the hypnotist's influence. Steadfast disbelievers in the doctrine of rebirth suggest that these so-called past-life memories are being formed under the direction of the hypnotist himself. Pointing out that stage hypnotists can lead people to behave in a bizarre manner, often performing plausible if stylised impressions of almost any person, thing or animal, these sceptics argue that under the much deeper hypnotism of regression more profound changes could take place in the human mind, perhaps opening up channels of creative thought and memory recall beyond the conscious capacity of the subject. Having subconsciously taken in so much information throughout their present lives, adults hypnotised in this way might conceivably be simply drawing from material acquired during their present existence. Moreover it has long been observed that the human brain is capable of storing in its darkest recesses virtually every sense impression that has ever entered it. This hidden memory, known as cryptomensia, has therefore been put forward by sceptics of reincarnation to explain some of the more intriguing examples of past-life regression.

Supporters of the regression technique, however, have been quick to point out that the more impressive regressions have involved facial transformations and voice-pattern variations consistent with the presence of an alternative personality. Often to the amazement of those who have witnessed it, people recalling periods of a former old age have become haggard or drawn while creases in the faces of older subjects have sometimes seemed to be smoothed out when they recall a previous youth. Physical changes can be even more dramatic: some researchers have recorded instances in which regressed individuals manifested the appearance of medical conditions consistent with past-life memories, such as muscular spasms in the faces of stroke victims. One British subject even developed a livid rope burn around her neck when recalling her hanging while another, who died from a beating, manifested extensive bruising all over his body.

Inevitably, however, it is always the specific details of the regressed individual's former-life recollections which have proven to be the most convincing evidence of the reality of the phenomenon.

In March 1983 an Australian TV documentary on the subject of reincarnation gripped viewers across the subcontinent and impressed many who had hitherto been sceptical about the possibility of soul migration. In *The Reincarnation Experiments* four ordinary housewives from Sydney, each chosen at random, were apparently transported back through the centuries under the influence of hypnotherapist Peter Rouser. One, Cynthia Henderson, recalled her life as a French aristocrat using colloquialisms not heard in France for centuries. She revealed her former home to be a château situated near the small village of Fleur. Although the woman had never visited Europe herself, she was able without difficulty to lead a film crew to the location, where, sure enough, a ruin of the building still stood. Another housewife tested, Helen Pickering, recalled her previous existence as James Burns, born in the Scottish town of Dunbar in the year 1801, a man who is known to have existed. As proof of her past life Mrs Pickering drew plans of Aberdeen's Marshall College, where she claimed – correctly – that Burns had studied; plans which, although very different to the building which currently occupies the site, bore an uncanny resemblance to a set of plans later discovered within the archives of the Scottish college. As the documentary pointed out, it would have been impossible for Mrs Pickering to have seen the records, and extremely unlikely for her to have researched the life history of the eighteenth-century Scot.

Coincidentally, the same year – 1983 – was to throw up one of the most convincing cases of past-life regression ever to be found in England. Liverpool medical hypnotist Joe Keeton had already conducted several thousand regressions before he met London journalist Ray Bryant in January 1983. Bryant had been asked by his local newspaper, the *Evening Post*, to write a number of features on paranormal matters, one of which he intended to devote to evidence of reincarnation. To add a personal dimension to his article he proposed that Keeton should hypnotise him so that he could describe to readers the actual sensations involved in being regressed. Although Bryant had never before been hypnotised Keeton was willing to allow his claims to be put to the test. In the event the journalist was to present Keeton with one of the most interesting cases he had ever studied.

Under hypnosis Bryant recalled several former identities, including that of a soldier named Reuben Stafford who fought in the Crimean War before returning to England to spend his last days as a Thames boatman. As recalled by Bryant, Stafford's life began in 1822 when he was born in Brighthelmston (Brighton) and ended when he was drowned in an accident in the East End of London in 1879. As his former self the London journalist's accent became thick Lancastrian, reflecting the fact that Stafford had spent much of his life in the north of England. Yet while impressive, this in itself offered no real proof, so after witnessing the manifestation of the Victorian soldier two members of Keeton's research team, Andrew and Margaret Selby, attempted to find documentary evidence of the man's existence.

In the Guildhall Library, London the couple were fortunate enough to find a roll-call of Crimean War casualties. Among those listed was one Sergeant Reuben Stafford, then serving with the 47th Lancashire Regiment of Foot, who was wounded in the hand at the Battle of the Quarries, a little-remembered skirmish that had taken place during the siege of Sevastopol. It also gave details of Sergeant Stafford's subsequent career, in which he won medals for bravery before being invalided out of the Army. At the next opportunity for regression these very same details came unprompted from the mouth of Ray Bryant. The date, location and name of the Battle of the Quarries were recalled by 'Stafford' as well as other facts of his regimental career. All were exactly correct.

This was by no means the end of the Selbys' research. Spending some days at the General Register of Births, Deaths and Marriages they eventually located Reuben Stafford's death certificate which showed that, having drowned (whether by accident or design was not ascertained), the ex-soldier had been buried in a pauper's grave at East Ham. Under regression the date of his earlier death and burial were also given by Ray Bryant.

Is there any way these facts could have been known without the operation of some form of reincarnation? In the regression of the journalist the possibility of cryptomensia hardly arises, since the details of the long-since dead soldier's war record would have remained safely out of the public gaze. Unless one assumes that Keeton and his volunteers abused their chosen occupation by perpetrating an elaborate fraud, the return to life of the Crimean War veteran in the body of the twentieth-century journalist would seem to be an odds-on bet.

1984

The Hole Story?

When large holes appear suddenly and unexpectedly in the ground a natural solution usually presents itself before very long. In ninety-nine cases out of a hundred the sudden earth movement is the result of subsidence caused by undermining, either natural (underground stream) or man-made (mine shafts). Occasionally, however, bizarre holes seem to appear for no apparent reason.

On 18 October 1984, brothers Rick and Peter Timm were rounding up cattle near Grand Coulee, Washington, USA when they came upon an irregularly shaped depression – about 10 feet by 7 wide and with a depth of some 10 feet – in land adjacent to a wheatfield. The Timms had harvested the area the previous month and were certain the hole had been made since. How, why and by whom was rather less clear. The brothers' astonishment increased when they found the missing earth still held together in a tight plug resting on the ground some 75 feet to the north-east. Small dribbles of fingernail-sized soil particles were found in a semi-circular arc linking the two places, thus indicating the direction of passage taken. But since the large clod remained almost completely intact and there was no sign that it had been rolled or dragged, it seemed to the Timms as though it had somehow been transported through the air and carefully placed in the position where it now lay.

The next week the puzzled farmers called in Don Aubertin, a mining director working for the Colville Indians, whose reservation bordered their property. To begin with Aubertin considered the possibility of a meteorite to be the most likely answer but changed his mind after a friend, geologist Bill Utterbach, suggested that the hole could not possibly be a crater. The geologist's reasoning was simple: the hole's vertical walls and flat bottom did not seem to have been formed by a downward impact but rather by upward lifting, yet the turf had evidently not been sliced or cut either, since roots dangled intact from the vertical sides of both the hole and the displaced slab. This detail confused the investigators even more. Rather than with the use of a mechanical tool it appeared that the block of earth had been removed through some form of careful levitation. But what force could possibly create such an effect? Although a whirlwind might conceivably have the power to lift such an object (estimated weight 3 tons), it could only have achieved it with a tearing motion. This would hardly account for the precise neatness of the action, nor the absence of damage to nearby fences.

And so the cause of the Grand Coulee phenomenon remained a mystery. When contacted a spokesman for the Smithsonian Institute Scientific Event Network admitted that they knew of no similar phenomenon and had 'no speculations' as to the force which had carefully lifted three tons of soil into the air and laid it to rest intact and virtually undamaged 75 feet away.

Extraordinary though this curious tale might seem it is not entirely without precedent. In October 1954 French newspapers described a peculiar egg-shaped hole which had appeared overnight in a field near Poncey-sur-L'Ignon.

Geological experts who visited the area were baffled and reporters who photographed the feature explained to their readers that it looked as if the earth had been sucked out by a giant vacuum. In February 1979, once more in America, investigators with the Utah Geological and Mineral Survey Group discovered a strange cruciform hole about 14 feet in diameter which exhibited many of the features that would be evident in the Washington phenomenon five years later. A report on the finding described the hole's origin in a single word: 'Mysterious'.

Yet by far the most bizarre story of all concerns three identical craters measuring 18 feet wide and 5 feet deep which appeared near each other in a field in Venice Center, New York, on exactly the same date – 12 November – in three consecutive years, 1966, 1967 and 1968. The holes were found after a loud explosion which could be heard several miles away, yet in each case neither evidence of an explosive charge nor any reason for its use came to light. As one writer remarked, 'It will probably be a long time before we get to see the hole story.'

1985

Portraits That Brought Misery

Of all mysterious coincidences few can be counted so bizarre, or so disturbing to the rational mind, as those surrounding the 'Crying Boy' fires which made headlines across Great Britain in the summer and autumn of 1985. Briefly the story can be summed up as follows: after a series of otherwise unconnected domestic blazes it was discovered that the same picture – a cheap reproduction of a young male child crying – had been present in each of the rooms where the fires had started. This detail might have been dismissed as an irrelevant if slightly odd chance occurrence were it not for the fact that in each case without exception the picture had escaped harm while surrounding materials had been almost entirely destroyed.

It was in early September that the uncanny phenomenon entered the public domain after a Yorkshire fireman, Peter Hall, was quoted in a national newspaper as saying that fire brigades across the north of England had found innumerable examples of the same picture remaining untouched in fires whose causes remained unknown. Hall had spoken out after his own brother, Ron, who had refused to take the story seriously and had even deliberately bought a copy of 'The

Crying Boy' to disprove the jinx, found his home in Swallownest, south Yorkshire, mysteriously burned down soon afterwards. Seeing that the picture had been removed intact from the charred ruins, Ron Hall swiftly put a boot through it.

Following publication of the initial story one national daily newspaper claimed to have had a flood of calls from 'TCB' owners suffering similar experiences. Dora Brand of Mitcham, Surrey, saw her home reduced to a pyre six weeks after she had bought the painting, and although it was among more than a hundred others she owned it was the only one to survive. Sandra Craske of Kilburn said that she, her sister, her mother and a friend had all suffered fires since buying copies of the picture. More stories came in from Leeds, Nottingham, Oxfordshire and the Isle of Wight. On 21 October the Parillo Pizza Palace, Great Yarmouth, Norfolk was gutted by fire although its prominently displayed TCB remained in pristine condition. Three days later the Godber family of Herringthorpe, south Yorkshire lost their home to an unexplained fire; the TCB displayed in their living room stayed unmarked while pictures on either side of it were completely consumed.

The next day in Heswall, Merseyside, a pair of the paintings hanging in the living room and dining room respectively of a house belonging to the Amos family were found intact after a gas explosion blew the building apart. Within twenty-four hours reports of another TCB fire, this time in the home of ex-fireman Fred Trower of Telford, Shropshire, led to renewed interest in the jinx and one newspaper went as far as to suggest that TCB owners attend a mass burning of the pictures on Guy Fawkes' night.

Though most people across Britain considered the story to be a piece of harmless 'silly season' entertainment others were less sure. By November several people appeared to have suffered nervous breakdowns apparently believing that the 'spirit' of the TCB they had destroyed was haunting them. One woman from Leeds seemed certain that the picture was to blame for the death in a fire of her husband and three sons, while another, Mrs Woodward of Forest Hill, London, similarly felt it to be responsible for the loss of her son, daughter, husband and mother in separate fire-related incidents. When approached to comment upon the growing hysteria surrounding the painting several fire brigades refused to discuss the subject or take part in the various mass burnings that were taking place around the country. Nevertheless, the peculiar stories refused to die.

On 12 November Malcolm Vaughan of Church Down, Gloucestershire helped to destroy a neighbour's TCB. He returned home to find his own living room ablaze for reasons which firemen were unable afterwards to explain. Several weeks later a mysterious fire that swept through a house in Weston-super-Mare, Avon, killing the occupant, sixty-seven-year-old William Armitage, made the headlines after it was revealed that a TCB was found intact lying beside the pensioner's charred body. One of the firemen who dealt with the blaze was afterwards quoted as saying: 'I've never believed in the jinx up until now. But when you actually come across a picture in a gutted room and it's literally the only thing that hasn't been touched, it is most odd.'

Odd to say the least, and, some might add, just a tiny bit frightening.

1986

Out-of-Place Animals

On the morning of 17 June 1986 a motorist driving through the Morange-Silvange area in the Moselle region of France was astonished to see a large kangaroo crossing the road in front of him at a distance of some 100 metres from his oncoming vehicle. When the driver reported the incident to police, enquiries were made at a new zoo near Hagondange which was due to open in several weeks. Officials at the zoo quickly discounted the possibility that the creature was one of their inmates, pointing out that their own promised shipment of marsupials had yet to arrive from Australia. Although sceptical of the kangaroo report they were intrigued enough to assist police with a search of the area and, much to their surprise, two of their keepers did see a creature of the characteristic kangaroo shape. Roughly a metre and a half high, it was observed jumping on its hind legs. The sighting occurred on the same afternoon that several local people had claimed to have seen a pair of kangaroos lurking in bushes near a village.

Not surprisingly the phantom kangaroos of the Morange-Silvange gained considerable media attention, particularly when puzzled gendarmes admitted that they had received no reports of kangaroos escaping from circuses or private collections. But when no further sightings were reported the story gradually faded from the public consciousness and by the following year few Frenchmen would be prepared to admit they had ever believed in the existence of wild kangaroos hopping around their countryside.

The story described above is but one example of a surprisingly common phenomenon – the appearance of out-of-place animals in locations far from their native habitat and in situations which defy logical explanation. In fact, every country in western Europe has seen its fair share of bizarre examples in which exotic insects, fish, snakes, reptiles and even some quite large mammals have suddenly turned up in the most peculiar circumstances. Although Europe is connected by land to other continents it is also densely populated. So it is difficult to imagine that animals could travel under their own steam across great distances without being seen, and the usual explanations for these unexpected arrivals (escaped or abandoned pets; escapees from zoos or travelling circuses; the misidentification of a native species) seem distinctly unsatisfactory. Meanwhile, the more elaborate paranormal scenarios (that they have been teleported across thousands of miles by some as yet little understood mechanism; that they are apparitional in nature; that they represent a spontaneous recurrence of creatures which once occupied the same countryside in ancient times) are unprovable.

But whether we lean towards the natural or supernatural interpretation for these sightings, the plain fact is that we cannot dismiss them wholesale as hallucinations, tall stories or media fabrications. During the present century the larger species of non-native mammals either seen at close quarters, photographed, captured or shot have included, in Europe alone, wolves, porcupines, jackals, monkeys, hyenas, racoons, African antelopes and Tibetan yaks. In the United Kingdom

– which is of course separated from the rest of the continent by water and should therefore be even less likely to find itself the habitat of exotic species – there have been sightings of boars, bears, crocodiles and wallabies in such numbers that it is impossible to write them off as hallucinations.

Some of the British species are without doubt real enough, and their appearance needs no recourse to consideration of phenomenal dimensions. There is to be certain a sizeable colony of wallabies which has lived in the Ashdown Forest of East Sussex since at the least the beginning of the 1940s, and individuals are occasionally caught by police and handed over to zoos or found run over on motorways in the home counties. How these wallabies got there remains unclear but their flesh-and-blood reality is not in dispute, even among the most sceptical zoologists.

Boars, though once common in England in the Middle Ages were, it was assumed, hunted to extinction around the end of the seventeenth century. However, by the early 1970s there had been too many sightings to discount and in the summer of 1972 a 200-pound male was captured alive in a garden at Odiham, Hampshire. Since then two more dead bodies have turned up, one shot by a farmer in Hampshire and another killed in a road accident near Nairn in the Scottish Highlands.

Brown bears are also assumed to be extinct in Britain, yet there have been several recent reports of bears seen running wild in Yorkshire, Bedfordshire, Norfolk and the outskirts of Greater London. Police took all of these reports seriously and conducted searches armed with high-velocity rifles. In no case did police officers actually see a beast for themselves, although on 27 December 1981, after four boys aged between nine and thirteen reported seeing a 'giant growling, hairy thing' on Hackney Marshes in London, Metropolitan police found bear pawprints in snow which, while not entirely conclusive, could hardly have been made by any other known British species. Given that the only witnesses were children little credence would have been lent to the London sighting had it not been for the fact that the corpses of two bears had turned up only a fortnight before floating in the River Lea in the London Borough of Hackney. This event has never been explained.

The possibility that large sub-tropical reptiles such as alligators and crocodiles could be roaming the British countryside seems on the face of it to be a preposterous suggestion. Nevertheless, like out-of-place mammals, they continue to be discovered from time to time. In August 1966 a 6-foot alligator was found snoozing peacefully in a garden in a quiet leafy avenue of Leicester. Police called in to deal with the creature had assumed it to be a hoax until they saw it for themselves. June 1970 saw seven sightings of a crocodilian creature basking on the banks of the River Ouse at Little Barfield, Bedfordshire, while another crocodile was seen five years later on the banks of the River Stour at Sandwich, Kent. A baby alligator was recovered alive walking along a road in Stevenage, Hertfordshire, during August of the same year, 1975. In March 1978 a schoolgirl found a 5-foot-long dead crocodile at the back of her parents' detached house in Caerphilly, Mid-Glamorgan, and the late morning of 16 May 1980 saw police near Preston, Lancashire hunting frantically for a 6-foot crocodile reported by a number of motorists to have crossed the M55 motorway. The hunt ended without a result. There have been no logical explanations for the presence of these creatures.

The anomalous appearance of out-of-place animals shows no sign of growing any less common. The past two decades have seen, in the United Kingdom alone, discoveries of creatures native to countries as far away and apart as Japan, New Zealand and New Guinea. As well as a considerable variety of smaller immigrants such as arachnids, butterflies, molluscs, crustaceans and tiny reptiles, the influx has included such diverse species as tropical fruit-bats, Arctic foxes, lynxes, racoons and at least one hyena. In none of these cases has it been possible to prove that the animals escaped from captivity within British shores.

1987

Frog-Falls on Great Britain

Falls of anomalous matter from out of the sky are a regular feature of the paranormal history of the twentieth century and would seem to have taken place in just about every country in the world. Since usually only one type of object falls it is hard indeed to imagine a natural solution for these mysteries. But when one considers collectively the wide variety of objects which have actually descended from out of the blue it is almost as difficult to come up with a supernatural one. Among the multifarious items to rain down during the last ninety-odd years we have reports of apples, hens' eggs (both raw and hard-boiled), soot, clods of earth, blood, cooked ham, various meatstuffs, peas, lumps of coal, moist flour, onions, tomatoes (fresh and cooked) galvanised nails, human fingers, crabs, clams, various crustaceans and other shellfish, baked beans, dried corn kernels, mustard and cress seeds, maize seeds, marble chippings, pieces of china crockery, red-hot chains, iron bars, golf balls, limestone spheres, melted glass, molten metal pellets and medium-sized mammals including crocodiles, a monkey and the inevitable cats and dogs.

Most of the above items have fallen to earth only once or twice during the past ninety years but some items of inanimate matter (most notably paper money and coins and stones) seem to appear from the skies with great regularity along with rather less easily identified substances, such as a wide variety of slimes, goos and jellies. Among creature-falls fish would seem to be well up there with the most frequently reported species. Yet unequivocally remaining at the top of the list – and this is true of literally every country one cares to mention – are frogs.

On 24 October 1987 two British tabloid newspapers, the *Daily Mirror* and the *Daily Star*, carried a report describing how an unnamed elderly lady had reported to the Gloucestershire Trust for Nature Conservancy the anomalous fall of large numbers of pink-coloured frogs upon her home town of Stroud during a torrential fall of rain the previous week. According to the woman's story, the tiny frogs bounced off umbrellas and pavements, hopping off in their thousands towards the sanctuary of nearby streams and gardens. The newspaper accounts went on to say that pink frogs of a similar description had been seen in large numbers in nearby Cirencester a fortnight before, although no one reported actually seeing them fall from the sky. The *Mirror* quoted the opinion of naturalist Ian Darling, who examined a number of the frogs. Darling believed them to be part of an albino strain whose strange pink colour was due to tiny blood vessels showing through their pale skins. Noting that Britain had been dusted by the red Sahara sand during this period, he personally believed that the frogs might have been lifted up by whirlwinds and carried thousands of miles in atmospheric globules of water. Others disagreed, and most newspapers which picked up on the story preferred to accept a more down-to-earth solution: namely that any frogs seen had simply hopped out of the grass or undergrowth (common behaviour during heavy rainfall) and that the elderly woman who claimed to have seen them actually fall from the sky was an eccentric and therefore unreliable witness.

It is not surprising that the majority of people, especially those disposed towards rationalist solutions for mysteries, should shy away from the implications of such a story. For here is a mystery whose logical contradictions not only defy every known law of science but which seems plain crazy at the same time. Why frogs should be the species which is most commonly seen to drop out of the sky is difficult to imagine, yet there have now been so many eye-witness reports that it is impossible to dismiss them as fabrications.

In his *Book of the Damned* Charles Hoy Fort collected literally dozens of examples that took place in the latter half of the last century and the early decades of the present one. Of these perhaps the most startling was the one which took place during a violent rainfall on the afternoon of 2 July 1901 in Minneapolis, Minnesota, USA. During the storm many hundreds of witnesses reported watching the descent of 'a huge green mass' which left an enormous volume of small frogs and toads across four blocks in such quantity that they were 3 inches thick in places and street travel was made impossible. Following Fort's death in 1932 the number of reports has if anything increased, although seldom have the creatures fallen in quite such prodigious numbers. On 12 July 1954 Englishwoman Mrs Sylvia Mowday was among many witnesses at a fair held in Birmingham's Sutton Coldfield Park who saw a large shower of khaki-coloured frogs measuring three-quarters of an inch wide come down during a light shower. The frogs were seen and felt thudding against umbrellas and when Mrs Mowday looked down she saw the ground absolutely covered with the creatures over an area of about 50 square yards.

In 1969 Veronica Papworth, a well-known newspaper columnist, was among several people who saw literally thousands of frogs arrive from the heavens over Penn in

Buckinghamshire. Ten years later, on 27 July 1979, another Englishwoman, Mrs Vida McWilliam of Bedford, found huge numbers of small green and black frogs covering her garden after a heavy fall of rain while the branches of the trees and bushes were covered in what appeared to be frogspawn.

Many people will scoff at these stories and there is nothing like a frog-fall to make scientists squirm. The phenomenon has never been investigated scientifically and I very much doubt if it ever will be. Among rationalists who are honest enough to admit that the sightings cannot be dismissed out of hand the vast majority prefer the type of sane explanation advanced by the naturalist Ian Darling: namely that the animals have been lifted en masse into the sky by a whirlwind and dropped elsewhere through the force of gravity. This, of course, in no way accounts for the peculiarly selective nature of the falls and the lack of other material such as pond debris found in the locations where the frogs come down. But if we reject this notion (as I personally do) what are we left with? Nothing that makes much sense, evidently.

And sometimes one is left to wonder whether there is a cosmic joker playing tricks on us all. It is interesting to note that in the early weeks of October 1987, which saw the falls of peculiar pink frogs of a species never identified upon the Gloucestershire towns of Stroud, Cirencester and Cheltenham, a film entitled *The Love Child* was showing in local cinemas. The poster advertising the film showed pink frogs tumbling out of space and the storyline of the movie featured a band who called themselves The Pink Frogs. A simple coincidence? Of course – well, what else could it be?

1988

The Nullarbor Plain Affair

Throughout Australia January 1988 saw the much-publicised run-up to the country's bicentennial celebrations. Yet vying for newspaper space with the national festivities was the story of a single Australian family who claimed to have undergone a terrifying experience while driving across the subcontinent's interior. Terrifying and inexplicable.

On 19 January the Knowles family were travelling from their home in Perth on a 2,000-mile car journey to Melbourne, where they planned to celebrate the anniversary with friends. Mrs Faye Knowles was accompanied on the expedition by her three grown-up sons, Patrick, aged twenty-four, Sean, twenty-one, and Wayne, who was eighteen. Since they were also taking their two dogs, their blue Ford Telstar Sedan was crowded and hot. So, sensibly, the Perth family decided to spend most of the journey travelling through the night when the desert air was cooler.

Having made good time along the coastal highway between Eyre and the South Australia state border, the early morning hours of Wednesday 20 January saw the Knowles begin to skirt the edge of the wide expanse of the Nullarbor Plain. Although the road was unlit the beautiful, starry, moonlit night afforded perfectly adequate driving conditions and in any case there was little or no traffic coming from either direction. But out of the dark sky an unexpected menace was about to descend upon them, a hazard not mentioned in any driving manual.

Seven or eight miles before they reached their next planned point of rest, the small township of Mundrabilla, their encounter began. First of all Sean Knowles, who was driving, noticed a peculiar kite-shaped object, glowing white with yellow tinges around the edges, come into his sight at an elevation some way above the highway in front. After a few moments it disappeared and Sean dismissed the matter from his mind, concentrating on the task in hand.

However, after he had travelled on for perhaps another mile the object reappeared much closer and apparently heading in their direction. It was moving very low, just a few feet above the road surface, which put it on a virtual collision course with their vehicle. Immediately the driver shouted and awoke his companions, who had been sleeping. The family came to their senses just as the glow swept down the road and into their path, landing just yards from their braking car. Sean Knowles swerved to avoid the object and in doing so almost collided with a car towing a caravan which had been heading serenely in the opposite direction, apparently unaware of the strange, glowing shape so obvious to the Perth family.

The Ford Telstar screeched to a halt, throwing its occupants into violent disarray, and when they had recovered their composure there was no sign of the glowing shape. After a brief discussion Sean Knowles decided to turn the car around and go back the way they had come, believing this to be their best chance of avoiding a further encounter. However, as he accelerated after the now distant tail-lights of the caravan a bizarre glow descended from above upon the Knowles' car together with a whirring, rotating, engine-like hum which reached such an extreme amplitude that the vehicle's metal frame seemed to be dancing up and down and shaking with vibration. It was immediately realised by the whole family that the same thing they had narrowly avoided only moments before had now virtually landed on top of them. Suddenly, a fine layer of black dust seemed to rush in through the half-open window, sending the passengers into even greater confusion, and for a few terrible seconds they all became convinced that the car was actually rising into the air, being drawn up as if by some incredible magnetic force. The dust brought with it a sickly sweet odour (like rotting flesh, the Knowles afterwards agreed) which filled their nostrils and made two of them vomit. Then without warning the ordeal was over: the car fell once more to earth, crashing with vicious force on its tyres and crunching the undercarriage and exhaust system on the bumpy road surface. Simultaneously, one of the tyres burst and the car swerved out of control, crashing through the brush and finally coming to rest with its front section embedded in a sand dune. When the family got out, full of fear, to search the sky above there were only the stars and the moon's luminosity to be seen.

The curious tale told by the family from Perth is far from unique in the annals of UFO literature. Vehicle interference (the breakdown of electrical circuits within cars driven by witnesses to UFOs) are now a standard part of accounts of alien visitations and there are even several other examples where drivers have claimed, like the Australians, that they were lifted along with their vehicles towards and sometimes even inside the ships of extra-terrestrial visitors. Generally these tales are dismissed as hallucinations, but the alleged incident which took place on the Nullarbor Plain in January 1988 is marked out by other significant details which seem to support the testimonies of the four witnesses directly involved.

To begin with the Knowles family were not the only people travelling along the Eyre highway that night to report seeing strange lights in the sky. John 'Porky' De Jong, a truck driver travelling towards Adelaide with his girlfriend Ann, saw a brilliant glow rising over the horizon near the Madura Pass at about 2.15 am, a time which corresponds closely to the incident involving the Knowles. Graham Henley, another lorry driver, claimed to have seen an object which bore direct comparison to that described by Sean Knowles. Henley was certain that the thing he saw in the sky was not a terrestrial aircraft or the reflection of a star.

Other corroborative evidence related to the condition of the Telstar and its passengers. Having filed a report over the alleged UFO sighting, Officer Trebilcock of the Port Lincoln Crime Scene Department confirmed to journalists that each member of the Knowles family had displayed great anxiety and was visibly shaken by the ordeal. Furthermore, Mrs Knowles, who was closest to the half-open window and who had put her hand outside the car at one point during the encounter, showed signs of an unusually severe skin inflammation. Officer Trebilcock had personally examined their car and found peculiar indentations in the roof consistent with it being lifted or pressured from above rather than the likely effects of a road traffic accident. Also, he found both the vehicle's interior and the outside metal structure to be covered in a thick grey ash whose origin he could not explain, a substance which gave off a particularly unpleasant smell, buttressing that essential part of the Knowles' story.

Several forensic analyses of samples of this ash were subsequently carried out, including one by a US aviation scientist named Dr Richard Haines and the Australian Mineral Development Laboratory working on behalf of the Channel 7 television network. Curiously, the substance was found to have a similar composition to that of worn brake linings, except that it also contained an extremely high proportion of chlorine. Of course the sheer amount of the substance found both within the passenger compartment and on the exterior bodywork of the Telstar could hardly have been produced by the braking of that vehicle alone. And therefore the dust element remained an unexplained feature of the case.

To some people the strongest corroborative evidence of all, though, was the fact that the vehicle's speedometer was found to be jammed at a full-scale 200km, a speed well beyond the capability of a 1984 Ford Telstar. Nevertheless, when investigators jacked the car off the ground for a test it was discovered that the wheels did spin at full speed, suggesting perhaps that at some point the car had been helped along the road surface by the force that travelled above it.

The wide publicity that followed the events of 20 January ensured that for a brief time the Knowles family were treated with something approaching celebrity status by the Australian media. The abject failure of sceptics to find a plausible alternative explanation for their encounter only served to intensify interest in the case. An initial suggestion – that they had seen the sun setting – was quickly refuted since the sun was already down by the time the object was first sighted. The possibility that the lights came from an electrical storm proved equally untenable after a nearby station owner and other motorists confirmed that there was no storm in the area at the time. A third explanation, which held that military tests of advanced missiles might be responsible, similarly fell apart when it was proved beyond question that no such tests were being conducted anywhere in the region.

Australians who watched the Knowles relive their terrifying encounter on television became convinced that the family had not staged the affair and even when later that year a reputed meteorologist from Flinder University in Adelaide,

Professor Peter Schwerdtfegger, finally came up with a natural explanation that apparently fitted at least some of the facts, few were convinced. Professor Schwerdtfegger's hypothesis was that the Knowles family had driven into the middle of a rare type of weather system known as a clear-sky electrical storm, which is typified by tumultuous and highly localised winds. The possible side-effects of such storms might, so the professor speculated, introduce into the atmosphere anomalous physical effects producing ash particles, by electrostatic attraction, of the type that covered the Ford Telstar.

As theories go the clear-sky electrical storm hypothesis was well worthy of consideration, but its impact on public opinion was lessened somewhat by the fact that no one had actually ever seen one in operation. And so the first and most obvious probability, that of a UFO link, remained a popular explanation in the consciousness of most Australians.

1989

The Haunted Hangar

When one claims to hear voices one risks being suspected of insanity. Yet most assuredly there have been many people who have heard voices coming from nowhere and who have not been the slightest bit mad. Some of these experiences can be explained in terms of auditory hallucinations, yet there remains a hardened kernel of inexplicable cases which defy such rationalistic theorising. In some cases the sounds are heard over a long period of time by multiple witnesses; in other cases they have actually been recorded. No amount of talk about hoaxes, self-delusions and so on can alter the fact that such anomalous sounds do appear from time to time and for reasons which remain largely incomprehensible.

During the autumn of 1989 British investigator Peter Thorneycroft conducted a study into strange events taking place nightly inside an aircraft hangar which housed a restored World War II Avro Lincoln bomber at RAF Cosford Aerospace Museum near Wolverhampton. Aural manifestations included bumps, scratches, squeaks, human sighs and girls' voices; other peculiarities included the sighting by museum staff of spectral air crews, the movement of switches and the rotation of wheels, plus dramatic drops in temperature. Investigating the eerie events along with technicians from BBC Radio, Thorneycroft himself heard and recorded anomalous sounds within the aircraft itself and saw the appearance of tiny bright moving pinpoints of light that could not be explained. When the sounds were analysed by BBC boffins, it became clear that outbreaks (most frequently noises associated with mechanical movements, such as the violent tugging of a ratchet, the closing of a door hatch etc.) always began with a discernible blip on the tape of a type similar to that produced by a sudden burst of static. The keeper of the museum, Len Wardgate, confirmed that the sounds could not conceivably have been produced by the 'dead' aircraft – which had no hydraulic pressure and was electrically disconnected – nor by the expansion or contraction of the aircraft hangar's metal panel structure. What was taking place within the hangar during the hours of darkness had no logical explanation, in Wardgate's opinion. Some people who have heard the Thorneycroft tapes have pointed out that the sounds themselves seem to be repeated in almost a sequential way and have therefore contended that what is being heard is something akin to a flashback recording rather than some kind of ghostly invisible activity taking place afresh. Certainly the unmistakable blip which began each series of noises would fit in with such a hypothesis, yet it is equally fair to say that if these sounds do represent some kind of recording then they are unlike anything science is familiar with.

The aviation museum at RAF Cosford is just one of many similar examples which have come to light during the past ninety years. For several nights running in November 1986 downstairs rooms in a small farmhouse in Somerset, England became filled with what appeared to be the voices of former residents. Witnesses who listened to these peculiar conversations from the past claimed that they began and ended with a distinct 'click', exactly as if a radio had been turned on and off. Yet neither receiver nor transmitter was found and no natural explanation was put forward.

Intriguingly, a similar metallic click preceded all manifestations which began to be heard inside Point Lookout, a converted lighthouse at St Mary's County, Maryland, in January 1973. The building's owner, Gerald J. Sword, found himself regularly awoken by a nightly cacophony of sounds which included doors banging shut, furniture moving and footsteps, although in the morning there was never any sign of disturbance. Concerned for his sanity, Sword set out to capture the sounds on tape, leaving a reel-to-reel recorder switched on. Sure enough, the replayed tape included many extraneous noises including spoken phrases, some of which seemed to be associated with the treatment of injuries. To Sword's astonishment a local librarian researching the history of his home confirmed that the building had been used as a field hospital during the American Civil War.

Sounds from the past which are deliberately captured on tape are fascinating; those which appear of their own accord can be very frightening. In 1978 a young woman named Joyce McCarthy from Whiteheath, Birmingham found that her home-recorded tape of a Donna Summer album had inexplicably been wiped off and replaced by noises of men screaming, crashing timbers and rushing water. McCarthy had played the tape normally on dozens of occasions before the eerie sounds were superimposed. The tape was analysed by a local university physics department who could offer no natural answer to the mystery. However, it had been noticed by local historians that the McCarthys' house lay above the site of a disused coal mine, known by the ominous name of Black Bat Pit. One historian, who was also a practising spiritualist, suggested that there might be a link between the anomalous tape-recording and a disaster which had occurred exactly one hundred years before in 1878. Sure enough, when the voices were magnified it was possible to make out the names of several miners who, records showed, had lost their lives in the flooded Victorian death mine.

The way certain locations seem to be able to store such occurrences and then release them many years later has led some members of the parascientific community to undertake experiments into the phenomena of anomalous sounds. Mostly these tests have proven less than conclusive, but recently some interesting results have come from the work of two British researchers, John Marke, an electrical engineer, and Alan Jenkins, an industrial chemist.

Hearing of reported manifestations in a Welsh public house, The Prince of Wales at Kenfig, Mid-Glamorgan, Marke and Jenkins proposed to test their theory that certain conventional substances used in building materials in the inn's walls had trapped sounds like a conventional recording tape (some bricks contain combinations of silica and ferric salts, both of which are used in tapes). Their practical experiment involved inserting powerful electrodes into the interior walls and running a huge current of more than 20,000 volts through the building in the hope of triggering electrons in the silica to release the trapped sound energy. The test worked. During a four-hour period when the current was turned on many extraneous noises were picked up by recorders, including faint organ noises, a barking dog and voices speaking in an old Welsh dialect.

Following the experiments of Marke and Jenkins some researchers have come to the conclusion that sounds indicating a place memory have nothing to do with traditional hauntings. They may very well be right. However, we still do not know why some sound impressions are held captive and not others; why only certain people seem able to hear them, and how they break free to become manifest years later. When we have finally answered these questions we will have moved a step nearer towards a greater understanding of the paranormal world.

1990

Circular Evidence?

During the summer of 1990 the appearance of more than 700 circles of apparently anomalous origin in fields containing various cereal crops sent the British media into a wave of hysterical excitement. They were not, of course, the first batch of markings to appear in this way. Indeed, as early as ten years before, in August 1980, several flattened areas of crops appeared inexplicably in Wiltshire fields, and similar 'crop circles', as they became known, had arrived ever since in the months before the annual harvest. Every year throughout the decade their numbers had grown, yet 1990 saw a radical departure from the previous phenomena, in terms of both the sheer number of mysterious designs and their artistic complexity. Now, instead of the usual individual circles and the occasional formation of three- or five-ring groups, there were spectacular combinations of rings and circles and even highly complex pictograms including bars, rectangles and arms which were quite breathtaking when pictured from the air.

Quite suddenly the phenomenon of crop circles, considered by most people to be of only minor interest and certainly of no particular relevance to their own lives, could no longer be ignored. Faced with the indisputable evidence of dozens of newspaper photographs, millions of people up and down the country began to debate the possible reasons for the existence of crop circles and the forces that had created them. Mainstream scientists who up until that time had quietly ignored the escalating phenomenon could no longer bury their heads in the sand and were forced to offer the bemused British population some form of explanation. When they did come up with tentative solutions, committed circle-watchers and mysteriologists were quick to point out their drawbacks (usually because the paranormal investigators who had been studying the phenomenon for years had themselves considered and eventually discarded those very same hypotheses). Today, as the mid-1990s draw near, we still have absolutely no real clue as to the force behind the crop circles, yet it is interesting and informative to review the short history of the century's most visible and startling phenomenon, and in doing so to make evident the reason why its origin is unlikely to be a natural one.

Although crop circles have been found regularly sprinkled throughout the counties of southern England (and a few have even been uncovered north of the Wash), the overwhelming majority seem to appear in the English counties of Hampshire and Wiltshire. Yet, it is not only a British phenomenon, for investigators have now uncovered twentieth-century cases from some twenty-four overseas countries and even a few other examples going back to 1503 in Holland. Even so there can be absolutely no question that the United Kingdom has fully earned its reputation as the crop-circle capital of the world and the two counties mentioned above, which in historical times formed the ancient British kingdom of Wessex, are the undisputed focus of the phenomenon, accounting for over ninety per cent of all known cases. Why this extraordinary concentration should exist is less than apparent, but then the same can be said for virtually every aspect of the circles' mystery. During the 1960s Wessex became a place popular with occult groups and UFO researchers alike, who fondly held to the belief that monuments like Stonehenge, ley-lines and other so-called mystic places provided the ideal locations for contact with earth forces and visitors from other planets. Quite why this should be was never fully thought through by those who adhere to the earth mysteries school of thought, yet when crop circles began to appear in increasing numbers throughout the early 1980s it seemed to such people to be proof positive that they were right all along. Tabloid newspapers were for their part only too happy to promote this version of events, and for a while hovering spaceships were the accepted non-natural explanation in the general public's consciousness. However, the hype surrounding the saucer–circle link did not produce even a single UFO sighting that genuinely seemed to relate to circle creation, and the theory gradually lost ground.

At the same time that ufologists were promoting their own pet hypothesis, scientific figures from a variety of disciplines were putting forward a series of scarcely more plausible speculations. The mating habits of hedgehogs, activities of amorous rabbits and even bovine flatulence were all at one time or another seriously considered. Some biologists contended that the circles were the result of unusual patterns of fungal growth while an expert on arms development suggested the marks might have been made by low-flying remotely piloted drones launched from nearby Wessex military bases. A leading French scientist believed the circles were the product of a secret weapon fired against aircraft targets and bouncing back to earth; in contrast, environmentalists cited holes in the ozone layer as being responsible.

None of the natural theories gained much credence, and people were increasingly drawn towards the possibility of a genuinely supernatural reason for the circles' appearance.

Until, that is, an English meteorologist named Dr Terence Meaden proposed the existence of an unusual current of air which he called a fair-weather stationary whirlwind. Likening his idea to the 'dust devil', which is known to suck up debris or sand in deserts and other hot locations, Meaden devised a combination of meteorological and geographical factors which he believed would be necessary for the creation of such a phenomenon in Britain. Lo and behold, they apparently matched those locations where crop circles had been formed in Wessex, and when several farmers came forward to add that they had themselves seen small whirlwinds picking up loose hay or corn on their land, the newspapers and the general public alike came to accept that the mystery had finally been solved.

But the formation of more complex circle patterns during the mid-1980s, including a particularly spectacular example at Bratton in Wiltshire, seemed to undermine Meaden's theory. In response the English meteorologist subtly altered his ideas by proposing that stationary whirlwinds might produce a miniature vortex which, under the right atmospheric conditions (during hot, calm days), would result in a build-up of electricity within the stationary column of downward spiralling air. Such a vortex, claimed Meaden, could conceivably lift and fall again, thus leaving the imprint of several circles in the field. Although such effects would undoubtedly also form over roads or water they would leave no trace in those locations. Once again most experts were convinced by the second theory, and even though to many people the intricacy with which the circles were made seemed to indicate the direction of an intelligence, scientists were quick to point out that many natural phenomena, such as snowflakes, were every bit as startling and perfect in design.

Yet even Meaden's upgraded theory provides no explanation for the quite bizarre pictograms which emerged across southern England during 1990. Triangular groups of circles, straight-sided figures, triangles, random groupings, linear groupings, asymmetrical patterns and even arrow heads were among the various carvings that appeared on the landscape of lowland Britain. The large-scale artworks (for there could be no other word to adequately describe them) immediately began another wave of media interest and people in bars and clubs all over the country were asking the same question: 'Where are these bloody things coming from?' Some paranormal investigators came up with a novel theory – that some invisible form of alien intelligence was spilling out messages – and some religious zealots saw them as a sign that the world was about to end. Scientists, having, it seemed, at last given up any hope of producing a natural theory for the ever more elaborate formations, now turned their attentions to probably the most obvious suggestion of all: namely that the circles were the result of a hoax. The problem with the hoax theory was that some pictograms were so complex and so enormous that only a precision army team could have brought them about.

Moreover, even if the methods existed to re-create these patterns – which was far from accepted – the effect would have to have been achieved overnight and without local farmers knowing. In fact farmers themselves had long before dismissed the idea that such teams of hoaxers were regularly trespassing on their property, and given the sheer number of large field carvings that appeared during 1990 it was very hard to imagine how such a group, or even several groups, could have been responsible for all the cases.

Three years after the mass outbreak of complex patterns appeared on the British landscape the crop-circle debate is no nearer a conclusion. Markings have continued to appear in ever more elaborate fashion and with increasing regularity. During that time several people have come forward claiming to have made the circles themselves and have appeared on television and before newspaper reporters to demonstrate their art. It is now beyond doubt that some of these features have indeed been hoaxes, though it would be very wrong to conclude that the activities of such individuals could account for more than a handful of the literally hundreds of examples on record. At the same time the appearance of truly extraordinary formations, including Maltese crosses and key images such as the Mandelbrot Set – the basic image of fractal geometry – have ruled out once and for all the possibility of a natural event. The idea that we are being contacted by unseen intelligences is appealing, yet the sad fact remains that if this is the case their messages are not being understood.

1991

The Phantom Burglar

There are some people who continue to believe that all purported ghost sightings come from the overheated imaginations of fantasy-prone personalities, and should be written off as optical illusions and other mundane anomalies of perception. To the non-survivalist tendency, apparitions exist only in the mind of the percipient and their apparent reality is simply a testimony to the extraordinary power of the human imagination. Although the witness genuinely believes that he has seen a ghost, its creation is purely from within himself, brought about perhaps by a subconscious wish to believe that he and his loved ones will survive death.

Those who have spent a lifetime studying psychic phenomena know very well that such simple pseudo-explanations can only rarely be applied to ghost sightings. However, interestingly, even many survivalist researchers have now come around to believing that apparitions have no truly objective reality. One theory which has gained ground among parapsychologists of the modern school contends that invisible spirits can make their presence known only by channelling thoughts into the mental processes of those still alive. In this way, discarnate souls create a picture in the receiver's mind, a vision which is so strong that the living person actually believes they have seen a ghost when really there has been no three-dimensional presence in the room.

Although the two models differ radically in their interpretation of what causes apparitions, each accepts that ghosts can only materialise through the agency of a living human mind. Both non-survivalists and survivalists of this school of thought would be quite certain that ghosts have no power to manifest in a place where there are no living eyes to see them. So on this point at least everyone would seem to agree. Yet recently fresh evidence has emerged which appears to challenge even this certainty. With the installation of remote-controlled closed-circuit television and video equipment as surveillance systems in various business premises, it is no longer necessary to have a human witness present when apparitions become manifest. And although it has come as a shock to many researchers, images indicating ghostly presences have been picked up on several occasions. Precisely this type of nocturnal visitor would seem to have made a fleeting yet significant appearance at an English nightclub in 1991. In the early hours of 27 October Cameron Walsch-Balshaw, the manager of Butterflies Nightclub in Oldham, Lancashire, locked up the premises with his assistant manager John Reid. It was a Saturday night and the place had been full as usual. Both men were tired but each was in good spirits and so, having set the club's burglar alarms and video surveillance cameras as usual, they stayed up drinking tea at Reid's home, which was just around the corner.

As it turned out neither man had gone to bed when just after 4.30am the local police phoned to say that the alarms were going off at Butterflies. The two employees quickly returned to the premises where they found several uniformed constables already on the spot. Sure enough the alarm system had been activated, yet when they entered the building the manager and assistant found no sign of a forced entry; indeed, everything seemed to be in place just as they had left it only two hours earlier. It was evident from a system check that the alarms had been triggered from inside the club's cash office, but as this was securely locked and a police search of the building had shown no signs of an intruder, it was unclear what had set them off.

It was then that one of the police officers suggested that they run through the video. What they found on the tape was to raise more questions than it answered. For when the men checked the security camera in the corridor outside the cash office they discovered that it had indeed filmed someone coming down the corridor, a male figure in a short-sleeved shirt and dark trousers. Yet this was no ordinary burglar. When the stranger reached the end of the corridor he simply turned and walked straight through the closed cash-office door. The bemused onlookers ran the tape back again and again, hoping that their eyes were playing tricks on them. But there could be no mistake. Without doubt the video showed the cash-office door to be shut – just as they had left it, and exactly as it had been found – yet the figure seemed to go through it without hesitation or difficulty. The time of this occurrence was shown on the video camera's running clock as 04:32:22 – the exact moment when the alarms had gone off at the nearby Oldham Police Station.

The unique film depicting the burglar from another world has understandably provoked much discussion in paranormal circles. Dismissed as a hoax by some, all available evidence suggests that it is genuine. In November 1991 an initial investigation was undertaken by representatives of the British Association for the Scientific Study of Anomalous Phenomena (ASSAP). Their researchers quickly discovered that Butterflies' premises, a Victorian building, had seen its fair share of ghostly happenings.

Several staff had experienced odd happenings of a poltergeist nature over the years and at least two men had met their death while working there. Because the fate of the ghost was not clearly shown on the video it was not possible to draw a definite connection with either of these earlier tragedies, yet following publicity generated by the incident and the publication of a still photograph in the *Oldham Evening Chronicle*, a local man, Derek Lloyd, came forward to speculate that the phantom might have been his father, who had died in the building while carrying out renovation work in 1936. ASSAP investigators were impressed by both the filmed evidence and the testimony of Walsch-Balshaw and Reid. Neither man had, it seemed, any motive for perpetrating a hoax and each came across as sincere. Journalists from local and national papers who interviewed them invariably came to the same conclusion as to the men's reliability.

But could there be another perfectly natural explanation for the enigma? some asked. Was it not possible that an earlier image had been trapped on the tape showing somebody walking down the corridor – in other words a double exposure? Cameron Walsch-Balshaw remained doubtful. 'All our tapes are demagnetised before they are used again. It's part of our insurance agreement. We have a bank of tapes, but what we start off with each night is basically a brand-new tape.' Researchers from ASSAP accepted his argument but in order to make sure they suggested that the tape be subjected to technical analysis to rule out even the slightest possibility of partial erasement. Fortunately, there was a simple enough test that could be made: if there is more than one image on a videotape there would also need to be more than one signal. When the Butterflies tape was examined by BBC technicians using an oscillator, the Corporation's experts were quickly able to verify that there was only one signal on the tape. Thus it was proved beyond doubt that a genuine image of a spectral figure walking down a corridor and passing through a solid door must have been filmed on the night in question. It was, in the words of BBC chief technician David Hall, 'a very startling video indeed'.

So what exactly did enter the Butterflies Nightclub during the early hours of the morning of 27 October 1991? The simple answer is that we don't know, yet whatever it was it must have had at least a partial element of reality. After all, the short-sleeved figure was not only captured on film but definitely triggered off the alarms at that precise moment. The system used in Butterflies worked by sending out a fan of infrared beams and the warning signal began when two beams in succession were blocked. Such a mechanism is subtle and it does not require anything particularly substantial to break the beams – indeed, even particles of smoke have been known to achieve this effect. But it is doubtful that a telepathically spawned illusion could work in the same way.

Whichever way we look at it, the only logical assumption we can make on the known facts of this case is that some form of objective presence was there – a presence which did not owe its existence to the subconscious mental processes of those who eventually saw it on film. A ghost, even.

1992

The Hueytown Humadruz

In January 1992 residents of the mining community of Hueytown, Alabama began to report hearing something distinctly peculiar in the middle of the night. Curiously, the sound which was described as a sort of droning, buzzing, background hum seemed audible to only one in ten of the population and although it was not particularly loud it was sufficiently annoying to cause headaches, migraine, nausea or simply bad nerves in some people. With Hueytown rapidly turning into a centre for insomniacs enormous public pressure was soon being put upon local authorities to find the source of the offending noise and put a stop to it. This, however, was easier said than done. For those who heard the noise could never seem to work out from exactly which direction it was coming and noise pollution experts didn't seem to have the slightest idea about its cause.

One by one possibilities were put forward. First traffic noise and industrial machinery were considered – and ruled out, since there was relatively little vehicle movement and hardly any industrial activity during the hours of darkness. A second theory – that the hum might be coming from electronic power substations and generators – was investigated and found not to be the case. A third hypothesis, that the sounds might be emanating from huge fans in the deep mineshafts that criss-crossed the subterranean realms beneath Hueytown, seemed to be a better bet; yet these fans were checked and easily passed the experts' tests.

The felling during the previous twelve months of a forest in a valley between the nearest mines and the town centre was linked to the mystery by some, one planning officer suggesting that a freakish combination of air pressure, humidity, temperature and terrain might create a sort of natural echo chamber. The idea was certainly a novel one, but since the hum was heard during both warm and cold nights it didn't convince many people. Whatever its cause, the Hueytown Humadruz continued to give people sleepless nights until it ceased to be heard in early 1993, ending suddenly and without explanation.

Although it can be of little consolation, the residents of the Alabama mining town were not the only people to have suffered at the hands of the humadruz that year. In England identical sounds were also affecting people across Gloucestershire, the highest numbers of complaints coming from around the upmarket suburban areas of Cheltenham and Stroud. Several hundred of those affected also suffered the more unpleasant physiological side-effects described earlier. There were no mine workings around the English examples and the same sort of checks to local power stations drew a blank. Some local people suspected that the noise was connected to the British government's top-secret spy and electronic communications complex GCHQ, which is situated near Stroud. Predictably the authorities denied any link and since the centre had been operating for many years without causing any bother they may very well have been telling the truth on this occasion. As with the examples cited earlier the Gloucestershire enigma ended some time in early 1993.

The humadruz outbreaks of 1992 are by no means the only time this peculiar phenomenon has caused misery. It is in fact a long-term problem which has sporadically plagued different communities in the industrialised world for at least thirty-five years. Early official explanations tended to focus upon the hearing of the victims themselves and for a while tinnitus, an eardrum condition which can sometimes generate sounds internally, was a widely accepted answer to the mystery. As it became more widespread, however, the humadruz defied this medical prognosis and people turned towards other external explanations, sonic booms and the spread of television sets being among the early favourites. In 1960 a British government enquiry was launched. Sufferers were locked in soundproof rooms in a laboratory yet still reported hearing the noise. The scientists investigating their plight remained baffled, many reverting publicly to the 'internally generated' explanation. Since only a minority of those living in any affected district actually heard the noise this line of reasoning might have seemed sensible, but it did nothing to explain why particular areas were singled out, why it was heard only during the small hours, and why it came and went so suddenly.

For some the humadruz was a minor nuisance; for others it represented something much worse. During the 1960s and 1970s the Department for the Environment received between 500 and 1,000 complaints annually and among these there were some terrible stories of people becoming clinically depressed and even mentally unstable as a direct result of the constant drone. The last notes of several suicides mentioned it as a reason for their despair. Clearly for some individuals the presence of a humadruz was something which could not be tolerated. Nevertheless, since all attempts to locate the source of the sound have proved futile, scientists preferred to ignore it.

Recently, however, there seems to have been a change of heart. In March 1992 the British government made available £50,000 to the Department of the Environment so that they could begin a new study. The department's first line of investigation focused upon a type of high-pressure underground natural gas piping located in many built-up areas of Britain, roughly 10 feet under the surface. British Gas refuted any suggestion that their pipes might be to blame, and since the laying of natural gas pipes post-dated the earliest reports of the humadruz by some fifteen years they were probably right to do so.

The next possibility to be discounted at long last was the hearing-defect syndrome. Twenty-five regular sufferers were painstakingly examined by medical specialists and found to have perfectly healthy ears. With this aspect of the matter finally settled the tinnitus explanation was ditched once and for all. But having decided quite conclusively what was *not* causing the hum the experts were once more stumped. By the time the money ran out the Department of the Environment was no nearer to comprehending this most persistent and irritating of curiosities.

1993

Saved by the Dead

As we have seen, ghosts return for a variety of reasons: to deliver messages, to honour death pacts, to seek justice and most commonly of all to reassure loved ones of their continued existence. Sceptics of apparitional encounters readily point out that optical illusions and wishful thinking can explain many cases, and even most believers will readily admit that a large proportion of phantasm sightings should be treated with caution before being accepted as worthwhile evidence for human survival of death. Nevertheless, examples where ghosts return with purposeful intent, perhaps to impart information of which the percipient can have known nothing, are more difficult to dismiss as hallucinations or hypnogogic images. Perhaps the most interesting phantoms of all, however, are those which not only display an intelligent purpose but are seen to intercede physically in human affairs. Such ghosts may be the rarest among all the subclassifications of the spirit world, yet they might provide the vital link which offers conclusive proof for survival. Reports of such occurrences have come in from around the world but probably the most recent took place in early 1993 in England.

Shortly before 6am on New Year's Day a fire began in the

downstairs living area of a three-bedroomed semi-detached house in Basildon, Essex. Sheila and Larry Duggin managed to escape down the smoke-filled stairs with three of their children but in the panic they had forgotten that their fourth child, Michelle, aged eight, was still lying asleep in her first-floor bedroom. By the time Larry Duggin had recovered himself enough to realise this the fire had spread and it was no longer possible to re-enter the house. Meanwhile, young Michelle had awoken and was banging hard upon the windowpane of her nursery, trying to attract attention. Though they could see her tiny hands waving frantically at the glass and hear her terrified screams above the roar of the fire, those outside were helpless. Neither the girl's head nor any part of her body was visible, for the window itself was too high for her to climb up to, and having only just alerted the fire service Michelle's parents knew that she would be overcome by the fumes long before she could be reached. It seemed as if only a miracle could save her.

Then, suddenly and without warning, that miracle happened. There was a crash of glass and a china ornament came flying through the window. A moment later the child herself appeared to be forcibly ejected in the same way, head-first straight through the hole in the glass that had just been made. Since there had been no warning, none of those below were able to break the girl's fall and she hit the ground with considerable force. And yet, astonishingly, she was totally unhurt and was soon being comforted by her relieved mother.

Though they were to lose all their possessions in the fire, the Duggins were simply glad they had all escaped with their lives. In particular, they were quick to praise young Michelle, who had shown such cool courage and speed of thought. But the eight-year-old girl was to recall a quite different sequence of events from the one which those standing below supposed had happened. First of all, rather than throwing the china ornament through the window herself it had, she said, been propelled by a man whose shining form had appeared next to her in the room as the smoke began to come under the door. Michelle had recognised the figure straight away as being her great-grandfather, who had died several years earlier when she was still a toddler. According to her testimony the ghost had then picked her up physically and pushed her head-first through the glass. The next thing she knew she was being cradled in her mother's arms.

At first the girl's parents found their daughter's story hard to believe, yet aspects of the incident certainly did seem strange. For one thing, the hole through which Michelle had made her dramatic exit seemed very small, too small for her to have passed through so easily. Secondly, the window itself was too high for her to have lifted herself up on to the sill. And what of the fall itself – over 15 feet on to the tarmac drive below, and scarcely a bruise to show for it? Talking to interested newspapermen several days later, Michelle's mother Sheila was quoted as having come around to believing the child's amazing tale. 'She was much bigger than the hole, which had jagged glass around it, and yet she came down with barely a scratch. All she keeps saying is that her great-grandad was there and helped her through. Her escape sounds so illogical when you think about it. Maybe he really was there.'

There was also a certain degree of circumstantial evidence to back up the girl's claims. Although most of the house had been gutted by the blaze the child's bedroom, which was at the front of the house, was among the least affected parts. Having succeeded in dousing the flames, firemen investigating the building had said that they found no chair, piece of furniture or other object below the girl's window, a detail which not only corroborated her version of events but made it extremely difficult to see how the eight-year-old could have pulled herself up high enough to escape. A fire brigade representative admitted that the whole affair seemed very odd indeed.

Can ghosts come back to save lives? One person who would be perfectly willing to believe the English child's story is Henry Sims, a retired farmer from Florida, who was himself saved from a house fire by the ghost of a dead relative. Around 10pm on a January evening in 1978, Sims said goodnight to his daughter and his grandchildren, who were staying with him and his wife Idela at their home in Live Oak, Florida. Though not a person who regularly experienced vivid dreams – and certainly not someone who had ever claimed any previous psychic experiences – the seventy-two-year-old ex-farmer was to see that night in his sleeping mind a clear picture of a dead child's face. It was the face of his nephew Paul, who had tragically been burned to death along with his baby sister when fire swept through their family home in 1932. In Henry Sims' dream, Paul was frantically trying to awaken him, shouting, 'Uncle Henry, Uncle Henry!' Sims awoke with a start and immediately caught the unmistakable smell of smoke in his nostrils. Yet it was not the only thing that alarmed him, for there beside his bed was the glowing form of the boy who a second earlier had been invading his dreaming mind. Within a second the apparition had vanished and Henry Sims was up and yelling to his wife, daughter and grandchildren to get out of the place. His cries awoke the other sleepers and all managed to flee the burning house just in time to save their lives.

Speaking after the incident the local Florida fire inspector, Lieutenant Frederick Lowe, said that it was miraculous no one had died. Had Sims not awoken at the vital moment it would certainly have been too late. In the opinion of Henry Sims, God Himself had sent his nephew's ghost to act as a guardian angel. 'The Lord wasn't ready for me to die,' Sims concluded. 'It was He who sent young Paul to warn of the danger and to pluck us all from that burning building.'

There is at least one other example in which a ghost has interceded physically in the material world. This incident – surely one of the most curious apparitional visitations of all – occurred some time in 1964, when a worker in an automobile assembly plant in Detroit narrowly escaped death after accidentally setting in motion a large piece of machinery above him. The endangered worker afterwards insisted – and his testimony was confirmed by others on the factory floor – that a tall, black figure had appeared at the vital moment to fling him bodily away from the threat.

The survivor did not recognise the man who saved him, but older men on the assembly line did. It was, they said, quite definitely the form of a worker who had been decapitated in a similar industrial accident more than twenty years before. The ghost had apparently returned to save a second victim from suffering the same fate.

The three stories related above show that ghosts *can* act intelligently – their behaviour indicates the probability that consciousness, awareness, memory and personality can be preserved beyond bodily dissolution. Through some process beyond our understanding these souls were able, temporarily at least, to draw together a combination of matter and energy which allowed them to clothe their ethereal selves with something which was for a few seconds both substantial and visible.

In other words, they were about as real as you or I.

Afterthoughts

God, we are told, moves in mysterious ways. So does the paranormal, though its manifestations often seem to have more in common with the Lord of Hades than a benevolent Creator. It is easy to see why many people shudder at the thought of unknown forces. Some preternatural occurrences, such as spontaneous human combustion, are frightening indeed and offer an unwelcome degree of personal danger. Others, like UFOs, appear to have wider implications for the survival of the race itself. But there are many more phenomena which provide no more than a nuisance to those directly involved, while the evidence surrounding apparitions, near-death experiences and reincarnations open up the possibility that we will all enjoy a more permanent span of life than our time on earth. The paranormal paints a far from uniformly dark canvas.

For those who retain an affection for the established principles of modern science, however, the paranormal seems like an unwelcome thundercloud blocking out the whole horizon. For virtually every mystery focused upon in this book forces us to question our present conceptual view of the universe, the physical laws which supposedly constrain it, and our own place as thinking beings within it. Faced with its multifarious paradoxes it is small wonder that mainstream science has yet to embrace the challenge of the paranormal world. For if we accept that the stories contained in this book are true, then basic fundamental assumptions such as the force of gravity, the linear movement of time, the mathematical law of averages and the limits of human sensory awareness may have little or no value. As the parameters of the possible become shifted again and again, so the ability of science to make sense of what is happening fades.

Subjective and objective perceptions merge and notions of reality are seen to have no permanent or absolute truth. The solid bedrock of decades of laboratory experimentation turn to quicksand and principles established by the greatest minds ever known can no longer be trusted. 'If prevision be a fact,' wrote one noted researcher in the early part of the century, 'then the whole theoretical framework of the universe is undermined.' But prevision *is* a fact, as so many people have long since come to realise. So is telepathic communication, the telekinetic manipulation of matter, personal levitation, spiritual healing and a whole host of mind-over-matter anomalies that science claims are impossible. The idea that an individual human consciousness can operate beyond the confines of the human body to directly affect the physical substance of the world around it throws the rationalist sceptics' carefully assembled jigsaw puzzle upside-down. So do near-death experiences, time-slips and other phenomena which suggest that the human soul can travel through time-space independent of the blood, bone and tissue counterpart, even surviving the supposedly final process of biological death and chemical disintegration.

It is hardly surprising, then, that most scientists have chosen to deny that such phenomena ever happen rather than to attempt to interpret it and integrate it into their own beliefs. To support the rationalists' case, the integrity and reliability of those directly involved in studying the phenomena are denigrated, and where such sources are impeccable it is mooted that a straightforward logical answer has simply been overlooked. The readers of this book must judge for themselves how far this approach can realistically be applied to the enigmas I have focused upon. Speaking personally, I offer no apologies for stating here and now that I remain unconvinced by the sceptics' line of reasoning.

UFOs are easily the most significant phenomenon of the past hundred years and probably also the most well witnessed. It should therefore come as no surprise to anyone that so many years have been devoted to different aspects of the flying-saucer mystery. Of the absolute reality of the phenomenon there can be virtually no remaining doubt, though it is probably true to say that most people still assume reported sightings to be hallucinations, misidentifications or hoaxes. I hope to have made it obvious to the reader that nothing could be further from the truth. Although there is no shortage of theories among ufologists, no one knows for sure where these machines are coming from or why they are visiting us. Yet the debate about UFOs should revolve around two issues – their origin and purpose – and not whether we should believe in them. As I have shown, the continuing public ignorance of hard UFO reality is due to the subtle (and sometimes not so subtle) debunking techniques employed by Western governments, military organisations and security agencies.

It has been estimated that over 5,000 UFO sightings have been made by fully qualified pilots, flying either civilian or military aircraft, yet this detail is largely unknown to the general public. The official policy is to stem the flow of information. So military personnel, civilian air crews, airport ground-control staff, police officers and other reliable witnesses in responsible positions are either sternly dissuaded against speaking to the press or prohibited from doing so by the special terms of their employment. It has recently emerged that during the 1950s and 1960s, when concern over the saucer situation in the United States was at its height, civilian pilots could be handed a ten-year prison term for simply passing on details of UFO sightings.

When civilians on the ground became witnesses to alien activity it was harder to gag them so the tactics changed. Usually such people were discredited by the media and establishment alike, while prominence was given to 'experts' whose natural explanations became widely believed, though they were often wholly implausible.

As I have written it would now appear that the policy of official secrecy in America began after the so-called Los Angeles air raid of 1942. Since then information has regularly been withheld from press and public alike, and only because of the United States Liberal Freedom of Information Act have many of the more sinister incidents, such as the deadly encounter of Lieutenant Thomas Mantell and the numerous crashes and disappearances which mark the period 1953–54, come to light. In Britain, where there is no comparable right of public access to the government's secret files, the public is denied even the smallest measure of truth. Although all official records tend to be made available after a time lapse of thirty years, these disclosures have never included material relating to UFOs. All specific requests for the release of this data have been denied and the British Ministry of Defence has now gone as far as to claim that all records relating to UFO contacts have been destroyed. Clearly Her Majesty's government has no intention of relaxing its hold of this most sensitive of all issues.

Of course, leaving aside the role of governments in debunking genuine encounters, one can understand why so many people remain sceptical of contactees' stories. The alleged Kelly–Hopkinsville visitations and the fantastic encounter of Antonio Villas Boas stretch the imagination, to say the least. Yet before we write them off as fantasies we should remember that similar encounters have been reported by witnesses from virtually every corner of the world in the thirty-five years since these events allegedly took place. We must also remember that much circumstantial evidence exists for UFOs, quite apart from the thousands of eye-witness reports. Blast patterns and other damage to surrounding areas have characterised the sites of alleged saucer landings and background radiation levels are regularly found to be high in these places. Humans caught in close proximity to alien craft have suffered physical illnesses consistent with those that would be expected to follow exposure to radiation discharge, and while the stories told by people who claim to have been abducted might seem ludicrous, several have returned bearing the scars of their remembered medical examinations.

When disparaging the testimony of such people sceptics typically portray them as being feeble-minded types, attention-seekers, alcoholics, drug addicts or people of highly unstable character. It cannot be stressed strongly enough that this is an entirely inaccurate profile of the average contactee. Indeed, all existing research into the backgrounds of those who claim encounters show that they represent a fair reflection of society, consisting mostly of well-balanced individuals who have no history of mental illness and, very often, no prior interest in paranormal phenomena. Moreover, it is now established that UFOs have been seen by people from the very highest strata of society, including senior civil servants, cabinet ministers, high-ranking military officers, senior churchmen and respected financiers. None of these people would have had anything to gain – and potentially much to lose – by concocting weird stories in order to attract attention.

Some sceptics (and even some ufologists) have now started to question the literal reality of UFOs from a rather different angle. This new breed of sceptic argues that, instead of being solid metallic vehicles driven by denizens of other planets, UFOs are in fact mentally induced projections of a hologram-matic type, emanating from a collective neurosis currently gripping the human race. Although the theory has its obvious attractions one can quickly see why it fails to stand up to serious examination. Mental images do not leave ground traces, cannot be captured on cine film or still photographs, and are unlikely to be picked up on radar screens. The non-physical hypothesis, originally put forward by the psycholo-gist Carl Gustav Jung, might explain distant objects seen high in the sky but certainly does not account for electrical power supply malfunctions, the mutilation of livestock and the occasional loss or disappearance of aircraft. As C.G. Jung was eventually to admit in one of the last letters he wrote before his death, the overwhelming probability is that UFOs are precisely what they seem to be – solid metallic objects of airborne transportation, manned or directed by intelligences other than human.

If the weight of collective evidence points to the hard reality of alien craft, then stories of saucer recoveries from New Mexico and elsewhere would prove the case entirely, should they turn out to be true. Just how much the governments of this planet know about the UFO phenom-enon remains a closely guarded secret but the 1980 sighting above Texas of a formation of USAF Chinooks seemingly escorting an object of non-human design offers the tantalising possibility that contact *has* now been established between Homo Sapiens and another highly developed lifeform.

While historical records show that men have been seeing peculiar objects in the skies since the days of antiquity, the vast bulk of sightings have come during the past fifty years, so it is unsurprising that most people think of UFOs as a peculiarly twentieth-century phenomenon. The same could hardly be said of ghosts. Tales of spectral encounters are to be found in the earliest writings of every major world religion and belief in phantoms would seem to have underpinned the superstitions of tribal cultures from the four corners of the globe. Yet while they are still a regular feature of popular fiction and film, public belief in the objective reality of ghosts has lessened during the age of scientific rationalism. However, at the same time apparitional visitations have, if anything, grown even more frequent. So what are we to make of this apparent contradiction? Many phantom encounters – especially those images made on the verge of sleep or immediately upon waking – may easily be explained in terms of a variety of natural explanations. Others, like the visions of phantom soldiers marching once more across ancient fields of battle, are genuinely mysterious, yet because they appear to reflect energy-impressions or images held in the ether they cannot really be held up as evidence of human soul-survival. But many phantoms *do* seem to provide just the evidence required by survivalists. Wilfred Owen's spectre appeared twice: originally to his father at the precise moment of his death in a French field hospital and again a week later to his brother on board a ship sailing through the waters off South Africa. Neither percipient knew of their relative's death at the time of their encounter. Likewise, Owen Harrison proved his survival by relaying information to an aunt which she could not conceivably have known, and Lieutenant Sutton, the American military trainee demanding vengeance for his murder by fellow students, also telepathically imparted a version of his killing which proved upon subsequent investigation to be true. None of these incidents can be accounted for by telepathy between still-living persons. At the same time, ghosts caught on film and video, or visages which appear directly in imprints upon physical matter, like the Belmez faces, cannot be contained within a purely rationalistic framework. The proof is there for all to see and it is impossible to deny its objective reality.

When a ghost is seen by a single witness the chance of misidentification or hallucination can never be entirely ruled out, even when the percipient's integrity seems unimpeachable. The same argument cannot be applied to examples where the apparition is seen independently by several people over a period of years or collectively by several witnesses at once (as in the case of the doomed flight 401). Hard though it is for some to accept, the most plausible explanation for these examples remains the supernatural one.

Given the prodigious number of spectral sightings made during the modern era the objective reality of ghostly phenomena can hardly be denied. The same could be said for poltergeists and other (possibly related) phenomena such as attacks by invisible assailants, phantom stone-throwers and fire spooks, although the precise nature of the force which generates these curious outbreaks remains rather more obscure. They may be the discarnate souls of evil-doers whose lack of spiritual development forces them to remain earthbound upon the plane of matter following their death (the spiritualist's belief), visible creatures from the nether realm the [pre-twentieth-century conception] or some strange form of psychic energy originating from the subconscious minds of the percipients, (a view now favoured by many parapsychologists). It goes without saying that none of these explanations can be encompassed within the present laws of physics, and mainstream scientists usually ignore such events or else offer the bland assertion that a perfectly straightforward natural solution must have been overlooked in the majority of cases. But the sheer scale of poltergeist activity belies such complacent pseudo-explanations.

What is more, the activity of invisible forces seems to be on the increase. Often, the arrival of these entities provides little more than a nuisance to the human witnesses caught up in the events. In other instances, the persistent violence displayed by the unseen force is terrifying to behold. Whatever the case may be, these bizarre activities make little sense to the rational mind. How or why a ghost or other invisible being should choose to send gallons of water shooting out of walls and ceilings is hard enough to comprehend, yet as we have seen mysterious flows and oozings regularly feature in paranormal reports from around the world. Fire spooks which bring about the spontaneous combustion of inanimate objects are even more frequently observed and their arrival is never welcomed. But more worrying are those forces which physically attack victims causing serious injury and sometimes even death. Few who have seen at first hand the mayhem and misery left by such invisibles will still doubt that their origin is supernatural.

As with the more extreme cases of apparent possession, there is little room here for believing in a purely psychological explanation. Extremities of mental hysteria may be unnerving to the lay witness, as doctors will confirm, but no aberration of the human mind can cause a person to sweat blood, levitate to a ceiling or vomit kilograms of excrement at one time. Nor would any form of known madness produce the external manifestations attendant upon some possession/poltergeist outbreaks, such as the appearance of blood or slime on walls, or the pervading stench of rotting flesh moving through the rooms of a house where a possessed person is sleeping. All these and many more repulsive effects have been reported by witnesses to unnatural incursions. They are not the stuff of mere fiction.

Depending upon your interpretation of each phenomenon, ghosts, possessions and poltergeists might all seem to point towards the probable survival of the human spirit beyond death. Further evidence of soul survival is held in related activities such as the electronic voice phenomenon or the phone calls from the dead occasionally received by those recently bereaved. Though much controversy surrounds these subjects, EVP research continues today and phantom phone messages go on being reported.

Should we talk in terms of life after death or life after life? Interest in reincarnation is now higher among Westerners than any time in the past and this fact should surprise no one given the prodigious number of people who have claimed former lives and described their earlier existences, in precise and accurate detail, either while under hypnosis or through conscious flashbacks. Sceptics argue that the mind's infinite capacity for storing knowledge in its subconscious vaults is the true source of past-life regression recall, yet they cannot find answers for specific cases like that of Virginia Tighe/ Bridey Murphy, or the Englishman Ray Bryant, who in 1983 recalled his life as Reuben Stafford, the nineteenth-century veteran of the Crimean War, in quite staggeringly accurate detail. While doubt continues to surround the method of hypnotic regression, the same objections cannot be made against the often staggering recollections of young children. Dr Ian Stevenson, the Californian psychologist, has collected over 2,000 case histories where infants from every race or religion have spontaneously recalled existences that match the known lives and deaths of actual people. In about ten per cent of these cases the living child bears the scars of the physical death injury suffered by the former host. A purely psychological explanation cannot be made to account for these examples and unless we look towards coincidence on a grand scale then some form of rebirth seems the most likely possibility.

Of course coincidence itself may very well play a less than

passive role in our destinies. Those who are labelled Jonahs or those unfortunate few who find themselves the subject of a personal jinx must wonder whether we are not, in Shakespeare's phrase, 'as flies to wanton boys' killed for sport by the cruel and unfeeling lords of fate. These underlying patterns may leave visible traces, as the examples focused upon have shown, yet like many other researchers I cannot help but wonder whether the same principles of synchronicity underlie all our lives while we only rarely come to notice them.

The apparent efficacy of some curses may well be linked to the jinx syndrome, if only because the deadly progress of each manifestation is both invisible and insidious. Whether it is simply the human mind's capacity to influence another's health and destiny, or whether there is really some supernatural agency assisting in the victims' destruction is not clear. But we can say with a fair degree of certainty that curses work whether the focus of the evil chooses to believe in them or not. Once again a purely psychological interpretation fails to fit all the available facts.

Another deadly force and one which is far more disturbing to the rational mind is the energy responsible for disappearing people – the apparent vanishment into thin air of living persons. Black holes, psychic whirlpools, cosmic liftshafts, time-warps and other various nightmare scenarios have all been mooted by a succession of paranormal writers, while mainstream commentators have generally looked towards more down-to-earth theories to explain these anomalies. To give the sceptics their due few disappearances are truly odd. Thousands of individuals go missing every year for a variety of perfectly unremarkable reasons and it is both foolish and unnecessary to look to unnatural causes for all but a handful of them. But when more than one individual vanishes without cause from a location where there is no obvious route of escape (as in the case of the Flannan Island lighthouse keepers), or where a large body of people go permanently missing (as in the cases of the Gallipoli regiment, the defenders of Nanking and the Lake Anjikuni Eskimos), such simplistic scenarios lose their meaning. Either the facts of these incidents have been embellished, fabricated or misconstrued to a point beyond recognition or there is something very sinister about them.

During the present century many eerie stories have come from eye-witnesses who have claimed to have seen people dematerialise into thin air. But since no evidence afterwards remains to support their incredible accounts sceptics tend to write them off as hallucinations. The same attitude cannot be taken when we come to examine the phenomenon of spontaneous human combustion, since the all-too-frightening evidence of this preternatural force is left behind in the form of the peculiarly burned bodies of the victims. Though medical science has long held SHC to be a myth, many forensic experts have now come round to accepting that the human body can burn on its own, under certain special circumstances. That is not to say that they accept a preternatural hypothesis, however. Instead, modern medical opinion asserts that the charred corpses of apparent SHC victims, like the English couple found in their Butlocks Heath home in 1905, have been reduced slowly and steadily to their bizarre state by the gradual action of a naked flame upon the human body's fatty tissue. This action burns the corpse down over a period of many hours like a wick in a candle. So, say the experts, SHC-type deaths may happen only under the following conditions: (1) Where the person has already died; (2) where a naked flame or other available source of heat is present; (3) where the corpse lies within an enclosed space and there is a limit on the available oxygen supply.

Many people who formerly rejected all talk of spontaneous combustion out of hand have now come around to seeing some merit in the 'wick theory' and now are happy to admit that the whole thing was not simply an urban myth, as they had previously supposed. Scientists are even happier because they believe they have accounted for one of the most disquieting elements of the paranormal without recourse to the unseen. In fact they have done nothing of the sort. Indeed, among all the natural pseudo-explanations for preternatural occurrences, the SHC 'wick' theory must surely take the biscuit for absurdity. First, its slow-burn hypothesis ignores the numerous witnessed testimonies of those who have seen SHC at work and declared the fire's progress to be astonishingly rapid. Secondly, it ignores the fact that SHC has regularly been seen to strike out of doors, affecting evidently still living victims (a few of whom have actually survived its onslaught). Thirdly, it does nothing to explain how human bone structure can be reduced to powder by the heat when nearby combustible material often remains unaffected. Fourthly, it cannot account for the numerous examples where human SHC victims have been found in situations where no naked flame or other nearby source of heat was apparent. All in all, this would seem to be yet just another example where mainstream science, failing to comprehend the facts as they are known to be, subtly alters them in order to concoct an alternative explanation based on an entirely false premise.

The Romans labelled spontaneous human combustion the 'fire from heaven', though hell would seem to be a more appropriate origin for these particular flames. Modern man has, of course, long since ceased to believe in such a place. So why, one wonders, do creatures of a demonic nature continue to appear with quite alarming regularity in our own era of microcomputers and space-age avionics? This is no exaggeration. Even leaving aside the hideous assaults of invisibles and examples of possession by unseen spirits, the twentieth century has seen literally dozens, perhaps hundreds, of examples where repulsive creatures of an elemental nature have appeared without warning to terrify witnesses. Some of these have been recorded in the earlier pages of this book. Many more are recorded in the Gazetteer which you will find at the end. What these supernatural monsters desire from humanity is not clear, and we cannot say how they make their fleeting entries into the world of matter. But it would appear to be perfectly evident that many of them are up to no good.

The black dogs of rural England and Wales may very well emanate from such an alternative level of reality since they have little in common with canines from the material animal kingdom. Though sceptics will readily assert that prior knowledge of ghost-dog lore and an overactive imagination can lead a witness to hallucinate such terrors, this explanation fails to account for the extraordinary consistency between reports made by witnesses in many different counties over several hundred years. And in any case, while many people may fear spiders and snakes few people are canine phobics. Were we to hallucinate in outward form some aspect of our innermost tensions or fears why should we create them in such a form? The rationalists have no answers.

At first glance tales of huge hominids like Bigfoot and the abominable snowman present mysteriologists with a distinctly different set of possibilities. The vastness and remoteness of their natural habitat makes the existence of such creatures as solid living flesh-and-blood animals a real possibility. Yet neither has ever been captured or shot, and while there are plenty of tracks, no physical remains have been found in the form of skeletal relics or skins. Interestingly, both the American Indians and the Nepalese mountain-dwellers seem to feel that these creatures also exist on a semi-phenomenal level. Could they be right?

Mystery cats which appear in such places as England and Australia may likewise emanate from a psychic plane beyond the human senses. Certainly this would explain why even more sightings are not made and why no carcasses have so far been found. Yet since field spoors and traces of fur have been discovered and identified on many occasions, their literal reality cannot be written off, either. Something, after all, must have savaged the livestock found partly eaten around the various spates of sightings.

Some out-of-place creatures definitely do exist. Britain alone has seen more than its fair share of non-native species turning up without explanation. Recent examples include an African spotted hyena shot near the Ashdown Forest of Kent in 1971; a 10-pound iguana run over in Dulwich, Greater London, the following year; an Arctic fox killed by a guard dog in Yorkshire during August 1983; and a South African tropical fruit-bat found clinging to a car radiator in the city of Exeter, Devon thirteen months later. No explanation has ever been put forward for the unexpected arrival of any of these creatures, but their flesh-and-blood existence cannot be disputed any more than we can deny the reality of those elephants occasionally found in the fishing nets of North Sea trawlermen.

Far more mysterious than the occasional out-of-place appearance of known existing species is the sighting of long-since extinct creatures. Many parapsychologists have adopted the view that the Loch Ness Monster and all lake-serpents are really spectral in origin. Such a hypothesis finds favour with many people not least because it helps us to understand how sightings can be made in small lakes in such countries as Ireland. It is quite inconceivable that huge animals could long remain undetected in shallow water, nor would these minor habitats provide adequate food for a large predator. Nevertheless, in a much larger body of water like Loch Ness a huge marine reptile might conceivably hide from man, and the world's oceans, having a mean depth of over two miles, provide perfectly adequate cover for truly massive creatures to remain elusive. Where great reptiles would find an abundance of food the chances of them existing remains a strong possibility, and since several unidentified corpses have definitely been washed up during the past ninety-odd years, the case for the objective reality of some sea-monsters would seem overwhelming.

Perhaps the existence of enormous reptilians in the world's oceans should not really be too surprising for zoologists. For the twentieth century has seen the sudden appearance of several unknown species as well as the re-emergence of others thought to have been extinct. New additions include the Japanese beaked whale, first caught in 1937; the Cochito porpoise, found in the Gulf of California during 1958; the huge Megamouth shark first seen in the waters off Hawaii in 1976; and a new species of Arctic killer whale which managed to exist quite happily beyond man's sight until 1983. The coelacanth fish caught in 1938, which was formerly believed to have died out 60,000,000 years before, is just one of several supposedly extinct marine creatures to have been discovered living in today's oceans. Even on land, where it is far more difficult for creatures to remain undetected, there have been significant modern examples of species returning from apparent extinction. The hispid hare and pygmy hog were relegated to history before the beginning of the twentieth century, yet both have been found living in Assam during the past decade. The Cuban ivory-billed woodpecker has been reported regularly since 1986, more than thirty years after it too was written off. The same year saw the re-emergence of yet another supposedly extinct species, the bamboo-eating lemur, whose home is in the mountainous rainforests of Madagascar.

Since most of these creatures had been thought to have become extinct quite recently there is no need to ponder long upon the mistake of their assumed demise. But the possible survival of much larger creatures from prehistoric times is far more difficult to contemplate and the likelihood of this scenario is scathingly dismissed by modern zoologists and those who study the fossils of dinosaurs themselves. So what are we to make of the occasional reports of such creatures that have been made during the last hundred years? While it is just conceivable that a creature the size of a brontosaurus might have remained hidden in the vast swamplands of the African interior, only the most credulous person would accept that flying lizards might have survived undetected in the mountains of north America. One is tempted to question the eyesight of witnesses to such creatures, yet as a trawl through the Gazetteer will soon show the spate of sightings in Texas during 1976 provides just one spectacular example of a much wider phenomenon. Insane though it may seem, pterodactyl-type horrors have been seen haunting the skies above several countries. Surely those who see them are not simply mis-identifying similarly sized man-made objects such as light aeroplanes?

Yet the alternative explanation – that the animals might really exist – must also be rejected. For if such an amazing fact were true we should expect to hear reports of sightings much more frequently. The idea that these visions might be a form of time-slip whereby the witness sees a replay of past events from prehistoric days could explain some sightings, but not all. It would not, for instance, make sense of those instances where the creatures have apparently attacked people or damaged property. All in all, surviving dinosaurs would seem to be a riddle wrapped in an enigma, which for the present at least cannot be unwoven.

Like so many paranormal phenomena, the appearance of mysterious creatures is fleeting and one is often required to assess the validity of the reports in the light of the witnesses' credibility. Crop circles provide us with a very different opportunity. So frequent are their appearance and so spectacular are the marks they make upon the British countryside that thousands have been drawn to marvel at their beautiful symmetry at first hand. Across the world millions more have read about them and seen the numerous published photographs in the hundreds of magazine and newspaper articles devoted to this most puzzling of modern-day mysteries. The phrase 'seeing is believing' is as true for the open-minded as it is for the sceptic, and it should not come as a surprise that crop circles have aroused unprecedented public interest. Can anyone reasonably maintain that something very odd has not been going on in the English countryside for some years? Incredibly, some still do, and many felt vindicated when in late 1991 a pair of retired artists named Dave Chorley and Doug Bower came forward to claim that they had been fabricating crop circles for years. Tabloid newspapers (all of whom seemed to readily accept their story) splashed headlines proclaiming that the game was up for the circle-watchers. No one seemed to question whether it had actually been possible for the two men to have personally faked all the markings, by that time numbering several thousand (672 in thirty-three English counties during 1990 alone). Still, incredible though the claims of Chorley and Bower evidently were, public interest in the circle phenomenon quickly dropped off and as a result of their confessions the suspicion of trickery has now attached itself to the fledgling science of cereology. Yet even now some mainstream scientists remain unconvinced by the natural solutions and crop circles remain one of the few paranormal events which are currently being researched by those outside the parascientific community.

Unfortunately the same cannot be said for many elements of the paranormal. Natural explanations for frotskis, the collective name given to falls of anomalous matter from the sky, are also commonly put forward, though with regard to these (with the possible exception of ice-falls) the rationalists' case seems more tenuous than ever. As well as the living creatures most frequently reported to suddenly rain down from the sky the twentieth century has seen odd showers of various matter, including peas, lumps of coal, onions, tomatoes, nails, meat and blood, human fingers, runner beans, pieces of china, marbles, a fused iron bar, golf balls, limestone spheres of various sizes and melted glass. A natural explanation for each and every one of these occurrences is basically the same. They have, say the experts, been lifted up by whirlwinds and deposited where they fall. I am sure that the reader will not require me to dwell upon the reasons why I believe this explanation to be most unlikely. Suffice it to say that whirlwinds would be expected to deposit all manner of debris over a widespread area, yet the most notable feature of frotskis is the way they tend to involve only one type of object or animal, the falls themselves usually being concentrated upon a very localised space, sometimes an individual person's house or garden.

The appearance of circular light forms, either the highly charged ball-lightning variety or the more low-level will-o'-the-wisp type, has also been explained by rationalists in less than satisfactory ways. The idea that ball lightning is merely an atmospheric phenomenon would be perfectly acceptable were it not for the fact that it sometimes shows obvious signs of intelligence. Similarly, the theory that low-level nocturnal lights might be formed from luminescent marsh gas fails to account for their idiosyncratic behaviour in following people or leading lost individuals towards safety or danger. Their tendency to haunt the vicinity of earlier tragedies also hints at a supernatural origin. Interestingly, the experiences of some witnesses to spook lights lends credence to the idea that they might be entities. In 1957 two English poachers walking along a supposedly haunted stretch of railway line between Crewe and Northwich were confronted by a hovering light form of the typical low-level variety. But instead of simply staying globular, the manifestation grew in size and transmuted itself into a 20-foot high angelic figure complete with long golden hair and large folded wings. Twenty-one years later, a strikingly similar story was told by an American psychic and metal-bender named Silvio who saw and followed a spook light while walking through woods. Silvio had a camera and photographed the object, but when the print was developed it showed something he had not expected – the anomalous image of a golden 'angel' enclosed in a yellow circle of light. Silvio himself linked the vision to the spirit of his mother, who had died only days before the incident took place.

The idea that light forms represent heavenly presences ought to find support among the many observers of Virgin Mary visions and other religious phenomena. For while most mysteriologists have failed to draw a meaningful connection between these two apparently unrelated enigmas, key elements remain central to both. Indeed, sometimes they actually coincide. In 1905 during an outbreak of religious revivalist fervour in south Wales, balls of light were regularly seen hovering above chapels in which a Welsh evangelist preacher named Mary Jones was taking services. Other manifestations which allegedly occurred during the revival included miraculous healings and spectral incursions. The appearance of light balls has also seemed to precede many visions of the Blessed Virgin Mary and other supposedly heaven-sent messengers. On 13 October 1917, the day the sun apparently danced before the eyes of 70,000 witnesses at Fatima in southern Portugal, a single luminous globe was seen to advance at low altitude from east to west and come to rest in the branches of the oak tree when Our Lady subsequently appeared to the children. Whether this shows evidence of alien involvement (as some ufologists have speculated) or whether it simply represented an unknown lifeform is impossible to say. But whatever else happened at Fatima the sun assuredly could not have literally danced, so the collective vision which so many people claimed to have seen must have been the result of some external influence upon their minds. Could this external factor have been heralded by the arrival of the light form?

Glowing spheres have been seen just before the beginning of many comparable miracles. In April 1968 two Muslim Egyptian car mechanics working in a garage next to St Mary's Coptic church in the Zeitoun suburb of Cairo saw a glowing sphere descend from the sky and come to rest upon the roof of the adjacent holy building. It proved to be the start of an extended period of curious activity where visionary figures surrounded by halos of glowing light would become manifest before the eyes of devotees and sceptics alike. The forms included fiery doves and females dressed in long robes who appeared to bless those watching below. These figures were interpreted by some as nuns and by others as the Blessed Virgin Mary herself. Whatever one's own belief, the fact remains that some very strange events did take place above the Coptic church. The nightly visions lasted until May 1971 and were seen in total by literally hundreds of thousands of sightseers who crowded the streets below. The manifestations were even successfully photographed. And when a similar light sphere hovered above a separate Cairo church, St Damania the Martyr in Shubra, on the night of 25 March 1986, it proved to be the forerunner of yet another of this century's most well-attested visionary experiences. On succeeding nights during the rest of that spring and summer a Madonna-like form appeared before the awestruck eyes of thousands of Egyptians together with fiery crosses, various angels and, finally, St Damania herself.

Religious phenomena of the type described above prove perplexing for the disbelievers since the sheer number of those who bear witness to them destroys the possibility of either a hoax or a misconception. The likelihood that such reports could be the result of collective hallucinations brought about by religious hysteria (itself an unproved theory) finds few supporters, since the religious figures were also seen by atheists and non-Christians. Evidently something odd was happening there and that something had a level of objective reality. To believe otherwise is to stand rational argument on its head. Whether it really was the mother of God returning to earth is, of course, another matter entirely.

Apparitional visitations, UFOs, disappearing people, poltergeists, frotskis – the list of impossibilities is seemingly endless. Scientists, having no way of embracing these mysteries within their own fixed set of rules, shy away from their implications, preferring to deny their existence. Parascientists meanwhile, those select few who have made it their business to enter the forbidden ground where others fear to tread, have been busily concocting their own theories with varying degrees of success. So what is the current state of thought among those whose lives have been spent studying the unexplained? Every mysteriologist has his own pet hypothesis and yet, broadly speaking, these theories now tend to fall within three categories, which can be briefly summed up as follows.

The first is known, somewhat colourfully, as the 'goblin universe' theory. Researchers who favour this hypothesis feel that alongside the visible world of matter we see around us there is a parallel universe which exists on an entirely different level of reality; a separate dimension where natural laws play no part and where virtually anything can and probably does exist. From such a place phenomenal creatures may pass briefly into our material world, become temporarily visible and then return to their own dimension, leaving behind the proof of their presence in the form of witnessed accounts, a blurred image on a photograph, or on an anomalous track on the ground. In the opinion of its proponents the 'goblin universe' is not entirely separate from our own, but interfaces on a mental level. Thus, at any given time, natural laws can be suspended in our own sphere of existence and vice versa.

Another school of thought which offers a slightly more mundane explanation for paranormal experiences links man's telepathic mental powers to naturally occurring but as yet unrecognised earth energies. Proponents of this theory contend that there is a clear pattern to be drawn between reported preternatural phenomena and seismic activity arising out of stress in rocks. Such stresses can, they argue, release powerful electromagnetic energy fields which in turn can move about in spherical glowing shapes. When these earth lights come into contact with people they alter a person's brainwave functions and induce hallucinations in much the same way that strobe lights can lead an epileptic to have fits. Under such influences affected people confabulate stories such as meeting supernatural creatures or being kidnapped by space aliens. They become convinced themselves, though in fact nothing of the sort has actually happened.

Although the 'earth lights' idea seems far-fetched one English ufologist, Paul Devereux, has written several impressive books containing apparently indisputable evidence showing how correlations between the appearances of UFOs and ball lightning are matched by known fluctuations in seismic activity across the United Kingdom. Those who follow the Devereux school of thought have been quick to point out that elsewhere in the world phenomena such as religious visions also seem to be more likely to occur in areas where rock tensions peak because of geological faults. For instance, during the above-described 1969 Zeitoun manifestations seismic activity in a 500-mile radius of Cairo was discovered to be ten times greater than in the surrounding areas. So what was actually happening above the church, say the Devereux group, was that light-form energy released by the seismic activity was later mistaken by witnesses for miraculous images because their sense of perception had been affected. Their minds simply reconstructed what they were seeing to fit in with their own religious preconceptions. God played no part in the process.

A third theory holds that unnatural incursions are actually mind-monsters, creatures from inner space, hologrammatic images which stem from within the reservoir of the collective human unconscious. Though these can be summoned up by shamans, occultists and witches, those with non-developed psychic powers are more likely to experience paranormal visitations under certain mental conditions or in places where a higher background level of psychic energy has been left behind. Those who accept this 'inner space' concept point out that the human mind interacts with the natural world in a far more direct way than is currently recognised by science. Thus human minds might actually be able to call forth telepathically spawned hallucinations which appear to have an element of objective reality, not only to those who created them but also to other observers. Such things might even for a short period of time manifest a hard or at least semi-material existence. Adherents to the 'creatures from inner space' philosophy reject the existence of discarnate forces in poltergeist outbreaks and are sceptical of the extra-terrestrial hypothesis for UFOs.

None of these theories finds favour with mainstream scientists, for obvious reasons. Are any of them sufficient to account for the numerous mysteries contained in this book?

The answer, I am afraid, is a clear and unequivocal no. Perhaps each has a certain validity and might explain some mysteries, yet none can account for each and every strange manifestation. Let's take each one in turn and examine its merit.

The 'goblin universe' idea might very well explain odd sightings of unknown creatures which seem to have a distinct phenomenal reality such as black dogs, and could also account for the unknown species that have proven impossible to track down such as the yeti, sasquatch and possibly even lake-monsters. But since several of these last examples have also been photographed, the spoors of the sasquatch cast in plaster and in the case of sea-going dinosaurs some corpses recovered, there is conflicting evidence which seems to point towards a rather more physical existence. The 'goblin universe' theory helps us to understand the action of some invisible entities but certainly not all apparitions, and much spectral phenomena would need to be treated separately. These would include those ghosts of human personalities which appear to be precisely what they seem to be – the ultra-physical vehicles of deceased human minds. UFOs present an even bigger problem, for if stories of UFO recoveries are true then they confirm once and for all the hard nuts-and-bolts reality of both ships and occupants. As I made clear earlier in this chapter, it makes more sense to interpret UFOs through the standard extra-terrestrial hypothesis or alternatively through the subterranean theory (my own opinion) – namely that they are operating from bases deep beneath the world's oceans. Finally, the 'goblin universe' hypothesis offers little explanation for such diverse enigmas as time-slips, spontaneous human combustion, precognition, jinxes, curses, bleeding icons, incorruptibility, cases of stigmata and miraculous cures.

Many of the same objections can be set against the

distinctly more 'natural' idea that seismic activity causes a reality-perception shift in the minds of observers to UFOs, ghosts, religious visions and various other infernal creatures. If these incursions are nothing more than illusions, how can UFOs be photographed, appear on radar, leave ground traces and increase background radiation levels? Seismic activity might conceivably knock out electrical power supplies but it could not mutilate animals, bring down aircraft or make ships disappear. Certainly the blanket of official secrecy that surrounds these incidents demonstrates that governments, military bodies and special intelligence agencies do not consider UFOs to be an illusion but a very real menace. The fact that a greater than usual level of seismic activity has characterised some areas which have become the focus for paranormal activity is certainly interesting, but it would be quite wrong to claim that this is always, or even usually, the case, still less the cause. Moreover, even when it is true, it still fails to adequately explain the phenomenon. Given that Cairo was at the epicentre of seismic activity in 1969 and accepting for argument's sake that this made the appearance of light forms more likely, why did the ball of light choose to descend upon a church and not another building in the city?

At first glance the 'inner space' idea which contends that the human unconscious can objectify phenomena on to the outside world seems the most promising theory. After all, the extraordinary ability of the human mind to control matter has been demonstrated on innumerable occasions and in various ways, by faith healers, metal-benders, thoughtographers, fire walkers and many psychics. However, while many peculiar events might emanate from the human mind's hidden capacities, others most certainly seem not to. Can we be expected to believe that a person might suddenly burst into flames because of an unconscious desire to immolate themselves, or that a community which suddenly disappears into thin air does so because they collectively imagine themselves out of existence? Some phenomenal creatures could be temporarily called up into a semi-substantial existence from the pool of humanity's collective subconscious, but as we have seen, others seem on the balance of evidence to be all too real, as do alien vehicles. Once more we are presented with a theory which seems to provide part of the solution but not all. It is all most unsatisfactory.

As the human race stands poised on the verge of the next millennium – which some believe will usher in a new age of spiritual enlightenment – the strange forces of the paranormal world remain little understood by those mysteriologists who have spent a lifetime attempting to make rational sense of them. The intellectual dishonesty of mainstream science, which manages to ignore everything which it cannot comprehend, has been compounded by the abject failure of parascientists to construct a meaningful set of laws from which we could build an alternative model of the universe. Yet, to be fair to myself and my peers, the difficulties involved in this branch of research should not be underestimated. Most paranormal manifestations occur in the outside world and without warning, leaving often frustratingly inconclusive and contradictory evidence. We cannot trap other-worldly creatures in a laboratory and dissect them at leisure. For most of us, the evidence we gather arrives through second- or perhaps third-hand accounts. This would be fine if one wished to research the basis of a horror story or science-fiction novel, but it is hardly the ideal methodology for a serious study. The reader will appreciate why we find this aspect of our work frustrating and when mainstream scientists cynically use our supposedly unscientific research practices to cast doubt upon all paranormal occurrences our sense of frustration grows all the more intense. In the face of such blatant unfairness and open hostility some researchers give up altogether. But most are made of tougher mettle. As long as odd things continue to be reported mysteriologists around the world will go on collecting data, comparing phenomena and drawing their own tentative conclusions. The search for proof of human survival will go on, evidence will continue to mount for the existence of UFOs, answers will gradually be uncovered for some of supernature's most baffling enigmas.

The twentieth century may have provided some of the most curious events that mankind has ever been faced with, and never before have they been so well documented. Yet most scientists remain wedded to the mechanistic view of the universe, with its fixed rules and certainties, rigid framework and unbending physical laws. What cannot be contained within the framework is labelled as impossible but as we have seen the so-called impossible is as real as anything else. All we need now is to look behind that reality and take an intellectual step beyond the limits of our own preconceptions. What we find there will, I am sure, prove as exciting as anything mankind has so far discovered.

Gazetteer

Unless a book of this type were to run to several volumes it would be impossible to include examples of every type of paranormal mystery. In fact some of my own favourites have of necessity been omitted. So to capture the fuller flavour of the century's oddities I have included brief entries of a few lines each in the form of a Gazetteer. From this last section it becomes obvious that the twentieth century has seen weird phenomena reported on a truly worldwide scale. Examples have been chosen because of their general strangeness or because of their significance in relation to mysteries focused on in the main section. But even here it has proved difficult to mention more than a tiny fraction of the more interesting phenomena. So individual sightings of ghosts, UFOs, mundane reports of spirit contacts through channelling with the dead, miraculous cures and experiments into metal-bending or telepathy are not included, simply because they are too numerous.

1900

USA, near Joplin, Missouri. A glowing phenomenon known as the Ozark spook light was seen regularly by local residents; typical of ghost lights, it moved away or disappeared when approached. Also in Missouri, near Wellsville, an Episcopal church struck by lightning during August thereafter displayed a portrait of the church sexton on its ceiling. The man had been several miles away when the lightning struck.

USA, Buffalo, New York State. On 29 September boys saw a rain of fish during a hard shower; the area was to register a similar fish-fall on 29 September 1939.

USA, Alexandria Bay, New York. In late November thousands of curious hailstones with the appearance of human eyes fell on to a widespread area.

1901

USA, Tillers Ferry, South Carolina. Hundreds of fish including catfish, perch and trout fell during a localised shower and were seen in cotton fields on 27 June.

Australia, Queensland. Substantial fall of gudgeon in August. This would be the first of ten anomalous fish falls registered in the state during the present century.

1902

USA, Chesterfield, Idaho. On 14 January a group of skaters were chased by an 8-foot hairy anthropoid wielding a club, the first of nineteen sightings in the state of a similar creature.

USA, off City Island, New York City. On 10 August a pilot ship commanded by Captain Alexander S. Banta was attacked twice by an unknown marine creature, black and much bigger than a whale, forcing it back to shore.

1903

USA, Bronx, New York. In May a large quantity of cash, jewellery and personal items went missing from an apartment owned by a Mrs Koch. For several days afterwards lights and shadowy figures moving about were seen in the apartment. Yet each time when police converged on the building no one was found to be present.

USA, Iola, Kansas. The appearance of a strange part-humanoid creature with horns, long hair and huge red eyes caused panic among miners on nightshift.

South Africa, off Hermanus. A gigantic snake-like sea-monster with eyes bigger than saucers approached a group of fishermen working 4 miles from the coastline.

1904

Ireland, Lough Erne, County Fermanagh. Large round lights were seen gliding across the surface of the lough every night for several months, beginning in March.

England, Wimbledon, London. On 2 April an unnatural darkness fell for ten minutes on the London suburb causing considerable panic and confusion. There was no sign of heavy clouds or smoke.

USA, near Philadelphia. The *SS Mohican* was enshrouded by

a strange phosphorescent cloud which caused the decks to glow as if on fire and played havoc with the ship's compass before it moved out to sea. 31 July. Also in USA, Memphis, Tennessee, a period of unnatural daytime darkness fell upon the city causing panic on 2 December.

1905

Wales, Froncysyltte, Clwyd. In early May a huge black bird was seen flying low over rooftops. Later that year, in October, an unidentified black quadruped was seen killing farm animals in England near Great Badminton, Gloucestershire.

USA, Kittery Point, Maine. Curious electrical flames were seen rising from the beach and sea surface making a crackling noise and leaving a strong sulphurous smell on 1 September.

1906

USA, Union Port, New Jersey. Sometime during June lightning struck a woman leaving on her arm a curious pattern of figures resembling a pheasant, a snake and Chinese letters.

England, Suffolk. On 8 February a huge circle of light was seen to form during a thunderstorm and hover low over a village. Several trees were damaged as well as a nearby church.

England, Gloucester. Mid-August saw the vanishment of three children from the same family while playing in a field adjacent to their parents' farmhouse. The alarm was raised and an extensive three-day search carried out by local constabulary and village helpers found nothing. Yet on the fourth day the missing children were found sleeping peacefully in a ditch less than 50 yards from their home. Remarkably, they had no explanation for their absence or recollection of the missing period of time.

1907

USA, Pittsburgh, Pennsylvania. On 27 January Albert Houck found his young wife lying on a table burned to a crisp – probably a case of SHC.

USA, Butte, Montana. A live toad was found encased in rock strata 200 feet down during the sinking of a silver mineshaft on 15 May.

USA, Alpena, Michigan. A lightning ball entered a house and caused mayhem, starting fires and smashing holes in the walls, on 1 August.

1908

England, Whitley Bay, Northumberland. An elderly spinster, Wilhelmina Dewar, was found combusted to ashes while asleep in her bed on the night of 22 March.

France, Vosges Mountains. On Trinity Sunday huge hailstones bearing an image of the Virgin Mary fell on a localised area, breaking over 1,400 panes of glass in the process.

Mexico, Gulf of Mexico. Passengers and crew on board the *SS Livingstone* watched a sea-monster with an estimated length of 200 feet on 21 June.

1909

USA, Trenton, New Jersey. An extraordinary monster with black leathery wings and a hideously formed head (nicknamed the Jersey Devil) was seen flying above the town and perching on buildings. Further reports from Camden, Woodbury, Burlington, Gloucester and other locations bordering Pennsylvania were made during January.

Portugal, suburbs of Coimbra. A violent poltergeist outbreak including loud percussions, physical assaults on adults and a baby levitated from its cradle to a table, took place in early October.

1910

Guyana, Konawaruk River. Gold prospectors were surprised by legendary 5-foot 'wild men' covered in reddish-brown fur in late February.

Wales, Ennerdale, Cambria. During February up to fifty sheep were slaughtered each night by an unknown predator. In every case the bodies had been drained of blood through small incisions in the animal's jugular veins but no flesh was eaten. Meanwhile, in England, a similar horror stalked farmland around Guildford during the following month, killing up to sixty sheep a night in the same strange vampiric manner.

1911

England, Bradford, Yorkshire. On the morning of 23 February a nine-year-old girl was lifted from her school playground by an unknown force 20 feet into the air and killed by the subsequent fall to earth.

USA, Louisville, Kentucky. Unnatural daytime darkness lasting for one hour fell upon the city, terrifying residents, on 7 March.

France, Mirebeau. During the Easter period a picture of Christ in a church began to bleed from its hands, heart and head. Tests proved that the blood was human.

1912

Australia, New South Wales. On 12 November a large quantity of fish fell from a tornado-like cloud on to the town of Quirindi. Other peculiar fish-falls across New South Wales during this century have included long marine worms, shrimps, winkles and crabs.

1913

France, near Charleroi. 30 January was the start of a four-day-long bombardment by stones of a farmhouse. No human agent was apparently responsible.

USA, Farmersfield, Texas. On 15 May a group of children saw a little green man less than 1 foot high which, according to reports, was then attacked and killed by dogs.

1914

Belgium, Mons. On 26 August retreating British forces were allegedly aided by phantom bowmen, thereafter known as 'the angels of Mons'.

1915

USA, south-east of Wann, Oklahoma. A large, hairy hominid with glowing red eyes was seen lurking near a house gate in mid-July, one of several dozen bigfoot sightings made during the twentieth century in the area.

England, Devon. Floating lights were seen over hills on Dartmoor throughout the summer and autumn.

1916

North Atlantic. An enormous sea animal was sighted by captain and crew aboard the German submarine U28 following the sinking of the British steamer *Iberian*. Seconds after the British merchant vessel had exploded the crocodilian-shaped creature, about 60 foot long, was blown out of the water among pieces of wreckage.

1917

Iceland, 70 miles south-east of the coast. In May officers and men aboard *HMS Hilary* saw a sea-monster with a neck estimated to be 30 feet long and a large triangular dorsal fin.

English Channel. The yacht *Zebrina* left Falmouth Harbour, Cornwall, in October for the small port of Brieux, France, on a voyage that should have taken no longer than forty-eight hours. No storms were reported but after four days the *Zebrina* was found deserted in excellent conditions and giving no clues to the fate of her missing crew.

1918

Australia, Lismore, New South Wales. A stone cross in a cemetery began to glow brightly at night. The phenomenon continued for sixty years and the monument was finally broken up by vandals. Also in the same state, farmers reported seeing giant 30-foot monitor lizards in the Wattagan Mountains.

1919

USA, Barron, Wisconsin. While walking to fetch some oil in August a thirteen-year-old boy, Harry Anderson, noticed twenty little men walking along towards him in single file. He estimated each to be no more than 18 inches tall.

English Channel. The schooner *Lucienne* out of St Malo was found washed up on Goodwin Sands, Kent. A half-eaten meal lay on the table yet those who sat down to the repast remained permanently absent.

1920

South Africa, Johannesburg, Transvaal. A large, round, glowing object, presumably ball lightning, was seen in June rolling up an incline emanating saw-toothed streaks of light. It exploded on meeting a wall, leaving a little damage and sulphurous vapour. Also that year came several water-monster reports from the Orange River and tributaries of the Vaal River.

England, London. During August showers of stones fell for three consecutive days on the suburb of Woodford.

1921

USA, New York City. On the evening of 9 March police found the corpse of thirty-six-year-old Isadora Fink in the back room of a laundry on East 132nd Street. Neither gun nor bullets were discovered in the room, which had been locked from the inside, yet Fink's chest exhibited two gunshot wounds. Police commissioner Edward Mulrooney later described the slaying as an 'insoluble mystery'.

Hungary, near Budapest. Throughout the year a thirteen-year-old boy found he could raise objects into the air just by looking at them. At night blue flames would flicker above his sleeping body and those who touched him often received electric shocks.

1922

Canada, near Antigonish, Nova Scotia. In January fires of probable poltergeist origin repeatedly broke out within an isolated farmhouse, including thirty-eight in one night.

Switzerland, Alpine region. During a March snowstorm exotic insects including South American spiders, caterpillars and huge ants fell.

England, London. Field Marshal Sir Henry Wilson was gunned down in a park on 22 June by Irish nationalists, ten days after a friend, wealthy socialite Lady Londonderry, warned him that she had seen the assassination in a dream.

1923

USA, Echo Lake, Nebraska. Two motorists camping close to the lake shore in July were awoken by a tremendous splashing and saw emerging from the water an animal with a neck longer than a giraffe's and a horn in the middle of its forehead. After the sighting local farmers blamed a spate of livestock disappearances on the monster.

England, Grimsby. In November a man was blasted by ball lightning and later died.

1924

Sweden, Bleckenstad. A large perfectly formed ball of limestone fell from the sky on 11 April. When examined it was found to contain marine shells and fossils.

USA, near Kelso, Washington. Prospectors staying in a cabin in Ape Canyon in July were terrorised by a horde of 'mountain devils' – presumably Bigfeet – which threw rocks at them. The prospectors drove the creatures away with gunfire, wounding one of their number.

1925

South Africa, Uitenhage, Cape Province. Large numbers of frogs and fishes fell together in the rain in March.

USA, off the coast of Massachusetts. On 24 May the crew of a fishing trawler watched a sea-monster they described as being like a gigantic eel, longer than their own 130-foot boat.

1926

USA, Evansville, Indiana. On 30 July thousands of nickel-shaped frogs fell upon a golf course during a thunderstorm.

One of seventeen rains of frogs reported in the United States that year.

Central Africa. Many sightings emerged of a 'water elephant' devouring hippos in Lake Bongweolo.

1928

USA, Elizabeth, Illinois. A 9-foot anthropoid menaced a family on 25 July. The first of thirteen Bigfoot sightings by multiple witnesses in the state during the twentieth century.

Canada, Ontario. Throughout the year came many reports of long-necked monsters from various locations including Lake Erie, Lake Huron, Lake Superior and the St Lawrence River.

1929

West Indies, Leeward Island, Antigua. For several weeks running in April and May clothes worn by a village girl ignited into ashes leaving her skin unaffected. While she was asleep bedclothes and mattresses similarly burst into flames. April–May.

China, Vientiane. During the summer months a plesiosaur-type animal was seen several times in rivers near the Loatian capital.

1930

USA, Kingston, New York. The body of Mrs Stanley Lake was found incinerated inside unscorched clothing in January. The inquest recorded an open verdict. In early February hunters trailed and wounded an unknown quadruped after it killed several pigs on farmland in Prince George County, Maryland, but the creature escaped.

England, Grayshott, Hampshire. On 29 December rain fell from a clear sky. A similar phenomenon is noted during the following three years.

1931

Ireland, County Derry. On 4 April a student from England saw a creature like a huge black dog with horrible teeth and eyes like burning coals swimming in a river. Possibly a pooka, a legendary Irish ghost dog.

Spain, Ezquioga. More than 150 people, including non-Catholics and agnostics, saw a vision of the Virgin Mary appear in the sky together with a host of angels and saints on 30 June.

1932

USA, Bladenboro, North Carolina. An invisible poltergeist fire spook entered a house causing damage to curtains, bedclothes and tablecloths, which burst into flames for no reason, in January.

Cameroon, Assumbo Mountains. Zoologist Ivan T. Sanderson was attacked by a giant bat with a 12-foot wing-span in May.

1933

USA, Niagara Falls, New York State. On 24 May a large quantity of fresh fish fell following an otherwise normal downpour of rain. One witness fed them to his cat. This was the first of ten fish-falls to take place in New York State during the twentieth century.

South Africa, Natal. A 90-foot monster was seen in St Lucia Lake on 7 July. The following night a similar creature was seen swimming in the sea a mile offshore.

1934

USA, Pennsylvania. During January strange lights were seen and eerie noises heard, including groans, wails and screams, in woods near Langhorne. When searchers entered the woods to investigate the sounds moved away. Later that year, in May, a farmer in South Dakota found strange tracks and watched a 'dragon-type' monster entering Lake Campbell the day after many animals went missing on his and neighbouring farms.

Italy, Pirano. In the spring human glow-worm Anna Manaro was investigated and photographed by doctors after she was seen to emit a blue luminescence while asleep.

1935

Grenada, Lowther's Lane district. A deserted cottage which had become the focus for ghostly manifestations and showers of stones the previous year was razed to the ground by a persistent fire spook on 14 January.

Canada, Saskatchewan. On 18 June three people saw a landed UFO in woods near Nipawin and watched humanoids in silver suits ascend a ladder into the craft. The following day scorch marks were discovered at the site and photographed.

1936

Kazakhstan, on the Black Sea off the Crimean coast. During January a ferocious black sea-monster with a horse-like head became entangled in fish nets and was cut free by fishermen who then fled ashore. Later the same year a woman in the Pavoldar region claimed she saw a flying winged female form dressed in black.

USA, Cleveland, Ohio. Heavenly music was heard emanating from a girl's grave in Calvary Cemetery for several nights during November.

1937

Mongolia, Gobi Desert. A reconnaissance unit of the advancing Japanese Army shot two large, red furred anthropoids of an unknown species in February.

USA, Saginaw River, Michigan. A fisherman suffered a nervous breakdown after being attacked by a 'big hairy thing' that walked on two legs. Further Bigfoot sightings came in from many locations in the same state during this year.

1938

Japan, Hokkaido. A wooden doll was placed in a sacred temple when it began growing hair after its owner's death. The growth continues to the present day and scientific tests prove that it is human hair.

Sweden, Parajaevarra, Lapland. In July several large fireballs appeared out of low clouds, killing one person and seriously burning many others as they tore through five houses before ascending skyward.

1939

USA, Loudenville, Ohio. During early summer ghostly light forms were seen flitting over fields and continued their activity for the next thirteen years. Later that summer an unknown force would seem to have manifested within a USAF transport aircraft en route from San Diego to Honolulu, killing five crew members.

England, Start, Devon. During November two women out walking saw a phantom manor house which they later tried to find the history of. To their amazement it was discovered that no such building had ever existed on the site.

1940

Ireland, Lough Bran, County Kerry. A black monster described as being a cross between a giant seal and a mythical dragon was seen onshore by a fourteen-year-old boy. Other lake-monster reports emerged from the nearby Lackagh Lake in early summer.

USSR, Gorki Region. Coins with a total value of several thousand kopeks fell upon the heads of local residents during a storm on 17 June.

1941

Australia, Wearyan River, Northern Territory. In February, after travelling to a remote area to assist a man who had been shot, an experienced nurse was helped by two men wearing white operating-theatre gowns who appeared literally out of thin air and afterwards vanished.

North Atlantic, Gulf of Lions. The Red Cross charter vessel

Icelandia was found drifting aimlessly upon the open sea, crewless yet totally seaworthy, in July.

1942

USA, Bloomington, Illinois. On 15 March bank worker Aura Troyer was found partially combusted in a basement and was unable to explain his immolation. Elsewhere in America men fishing in River Dale, Maryland, reported sightings of large crocodile-type creatures in Herring Creek on the lower Potomac River on 18 November.

England, Newbiggin-by-the-Sea, Northumberland. A man claimed to have been abducted by aliens on 18 December and forced to undergo a medical examination. Probably the first claimed UFO abduction of the century.

1943

USA, Deer Isle, Maine. On 13 January the combusted body of fifty-two-year-old Allan Small was found lying on his lounge floor. Although a round circle of carpet was also affected, no other fire damage was evident and no source of the fire's origin was found. Three weeks later, on 1 February, invalid Arthur Baugard was found dead in identical circumstances at his home in Lancaster, New York.

1944

Denmark, near Copenhagen. On 24 February violent splashing took place at a private boat pier on Lake Fureso and several 1-inch-thick planks of wood were smashed to smithereens by a creature which witnesses described as being like a giant pike.

Germany, Hagenau. Allied fighter pilots flying a mission over Europe on 22 December encountered large orange glows which paced their aircraft even when they took evasive action. The first of a number of reports made by pilots during the Second World War of glowing balls seemingly acting under intelligent control.

1945

Germany, Wildenstein Castle, near Heilbronn. Small creatures described as goblins were seen by residents along with several ghosts and outbreaks of other bizarre phenomena throughout the year.

USA, Pittsburgh. A one-hundred-year-old bronze bust of a Japanese geisha girl owned by art collector Allan Demetrius began to weep salt tears on the evening of 6 August, the day that saw the atom bomb attack on Hiroshima.

USA, Midland, Arkansas. A fire spook in a house caused damage to curtains, clothing, wallpaper and furniture on 9 September before burning down a nearby barn.

1946

Austria, Eisenberg. In early spring young coma victim Alosia Lex woke up claiming to have seen visions of the Blessed Virgin Mary, who gave her messages containing information which the girl could not have known.

Yugoslavia, Pasman Dalmatia. Another Virgin Mary apparition, this time crowned with stars, appeared in a cloud and was seen by many witnesses on 11 June.

Across Scandinavia. There were numerous reports of ghost rockets flying low and terrifying local people. The majority of accounts come from Sweden, where the projectiles invariably appeared to fall into lakes and fjords.

1947

Brazil, Manous, Amazon River. A traveller encountered five enormous birds resembling pterodactyls, with leathery bodies and wings, in February.

USA, Security Bay, Alaska. A sea-monster with a cow-like head and fins on its back was seen looping through the water during April and again off Pennock Island in May.

South Africa, Tiger Rocks, Natal. A 60-foot sea-monster was seen over a dozen times during the summer by fishermen in boats, and then in September by a man walking along the beach at Isipingo.

1948

USA, Maycomb, Illinois. Over 200 fires broke out mysteriously in a single week in August on an isolated farmstead, eventually causing the total destruction of cottages and barns.

England, Barton-on-Sea, Hampshire. A couple on a golf course were bombarded by hundreds of live fish which fell from a cloudless sky in September.

Philippines, Lipa. Following visions of the Blessed Virgin Mary seen by convent nuns, many miraculous showers of rose petals fell upon the town during the months of October to December.

1949

Brazil, Rio, Araguaya region. A 150-foot long monster snake with glowing green eyes, known as the *Sucuriju gigante*, was seen and photographed.

USA, Manchester, New Hampshire. Mrs Ellen Coutres spontaneously turned into a human torch for no apparent reason in December.

1950

England, Exmoor, Devon. A farmer awoke one morning in February to find his fields littered with ice lumps the size of soup plates, one of which, weighing 14 pounds, was embedded in a ram's neck.

USA, Benson Harbor, Michigan. On 23 June witnesses on the ground saw a DC4 aircraft destroyed after a collision with a glowing object which had been chasing it.

1951

Germany, Dusseldorf. On 10 January a carpenter working on a roof during a hailstorm was found impaled by a 12-foot-long ice spear which apparently fell from the sky.

USA, St Petersburg, Florida. On 1 July sixty-seven-year-old Mrs Mary Reeser was discovered as a pile of ashes on the floor of her one-bedroomed apartment, her skull shrunken to the size of a baseball.

1952

Russia, Vorozneh. From reports that have reached the West only quite recently it would appear that sometime during the summer a glowing ball of fire slowly descended upon a factory producing heavy armaments in this city of over 1,000,000 residents. The resulting explosion apparently devastated the factory and surrounding area, and although there were no official figures for dead and injured we can safely assume that casualties must have been considerable.

USA, Nashville, Tennessee. On Thanksgiving Day Mr H. Cantrell was struck by lightning and thereafter found to be cured of the brain cancer which was threatening his life.

1953

USA, Greenville, South Carolina. On 3 March motorist Waymon Wood was found 'crisped black' inside his otherwise undamaged car, a probable victim of SHC.

USA, Los Angeles, California. Another probable case of spontaneous human combustion involved Mrs Esther Dulin, aged thirty, whose charred remains were found on 6 May having fallen through a burned floor into the room below, even though other nearby combustible objects remained untouched. Later that year, on 18 June, in Houston, Texas, a curious creature like a man with leathery wings was seen landing in a tree by more than one witness.

1954

Italy, Boaria Rouigo. On 15 October an egg-shaped UFO flew low over farmland emitting heat blasts which burned cattle, injured one farmer and set fire to buildings and haystacks.

Canada, Flat Rock, New Brunswick. A house was attacked by a fire spook in November, and books, foodstuffs and furniture burst spontaneously into flames.

1955

USA, Cincinnati, Ohio. On 22 July blood fell from an oddly shaped cloud upon a group of gardens, killing trees and grass and burning the skin of one witness.

USA, Westchester County, New York. A couple night fishing on Titicus Reservoir on 17 September saw a luminous sphere rise from the water and move about in a way suggesting intelligence, for more than an hour.

Philippines, Tokelau Isles. On 10 November the pleasure cruiser *Joyita* was found abandoned a few miles from the coast of Fakofo. Its twenty-five missing passengers and crew were never seen again.

Wales, Wrexham. On 5 February rain fell from a clear sky. Ten days later there was a clear-sky fall of snow on the same district.

1956

Atlantic Ocean, off the west coast of Africa. In August 'straight, slow lightning' was seen crossing a clear sky by observers aboard the *SS Oronsay.* The peculiar phenomenon was repeated at regular intervals for over an hour.

USA, Dry Harbour, Alaska. A 100-foot-long carcass of an unknown animal covered with reddish-brown hair was washed up in late autumn.

England, Hanham, Avon. A fall of pennies and halfpennies was noted by children and adults during November.

1957

USA, New York State. On 22 June witnesses at Rye saw a lighted ovoid object descend into the water off Long Island Sound and leave again a few minutes later.

USSR, Caucasus Mountains. In July Professor V.K. Leontiev sketched a 7-foot tall Neanderthal man he encountered near the Jermut River area, one of many man-beast reports to come out of that area during the summer and autumn.

1958

USA, near Riverside, California. Motorist Charles Wetzel reported being attacked by a round-headed entity with shining eyes, long claws and scaly skin as he drove across the Santa Ana River on 8 November.

Northern Ireland, County Antrim. On 28 December a farmer witnessed low-flying UFOs above his land, one of which cut a 40-foot-tall tree in half some 10 feet from the ground.

1959

Poland, Kolbrez. Soldiers based near the coast saw a triangular UFO rise out of the sea and then circle their barracks several times before shooting away, in March.

Papua New Guinea, Boianai. The leader of a Christian mission, Rev. W.B. Gill, and many other Papuan witnesses saw UFOs and their occupants on three successive nights from 26 June.

1960

USA, Lake Whitney, Texas. On the clear apparently normal evening of 15 June thermometers recorded a temperature rise of 70 degrees Fahrenheit for ten minutes in a highly localised area of the Lone Star State. The intense heat activated sprinkler systems and terrified locals who went outside to see the sky glowing a bright orange colour. The following morning farmers awoke to find their crops scorched black. Later that same month in the Chief Cornstalk hunting grounds of West Virginia a winged man-like figure was seen standing on the main inter-state carriageway of Route 2 before taking off vertically and disappearing into the night sky.

1961

Italy, San Damiano. On 29 September, close to death from a terminal illness, Rosa Quattrini was miraculously cured by a vision of Our Lady, the first of many apparitions seen to become manifest in her presence by other witnesses.

USA, California. On 18 August thousands of migrating oceanic birds called sooty shearwaters fell upon a 6-mile stretch of the Californian coastline along Monterey Bay. Autopsies showed no signs of sickness or poison and their sudden arrival from out of the night sky remained unexplained.

USA, Elizabethon, Tennessee. 25 November saw anomalous falls of a substance like polyethylene film reckoned in total to weigh above 1 ton.

Canada, Montreal. On the evening of 10 October the merchant steamship *Roxburgh Castle* was covered in millions of white filaments which were seen to fall from a clear sky and dissolve after approximately half an hour.

1962

Argentina, near Bajada Grande, Paraná. A student on a motorbike reported being attacked by a round-headed being with white hair and three eyes on 28 July.

Brazil, Rio de Janeiro. On 20 August peasant Rivalino Da Silva was seen being kidnapped by aliens and taken aboard their craft, which blasted off leaving ground traces. Da Silva was never seen again.

1963

USA, Porterville, California. A seventeen-year-old girl who had been swimming in a pool emerged with a shocked expression on her face, screamed and collapsed dead for no apparent reason in front of onlookers. An autopsy failed to identify the cause of death. On exactly the same date five years later her sister died in identical circumstances, the cause once again unknown.

New Zealand, Brooklyn, Wellington. A house was bombarded with coins and stones for three successive nights during March.

England, Norfolk. A motorist driving between the twin villages of Little and Great Snoring in early summer hit a black dog which exploded in a sheet of flame.

1964

Off Western Australia. On 23 January large rotating lights were seen under the sea at a point north-east of Groote Eylandt, causing the compasses of passing ships to go haywire.

England, Gateshead, Tyne-and-Wear. A group of children playing on farmland on 2 June reported a sighting of creatures they described as 'little elves' frolicking over haystacks.

USA, off the coast of Florida. American pilot Chuck Wakely found a strange luminescence enveloping his twin-engined plane during a solo flight from Nassau to Miami in November. Similar phenomena were reported by other fliers passing through the notorious Bermuda Triangle.

1965

USA. Over 10,000 separate reports came in from a dozen states after a frantic wave of UFO activity began on 24 July.

Mexico, Coatepec. A part-human entity with cat's eyes was seen by four independent witnesses during a single night in September.

1966

England, Walthamstow, Greater London. A crucifix in a church shed tears for ten weeks between May and July.

France, Lachaud Correze. On 15 July a farmer in a field heard a bang and then found himself covered in sticky dust which left him with third-degree burns, partial blindness, giddiness and acute anaemia.

USA, Miami, Florida. A poltergeist in a warehouse resulted in over 220 incidents of goods falling off shelves, beginning in December.

1967

Italy, Cefala Diana, near Palermo, Sicily. Around fifty people saw visions of the Virgin Mary in the window of castle ruins for seven days running during May.

Brazil. Farmer Inacio Da Souza disappeared and when he was seen again recounted being taken aboard an alien ship and examined. He was found to be suffering from vomiting and other symptoms of radiation sickness and died of leukaemia one month later.

1968

Brazil. At a location near Copana substantial quantities of meat and blood fell from the skies for about five minutes on 27 August, while elsewhere in the country, at Ipiranga, one of the most bizarre poltergeist cases ever documented was beginning with the visible passing through solid walls, floors and doors of heavy pieces of furniture.

Ireland, Sraheen's Loch, Achill Isle. On 1 May two men saw a lake-monster moving on land across a road. A week later a boy cycling by the side of the lake saw a large black creature crawling out of the water towards him and fled.

Argentina, Correa, near Rosario. On 14 October a rancher discovered mutilated dead cows near a burned circular patch of grass and the following day found fungi the size of basketballs growing there.

1969

Colombia, Anolaima. On 4 July a landed UFO was approached by eleven witnesses, one of whom managed to touch it. Two days later he was taken ill and died quickly, possibly due to exposure to radiation.

Vietnam, near Da Nong. A creature described as a 'bird woman' with leathery black wings was seen by US Marine guards during August.

USA, Punta Gorda, Florida. Golf balls rained from the sky in prodigious numbers on 3 September.

1970

In February an eighty-nine-year-old woman, Mrs Margaret Hogan, burst spontaneously into flames while standing at a bus stop outside her flat in Prussia Street. Astonished bystanders attested to the rapidity of the fire which destroyed her, and Dublin city coroner Dr. P. Bofin accepted that her death 'conformed to the phenomenon known as spontaneous combustion'.

Belgium, Brussels. A luminous area 25 feet long and 5 feet high, formed of tiny phosphorescent green vibrating particles, caused chaos in the city centre on 24 January before changing shape and moving away.

Finland, Imjarvi. On 7 January two skiers saw a landed UFO and an entity 3 feet tall which directed a pulsating light at them, hitting them and knocking them down. The men needed hospital treatment for burns and were ill for some time afterwards.

1971

Italy, Mapopati. Beginning on 3 January, a painting of the Madonna wept human blood from eyes, heart, hands and feet, which formed into crosses on the wall below.

USA. In August a cat-like animal with the ability to appear and vanish at will slaughtered a variety of farm animals in Canton township, Michigan. In the same year at Port Richey, Florida, hundreds of small silver fish fell from the sky on 7 September.

1972

Italy. An extraordinary outbreak of weeping and bleeding religious icons included a statue weeping near Assisi, a weeping Madonna at Regio Calabria, a weeping picture at Adria-Rovigo and Madonnas that wept or oozed blood in the towns of Bergamo, Salerno, Florence and San Vittorio.

Mexico, Monterrey. A statue of the infant Jesus breathed, perspired and wept daily in front of crowds of up to 15,000 during January.

USA, Defiance, Ohio. A 9-foot 'werewolf' with fangs attacked a railway worker on 31 July.

1973

USA, East Hartford, Connecticut. In March a doll appeared to be possessed by the spirit of a dead girl, causing sometimes violent poltergeist activity in an apartment. Later that same year, 8 December saw the preternatural combustion of the corpse of Mrs Betty Satlow of Washington, who had died the previous day of carbon monoxide poisoning. Her remains were taken to a laboratory for a series of tests following which a state department spokesman admitted that the cadaver had been subjected to a force 'outside the laws of nature'.

France, Brignoles. Thousands of small toads and frogs fell from the sky in a freak storm on 23 September.

1974

Canada, Saddle Lake, Alberta. Sightings of a lake-monster 150 feet long with a horse-like head came during January, the first of over one hundred sightings of the creature over the next ten years.

England, Isle of Wight. Throughout the summer an old oak tree situated near east Cowes was seen billowing out smoke, causing firemen to make several investigations. However, no sign of fire or source of heat was found to explain the well-witnessed enigma. Later that year, also in Britain, a Welsh motorist driving alongside Bala Lake, Gwynedd, on the night of 4 October saw a bright disc descending upon his car. The vehicle was afterwards found to be covered in a peculiar thick film of grey dust.

1975

USA, New York. Mr and Mrs Jackson Wright stopped in the Lincoln tunnel to allow Mr Wright to wipe snow from his windscreen. When he got back inside a few seconds later his wife had vanished. Elsewhere in America, Queenstown, Alabama saw visitations by a mystery animal which killed a 250-pound Shetland pony and a 130-pound pig during the same month, January. Later that year, on 21 October in Colorado, a 1,500-pound bison was found dead in its enclosure at the Cheyenne Mountain Zoo. One ear and the udder had been cut off, its genitals mutilated and a 24-inch-square section of the animal's hide had been removed. Zoo officials found the enclosure secured and there seemed no explanation for the attack and little possibility that a human intruder could have entered the area unnoticed.

Puerto Rico, Moca area. The mysterious deaths of animals including dogs, cats, geese, rabbits and goats followed hard upon UFO sightings in the same area during the period February to July.

1976

USA, South Carolina. Many sightings were reported of man-sized green-skinned creatures haunting the swamps. The 'South Carolina lizard man', as it was dubbed, is to date just one of at least sixteen abominable swamp creatures to have been seen by multiple witnesses in mainland USA.

Hong Kong, Sai Kung. A large black cat-like animal was seen by many people and would appear to have attacked and killed several large dogs between October and December.

England, Tollerton, Nottingham. In late July two milkmen on a morning delivery round were surprised by a fully grown lioness. Sixty-four other sightings followed in a three-week period in the surrounding area.

1977

Wales, Dyfed. A major UFO flap erupted during February after a glowing saucer said to be roughly 15 metres in diameter landed next to a rural county primary school near

Broadhaven village. Following this initial sighting strange objects continued to appear all over Dyfed, coinciding with electromagnetic disturbances and regular breakdowns in the county's main electricity supply.

USA, Logan County, Illinois. Several sightings were made of huge birds like overgrown vultures during July and August. In the most bizarre incident, which took place on the evening of 25 July, two of the creatures apparently swooped down and attempted to pick up ten-year-old Marlin Lowe, carrying him for some 20 feet before dropping him to earth.

USA, Chicago, Illinois. During late summer well-witnessed sightings of a female ghost known as Resurrection Mary were followed by the discovery of handprints embedded into metal railings surrounding the cemetery where her body is buried.

1978

USA, Galax, Virginia. In a poltergeist-style outbreak a garage was bombarded with nails for four days from 10 July. During August and September a house in Spokane, Washington, was bombarded for a week by golf-ball-sized rocks.

Nepal, Hinku Valley. In November British climbers heard strange screams and found footprints, possibly made by a yeti, at an altitude of 17,250 feet. Meanwhile at the Khumbu Glacier an expedition led by Lord Hunt photographed yeti tracks 14 inches long. Earlier, at a location near Pheriche, a girl tending a yak herd was attacked and knocked unconscious by a yeti which killed several of her herd.

Italy, Adriatic Sea. Fishermen reported strange columns of water over 100 feet high and unidentified objects emerging from and submerging into the water in October.

New Zealand, South Island. Unidentified targets on radar indicated UFO activity off the north-eastern coast near Wellington Airport, and pilots reported anomalous lights for several nights. The phenomenon was filmed on 30 December and shown on television across the world.

England, Risely, Cheshire. On 16 December, a service engineer returning home from a union meeting found his vehicle enveloped by a glowing mass of unknown origin. Shortly afterwards the driver contracted multiple cancer and died.

1979

Malaysia. Schoolchildren at Bukit Mertajam allegedly saw a small landed UFO and minute entities on 19 May. Another small saucer landed at Kampung Nagalit and shone light at students, temporarily blinding them, on 26 May. Elsewhere in the country, at Lymut, several witnesses saw 10-foot-tall hairy creatures with red eyes, which had the ability to disappear into thin air, on several succeeding days beginning on 11 August.

India, Behar. A UFO which hovered over a school near Islampur Town on 12 July was reported to have drawn up large sections of roof from the main building.

France, Seron, Hautes Pyrenées. A spate of odd fires in a farmhouse (about ninety in one month) began on 6 August and ended only after a priest blessed the place and sprinkled holy water on the ground.

1980

Tibet, Menbu Lake. Many witnesses, including communist party officials, saw a long-necked lake-monster pulling a cow from the shore in June. Later, in a separate incident, a farmer rowing on the lake was dragged down.

England, Ashfield, Nottinghamshire. On 13 July, 200 people collapsed during a show involving junior brass band parades in fields near Kirby. They were ferried to four hospitals with symptoms including running eyes, sore throats, dizziness and vomiting, but doctors were unable to identify a cause for the peculiar events.

Australia, near Rosedale, Victoria. A farmhand woken on the night of 30 September by cattle bellowing saw a domed UFO hovering over a water tank. The next day he discovered that 10,000 gallons of water had gone from the tank.

1981

Across the USA. A rush of Bigfoot sightings began on 6 February, when an 8-foot hairy anthropoid was seen sorting through rubbish behind a restaurant near Rocks State Park, Maryland. Towards the end of the month a courting couple saw a similar beast 5 miles north of Veedersburg in Indiana, while also in the same state, this time 2 miles south at Spraytown, another big hairy creature was seen skulking around gardens on the night of 16 April. More sightings that year were to come from several other states, including Montana, New York, Louisiana, Wisconsin and South Dakota. Again in the USA, in Chesapeake Bay, Baltimore, a long-necked monster known as Chessie was photographed swimming through the Upper Choptank River during May. It was the first of several sightings of the same creature during the 1980s.

Wales, Dyfed. Dozens of sheep were savaged on three successive nights in June on farms around the village of Ysbyty Ystwyth. During the next six weeks several sightings were made of enormous felines, one of which killed a henhouse full of chickens and the guard dog left chained up to protect them.

1982

Russia, Novaya Zemlya, Bennet Island. Large icy clouds of mysterious origin formed and dissipated within hours on 12 March, moving against the wind and looking unlike anything occurring naturally.

New Zealand, Auckland. Workers constructing a tunnel on New Zealand's North Island found live frogs embedded in a sedimentary mud-stone layer some 4 metres down. One of many examples during the twentieth century and before where live amphibians or fish have been discovered imprisoned in seemingly impossible situations.

1983

England. During June there were extensive falls of strange objects from the skies above southern England, ranging from crabs in Sussex to pennies in Norfolk and small pieces of coke in Dorset. Freak weather conditions were blamed for this peculiar phenomenon.

Zimbabwe, near Harare. During the whole of the year residents of Warren Hills believed their homes to be haunted by the spirits of the people buried in the graveyard beneath their houses. Many reported poltergeist phenomena such as showers of stones, broken windows, temperature falls and movements of furniture.

USA, near Los Fresnos, Texas. An ambulance driver helping someone in a road-traffic accident reported seeing low swooping pterodactyls on 14 September. The following month several people saw a humped sea-monster which they judged to be about 100 feet long swimming off Stinson Beach, California. A similarly described creature was sighted by surfers off Costa Mesa three days later.

1984

USA, Fort Worth, Texas. On 8 July, according to hundreds of witnesses, one of the city's main streets developed a 20-foot-long bulge (not unlike that which would be made by a giant earthworm) which swayed back and forth for several minutes before disappearing. It was initially assumed that a gas abnormality was the likely culprit, yet excavations proved otherwise and the soil layers beneath the street were discovered to be intact.

England, York. During the early hours of 9 July a strangely shaped cloud formed above the city and unleashed a single bolt of lightning which struck the Minster Cathedral, causing extensive fire damage. Speculation grew among the Anglican community that the event was a sign of God's wrath at the heretical opinions of a newly appointed bishop. Meteorologists insist that no electrical storm was present over the north of England that night.

France, Montpichon Manche. Many local people reported seeing a floating vision of the Virgin Mary haunting lanes during mid-September.

Iceland, Lake Kleifarvatn. In November a group of bird-hunters watched two unknown creatures which 'moved like dogs but swam like seals' emerge from the lake. Bizarre footprints were afterwards found.

1985

England. The same year that saw the rush of 'crying boy' mystery fires also produced a spate of SHC examples. On 28 January a young girl student walking down a corridor at a college in Widnes, Cheshire, burst into flames in front of eye-witnesses and afterwards died, although her friends managed to put out the blaze. Another victim was Mrs Mary Carter, an elderly widow found dead in the hall of her flat in Ivor Road, Sparkhill, Birmingham, on the evening of 23 April. Though there were matches in the rooms none were found near her body and the fire lacked explanation. A month later, on 25 May, Paul Hayes, a nineteen-year-old computer operator, burst into flames from the waist up as he was walking along in Stepney Green, London. In his case the fire lasted only thirty seconds and he had managed to stagger into the London Hospital, where he received treatment for burns on his hands, forearms, face, neck, chest and ears.

Australia, Concord, Sydney. In February oil oozed copiously from both a statue and a picture of the Lebanese saint St Charbal. When touched by a crucifix on 15 March, the crucifix began to drip blood.

Ireland, Asdee, County Kerry. Children and adults saw statues of Jesus and Mary moving on 14 February. Later in the year, in July at Ballinspittle, County Cork, a statue of the Virgin was seen to move supernaturally by many witnesses.

1986

France, St Quentin, Aisne. A curious poltergeist outbreak, including droplets of blood appearing on walls, carpets and a bed, occurred in January.

Canada, South Burnaby, British Columbia. Evil-smelling slime fell from the sky on to an elementary school for three days during February.

USA, Essex County, New York. On 27 April a fifty-eight-year-old retired fireman was reduced to 3½ pounds of ash – a probable case of SHC.

Greece, Asterussia Mountains, Crete. A huge pterodactyl was seen flying low by hunters in the early summer.

England, Swinton, Greater Manchester. Two men cleaning the cellar of a reputedly haunted public house were attacked and hospitalised by an invisible assailant in the late autumn.

1987

India, northern Kashmir. On 31 January workers on a mountain sheep farm heard cries for help and found a boy who had been attacked by a yeti.

Germany, between Baden-Baden and Frankfurt. On 14 October drivers on an *autobahn* witnessed a dark sedan car vanish in an explosion of flames and smoke. Yet afterwards no wreckage was found.

England, Bridlington, Humberside. Trawlermen called in a priest after their fishing boat appeared to be haunted. The radar ceased to function; the steering sent the ship round in circles; there were ghostly apparitions and various other weird occurrences. The phenomena ended after an exorcism was performed in December.

1988

England, Wheatly Hill, Durham. A seventy-one-year-old woman survived SHC but her husband was badly burned putting out the fire. During July in Cheadle, Cheshire, a group of martial arts enthusiasts practising in the grounds of Asney Hall saw a hideously formed dwarf-like figure lurking in bushes. Subsequently several members of the club suffered physical assaults and possession by an unseen force.

1989

England, Oxfordshire. A strange outbreak of respiratory problems as well as nosebleeds and sore throats afflicted the villagers of Calham after a curious thick cloud descended upon their homes on 3 May. Also in England, on the night of 3 June in Nottingham, a casino manager disturbed an egg-headed alien looking in through a first-floor window. The manager was paralysed by a burning sensation in the forehead and the entity escaped before the alarm could be raised.

Hungary, near Kerescend. A twenty-seven-year-old engineer travelling with his wife to Budapest on 27 May stopped his car to urinate at the roadside. His wife saw him fall down dead after being enveloped in a blue mist. Although he appeared outwardly unscathed, an autopsy on the man revealed that his intestines had turned to carbon.

Mediterranean Sea, north-west of Crete. At dawn on 7 August the crew of the Sicilian fishing boat *Fransesco* began firing distress flares. After being rescued and towed to Kastelion Harbour on the Greek island of Crete, they reported a night-long attack by spectres and evil spirits which threw gear overboard and destroyed radio and navigation equipment. Even after the boat was exorcised by three priests the crew refused to return aboard and were flown home via Athens.

1990

England. Muslim immigrants across the country sliced open aubergines and discovered seeds spelling the holy name of Allah in Arabic. In Hurstpierpoint, Sussex, in early September a thirty-four-year-old man was found dead in his bedroom with SHC-type burns to his arms, legs and upper torso.

Iran, Isfahan. On 24 March a picnicking family were attacked by a huge unidentified bird, larger than an eagle, which carried off their two-year-old child in its talons. An intensive search failed to find the child or the bird's nest.

China, Hunan Province. In April four-year-old Tong Tangjiang partially self-ignited on several occasions. Tiny, intense jets of blue flame burst through circular holes in his skin.

USA, Los Angeles, California. Twenty-six-year-old Angela Hernandez, a female patient undergoing surgery at the UCLA Medical Center, exploded in flames while on the operating table and died on 29 May.

1991

Jordan, Zarka, near Amman. A priest preparing communion on 21 April discovered fresh blood flowing from the bread, prompting worshippers to spread it upon their bodies hoping for miracles.

England, Kent. An Alitalia MD-80 passenger jet narrowly missed a dark missile-shaped UFO at an altitude of 22,000 feet on 4 April. Later the same year, on 15 July, a Britannia Airways Boeing 737 descending towards Gatwick almost hit another mysterious object at a height of 14,000 feet. In both these incidents the UFO was tracked on radar.

England, Leicester. Throughout the year the Boulter family were plagued by curious spirits which left behind copious quantities of a yellowy slime, usually oozing through walls. The substance was analysed at Nottingham University and found to be urine from an unidentified animal, though definitely not human.

England, Manchester. A businessman returned home on 9 September to find a demonic voice had left an indecipherable message on his answerphone. Sophisticated analysis of the tape showed that it began with the words 'I hate you'.

1992

Japan, Kyushu. A 35-foot-long humped water-monster known as Issie was caught on a camcorder film by a motorist driving beside Lake Ikeda on 4 January.

Sweden, Lake Storsjon. Bridge construction workers and a group of thirteen students on Froson Island saw a large marine reptile.

Mongolia, near Chinese Border. On 12 June climbers led by experienced Englishman Julian Freeman-Atwood encountered long-haired man-beasts known locally as *almas*. Fresh tracks were found the next morning.

Scotland, Lothian region. Throughout the year low-altitude green fireballs were regularly seen shooting at high speed over moors.

1993

England, Leigh-on-Sea, Essex. A long-necked reptile was seen by several witnesses swimming towards the sea in the northern part of the Thames Estuary in February. Later the same year, in October, a group of wild boars, previously thought to be extinct in Britain, were captured on a camcorder film by a tourist in the Derbyshire dales.

Eire. Throughout the autumn there were many reports of moving statues at shrines across southern Ireland.

ɔw offers an exciting range of quality titles by both established and new authors. All of the books in this series are available from:

Little, Brown and Company (UK) Limited,
P.O. Box 11,
Falmouth,
Cornwall TR10 9EN.

Alternatively you may fax your order to the above address. Fax No. 0326 376423.

Payments can be made as follows: Cheque, postal order (payable to Little, Brown and Company) or by credit cards, Visa/Access. Do not send cash or currency. UK customers: and B.F.P.O.: please send a cheque or postal order (no currency) and allow £1.00 for postage and packing for the first book, plus 50p for the second book, plus 30p for each additional book up to a maximum charge of £3.00 (7 books plus).

Overseas customers including Ireland, please allow £2.00 for postage and packing for the first book, plus £1.00 for the second book, plus 50p for each additional book.

NAME (Block Letters) ....

ADDRESS..

....

☐ I enclose my remittance for ____________

☐ I wish to pay by Access/Visa Card

Number | | | | | | | | | | | | | | | | |

Card Expiry Date | | | | |